W9-AQG-980

THE SHAPING
OF AMERICAN RELIGION

PRINCETON STUDIES

IN AMERICAN CIVILIZATION

NUMBER 5

VOLUME I

RELIGION IN AMERICAN LIFE

THE

SHAPING

OF AMERICAN

RELIGION

EDITORS: JAMES WARD SMITH

AND A. LELAND JAMISON

PRINCETON, NEW JERSEY

PRINCETON UNIVERSITY PRESS

Copyright © 1961, by Princeton University Press
All rights reserved
L. C. Card 61-5383
SBN 691-01965-7
First Princeton Paperback Printing, 1969

The Editors wish to express their gratitude
to the Carnegie Foundation
for a generous grant which made these four volumes possible,
and to Mrs. Helen Wright
for her continuous invaluable assistance in many ways.

This book is sold subject to the condition that it shall not,
by way of trade, be lent, resold, hired out, or otherwise
disposed of without the publisher's consent, in any form of
binding or cover other than that in which it is published.

Printed in the United States of America
by Princeton University Press, Princeton, New Jersey

CONTENTS

CONTENTS

THE SHAPING
OF AMERICAN RELIGION

NOTE TO THE PAPERBACK EDITION

THE SHAPING OF AMERICAN RELIGION is the first of a series of volumes published in 1961 under the title "Religion in American Life." It is important that readers of this volume be aware of the whole of which it was designed as a part. Some history will help to throw light on the Introduction which follows.

Each year the Special Program in American Civilization at Princeton University offers an upperclass seminar on some aspect of American life. Two elements are essential in the choice of subject. First, it must be an aspect of general and pervasive importance. The conference draws upon students and faculty from nine departments of the university: Art, Economics, English, History, Philosophy, Politics, Psychology, Religion, and Sociology. It is essential that the subject of the seminar cut broadly across these departmental lines—a requirement which virtually guarantees a subject of major importance. Second, it must be an aspect of American life which the faculty feels has not been adequately surveyed in existing literature. This requirement is essential to capture the interest of busy scholars who are asked to devote their time and energy to an undertaking which forces them to transcend their normal departmental interests. There will always be copious existing literature upon any topic of the kind specified, but there will normally be no adequate comprehensive coverage. The topic will be one in which over-all perspective is needed.

It is not accidental, then, that from time to time the Program has broken ground in areas where it has felt that its results warrant the effort to initiate publication in the area where the gap is felt. Three times in the past, volumes have eventually emerged from the research and teaching in the Program—most recently in the two-volume study published in 1952, *Socialism and American Life*.

In the academic year 1948–1949 the Program first offered a seminar entitled "Religion in American Life." Few conferences have been more successfully interdepartmental in character, involving the special interests of every one of the departments listed. Moreover, one year's experience was sufficient to convince us that here was an area where publication was definitely desirable. The conference was repeated in the academic year 1953–1954, and again in 1957–1958. The conception of this four-volume work is in large part the result of the research and teaching of those years.

In presenting the seminar three times it was convenient to divide the particular areas of student research into various compartments. We used, in general, two overlapping principles of division. First, the division of problems into those which are primarily (a) institutional, (b) artistic, and (c) theoretical; second, and cutting across the former three, the division into (1) historical and (2) contemporary analytical.

These categories of division proved convenient for teaching purposes, and they have to some extent persisted and been maintained in the arrangement of topics in the bibliography of Volume IV. In the early stages of our planning we had assumed that some such categories of division would also govern the arrangement of the essays collected in the first three volumes. It is perhaps significant that we found this increasingly impracticable as time went on.

Part of the reason for this is discussed in a more theoretical fashion in the Introduction to Volume I. The divisions institutional, artistic, and theoretical turn out in the long run to be somewhat artificial. It was increasingly obvious that our authors should in certain cases be allowed to range freely across such lines of demarcation. And the same may be said for the distinction between historical and nonhistorical. Nonetheless, the fact that we began with such divisions in mind, though we tended increasingly to move away from it, does help to explain the final arrangement of essays here offered.

A further remark is necessary before we explain this arrangement. In one sense our purpose in preparing these volumes has been to make the reader aware of the vast range of problems on which attention must be focused by an adequate study of religion in American life. But the plan for Volume IV, the descriptive bibliography, seemed to us to obviate any need for "completeness" in the coverage of problems in the volumes of essays. Our motivation in inviting the essays was to provide signposts rather than encyclopedic coverage. We do not include essays on all important topics; far from it! We have tried rather to put together a series of essays which, viewed in relation to the encyclopedic coverage of the bibliography, will throw light not only on what we know about this subject but also on a great deal that we do not know, yet need to understand more fully if our conception of religion's role in American culture is to be well-rounded and well-informed.

The essays of Volume I set the stage for those that follow. The first four survey the institutional structure of the four general segments of American religion: Protestantism in its more clearly "classical" forms, Roman Catholicism, Judaism, and the less easily classifiable varieties of "new" religions. The latter have mainly proliferated from the Protestant stem, but attention is also given to movements which have turned in other directions. The chapters on Judaism and Roman Catholicism follow rather closely the order of historical development. H. Richard Niebuhr, by contrast, assumes some knowledge of

5

the detailed history of American Protestantism, concentrating his analysis on the structures and dynamics of the complex Protestant movements. The "splinter groups" have been treated in part historically, in part with reference to their typical emphases. These essays, in any case, make no claim to provide a full conspectus of American church history. Matters of considerable importance have been regretfully but intentionally omitted. Among these are the achievements and influence of the early French and Spanish explorations and colonization, and the role of the several branches of Eastern Orthodoxy in the religious scene. On the credit side, the comprehensive bibliographical observations of Volume IV contain at least the outlines of a full history of religion in America. We have not attempted anywhere in these volumes to offer a substitute for the standard histories of religion in America.

The second group of essays in Volume I surveys the course of American religious thought. Sydney Ahlstrom summarizes the major phases of "professional" theology. Perry Miller, Stow Persons, and Daniel D. Williams examine particular periods and movements of American religious thought, highlighting those features which have developed within the peculiarly American context. The chapter on religion and science discusses, from the point of view of a philosopher, a conflict which has bedeviled traditional theology from the time of Copernicus to the present. Here, again, Volume IV furnishes enough additional information to comprise a reasonably adequate outline of the history of religious thought in America. This story has yet to be told in its entirety by any single volume, so that the present essays may serve usefully to lend perspective, if not completeness, to the accumulated knowledge of American intellectual history.

In 1969 the reader of the several volumes of "Religion in American Life" may feel that some of the essays are dated in tone and outlook. Both America and religion passed through revolutionary transformations during the intervening years. The Second Vatican Council, the intensification of our urban

6

traumas, the rise of Black Power, the ambiguities of an unpremeditated and unpopular war—these and other developments, imperfectly discerned in the late Fifties, have profoundly affected both our national unity and our attitudes toward traditional religious concepts. The religious situation needs reassessment year by year. Nonetheless the truism holds that "what's past is prologue," and the ongoing drama can best be understood if something is known of what went before. The present volume, together with its fellows, modestly hopes to cast light on the creative antecedents of the contemporary scene.

JAMES WARD SMITH

Princeton, New Jersey
May 1969

INTRODUCTION

A SERIES of volumes entitled "Religion in American Life" should surely begin by clarifying the sense in which the word "religion" is used, for the word has been used, and still is used, in a wide variety of ways. An attempt to legislate a single "proper" meaning would be ill-advised from the start. The unabridged Webster provides nine definitions of the term, of which three merit our quoting in part:

"1. The service and adoration of God or a god as expressed in forms of worship, in obedience to divine commands. . . ."

"6. An apprehension, awareness, or conviction . . . of supernatural powers or influences controlling one's own, humanity's, or nature's destiny. . . ."

"8. A pursuit, an object of pursuit, a principle, or the like, arousing in one religious convictions and feelings such as great faith, devotion, or fervor, or followed with religious zeal, conscientiousness or fidelity; as, patriotism was to him a *religion*."

Webster's eighth definition, or rather the use that it records, raises the first problem which calls for comment. We do sometimes speak of a man's religion, meaning thereby any ultimate and overriding commitment which is central in his life. So, too, we may speak of the religion of a nation or a culture. We might be told that the religion of America is democracy, or success. We hear on all sides such phrases as "the religion of communism" or "the religion of science." These latter two phrases are ambiguous. The former, for example, might refer to the cosmic world view (albeit the atheism of dialectical materialism) which communism officially propagates. It might, on the other hand, refer simply to the fact that action for the party goals constitutes a dominant focus of fervent and devoted attention for a great many purposeful people. So, too, with the phrase "religion of science." It might refer to the cosmic world view implied, or held to be implied, by science; it has even been used in the context of claiming that physics supports such special doctrines as theism.

More often, however, it seems to be used as a way of saying that more than a few modern intellectuals have devoted their lives to science with something of the same self-sacrificing fervor which we have traditionally associated with the devotion of the "believer" to God and His purposes.

There can be no point in arguing that such a very general use of the word "religion" is improper, but in marking out our subject matter for these volumes we have had a more specific use in mind. Clearly, if we meant by "religion in American life" every tendency on the part of this culture to devote itself to ideal purposes, our subject matter would be nothing short of a complete social and intellectual history of the nation. Our concern is with something narrower than that; it is, to put it roughly, with the tendency on the part of our culture to devote itself to ideal purposes which stem from the Judaeo-Christian tradition. One value of an undertaking such as this is that in getting down to details we find that our distinctive religious heritage resists oversimplified generalization. Until comparatively recent times this has been a predominantly Protestant nation, but Protestantism itself is a manifold and fluctuating phenomenon. Thus, in one way or another, Protestantism receives major attention in most of the essays here collected. For three centuries the main thrust of American religion stemmed from the Reformation, and Protestantism in all its heterogeneity must be the object of whatever praise or blame attaches to religious influences in American culture during that period. Floods of immigrants, especially after the Civil War, breached the wall of Protestant dominance. During the past half-century the rise of Catholic influence has been phenomenal, and it appears likely that a study of religion in American life a century hence would need to place far more stress upon Catholic influences in culture. The Jewish tradition, like the Catholic, has attained full partnership in the American enterprise only in the twentieth century. For these reasons, our treatment of the Jewish and Catholic traditions has been far less detailed than our treatment of diverse

Protestant trends.

In any event, we shall be concerned in these volumes with the manifold ways in which a traditional, and largely Protestant, version of religion in Webster's first and sixth sense of the word has both created and been transformed by the fervor, the zeal, and the devotion referred to in the eighth sense.

At the close of the sixth decade of the twentieth century, commentators on the American scene seem to be of two minds in regard to the status and significance of religion in our culture. On the one side there are those of the intellectual avant-garde who insist that "God is dead," and that Western culture has entered into a "post-Christian era." On the other side are those who call attention to "the surge of piety in America," with its accompanying increase in religiosity (if not of authentic religious faith) and an unprecedented rise in the fortunes of institutional churches. The latter observers, to be sure, usually argue that God has been domesticated rather than exterminated, a taming which results in the same kind of secularization of life produced by the loss of any consciousness of God in the modern mind. In short, sophisticates seem to have given up on God altogether, while the naïve masses simply "infinitize" their personal and social values and call the nebulous aggregate "God." Both tendencies are more than once discussed in the ensuing essays.

The obituary for God may be premature. The present volumes, in any case, have been prompted by the conviction that what Americans have at least thought to be their various forms of religion has been vastly and profoundly significant in the total American cultural experience. The several essayists have rigorously eschewed any attempt to demonstrate the truth or falsity of religious propositions—or even to defend the metaphysical validity of any religious apprehension of reality. Their chief concern has been to identify, document, and occasionally evaluate the two aspects of what is surely a unitary process: the religious dimensions of American culture, and the cultural dimensions of American religion. All have assumed that the phenomenological features of religion—the explicit ideas, acknowledged values and norms, institutional forms and activities—have been intimately related to the actualities of American life. In the main, of course, American religion is derivative; at the base lie both the Bible and the long evolution of European Christianity (and European Judaism, too, for that matter). Yet America has produced its peculiar variations, emphases, nuances, all stimulated and made possible by the specific circumstances of American geography, social composition and mobility, political development, economic resources and opportunity, and the like. The American religious ethos has a flavor of its own, unmistakably different from the ethos of European religion of whatever persuasion. The title of Harry Golden's book *Only in America* has point for religion no less than for other facets of culture. Almost nowhere else in the world, for example, have "free" churches known and embodied quite the measure of freedom which an isolated continent and an unfenced frontier provided the churches as they advanced across the American continent. Whatever the theological pretensions of any particular group might be, the restrictions of a monopolistic establishment simply could not be enforced where dissidence could find relief in mobility. Similarly, the tides of immigration assured a religious pluralism quite independent of preconceived theory. Although nearly every religious group may consider itself to be the possessor of the whole religious truth, the theory is innocuous apart from constitutional means of enforcement. Thus, a virtually boundless frontier and unrestricted immigration quite adequately account for the various adjectives most frequently applied to the American religious pattern: pluralistic, voluntaristic, individualistic, democratic, pragmatic, activistic, revivalistic, and enthusiastic. Which is to say that every type of religious temperament, as well as all religious ideologies, found opportunity for expression and growth here. Other causes and conditions have operated to create the distinctive patterns of American religion, and these, too, are discussed in these volumes. It should be useful to have precise and extensive documentation of the generally acknowledged fact that the *forms* of religion, if not its substance, are powerfully molded by the environment in which religiously minded persons function.

The obverse, however, may be equally true, namely, that religious ideas, values, and motivations significantly influence the social and cultural forms. Such a proposition, of course, is nonsense to those who consider religion as always epiphenomenal. Many serious interpreters of the human situation discount as illusory the common transcendental reference of all religions. The province of human experience which religion claims as its unique possession—all that may be subsumed under the category of the numinous—is attributed to psychological aberration, while the beliefs and doctrines asserted by prophets and theologians are viewed as reflections of dominant political, economic, and social interests within a given culture group. Thus, it has been argued that the lofty teaching on predestination was only an effort by Puritan-Calvinists to lend supernatural sanction to the dominance of an elite in Massachusetts. The example is farfetched, to be sure, and does not fairly represent the persuasive arguments of those who, often quite correctly, see religion as either an opiate of the masses or as a supernatural sanction of fundamentally secular interests. Our essayists do not neglect relevant instances in which this reductionist view seems to be substantiated in the American experience.

The contrary opinion, nevertheless, can be documented and defended. Most briefly stated it is this: high (as distinguished from primitive) religion also maintains an autonomous position in every culture. Religion is creator as well as creature, critic as well as conformist, revolutionist as well as conservative. It is true that men very readily search out religious reasons for whatever they already want to do (as the ante-bellum defenders of slavery appealed to dubiously appropriate Biblical texts in support of a profitable form of social organization); but religiously derived ideas and motivations also lead men to break through the barriers of custom, even at great personal cost, in quest of what is believed to be the will of God in particular circumstances. The cynic may protest that the religious idealist is self-deceived, that his faiths and beliefs are no more than rationalizations of less noble desires suppressed and masqueraded in the subconscious. Whether such a judgment is true is not the point. Rather, full weight must be given to the convictions which men *profess* as their guides for conscious action. Even false ideas have consequences. The cultural historian is content to record the ideas ("true" or "false," as the case may be) and the results which presumably have emerged from them. Thus, it is surely demonstrable that some of those who fashioned American freedom and the democratic system did find encouragement and even compulsion in the Judaeo-Christian view of man and society under God. In his *The Kingdom of God in America*, H. Richard Niebuhr has made a strong case for the critical and creative force of one central item of Biblical faith, the Kingdom of God, in the shaping of the American pattern of culture. Perhaps the Biblical faith that "the kingdoms of this world shall become the kingdom of our Lord and his Christ" is a fairy-tale fantasy. Many Christians and Jews, however, have believed it to be a right reading of historical existence, and the belief has determined in significant measure what they have done in politics, business, and the arts.

Hitherto we have been using the phrase "religion in American life" as though it referred primarily to institutional matters. And so indeed in one of its dimensions it does. To discuss the role of religion in American life is to discuss, either historically or by survey of the present, the role of religion in our socio-political institutions and traditions. There are, however, two other dimensions which need to be mentioned. Behind the impact of religion upon our institutional life there lies a body of speculative theory—constantly changing, especially in a Protestant culture—which can be approached systematically from standards that are independent of social and institutional concern. We have had, after all, our speculative theologians; a second dimension of any study of religion in American life must face the question whether

13

American theologians and philosophers have made any significant contributions at the speculative level to the religious thought of the West.

These volumes contain, therefore, several essays which are concerned specifically with the theological and speculative. The line of demarcation between the speculative and the practical is by no means sharp, for most intelligent speculation is acutely aware of the cultural context within which it arises. On the other hand, the "Social Gospel" theology is a special form of theology. It is not always the case, nor even typical, that theologians adopt as their main line of justification the demand that their speculation meet the needs and requirements of social and institutional life. The demand more normally proceeds in the opposite direction: that theological speculation independently justified provides a basis upon which social and institutional life is to be judged. For this reason, no study of religion in American life would be complete which confined itself to the merely institutional and social. For all its emphasis upon the practical, American life has had its speculative moments, and we have set as one of our goals the attempt to identify in the vast kaleidoscope of American thought some of its more important contributions in the area of speculative theology. As in all other matters, our attempt has not been synoptic but rather selective and suggestive.

There is a long tradition in Western philosophy of drawing a threefold distinction among man's concerns. The technical terms which once were used were "cognition, conation, and affection," or simply "thinking, doing, and feeling." Recent analytic philosophy, at any rate in English-speaking countries, has been very suspicious of this triad (and indeed our present remarks may help to show why), but it may still perhaps serve a purpose. We have thus far been discussing religion as a force in institutional life and as an undertaking with speculative concern. To the extent that we find separation difficult we are giving force to the claim that one cannot in the long run divorce questions of "thinking" from questions of "doing" or vice versa. But what of the words "feeling" or "affection"?

How in a study of religion in American life may such words be brought into play? This question brings us to the third dimension of our title.

To begin with, and again questioning the traditional triad, the way a man or a culture "feels" will persistently find expression in what he "thinks" and "does." On the other hand, there are several ways in which a scholar might seek to isolate the emotional side of man's life in a study of religious phenomena. One way would be straightforward psychology. We had at one time hoped to include in these volumes at least one essay by a scientific psychologist, considering the high points in the emotive expressions of the American religious consciousness. It is perhaps worth recording that none of the scientists we approached felt qualified to write such an essay. The repeated excuse was that they were unacquainted with American history—only vaguely aware, for example, of the phenomenon of the Great Awakening of the 1740's. There being no dearth of literature on this subject by the theologians and historians, we have had to be content to cover a copious existing literature in the volume of bibliography, the last volume in our series. We record here our feeling that one of the gaps our undertaking has most glaringly revealed—revealed to the extent of its remaining as a gap in our own volumes—is the failure of trained scientific psychologists outside the seminaries to examine American history to provide themselves with empirical data on which to base scientific hypotheses describing the religious dimensions of man's life.

We have, however, been able to include several essays which refer in one way or another to the emotive or affective side of religion from a purely historical standpoint. The Great Awakening is a part of our story, though unexplored by psychologists. Moreover, the very record of contributions to theology in a country which produced Jonathan Edwards in the early eighteenth century and William James in the late nineteenth cannot fail to direct attention to the religious affections. Not only in its institutions, but in its reflective thought, America has followed paths which keep the emotive side of religion constantly in the foreground.

It is often said that art is unique in its capacity to express the emotional side of man's life. This suggests a final way in which a study such as this might draw attention to the affections. Five of the essays we have gathered are specifically concerned with American art—two on the novel, one on poetry, one on music, and one on architecture. In these essays, perhaps more than elsewhere, will be found the guideposts to an understanding of how Americans have *felt* about religion. This is, of course, a complex matter, ranging all the way from an understanding of the highly intellectual and esoteric feelings of a little-understood poet to an understanding of the feelings of the millions of Americans who made Lloyd C. Douglas' *The Robe* and Joshua Liebman's *Peace of Mind* best sellers.

One must notice, however, that once again the triad of "thinking, doing, and feeling" tends to fall apart. To give but two examples: it will be found that no treatment of the American religious novel can ignore the extent to which the novel as an art form functions as a commentary on the institutional forms of American life. The expression of "feeling" cannot be dissociated in the last analysis from commentary upon our "doing." As a second example, Richard Blackmur's essay on poetry makes it brilliantly clear that the main thrust of the question whether poetry is or is not religious involves us in the attempt to identify the thought behind the feeling. Feeling may be of the essence, but we do not achieve religious poetry by such feeling as is expressed in doggerel upon Biblical themes. Religious poetry must, like all poetry, express emotion, but it must also have religious depth. This kind of emotion does not spring into full bloom out of nowhere; it grows from roots deep in man's nature as a contemplative being.

One of the many services we hope these volumes will provide is to make all of us more aware, first, that there *are* these several dimensions of the role of religion in American life; second, that there is a constant interplay among them and that a one-dimensional treatment will never be adequate. The speculative theories, the institutional forms, and the artistic and emotional expressions of American religion are all parts of a complex and organic whole. A fair assessment of religion in American life requires us to keep all of its components continuously in mind.

The editors are not so rash as to attempt a final summary of the generalizations suggested by the contributors to these volumes. As the materials are various, so are the conclusions. To be sure, certain very broad observations may be made: American religion has tended to emphasize freedom and the individual over authority and the institution; it has been rather more concerned about the practical fruits than the theoretical roots; it has valued the active over the contemplative, the moral over the aesthetic, time and this world more than eternity and heaven. Yet notable exceptions neutralize every such generalization. The two indigenous religious movements of importance, Mormonism and Christian Science, both exhibit a high degree of ecclesiastical discipline and dogmatic rigidity; the emotional extravagances of revivalism have been counterbalanced from the start by a succession of serious (if not always original) theologians, from the spokesmen of "the New England mind" to Reinhold Niebuhr; the this-worldly focus of both the Social Gospel and the cult of "positive thinking" has never quite supplanted the yearning for salvation by sin-obsessed souls. The fact is, in religion as in all else, America has embraced almost every conceivable tendency, idea, and ideal.

This religious pluralism has been often trivial, surely never uniform and coercive in its effects on American culture as a whole. It has shaped no great literature, inspired no classic creations in art or music. Its influence on political experience has been altogether ambiguous. The organized churches, at least, have too often failed to accept the responsibility of leadership. Nevertheless, it is the thesis of these studies that religion has both powerfully and pervasively affected the complex development of American culture. The effort has been made in every essay to demonstrate the ways in which religious concepts, values, and institutions have left their mark on American life. Our main purpose has not been to invent novel proposals; rather, we have desired to reflect further upon what the evidence of cultural history suggests. And above all we acknowledge that the most potent effects of religion in any culture can never be quite accurately or adequately described—the effects produced by religious motivation, the religious dynamic in human behavior. If America can in any meaningful sense be described as a "religious civilization" it is because the nation has been composed of large numbers of men who have found meaning and incentive in religious faith. All too frequently with more zeal than knowledge, seldom with full consistency, certainly never without the corruption of petty self-interest, countless Americans, of high and low estate, have (together with their counterparts everywhere) affirmed their ultimate loyalty to God somehow conceived—most characteristically and publicly to the Biblical God of Moses, Jesus, and Paul; the God, too, of Luther and Calvin and Jonathan Edwards, even of Joseph Smith! The Judaeo-Christian tradition, as it evolved through a millennium and a half of European experience, has furnished the dominant concepts of God, man, the good society, and human destiny. These ideas have been "in the bones" of Americans and are reflected in every facet of American life. But ideas are only as socially potent as the men who espouse them. A culture may be described as authentically religious only to the degree that its members are moved by a sense of commitment to the infinite, by a conviction that the living God is at work in human history. Such a faith may breed fanaticism, parochialism, complacent self-righteousness; uncritically held it may lead to an idolatry of place and people—even Biblical history gives ample evidence of that kind of self-deification. Yet any faith, beyond mere superstition or chauvinism, contains within itself at least some admixture of transcendence, providing the imperatives and the criteria of prophetic judgment. Thus, Americans have ever been the most trenchant critics of America, measuring themselves not only by the standards of dispassionate rationality, but also by the perfections proposed in their visions of the infinite and eternal. The visions have been disparate and blurred, so that we must speak of American *faiths*, rather than an American faith.

It is certain that Americans have more commonly professed some kind of faith than not. Some of them have sought to express their faith in theological systems, although outside a few periods (as in Puritan New England) and denominations (as among Presbyterians and Lutherans) theology as such has seldom been a prime concern of the average American. Religious institutions, the churches, have been important channels of religious effort—the numerical total of voluntary church membership in America is unparalleled elsewhere in Christendom. Yet, as often as not, Americans have implemented their visions in associations, crusades, and movements quite divorced from the conventional church organizations. The one way is not necessarily more "religious" than the other. Indeed, in enterprises of human idealism, as in poetry and the arts, the purest intensity of religious apprehension and motivation may often deliberately reject the clichés and symbolic stereotypes of classical orthodoxy. Thus what appears at first glance to be secular may be, rather, genuine faith in a new and perhaps misleading disguise. A study of religion in American life, while it cannot concern itself with every use of the word "religion," is vastly more than a history of American religion in the conventional sense: it must embrace all those interests and activities which have to do, however indirectly, with the life of man as a spiritual being, man in terms of his ultimate significance. The range of such interests and activities may stretch from matzoth to millenarian hopes.

The present volumes are issued with the humble recognition that the religious dimensions of American life have here been only tangentially explored. The editors and essayists will hope, however, that these recollections of familiar matters and this partial documentation of available evidence will encourage more thorough research in areas of first importance to Americans in understanding and preserving their rich inheritance.

THE PROTESTANT MOVEMENT
AND DEMOCRACY IN THE UNITED STATES

H. RICHARD NIEBUHR

ANY attempt to interpret Protestantism in its relations to American democracy is somewhat presumptuous. In common usage each of the terms refers to a great multiplicity of phenomena in which it is difficult to discern a unifying pattern; the manifold associations between some processes ordinarily called Protestant and others usually called democratic do not allow themselves to be ordered in neat schemes. Accurate yet also comprehensive definition of the terms is impossible, so that to those who insist on precision as the condition of rational discourse all discussion of the theme must seem somewhat nonsensical.

By Protestantism we generally mean a great congeries of historic movements, of religious associations and institutions, of convictions about God and man, of interpretations of divine and human actions, of creeds and rites, of ethical principles and patterns of behavior, and of antagonisms to other convictions, associations, and modes of action. To define this complex by selecting some idea, or value, or form of organization as central is always to act rather arbitrarily. Democracy designates a no less multiform and complexly interwoven set of experiences that, though seemingly a whole, has no obvious common center. Beliefs about human rights and equality, principles and arrangements of government, the pursuit of happiness, freedom in economic enterprise and in religious practice, frontier individualism, the party system, respect for minority rights—all these and much more belong to the complex. To select some idea or practice as the essence of this aggregate is also to exercise subjective and arbitrary choice. Since neither Protestantism nor democracy presents to us a clearly portrayable face with determinate features, we tend to define them negatively as anti-Catholic and anti-authoritarian movements. Yet this is manifestly inadequate, for their antagonisms are secondary to their protagonisms as often as their affirmations depend on their negations. Unique "somethings" in past and present, they cannot easily be subsumed under even such general categories as religion and politics, or church and state. Protestantism is not only religion but presents itself also as political action; democracy appears not only as a form of political organization but as a kind of faith.

Great as are the difficulties of definition, the obstacles in the way of an interpreter of Protestant-democratic relations seem even more frustrating. He has before him a puzzle something like the riddle of psychosomatic relations. Having made an initial, apparently necessary, distinction between two entities or processes that offer themselves to him as united, he asks himself whether the relations are those of interaction, or of parallelism, or of epiphenomenalism, or whether indeed he is dealing with two aspects of a more fundamental reality. He notes the interaction of Protestant churches and democratic states in political battles for the disestablishment of churches and in popular agitation for municipal reform. He finds parallelism rather than interaction in democratic interest in natural or common law on the one hand, Protestant reliance on the revealed law of God on the other. Some occasions suggest that the significant movement occurs in one process while an accompanying appearance in the other presents only a superficial symptom, as when Protestantism reflects democratic interest in secular progress. Yet in still other cases both Protestant and democratic phenomena are most intelligible when interpreted as the similar-dissimilar aspects of something more fundamental than either—for instance, of economic process, or of one of those strange tides in history called "climates of opinion." As in the case of mind-body relations, all the various patterns of interpretation must be used because none suffices for every occasion. Whatever dogma the interpreter has accepted, he finds that he must use now and again modes of interpretation that clash with it as he seeks to remain true to his objects. The economic determinist must discuss the interaction that takes place between elements in the cultural superstructure; the analyst of political power must recognize in passing that in religion there is something not wholly explicable in terms of self-interested will-to-power; the believer in the independence and primacy of spiritual, religious life must concede at certain points its great dependence on politics and economics.

Despite such difficulties that make every interpretation of Protestantism in its relations to democracy in America provisional and uncertain, the effort must be made repeatedly to discover and describe intelligible pattern in these areas of our confusing world of historical and social experience. Theological and historical, like literary, criticism undertakes its task anew in every generation because the unexamined life is not worth living and because self-knowledge is an intrinsic as well as instrumental good. So, recognizing that subjectivity and partiality cannot be avoided but only controlled, we venture on the effort to interpret Protestantism in its relations to American democracy. The business of the critic, it has been well said, "is not the avoidance of subjectivity, but its purification; not the shunning of what is disputable, but the cleansing and deepening of the dispute." [1]

I. Protestantism as Movement
and as Order

A. Protestantism as Movement. Between the polarities of order and movement, of structure and process, the Protestant finds himself and his communities always drawn toward the dynamic side. It seems to him that his partner in Christendom, the Catholic, orients himself with equal constancy toward the opposite pole. Does not this Catholic have a sense, expressed in all his actions and utterances, of being part of an established order of things, member of an enduring and fundamentally unchanging church, recipient of

[1] Erich Heller, *The Disinherited Mind*, New York, 1957, p. ix.

a truth once and for all revealed, believer in a well-defined and articulated "true religion," subject of constant and known laws, follower of leaders who stand in an unchanging office and succession? Does not that individual believer seem to "pass through things temporal" as through a well-mapped territory, under the guidance of shepherds who know not only in what direction to lead but are acquainted with the forks in the road, the traps and ambushes beside it? To the Protestant, however, life seems a pilgrim's progress which, whether made solitarily or in company, proceeds through unpredictable contingencies and crises toward the destination beyond life and death where all the trumpets blow. Though his Bible is also a book of doctrines and of laws, it is this less than the story of past pilgrimages now continued, and of encounters between God and man to be re-enacted in every generation. He, too, believes that the church is founded on a rock, but the rock is Peter's act of faith rather than substantial Peter himself; and the church of his experience is not so much a millennial structure defying the storms and floods of the years as it is a tabernacle set up on the march night after night, struck down again morning after morning. That its frail walls withstand the gales and rains is due to no inherent strength but is always a miracle of grace. The Protestant memory of the past is not focused in one grand event when the true human community was reconstituted by the Lord and when the church came into being as representative and guardian of that community. The great event was one of arrivals, departures, and promises of return; it has left behind in history not so much a visible, resurrected Body of Christ in the form of the church, as faith and hope and love, becoming incarnate now and again, but essentially as invisible as are all the movements of the spirit. The story of the church itself has for him a double center, its founding and its reform. The symbolic pattern in his mind as he looks on general as well as on church history is not that of a new creation, but of creation and fall and re-creation; church and world and individual life are forever being created, forever falling, forever being raised again. Hence also his expectation of the future is not anticipation of life continuing in enduring structures, but of shaken foundations and new construction on ruins. Everything for him is movement; everything a becoming.

Orientation toward the dynamic does not mean that reliance on structure and concern for order are not also present to the Protestant mind. The polarity in which he moves does not allow exclusive reference to one pole. Nor can he think of the Catholic as so oriented toward structure and order that participation in movement is not also part of his life. Yet what is dominant in the mind of the one seems recessive in that of the other.

The Protestant in America may be even more conscious of involvement in a movement than is his European brother. He is aware of the society in which he holds membership not only as relatively recent in origin but as subject to even more recent changes. If it traces its beginnings to Europe, it also records its refounding in America. If it is native-born, and so very young as church history counts time, it has in most instances passed through some crisis of cleavage, or reunion, or reorganization. The church history in the American Protestant's mind is one of many reformations. He is aware also of modifications in the creed, the polity, and the interests of his religious group in consequence of its interaction with other Protestant societies and with democratic, scientific, and industrial civilization. The theology with which he is more or less acquainted through instruction from the pulpit seems to be subject to constant change as it moves toward rapprochement now with biology, now with psychology, now with the mind of the day as expressed in literature. It emphasizes now the moral, now the doctrinal principles of Christian faith; it is orthodox and liberal and fundamentalist and neo-orthodox in turn. There is no standard theologian, no Protestant St. Thomas Aquinas, to whom all his religious interpreters refer. His theology, with a few exceptions, is not oriented toward the fathers but toward contemporaries. As with theology, so with ritual: ancient rubrics, banned by Puritan reformers, are reintroduced into the common prayer of their followers; high- and low-church practices compete with each other in the highest and lowest of churches. Moral concerns also succeed each other as humanitarianism is replaced by crusades for social reform through political action and these by campaigns for temperance and these by discouraged acquiescence in popular mores and defensive praise of the "American way of life."

The unfixed, moving character of American Protestantism seems even more striking when its phenomena are regarded objectively than when we attempt to enter empathetically into the Protestant mind. The churches in the United States called Protestant are not foundations established at one time in history when the long-enduring reign in the West of the Roman Catholic church was challenged. To be sure, of these more than two hundred organizations, many trace their origins to the sixteenth-century Reformation. But others had their beginning in a somewhat different reform movement in seventeenth-century England; others go back to the Awakening and the Enlightenment of the eighteenth century, to Pietism, Evangelicalism, and Methodism; still others were founded early in the nineteenth century during the Second Awakening, or in revivals and reformations of more recent decades.

A classification of Protestant denominations in the United States based on the times of their origins might turn out somewhat as follows:

1. The churches of the sixteenth-century Reformation: the Lutheran, the Reformed, the Presbyterian, and the Protestant Episcopal churches; left-wing Reformation groups such as the Mennonites and some Baptist societies.

2. The churches of the seventeenth-century Puritan Revolution: the Congregationalists; the Society of Friends.

3. The churches of the eighteenth-century Awakening and Enlightenment: the Methodist church; the Moravians;

25

Evangelical United Brethren; Dunkers; most Baptist groups; the Unitarians.

4. The churches of the nineteenth-century Revivals in America: the Disciples of Christ; the churches of Christ; the Cumberland Presbyterian church; the Seventh-Day Adventists; many Pentecostalist denominations; the Church of the Nazarene.

A fifth group might be added, partly on the basis of chronology. It would consist of those Protestant groups that had their inception in the late nineteenth and early twentieth centuries. Many of these, though not all, show to an unusual degree the mark of having been founded by an individual "prophetic" or "charismatic" personality. Among them are Jehovah's Witnesses (the Russellites); Mary Baker Eddy's Church of Christ, Scientist; Bishop A. J. Tomlinson's Church of God; Aimee Semple McPherson's International Church of the Four Square Gospel; Mrs. Alma White's Pillar of Fire; Alexander Dowie's Church in Zion; Benjamin Purnell's House of David, and many another. Somewhat akin to this group, so far as unusual dependence on a prophet is concerned, though founded at an earlier date, are the two Mormon societies.

When the pluralism of Protestantism is so regarded, then the manifold seems to represent the successive phases of a process as much as division among the elements of one structure. It is as though we had before us the representatives of many generations rather than divided siblings equally in revolt against common parents. Division within one brotherhood, schism in one society, is undeniably present; but the evidence of one process that has resulted in these several institutional concretions is also noticeable.

If we attend to this evidence, a question arises about the nature of that process. The term "Protestant" offers us one clue. Though very few of the churches classified under that name use it officially, they seem content to be called by it en masse.[2] But Protestantism in its many varieties is not the product or carrier of a single protest against one order of religious and political life; it represents rather a whole series of protests directed against many successive established orders of Christian faith and against their political guarantors. The protest against the Roman church and the empire gave Protestantism its name, yet at the same time, when the evangelicals (as they preferred to call themselves) who followed Luther, Zwingli, and their associates were voicing that dissent, a second group of protesters—now often called the left wing of the Reformation—challenged the first group and their political supporters. As the former objected to the papacy, the ritual, the ethos, and the doctrine of the Roman church, and to political measures enforcing conformity to these, so Anabaptists, spiritualists, and rationalists protested against the manner in which the Reformers were interpreting the Scriptures, organizing churches, and relying on political powers to enforce their measures. A third protest arose when Puritanism in its various forms objected neither to pope nor Roman cultus in the first place, but to Archbishop Laud and the Anglican establishment, to the Stuart monarchy, the Star Chamber, and the Court of High Commission. But that remonstrance again was accompanied by objections raised by Independents, Quakers, and other religio-political groups, not against Anglicanism but against Presbyterian Puritanism. So protest against Rome was followed by protest against Wittenberg, against Zurich, against Geneva, against Canterbury, against Westminster. A century later Evangelicalism, Pietism, and Methodism took anti-Romanism for granted, but raised primary objections against the traditional forms of religious life that had become established in the state churches of Europe, Great Britain, and the American colonies. Finally,

[2] Among major American denominations only the one closest to Roman Catholicism in some respects, the Protestant Episcopal Church, uses the word "Protestant" in its official title.

the nineteenth-century protests were directed against all preceding orders of religious life, including those that had issued out of the eighteenth-century crises. Not only "Republican Methodists" with their dissent from the episcopal polity of the Methodist church, but other groups more concerned with "second blessings," with "going on to perfection," with the reconstitution of churches as gathered communities of the regenerate only, challenged traditions that were far from hoary. In this whole series of protesting movements there were scarcely any that returned to the position which had originally aroused opposition. And this seems strange, since in the history of human change a kind of rhythm often prevails; Romantic objectors against classicism find themselves challenged by new classicists; liberal protest against governmental control of economic activities is followed by social protest against individualism; the opponents of nominalism return to a form of realism. There may be traces of such a rhythm in the story of Protestantism, but the very large majority of all the new churches remained Protestant in the original meaning of the term. Though they turned against the challengers of Roman Catholicism, they did not return to Rome or to the principles of its Catholicism.

What is the source of these recurrent dissentings? Is the movement of protest carried by a more positive factor than mere dissatisfaction with existing order? Any effort to answer such questions could lead us deep into the consideration of Hobbesian and Freudian, of Aristotelian and idealistic, or of Hebraic and Pauline, theories of human nature and of society. A simpler approach is possible, however, through consideration of two main types of explanation of the movement of protest, as offered on the one hand mostly by its theological critics, on the other mostly by its exponents.

The source of the protests, says the critic, is simply self-will or the will-to-power. Anti-authoritarianism has its roots in the desire of every man to be God, the master of his own fate, the sovereign of his own life. But once the process of revolt against order and self-transcendent sovereignty has been begun it cannot be stopped. It cannot be stopped in society or in the soul. National churches that begin with the rejection of the universal church find themselves rejected by groups in the national society that discern in them representatives, not of divine authority, but of temporal princes or of dominant social classes. The generation that revolts against ancestral order must experience the revolt of its children who find parental domination to be supported by nothing but the diminishing prestige and power of senescent adults. The process of anti-authoritarian revolt cannot be stopped within the person himself. The individual who has set up his conscience in rivalry to the God-given law of the church discovers that conscience, subject to no sovereign, becomes prey to rebellious desires within him. So the source of the continuing revolt, in theological terminology, is sin: the lust of the flesh, the lust of the eyes, and the pride of life; or self-will and sensuality. And the doctrines proclaimed in revolt are to be interpreted as rationalizations, smoke-screens behind which destructive forces operate.

Much direct and circumstantial evidence seems to support such an interpretation of Protestantism as a movement toward anarchy exhibiting not only nationalistic but also partisan and class will-to-power, exhibiting not only individualistic but also egoistic, and not only egoistic but also sensualistic, revolt against an authority that represents the wholeness of human society. The histories of modern nationalism and of Protestantism are closely intertwined, and the relations of capitalism to Protestantism seem to lend credibility to the gibe that the Reformation was the revolt of the rich against the poor. As for personal motives, muckraking histories of Protestantism can point with mixed sorrow and glee to Luther's repudiation of the vow of celibacy and his marriage with a nun, to Henry the Eighth's desire for a divorce, to Philip of Hesse's bigamy, and to many another adventure in love or marriage which culminated in some grand experiments in the country where Protestantism has been most unconfined: group marriage in the Oneida community, polygamy among the Mormons, and a high divorce rate among Protestants in general, not to speak of rumors about the prevalence of incontinence at frontier revivals, or the private morals of certain prophets and prophetesses. If the private profit motive is considered, the trail of cupidity is not hard to follow; it leads from the seizure of church lands by Henry's earls and barons to the founding of "free enterprise" religious establishments purporting to purvey cures for all physical, mental, and spiritual ills. The power motive, too, can be amply illustrated by reference to all the "theocracies"—from Geneva to Father Divine's heavens—in which not God, but someone claiming plenipotentiary power, is said to have exercised sovereignty. To all such incidents in which Protestant protest against established authority can be associated with the motions of sin, a psychological analysis of unconscious motivation could add a very formidable series of case studies.

Such moral arguments, or psychological and sociological analyses of the sources of protest, are, however, always ambivalent and inconclusive. The sorts of motivation that can be pointed to in accounting for revolt against authority can be discovered with equal frequency in its exercise or in obedience to it. Granted that the break-up of a unified system of order has given men, particularly within the spheres of Protestantism and of democratic societies, large opportunity for the exercise of the will-to-power and of passion, and that it has allowed to come into open appearance forces previously repressed and disguised; it does not follow that these are the sources rather than the concomitants of protest, or that they are the sources of all protests. They, and even protest itself, may be the accompaniments of a movement that has within it another drive than that of self-will, and another interest than the rejection of authority. It may be that American Protestantism with all the evidences of antinomianism that abound in it, like the democracy with which it is associated, represents not so much a movement from order to disorder as one from the order of authority to the order of freedom, or from the mode of life primarily interested in structure to one primarily directed toward action.

In distinction from their critics, Protestants have not thought of themselves primarily as protesters or as anti-authoritarian. For them the negations have been only incidental to the affirmations. And the positive thing they believed they were affirming was not some new authority in place of the old, whatever authorities needed to be acknowledged. It was rather the near or immediate possibility of a kind of life that was not subject to authority because it was free, that did not require an external ordering because it was ordered by the attractiveness of the good. Freedom did not mean negative liberty *from* authority so much as it meant positive liberty *toward* the goals of action. To describe his movement, his churches, his beliefs in terms of authority; to speak of them as anti-authoritarian or as substituting the authority of Bible or of conscience for ecclesiastical authority; or otherwise to deal with the gospel, the Scriptures, and the church as though the main human or Christian question were the one about authority, is always to require the Protestant to think of himself and account for himself by means of categories that are essentially strange to him. They are strange not because they are not applicable, but because they do not touch the central issue with which he is concerned and around which his internal debate takes place. To require him to explain himself in answer to the question, "By what authority do you do these things?" is like asking a poet to justify himself in terms of logic, to answer the question, "By what logic do you say these things?" Such questions are relevant, but they impose upon the answerer the value preferences of the questioner who in the one instance regards social order, in the other instance, logical order, as the fundamental good.

The protests of Protestantism—always allowing for the

31

presence in them of rebellious self-assertions—have been secondary, for the most part, to revivals. The movement of protest from generation to generation has followed, not preceded, a movement of reformation, regeneration, awakening, and renewal. And the protest was raised not against the authority of the old, but against its acceptance and establishment of a mediocre form of men's moral and religious existence.

The first question in the mind of those sixteenth-century men who became the Reformers was not the one about correcting the errors and healing the diseases of the church. That question had been long in the air and was to continue indefinitely. Their problem was rather how the reformation, the renewal, the regeneration of human life was to be achieved. How can man, rebellious, full of suspicion of all powers including the ultimate power, full of anger and fear, become reconciled to life and to God? How is it possible for moral man, the incorrigible lover of self and continual victim of his passions, whether ruler or subject, whether exercising or obeying authority, to become a lover of God and of his companions? How can he become free not of external restraint, but of those internal conflicts and that alienation from himself which justify external restraint and are increased by it? To think of such freedom was also to think of eternal happiness, of the attainment of that true life of which men are aware as a promise implicit in their existence. The statement of the human problem in such terms was possible only because hope had been revived.

The rebirth of hope had two aspects: for one thing, the redemption of life's promise was very near; for another, the promise was for a new quality of existence. The forgiveness of sin, release from guilt, joy in existence, life in confidence—these were gifts offered now, not prizes promised in another world. To be sure, the final release of souls from internal division and external estrangement from God and one another was a future event; but the great salvation was not far off; it was now in process and men could now participate in a victory that was very sure. The good news these evangelicals heard and preached was not the news that at a past time salvation had come to men and had been conserved in the holy institutions of the church, nor yet that at some future date men were to be healed of their diseases. It was rather that the past and the future salvation were effective in the present. Forgiveness was offered now; God was electing them now. As in the early days of the church, though with differences in symbolism, the ultimate hope for the great redemption from evil was fortified, enlivened, and enriched by being brought very near in the present experience of anticipatory signs of its coming.

The renewal of hope was not a revival of the expectation of immortality and of eternal happiness. These were in a sense included, but the prospect that had opened to the eyes of the Reformers and their followers through the mediation of the Scriptures was one of a certain quality rather than quantity of life. The characteristic words for it were taken from the apostle Paul; it was life in the spirit, in grace, in freedom, in reconciliation. The hope was for "the glorious liberty of the children of God." The meaning of such liberty depended, of course, upon the whole context. It was the freedom to which Christ set men free. It was freedom from the rule of Satan, sin, and death; from the compulsions of obedience to superpersonal forces of evil; from domination by self-interest and the passions; from the necessity of fighting off death and all diminution of life. It was freedom from law and authority only in a secondary sense, as freedom from a restraint no longer necessary to selves who joyfully accepted their lives and fortunes as free gifts of grace, and who lived in gratitude to God and their companions. Such moral freedom was related to the flouting of law on the one hand, and to meticulous obedience to it on the other, as the free exercise of poetic genius is related to the willfulness of nonsense rhymers and to the pedantic, imitative work of prosaic minds, both ignorant of the artist's vision.

The Reformation was a revival of confidence even more than a renewal of hope. To its great and little leaders and to many simple folk there came a new certainty that no dogmatic formula could express. They had lost confidence in the church, to be sure; they had lost confidence in themselves as able to lift themselves to sainthood. But this loss of confidence in institutions and in men had been followed by a new reliance on the Determiner of Destiny, on the power whence all things proceeded and by which all were governed. The far-off God was very near; the silent Eternal spoke; the holy Judge was gracious; the mystery had become incarnate, experienceable, knowable. As revival of confidence, the Reformation, despite its doctrine of predestination, was not the birth of assurance in a few men that they had been elected to escape the great frustration and destruction of existence, but was a wide sense of the meaningfulness of all life, of all creation, which—despite and through treason, agony, and death—was being, as it had been and would be, resurrected to glory.

The renewal of hope and confidence was accompanied, if not preceded, by a revival of the "hunger and thirst for righteousness." Increased desire for integrity in the self and in the common life, increased sensitivity to hypocrisy and divided loyalties, increased revulsion against the compromises and deceptions of "normal" human conduct in part precipitated the mental crises in which the revival of faith and hope occurred. In part they followed, since men tend to suppress those desires that have no prospect of fulfillment and to experience the release of suppressed wishes when the goal comes into view. Hopeful men also anticipate the expected state of affairs and pre-enact in the present what they confidently expect as future gift. That the Reformation included a strong element of moral renewal, of ethical seriousness, of concern for private and public faithfulness, is not subject to doubt. In the case of Calvin and Geneva the evidence is clear; Luther, more subject to misunderstanding and more exposed to attacks, does not fall short on this score when fairly read and studied.[3]

[3] See in particular Karl Holl, "Der Neubau der Sittlichkeit," in his *Luther, Gesammelte Schriften*, Vol. i.

The early and late intrusion into this first Protestant revival of enthusiasms too sanguine to be safe, of private ambitions disguised as hope of freedom, and of dogmatic opinions masquerading as faith is evident enough. In this respect the situation did not differ, except in magnitude, from the one presented in the Pauline letters. Yet revival there was—of hope, and confidence, and moral seriousness. And not only those who became members of the rejected and protesting churches participated in it; it was an event in Christendom which affected Catholicism, the nations, the folk-mores, the climate of opinion.

Each of the later great protests can be traced to a renewal somewhat similar in character to that of the sixteenth century. The differences among the reformations, awakenings, and revivals were such that the right of a later inspiration to call itself a renewal of an earlier one could be cogently questioned. Lutherans could see in Pietism a return to the spirit of monasticism rather than to that of the Reformation; Calvinists suspected Methodists of reintroducing into the Christian mind the thought that redemption could be achieved by the willing individual. The Great Awakening in America; the revivals that spread from Cane Ridge; the Pentecostalist movement; Jonathan Edwards, Timothy Dwight, Stone, Campbell, Finney, and Moody—all these have been subject to criticism in turn by the guardians of traditions begun in earlier reforms and by eye-witnesses of an earlier resurrection of Christian life. The differences are evident; sometimes they are matters of degree, sometimes of emphasis, sometimes of purity. The renewal of hunger and thirst for righteousness was more prominent in some movements than in others, as we note when we compare Wesley with Zinzendorf, or Finney with Whitefield; in the millenarian eruption the renewal of hope was more pronounced than the renewal of confidence; no other awakening of love of God and neighbor compares with Edwards'; no other rebirth of confidence in God seems to reach the heights found in Luther's and Calvin's Reformation. Yet

35

the successive renewals all shared to a considerable extent in all these reorientations and reshapings of fundamental attitudes toward man's ultimate environment. All of them interpreted through the Scriptures the past, present, and future of existent men and the power that ruled them in all their times. However various in authorship and theological thought, however subject to different interpretations, those Scriptures presented a significantly distinctive and unitary understanding of God, man, and history. The unity of the Protestant movement was like the unity of the Bible, whence it derived its successive inspirations.

The emergence of American Protestantism out of reformations that had this character, and the continuation in it of similar renewals, does not account for all of its features. But to interpret it without reference to the critical occasions in which its organizations and institutions were developed, or to interpret those occasions as primarily protests against authority, is to neglect a patently actual force in its history.

Protestantism everywhere, and in America in particular, presents itself as a movement rather than an organization. And as a movement it is less one of protest than of revival, for revival precedes protest. Revolt against authority is only incidental in a movement for which freedom is a positive thing—freedom for faith and hope and goodness, rather than a negative liberty from external control.

B. PROTESTANTISM AS ORDER. In the polarities of process and structure, of movement and order, there is no dynamism that has no static and structural aspect. Whatever is true about physical or metaphysical process, in human history the dynamic seems always to be followed by the static, and there is a requirement for order in every movement. Though Protestantism seems intelligible only if it is regarded primarily as a movement in Western Christendom, it also presents itself as an order or as congeries of orders. It is our name for a collection of Christian organizations with habitual modes of government and obedience, with doctrinal statements about what is or ought to be believed, with methods of economic support, with recognized officials and offices, with stated forms of prayer and ritual, with established ways of education in Sunday Schools, colleges, and seminaries. These orders and structures have not, for the most part, been specifically designed or intended by founding fathers; it was not for the sake of establishing them that the movements of protest, least of all the revivals, took place. In part they represent the continuation of modes of behavior established prior to reformations and revivals; in part they are re-enactments of activities first undertaken in the midst of revival, repeated thereafter almost as a matter of course; in part they have been invented to meet unforeseen difficulties and opportunities. Ideas of new order do not seem to come first in the Protestant mind. They are accepted or developed as the need arises, and, for the most part, have something of an emergency character. They are instruments, not ends. Exceptions to the general rule must be allowed in view of the scope given in the permissive world of Protestantism and of democracy to Utopianism as well as to the free enterprise of religious inventors and entrepreneurs. But these operate at the fringes rather than in the center of Protestantism.

Two sets of conditions in particular seem to lead to the development of orders in Protestantism. One of these is offered by the conflicts that appear in every moment of revival as the movement comes into collision with the established order and as a number of somewhat divergent forces are freed from the control of that order. The other set of conditions is found in the need to conserve the attainments of a moment of inspiration and to transmit them as well as the spirit of the movement to a new generation.

Each revival out of which the institutions of American Protestantism have issued has been marked by a triple conflict and agreement. The first was among the friends of the reformation; the second with the established order; the third with allies that joined the reformers more in their protest than in the reformation. The participation in each major movement of a number of like-minded but not unanimous groups with their leaders meant that variety of concerns was present in the midst of general agreement. The Reformation, the Puritan revolution, the Great Awakening, Pietism, Methodism, Evangelicalism, the nineteenth-century revivals, all had multiple origin and leadership. Luther, Zwingli, Bucer, Calvin, Melanchthon, and many others are the fathers of the Reformation; Puritanism in England came through so many channels that it celebrates no major founders; Spener and Francke are associated in the coming of Pietism; John and Charles Wesley and George Whitefield are the preachers of the Methodist revival; Edwards, Whitefield, the Tennents, and others, of the Great Awakening. These leaders, moreover, are representative of the experiences, concerns, hopes, and convictions of many groups of inconspicuous believers. Among such diverse like-thinking and like-acting people, agreement must be formulated just because there is unity in diversity and diversity in unity. Confessions of faith, allocations of responsibility, provisions for the treatment of ever-present recalcitrants and delinquents, agreements about the ways of common action result. Later the confessions become creeds to be enforced; the governmental arrangements harden into polities and disciplines; ways of worship and of evangelization are standardized as rites.

Agreement and conflict with the established order also lead to organization and the establishment of new structures. The movement of revival arises in the midst of ordered and habitual religious action. It is not concerned in the beginning with the replacement of the old order by a new, but with the reemergence of that spiritual life out of which it believes the old order had issued. It seeks only the elimination of those elements in the traditional way that seem corrupt—

adjustments made by the church to the ways of the world for the sake of survival or success. The new movement believes itself to be in agreement with the fundamental intention set forth in the old order. Then follows the rejection of the new by the old; the protest of the new against the old; and a short or long period of conflict. Defense and offense in the ensuing struggle require organization and the adoption of strategical and tactical measures. Issues about minor questions of order acquire symbolical meaning and become rallying points of the contesting forces. In time, emergency provisions become habitual. Yet, despite conflict, agreement of the new with the old remains evident in the silent continuation among reformers and protesters of many traditional ways.

The third sort of conflict and agreement may be the most important in the development of Protestant institutions. Protest against the established order attracts into the camp of reformers and awakeners individuals and groups with motivations very diverse from their own save at the point of antagonism against the prevailing institutions. As Paul's resistance to Peter and the pillars of the early church offered opportunity to antinomians and Gnostics, so Luther was joined by enthusiasts, by knights, and peasants more interested in protest against the old order than in the gospel of faith and forgiveness. The Puritans had at their side Levellers and Fifth Monarchy men; Edwards had his Eleazar Wheelock; Finney had Garrison and the Abolitionists and the perfectionists; Channing had Parker and the Utopians. These allies of the reformers in their conflict with the old are of various sorts. One kind is primarily political; its members are concerned with immediate deliverance from some particular injustice under which they or their companions suffer. They tend to regard that injustice as the root of all evil and the traditional form of religion as its guarantor or protector. Another group of voluntary allies consists of religious enthusiasts for whom the present moment constitutes not the beginning of a new process but the culminating point in

39

historical human existence. For them the kingdom of God has not only come very near but can now be taken by force, whether physical force or the resolute concentration of spiritual power. A final judgment in which divine righteousness will be established has not only become certain but is now at hand; sheep and goats are now to be divided, and if God still hesitates to do so, men must undertake the task. For such men, the time of revival is not one of hope's renewal but of its realization; not of faith's resurrection but of its transformation into sight; not of revived hunger for integrity but of hunger's satisfaction. To such impatient souls the reformers always seem to be dragging their feet and to be compromising with an evil old world. Every revival and protest has given opportunity for the rise of such groups that assumed the reformers' real cause and their own to be identical. But there was no identity and the reformers partly agreed with the old order in rejecting the enthusiasts. In consequence the reformation needed to be ordered, its beliefs formulated, its organization developed, its discipline enforced.

The second series of conditions under which the problem of structure becomes acute for the leaders of the evangelical movement is provided by the rhythmic alternation, in personal and social life, of moments of inspiration, insight, and resolve with times of dryness, doubt, and resignation. When the creative moment has passed, all the habitual, long established modes of thought and action tend to reassert themselves; hence the effort must be made to give concrete and structured expression to the new inspirations, insights, and resolves. This leveling off on a new plateau is not what was intended in the movement, but the necessity for it must be accepted. So Paul found his converts from Judaism and paganism subject to relapse from life in freedom to life in bondage to passions, or to the old law, or to both. Hence he formulated for them a kind of minimum, negative morality that proscribed attitudes and acts incompatible with life in freedom, and he described the kind of conduct that signalized the presence of the Spirit. Now a standard had been set up that could become a new law.[4] Paul's problem has been recurrent in all the Protestant, and in all the pre-Protestant, evangelical movements. As with ethics, so with faith. The confidence in God that is renewed in the revival of faith is not a new set of beliefs which can be substituted for an older creed; but the effort to conserve it seems to require its translation into propositions about the power, the faithfulness, the graciousness, and holiness of the Father, Son, and Holy Spirit, by whom the confidence was elicited.

Another factor that affects the trend toward conservation of the contents of creative moments is, of course, the rise of a new generation, and the desire of fathers to transmit to children the fruits of their experiences. New freedom, no less than old order, becomes a tradition in two generations. Catechisms are written for the sake of mediating through creed and commandment the faith and ethos of a time of renewal. The story of that time is ordered, endowed with high symbolic meaning, inculcated into the memories of those who did not participate in the events. Loyalty to the society that issued from the reform is identified with loyalty to its cause. The apparent necessity of conserving the gains of the past takes precedence over the past's outlook toward the future.

How these various influences have operated in American Protestantism, so constantly involved in movement, to produce a kind of pragmatic order can be illustrated in a whole series of case histories. Perry Miller has described what happened to American Puritanism in its transition not only from colony to province but from movement to establishment.[5] The pioneers in a campaign that had the renewal of English and, indeed, of all Christendom as its object became the isolated detachment of an army that had made a

[4] Cf. especially Galatians 5.
[5] In *The New England Mind: From Colony to Province*, Cambridge, Mass., 1953.

compromising truce. Now nothing remained but to try to conserve in the outpost the limited gains that had been achieved. The adoption of the Half-Way Covenant, arising out of the need of making provision for the new generation, was the symbol of transition from a movement toward the future into an order conserving the past. Later, Jonathan Edwards, meeting the criticism directed against the disorderly accompaniments of the Great Awakening, wrestled with the problem of standards of Christian and clerical conduct compatible with the experience of true regeneration, and with the question of the kind of church organization required for the conservation of the fruits of revival. In English and American Methodism the class-meetings, the chapels, the new hymnody, the revision of the Thirty-nine Articles, the development of the discipline, the adoption of the episcopal form of government, and the organization of the clergy do not represent institutions for the sake of which the Wesleyan movement broke with Anglicanism. They were rather measures that developed in the midst of the revival or that were adopted to meet the emergent requirements of a situation full of unwanted conflicts and the need for conservation. The orders of the Baptist churches, of the Disciples of Christ, and of Pentecostalist and millenarian groups may be understood in similar fashion.

Protestantism in general, but American Protestantism in particular, seems to have developed its institutions and orders not as its ends in view or as representative of its purpose, but as the necessary instruments and pragmatic devices of a movement that could not come to rest in any structure. In the language of theology the movement is essentially eschatological, looking forward toward the great consummation of a promise of freedom in love of God and neighbor, not, however, as a distant event, but as one which has begun and is being re-begun generation after generation.

The structures or the orders of Protestantism, however, cannot be understood as pragmatic devices only. The expediency, after all, has been that of a movement which, however manifold in temporal and spatial and social manifestations, has had a unified source of inspiration, namely the Scriptures. It has been subject also to the pressures of a number of limiting, formative forces including the long Christian tradition, the interaction of the various movements and groups upon each other, and the common influence of the cultural and political environment.

It is often said that Protestantism has tried to replace the authority of the church by the authority of Scriptures and that, as Catholics look to the pronouncements of councils and popes for imperatives prescribing what must be believed and done, so Protestants look to the Bible. It is also often remarked that, in the absence of a supreme judiciary whose decisions about the meaning of Scriptures are accepted, the result of Biblical authoritarianism for Protestantism has been conflict among many equally authoritative, equally relative interpretations of the supreme law. There is much truth in both assertions. Not a few Protestants have been and are upholders of Scriptural authority in this sense and have contended with others about the true interpretation. But this view of the Bible, whether held by Protestants or by their opponents, seems to contain a fundamental misconception of the kind of power or authority Scriptures have exercised. The emphasis is wrongly placed; a secondary function is regarded as primary. In all the great seminal reformations and revivals of Protestantism the Scriptures have been of central importance. But as these renewals were not in the first place efforts to impose new order on church or personal life, so also the Bible read and expounded in them was not a law book or a repository of creedal formulations. It was rather the book of promises—of life's promise, of God's promise to men, of promises made, fulfilled, and to be fulfilled. The Bible was effective as the story of that liberation of men from all enslavements which, beginning and enacted in the past, was being accomplished in the present and would most certainly be completed. To use the inadequate analogy of American democratic society, the Scriptures for Protestants are not like what the Constitution is for Americans, but more like the collection of all the documents from Magna Charta to the Atlantic Charter that record the story of secular liberations. The authority of the Bible has been more like that of the prophet than that of the law-giver. It has called to repentance and change of mind, to sorrow for transgression and waywardness, and to joy in the hope of redemption from evil, to dissatisfaction with all half-life, and to anticipation of authentic, death-overcoming life with Christ. The authority of the Bible for Protestants—no doubt for all Christians—is the authority or power of promise in process of fulfillment, rather than of law.

With many differences of emphasis on various elements in the promise and its fulfillment—such as the forgiveness of sin, the gift of the Spirit, perfection of life, the Second Coming of the Christ—Protestants from Lutherans to millenarians have lived under the authority of Scriptures as such a book. It has been for them not a compendium of imperatives about what ought to be believed and done, but a description of what had been, was being, and would be done in the course of human events. But it has also been used by them in a secondary way as a kind of constitutional authority. As problems of discipline and order have arisen in the wake of reforms and revivals, Protestants have turned to it for counsel and imperatives regarding the things now to be confessed in word and deed. Though they have found various injunctions and models in a book presenting so long and complex a history, and though they have quarreled with each other about interpretation, still those various commands and examples all belong to one context and are qualified by their association with one set of first principles. There are general principles of "faith and order" that practically all Protestants hold in common, not only because they have inherited them from the long Christian tradition but because that tradition has been renewed and reinforced by the Scriptures. Among them are such fundamentals of belief as the faith in one God —Father, Son, and Holy Spirit; in the creation and redemption; in the incarnation, sacrificial death, and resurrection of the Son of God; in forgiveness of sins and everlasting life. Among them, too, are such general rules as that transgression of both the Ten Commandments and the summary law of love of God and neighbor is incompatible with the life of faith; that all believers are to be considered as members of one body, and each of them, indeed every man, to be valued as the direct object of the divine love; that the chief business of the church is the proclamation in word and action of the promise and reality of liberation through Jesus Christ. The varieties of Protestant belief and ethos are varieties within one genus, and that this is so is largely due to the Scriptures.

Protestant order, as has been noted, owes much also to the tradition of the early and the medieval church. Protestants have accepted to a large extent, though often without great insistence on their importance, the early creeds of undivided Christendom. Their liturgical practices, their sacraments and preaching, though primarily authorized for them by Scripture, sometimes show indebtedness to the long tradition. Even the ordering of the clergy and the relations of laity to clergy retain, apart from extreme groups, some vestiges of the old habits.

A third set of influences that have shaped Protestant order appears in the interaction of the various movements and groups which together constitute the historic phenomenon. This interaction has been especially effective in America, where the groups have been held together in one political society. Pietism, Evangelicalism, and the Awakening not only brought forth new churches that defined themselves in protest against established Protestant societies, but were movements within the latter. The Methodist revival was continuous with the Evangelical movement in the Church of England. The revival of the early nineteenth century not only produced new denominations, such as the Disciples, but also affected the practices of Baptists and Methodists. The conservative fundamentalist movement in the twentieth century had a similar double effect. This interplay of groups and movements has not produced uniformity in American Protestantism, but has led to considerable likeness in the creedal, cultic, and governmental ordering of a large part of it. Even conflicts in it tend to be less interdenominational than intra-Protestant, with similar parties appearing in many churches.

Consideration of the great effectiveness of a common political and cultural environment in shaping Protestant order in the United States must be postponed for later consideration. In the present context it seems necessary only to call attention to one final element that has exercised much influence on the tendency toward pragmatic and fluid ordering which seems characteristic of Protestantism. The element is the often unconscious but tenacious and pervasive confidence of believers that all their religious and secular movements and institutionalizations take place within a world actively governed as a universal commonwealth. For minds nurtured by the Scriptures the rule of God is neither a set of laws to be enforced primarily by men, nor yet an ideal to be realized by them at some future time, but a present administration of affairs. The cosmic administration is functioning, however mysteriously and hiddenly; divine justice is being done, divine mercy exercised amidst all the suffering of the innocent and God's long-suffering of the wicked. This confidence must wrestle with many intellectual and moral problems as through the centuries it confronts scientific and philosophical movements and is shaken in the catastrophes of social or personal existence. It is subject also to perversions, as when reliance on the work of the unseen hand is used in excuse of complacency and in justification of conduct careless of distant consequences. Yet where the confidence in the actuality of the divine government is present, the ordering of life must go on as a serious yet somewhat tentative and temporal affair.

New measures are called for to meet new opportunities or to exercise new repentance for sin. The impending judgment of God on the sin of slavery, of racial discrimination, of international conflict, or of Protestant disunity itself, must be anticipated rather than some moral law of nature enforced. At the same time, within a world under the government of God a considerable freedom prevails: not a freedom to decide the ultimate issues, but the freedom of those who are responsible in limited spheres of action and who can devise seriously meant yet temporal and tentative organizations or modes of action somewhat adequate to the occasion. The forms of faith and order, creed, polity, liturgy, and discipline in Protestantism in America are all affected by the sense of tentativeness that is due as much to the certainty of God's continuous governmental and creative working as to the temporal climate of opinion in democratic society. More light is always to break forth from the Scriptures; new occasions will teach new duties. The pragmatism, the experimentalism, and the changefulness of order in Protestantism, perhaps particularly in America, may be due in considerable part to this sense of orientation in a dynamic, divinely governed world. There are reactions ever and again toward more fixed rules of belief and practice, but they seem to be reactions that testify to the main tendency of a moving order, or of an ordering that goes on within a movement.

II. Protestantism in Relation to Democracy

Protestantism has not proceeded on its way in isolation but only in constant interaction with other movements. Its order has been the product not only of decisions made within it, but also of pressures exercised upon it. The Reformation was accompanied by the revival of learning, the Counter-Reformation, the growth of capitalism and of nationalism; the Awakening by Enlightenment and Romanticism; the revivals by political, scientific, and industrial revolutions. Orders of belief, discipline, and worship in Lutheran, Anglican, and Reformed churches were in part imposed upon them by political powers more concerned with problems of political unity and independence than with the forgiveness of sins and righteousness of life. The churches arising out of later revivals were usually less subject to political, but more amenable to social, pressures.

In America the primary companion with which Protestantism has had to deal as friend and rival and foe has been democracy. Democracy has not been the only associate of Protestantism on its march. The great migrations from Old World to New and, within America, from east to west, from country to city, have left marks of their influence on the map of the Protestant journey. The industrial revolution, going on with accelerating tempo decade after decade, and the scientific revolution, with its critical moments for the church in the Darwinian, Freudian, and sub-atomic discoveries—these, too, have profoundly affected the Protestant course. Sometimes they have brought confusion, sometimes have led to ventures down by-ways, often have brought great defections from the ranks of Protestant churches. All these cultural movements have been interwoven, so that Protestantism as church has confronted them all as "the world." With the possible exception of science, however, it has been democracy which, among them all, has been Protestantism's most important ally and opponent. It has offered to this religion its greatest opportunities and its greatest temptations to forfeit its own soul.

Theology must leave to the historians and critics of political institutions and democratic thought the task of assessing the influence of Protestantism on democracy. It may discern certain parallels, for instance, between the line of democratic revolutions and the line of Protestant protests; between Protestant revivals and democratic liberations; between Protestant reliance on Scriptures under the government of God and democratic dependence on written constitutions under the reign of natural law; between Christian rejection of the significance of human differences in men's relation to Christ and their Creator, and the democratic doctrine of equality; between democratic suspicion of power and Protestant belief in the prevalence of original sin; between evangelical wrestling for freedom from sin and death, and democratic striving for liberty from external compulsions. It will often seem to the theological point of view that democracy is Protestantism in its secular form, that is, in the form relevant to the concerns of the present age. It becomes secularized only when this age is isolated from the age to come; when time is lived through as though unsurrounded by eternity. But when we are aware of the multiple causalities that operate in history, we content ourselves with notice of the parallels without ascribing democratic effects to religious causes. Moreover, one has reason to suspect that when Protestant theology undertakes to show how much Christianity in general and Protestantism in particular have contributed to democracy, it has already exchanged Protestant for democratic faith, has found the justification of religion in its promotion of a human and temporal cause, and has confused the power of religion with the power of God. So it seems that the only question a Protestant theological critic can properly undertake to answer is the one about the effect of democracy on that Protestantism whose nature he has tried to understand from within.

By democracy we shall mean here not, in the first place, a series of doctrines or fundamental beliefs about human equality and freedom, but rather those institutions of government, those settled social habits and modes of thought that tend to prevent the absolute control of individual citizens or of groups in the American nation by any individual or communal power. In this sense democracy is not so much what the word literally means, government by the people, as, negatively, the prevention of absolute or decisive control of any part of the people by any other part. Respect for minority rights is as essential an element in its practice as consent by the minority to government by majority. Among the legal measures that tend to secure the negative purpose of democracy are the separation of the powers of government and of church and state, the restriction of governmental powers by constitution and Bill of Rights, the mutual restrictions of local, state, and federal powers, and frequent, secret elections. By democracy we mean, therefore, the ordered practice of protecting the people's liberties, the people being considered not as a unanimous whole exercising a general will, but as a community of individual selves and a community of communities. On its positive side this democracy provides for the expression of the desires and demands of individuals and groups, as well as for their cooperative action in the pursuit of common ends. It does this not only by means of legal measures and governmental arrangements that secure the right to petition and provide for representation, but by habits of association established and recognized in the mores of democratic society.

This democracy cannot easily be described by a simple phrase. It is not government of the people and by the people, since the people are not a single whole; it is not merely government by the consent of the governed, since the system provides for much more active expression of will and desire than consent; neither does democracy seem to be merely a constant struggle for power among competing groups, since it provides rules under which that struggle is carried on and has cooperation no less than conflict in view. Such democracy, as known in America, cannot be defined, either, by reference to certain doctrines. Doubtless its practice presupposes certain great premises, but what they are or how they are to be formulated is often subject to dispute. The context and background of democratic practice may be stated now more in Lockean, now more in Rousseauistic, now more in Calvinistic terms, or even in semi-Hobbesian or Machiavellian fashion.

Historically, this democracy has come to expression in a series of violent and non-violent revolutions in which power that threatened the people's liberties has been checked or overthrown. The movement of democracy can scarcely be called progressive, since ever-new forces arise within and outside the nation to exert disproportionate power over the people or some of their communities. In meeting such challenges democracy, like Protestantism in this respect, develops an ordering of common life that seems largely to have pragmatic character and that shows signs of having issued out of emergencies.

A. The Increase of Protestant Disorder and Dependence. The answer to the question how democracy has affected Protestantism in the United States seems obvious. It has given the Protestant churches as well as Catholicism and every form of religion or irreligion almost complete freedom; furthermore it has allowed freedom in religious matters to every individual. The consequence seems to have been increased disorder in Protestant Christianity. Democracy, however, has also thrown Protestantism, along with every other form of faith, on its own resources, unsupported by any government. Under these circumstances Protestantism, much divided, without a long tradition, loosely related to its Old World organizations, has become a highly adaptive religion tending to forfeit its own character in adjusting itself to the wishes and felt needs of the people on whom it depends for support. It is said to have become a "Culture-Protestantism" in which all inner direction was lost as the price of conformity was paid for the sake of survival. Thus democratic freedom, it may be argued, has led Protestantism toward anarchic pluralism, and to dependence on the voice of the people rather than on the Word of God.

These fairly common observations about American Protestantism have a considerable measure of truth, and their elaboration will assist toward an understanding of the non-

Catholic churches in their New World forms. But they do not constitute the whole truth and must be supplemented by the consideration of the unifying tendency in American Protestantism and of the growth under the conditions of freedom of an independent evangelical movement.

When the American religious scene is compared with that offered by other nations in Christendom, the obvious feature that strikes the eye is the multiplicity of churches in the United States. Elsewhere also, national Protestant folk- or state-church organizations are usually accompanied by dissenting groups but these, as a rule, are comparatively small and there are not many of them. Denominationalism—the system of many apparently competitive churches equally recognized by state and people—is a peculiarly American phenomenon. This denominationalism seems to be the consequence for Protestantism of that liberty in religion which American democracy has accepted and encouraged. Democratic freedom has not been the cause of multiplicity, for Catholicism has maintained its unity in the land of religious liberty, but it has supplied the conditions under which inherent tendencies toward fractionalization and division in Protestantism could have free sway.

In the first place, democracy has permitted every national form of Protestantism that had been developed in Europe to maintain itself in America. Of the more than two hundred Protestant denominations in the United States, a considerable number represents the continuation in the New World of state or national churches. The Church of England; the Lutheran churches of Germany, Sweden, Norway, Denmark, Iceland; the Reformed churches of the Rhineland, the Netherlands, and Scotland; the united church of Prussia—these have all survived in a nation that permitted immigrants to follow their own religious convictions and traditions. Furthermore, the dissenting churches of the Old World were placed in America on an equal footing with the successors of established churches, and under these circumstances often enjoyed a growth impossible to them under the restrictions of existence as tolerated but not approved religions. Congregationalism in the United States does not offer an unambiguous example, since it was once established in Massachusetts and Connecticut. Since its disestablishment, however, it has become a strong denomination, far outranking, when measured by usual standards, the dissenting Congregationalism of England. The Methodists, remaining relatively weak alongside the Anglican church in the country of their origin, have become the largest single Protestant organization in the United States, with a membership many times larger than that of the Protestant Episcopal Church. Baptist dissent in Europe, subject to much political and social repression, neither attracted large numbers nor achieved significantly strong organization; in America almost one third of all Protestants are Baptists, and though they are divided into many groups, their two largest associations are cohesive and influential. Alongside such dissenting denominations that in the New World have enjoyed great growth, more than a score of other European non-conformist groups have continued their existence in America. Among them one can count the Mennonites, the Society of Friends, Moravians, Schwenkfelders, River Brethren and Plymouth Brethren, the churches of the New Jerusalem, the Associate Presbyterians, the Swedish Evangelical Mission Covenant church, and Dunkers. While migration to the United States is the antecedent cause of the presence of such groups, the promise of freedom in religion often motivated their migration, and under the conditions of freedom they have flourished in a way impossible to them in situations where uniformity of religious belief was prized and enforced by social, if not political, pressures.

Democracy has not only permitted the continuance of all the old divisions of Protestantism; it has also allowed, if not encouraged, the growth of new groups. Large as the number of naturalized denominations is, it is exceeded by the number of the native-born. Most of them trace their origin to some extensive or localized revival in America such as the Second Great Awakening, out of which the Disciples of Christ and the Cumberland Presbyterian church issued, or the renewal of hope in millenarian form that produced the Adventist groups, or the Pentecostalist and Holiness movements whence came the Assemblies of God, the Church of the Nazarene, and similar groups. Their organization in separation from the older churches and their division from each other were due to many causes. Under the conditions of freedom those who felt themselves to be like-minded, to be moved by the same spirit, and who believed that the old organizations did not adequately represent what to them was all-important, tended to unite in associations for the promotion of common causes without contemplating the development of another denomination. But in time a new church developed and in the environment of freedom and religious multiplicity there was no internal or external pressure to prevent schism or enforce unity.

Geographical locality and regional culture has also contributed in the American situation toward the multiplication of native-born denominations. Groups of Protestants living in the same more or less restricted area, affected by some movement in religious conviction and emotion—including reaction against denominationalism—have tended to associate with each other and to develop common forms of thought and practice. Or Protestants previously members of one church have been divided from each other by social conflict, such as that of the Civil War, or by geographical and social distance, such as that between old and new settlements. Such groups may represent less the rapidity of the process of fission under democratic conditions than the slowness of the fusion process in a situation in which church unity is wholly dependent on motivations internal to Protestantism itself.

Again, many new forms of Protestant church life have been fashioned in democratic America by individuals. Elsewhere the individualism that seems always to be present in Protestantism has been checked by the force of the continuing Catholic tradition, by the presence of a dominant state or people's church with a widely recognized official clerical leadership. But in democracy, individuals endowed with strong personal convictions, or great personal force and attractiveness, or unusual ambition, or with all of these at once—true prophets and false ones—have enjoyed peculiar opportunities to gather bands of disciples, to set themselves up as reformers of old faith or as founders of new religions. In many instances the groups that have gathered around such leaders and eventually become denominations have been very much like the revival churches. In some the presence of economic motives suggests similarity to business enterprises; in still others a likeness to communal Utopian experiment appears.

Finally, some of the multiplicity of forms of faith and order in American Protestantism may be traced to the operation of free initiative in religious and moral enterprise. As special needs have attracted the attention of members of old churches, they have organized societies to provide religious, moral, and humanitarian services to parts of the population not under the pastoral care of existing institutions. As the Salvation Army —originating in England, to be sure—began with the effort to bring religious and moral help to neglected slums but became an organized religious body, so other groups that consider themselves to be primarily evangelistic or missionary or educational organizations have come to function as independent churches with their own membership, clergy, and common order.

The organizational pluralism that prevails in a Protestantism left free by democracy to develop in its own way seems to be matched by the pluralism of beliefs professed, hopes entertained, ways of salvation preached. Though the great mass of American Protestants continue to assert that the Scriptures are their authority, so many principles of Scriptural interpretation are used among them that diversity is the consequence. Literalism and liberalism; historical and confessionalistic interpretation; confessionalist explanation in Lutheran, Calvinist, and fundamentalist forms; mysticism and rationalism—all are represented. Officially these Protestant churches remain mostly Trinitarian in their doctrine of God, but deism and Unitarianism, immanentism and spiritualism, as well as exclusive concentration on the deity of Christ, are widely taught. Hopes of the vision of God, of His kingdom coming to earth, of brotherhood and peace, of heavenly bliss, of a millenarian reign by the returning Christ, of the progress of civilization, and of personal health and prosperity—all are promised as future gifts of God or as rewards of faithfulness in conduct and belief. Freedom in worship seems to lead to undisciplined inventiveness and formlessness. While the sermon remains the central feature in most Protestant meetings, the term "preaching" now includes not only the proclamation of the gospel and the interpretation of life in the light of Scriptural knowledge of God, man, and history, but lecturing on political, humanitarian, and literary themes, ritualistic rhapsodizing, and rote repetition of holy phrases. Not only the sacraments of baptism and the Lord's Supper, but feet-washing, holy rolling and ecstatic dancing, speaking in tongues, and the handling of snakes may be found by the curious student of religious customs as he visits the meetings of groups in America that call themselves Protestant.

All such observations of the multiplicity of organizations, beliefs, and rites support the suspicion that tendencies toward schism and disorder are inherent in Protestantism, and that the conditions of freedom in democratic society have allowed them to come to full expression.

In the sixteenth century, Europe's Protestant churches, declaring their independence from Rome, became largely dependent on national states that both supported them and used them for political ends. In America, democratic political society either yielded to their desire for complete freedom or thrust independence upon them. The corollary of freedom, however, has been self-support, and the corollary of self-support seems to have been dependence, not now on government but on popular good-will. All Protestant groups, whether originally constituted as churches that include all citizens or as sects that gathered into an exclusive society only the manifestly converted, have had to become voluntary associations in the United States. Seeking to survive, thrown into competition for attention, membership, and economic support, not only with each other but with secular enterprises claiming the same resources, they appear to have adjusted themselves all too well to the wishes of the people. Hence they have functioned among immigrant groups as conservers of the old national cultures, maintaining, for instance, the languages of motherlands and fatherlands long after their people had abandoned such usage in daily secular relations, even in their homes. Sometimes they have fostered old national loyalties long after their members had become American citizens. As churches serving prosperous classes they have presented in sermon and rite a spiritual religion only remotely relevant to the commercial, industrial enterprises in which their people for the most part were engaged—a kind of luxury faith that neither challenged the mores of secular life, nor deeply affected men's sense of their fundamental orientation in the world, but supplied them with special though mild ecstasies. Religion, like art, in this setting has been presented as something that belongs to "gracious living." Elsewhere Protestant churches have supplied to oppressed, unhappy classes, such as Negroes in garbage-strewn slums, imaginative visions of a Beulah-land to come, or enchanted them into seventh heavens by rhapsodic rites. They have sought the support of industrial workers by proclaiming a gospel that called for repentance on the part of owners and employers, pronounced blessings on the virtues of labor, and preached a crusade for a socialized economy. In rural areas they have led worshipers in adoration of virgin mother earth; in the cities they have sung the praises of man the builder, as though he were constructing the New Jerusalem. When Americans wanted above all else to remain isolated from the wars of the Old World, Protestantism was largely pacifist; when the nation was drawn into international conflict, "preachers presented arms." When people were made deeply conscious of their anxieties, churches offered them peace of mind; when they were lonely after old and new migrations, then community, fellowship, and friendship were presented as Christ's essential gifts mediated through his church.

Amidst all this adaptiveness there has been, however, a more basic adjustment of Protestantism to the spirit of American culture. In the United States, as elsewhere, the dominant religion is probably the social faith, for which society itself is the great cause to be served, and the source whence men hope to draw whatever significance they have. Democracy for this religious attitude is not a way of government; it is a way of life and a way of salvation. It is believed in, counted upon, trusted as a spirit immanent in the society, or as idea incarnated in it. The hope that accompanies this faith appears as the American dream, or as the fulfillment of Manifest Destiny, or simply as progress toward peace, prosperity, and plenty. American social religion has its sacred scriptures, its doctrines, symbols, and rites. To what extent it emerged out of Protestantism, out of other religious traditions and out of unconscious depths will long remain questionable, but in its progress and development it has been closely interwoven with Protestantism. And the latter, in many times and forms, has so adjusted itself to the American faith that it has been difficult to distinguish the one from the other. Not infrequently Protestants have defined Christian freedom in democratic terms, not as freedom from sin and death and as that bondage to God which is perfect freedom, but as liberty to worship as one pleases or, better, as deliverance from political tyranny, from want, and from fear. The gospel of a love that seeks out the lost and lowly, that concerns itself more for the one per cent who are sick, astray, or in prison than for the ninety-nine per cent healthily at home, is translated into the doctrine of equality. The Word of God, and the voice of the people; the hope of the kingdom of heaven, and the American dream; the forgiveness of sins, and toleration; the grace of our Lord Jesus Christ, and affable manners are confused and confounded. Such cultural Protestantism takes on many forms; fundamentalist and liberal, nationalist and internationalist types may be distinguished. But the variations are distinctly those of the social faith to which Protestantism has adjusted itself.

Thus it may well be argued that under the conditions of freedom the inherent weaknesses of Protestantism have become fully apparent. Protestantism in America seems to have moved from schism to schism, to have fallen prey to individualistic self-assertiveness, to have lost its character as independent church.

B. THE INCREASE OF PROTESTANT UNITY AND DYNAMIC. While such tendencies in Protestantism in America are too evident to be denied, an interpretation that would take only them into consideration would not do justice to the ambivalent, complex phenomenon of evangelical religion in the United States. For, alongside the trend toward fractionalization, there has been in this Protestantism a countervailing movement toward unity; and alongside the tendency toward dependency on the people, there has been the constant effort to make the people fully aware of their dependence, not, indeed, on the church but on God.

The movement toward integration in American Protestantism is no less striking than the movement toward disunity. It has organizational, doctrinal, ethical, and ritual aspects, but is perhaps particularly a movement toward the attainment of a common temper, outlook, and purpose that do not need to be precisely formulated.

While democracy made it easy for successors of European national churches to continue their separate existence in the New World, it also provided conditions under which unforced union could take place between groups that, issuing from the same historic revival, had been sundered by political decisions and cultural differences. Lutherans, who in Germany were divided into many territorial churches, have come together in America. The Lutherans of Sweden, Norway, Denmark, Iceland, and Finland move slowly yet with accelerating speed toward combinations in which old political and cultural distinctions are forgotten, while the common religious heritage is maintained. Through denominational mergers and the organization of conferences, councils, and federations, Lutheranism has advanced for many a year and continues to advance toward a unity denied to it on its home continent. So also the Reformed churches of the Rhineland, the Netherlands, the Swiss cantons, and Scotland, through enacted or planned unions, close ranks that were broken by political rather than religious conflict.

A similar movement has long gone on and continues among the organizations that, though originating out of similar revivals or traditions, were separated from each other by geographical distance. The loosely knit Baptist churches, particularly subject to regional influences, have long been gathering themselves into ever larger and more inclusive associations. Churches of the North and the South, separated by political conflict but also by differences of development in different environments, and churches of the East and West, have united in the past and move more rapidly toward union as the nation itself becomes more homogeneous.

Reunions after revivals have been almost as frequent as separations during revivals and, indeed, the awakenings themselves have been integrating in their effect as well as divisive. They have rarely occurred in one denomination only, and they have brought together in new association members of previously estranged churches. They have been effective in overcoming geographic barriers that separated not only churches but regional societies. It has been noted that the Great Awakening contributed considerably to the development of a common mind in the isolated colonies of eighteenth-century America. But more significant for the church union movement was the rapprochement between Presbyterians and Congregationalists it brought about. The development of the Disciples of Christ and the Christians, denominations that seek Christian unity, as a result of the Second Awakening, also illustrates, though somewhat ambiguously, the union movement that has been present in revivals.

The story of almost every one of the larger Protestant denominations in the United States can be read as a story of Protestant re-union quite as well as a story of division. The history of the Presbyterian church in the United States is not untypical. Beginning with the account of the founding of English, Scotch, and Scotch-Irish churches in Virginia, Massachusetts, New York, Pennsylvania, and other colonies, it relates their organization into presbyteries and synods early in the eighteenth century, tells of the founding of new churches during the Awakening, of the subsequent rift between "old side" and "new side" groups, and of their reunion after a few years. Later chapters record: the acceptance of the Plan of Union with the Congregational churches, effective for many years; the appearance of a new strain on the family tie as Old School and New School Presbyterians take issue with each other during the Second Awakening; their reconciliation; the division between Northern and Southern Presbyterians by the war between the states; union with the Cumberland church, which had issued out of the Kentucky revival; union with the Welsh Calvinist Methodists; union with the United Presbyterian church, which was the American successor of a dissenting church in Scotland. The later story also includes accounts of participation in the founding and work of the Federal and National Council of Churches of Christ in the United States, the International Missionary Council, the Alliance of the Reformed Churches Throughout the World Holding the Presbyterian Order, and The World Council of Churches. The movement toward cooperation and organic union with the southern wing of American Presbyterianism has been continuous and fruitful for several decades.

Another type of movement toward integration within denominational boundaries is illustrated by the histories of the American and the Southern Baptist Conventions. Though they contain the accounts of many schisms, they report to an even greater extent the drawing together into ever more inclusive and active fellowships of independent local churches and of regional associations that had grown up in isolation from each other. Thus the stories of the denominations in America give evidence of the presence in Protestantism of a continuous movement toward unity that is no less characteristic than the tendency toward division.

That movement has its interdenominational as well as denominational forms. In the climate of democracy, free associations of Christians concerned with the prosecution of some limited ends have sprung up decade after decade. Members of Presbyterian, Congregational, Baptist, Methodist, and many other churches have united to form missionary, educational, charitable, and reform associations. The organization of colonization and anti-slavery societies of peace leagues, temperance unions, hospital associations, Sunday School unions, rescue missions, and a host of similar ventures is a unique and important element in American Protestantism. Some of these, such as the Young Men's and the Young Women's Christian Associations, have become established institutions; some, such as the American Board of Commissioners for Foreign Missions, have become arms of denominations; some have lost their relationship to churches and become secularized. Some of the associations have flourished during periods of crisis such as the Civil War; others have maintained themselves for decades. If order is to be found only where there is planning and central control, the multiplication of such groups will seem indicative of disorder; but if order and unity are also visible in the rise of spontaneous cooperation for the achievement of limited ends, then these associations are as representative of Protestant order and unity as the many orders and sodalities of Roman Catholicism are of the unity of the Roman church.

Another sort of integration in Protestantism has taken the form of federation. The federation may be that of whole denominations, of similar agencies of such denominations, or of local churches with varying denominational affiliations. The first type is represented by the National Council of Churches (which was preceded by the Federal Council), the National Association of Evangelicals, the National Lutheran Council and the Pentecostal Fellowship; the second by the International Missionary Council, the World Council of Christian Education, and the United Christian Student Council; the third by scores of municipal, county, and state councils of churches. The development of such federations and councils is slowly giving to American Protestantism a double organization. On the one hand it is organized into denominations, for the most part national bodies, cooperating with each other through denominational offices and officials; on the other hand it is developing a geographical organization, in which local churches with various denominational affiliations combine in city and state organizations and slowly acquire agencies and offices through which to administer common concerns.

Other aspects of the tendency toward unity among Protestants come into view when one considers the growing similarity of the various groups in internal organization, religious attitudes, and action. Though many denominations distinguish themselves from others by reference to their congregational or presbyterian or episcopal polities, these terms often have more of a sentimental than descriptive value, as in actual operation the historically variant forms of government tend to approximate each other. The most evident influence leading toward agreement in this area is that of American political and social organization. Equality in voting rights, representative government, the recognition of the separate yet interdependent duties and rights of local, regional, or state and national societies, the separation of executive and legislative powers, provision for strong executive power, the multiplication of executive commissions—all these are recognizable features in the changing internal order of the denominations.

While the history of religious convictions on the part of Protestants in America must take into account the continuation of the variant emphases of the more doctrinally and the more practically oriented groups, it needs also to describe changes in common outlook. The general tendency, for decades if not for centuries, has been toward disinterestedness in highly developed creedal formulations. This has been accompanied by a great emphasis on practical activity so that, from the point of view of Europe, American Protestantism seems characterized, despite all denominational variants, by its pragmatism. There is, however, another common strain in this American religion, less evident to the casual view but perhaps more significant. A strong concern for individual, personal appropriation or internalization of faith and hope and love of God and neighbor has manifested itself many times in the New World revivals and remains the great interest of churches that issued from them. Moreover it is just these churches that have grown into the strongest religious groups in America, and even the more creedal groups have been influenced by them and the revivals. Hence emphasis on personal Christian experience and commitment has become a great common denominator in American Protestant conceptions of Christian faith and life.

The consequence of these various integrating and harmonizing tendencies has been the emergence in the United States of a kind of "core Protestantism" that is still too loosely knit together to be called an American Protestant church. This core Protestantism is surrounded, here as elsewhere, by dissent, but just as the core represents an indigenous development, including the successors of old European dissenting groups as well as of old established churches, so also the dissent is largely of native and recent origin. The considerable diversity present in the central, unifying organization of interlocking activities, of interweaving interests and ideas, is probably no greater than that which is contained within ecclesiastical structures that appear to be more nearly monolithic.

In view of such considerations it can be fairly maintained that Protestantism, left free by democracy to develop in its own way, has shown as strong a bent toward unification as toward atomization, and that the process of diversification of religious conviction and action in it has been balanced by an accompanying process of integration.

The movement toward integration may, of course, be interpreted as a result of the Americanization of Protestantism, and so be regarded as offering proof of the contention that free Christianity, unregulated by an overruling ecclesiastical or political authority, tends to fall into dependence on the social culture. It seems unquestionable that the Americanization of European immigrant groups has been important in bringing their churches closer together and that the development of a national culture, erasing regional patterns of thought and behavior, has effectively promoted the association of geographically separated religious societies. The operation of social forces may nevertheless be traced in all movements toward diversification, as well as in unifying tendencies; adjustment to culture is a constant phenomenon in the history of Christianity. It would be difficult to find methods of analysis by means of which to discover whether the "core Protestantism" of the United States is more American than Lutheranism in Europe is German, Swedish, or Norwegian; than Anglicanism is English; than Calvinism Dutch or Scotch. The diversity and unity of Roman Catholicism, with its Spanish, Italian, Polish, Irish, Gallican, and German churches, with its historic relations to the Roman empires and Romanized culture, also show the influence of social forces on Christianity. The question about American Protestantism, then, is whether dependence on culture is unusually manifest in it, or whether the tendency in that direction is also balanced by a countervailing action.

The Americanization of Protestantism has been accompanied by its re-evangelization, and by the evangelization of the nation. The tendency to equate the gospel with the democratic social faith has been balanced by the effort to Christianize the democratic mind. The other-directedness or heteronomy of American Protestantism has been matched by self-directedness or autonomy.

Autonomy and independence are somewhat misleading terms when applied to Protestant Christianity. They designate ideas and tempers that belong in the context of democratic faith. Protestantism in all its original forms has been concerned to emphasize the direct and absolute dependence of all men and their societies on God, and only in that setting has it affirmed independence from finite powers. Its protests against churches and states have been directed less against invasions of the rights of men than against usurpations of the absolute sovereignty of God. Hence its relations to a democratic movement that begins with a dogma of inherent human rights have always been somewhat ambivalent. Though it has tended to agree with democratic challenge of the divine rights of kings or churches, it has been required to challenge every doctrine of the divine right of the people. It has made common cause with the democratic claim that men had rights prior to those granted to them by any government, but it has regarded those rights as issuing only from duties prior in obligation to any duties imposed on men by governments. The right to freedom of worship for such Protestants has been based on the duty to worship God; the right to freedom in speech on the duty to speak the truth as the truth is known; the rights of conscience have been derivative, for them, from the human duty to obey God rather than men.

An "independent" Protestantism, true to its own convictions, doubtless represents other principles, such as the authority of the Scriptures, justification by faith, the duty of serving

God in daily work more than in special acts of religious devotion. But in its relations to democratic culture it will show its independence vis-à-vis that culture primarily in the constancy with which it upholds the principle of divine sovereignty. It may refer first of all to Scripture or first of all to conscience as mediator of divine commandments, but in either case it affirms the immediate presence to every individual of the divine law, and it must protest against the assumption by any human authority—whether priest, preacher, magistrate, people, or popular majority—of the right to speak in the name of the absolute. It may regard the execution of the divine will as concentrated in a few critical events in history—especially in Jesus Christ and the final consummation—or it may see it pervasively present in all events; in either case it notes that all self-government is responsible to power beyond all selves and subject to overruling Providence. If Protestantism in America has lost sight of these points and accepted instead the dogmas of democratic faith, then indeed it has lost its independence; then it no longer challenges the social faith but is a passive representative of the culture.

Now, as has been noted, it is not difficult to find in the sermons and church pronouncements of Protestants many proclamations of the dogmas of democratic faith and many glorifications of the rule of "the common man," or of the beneficent effects of guidance by self-interest, or of freedom independent of responsibility. But there are few periods in history in which such themes are not overborne by vigorous and constant witness to the overruling sovereignty of God, by exposition of the divine demands and actions, by calls upon individuals and groups for obedience and repentance before the ultimate holy and gracious power.

Among the occasions in American history in which the presence of such an independent Protestantism has been evident are the Edwardean challenge to New England individualism; the Calvinistic protests against the doctrines of the French Revolution (which a Timothy Dwight found represented in Jeffersonianism, but which dissenting allies of the latter also fought vigorously); the attack made by Finney and his many associates and successors on the doctrine and practice of self-interest as the basis of the good life; the social gospel's call to repentance, directed primarily to the commercial and managing segments of the population. These, however, mark only high points in an activity of exhortation, proclamation, and education that has been constant.

Throughout American history independent Protestantism has been involved in the conflict about the context in which democratic institutions are to be used and understood. These institutions in themselves show no clear, logical relations to either the principles of "democratic faith" or to those of Christianity. They have been interpreted and employed as expressions of both. Representative government has meant delegation of the people's or a majority's authority; it has also meant the selection by the people of men they trusted to be obedient to ultimate principles of right and to be concerned about the welfare, not of constituents only, but of the whole nation—indeed of mankind. Separation of church and state has meant in one context that the state can be indifferent to religion because only individual and subjective matters are involved; in another, it has been recognized as the measure that must be taken because men's relation to God is too important a matter, too significant in consequences, for society as well as individuals, to be subjected to the short-sighted administration of political office-holders. The Bill of Rights has been interpreted within the framework of a philosophy of individualism and also in the context of the individual's obligation in a universal commonwealth. Democratic institutions in general have been set now in this context, now in that. The tactics of democracy have been employed within a grand strategy of one or the other type, and the conflict about the strategy or the final principles to which all technical uses are subordinated has been constant in American history. In that conflict American Protestantism has not indeed been unanimously on one side of the issue, but there can be little doubt that the preponderance of its influence has been toward the side of universalism rather than of individualism, of moral obligation as prior to freedom, of representative rather than delegated government.

This has been perhaps particularly evident in connection with the interpretation and use of the Constitution—whether the fundamental law is to be interpreted as expression of a general social will subject to historic change, or as an interpretation of ultimate, natural, or divine law. Protestantism, joined later in America by Roman Catholicism, has insisted on the latter idea. Its highly Biblicistic wing has, indeed, endeavored to have the American state acknowledge the Scriptures as the written formulation of the ultimate law to which all nations are subject. The major tradition in Protestantism, as in Catholicism, has appealed to a law knowable by reason, a law of nature, which, however difficult to formulate in changeless phrases, must be constantly searched out by the people and their judges. The influence of this "cosmic constitutionalism" on American democracy in the nineteenth century was profound; it has waned in the twentieth, but Protestantism has not abandoned it. One may trace to it those practices in politics and diplomacy that political realism at home and abroad deplores as "moralistic." Yet it is not evident that it has been the source of self-righteousness more than of self-criticism.

Another area in which the presence of an independent Protestantism vis-à-vis democratic society has been manifested is that of social reform. More than in the case of state-supported or state-recognized churches, probably more than in the case of non-Protestant churches, free American Protestantism, apparently so dependent on the social culture, has functioned as the critic of that culture. Directly, or through the exercise of pressure on governments, it has undertaken to inaugurate reforms in social customs and institutions. Some church crusades against evil have been guided by narrow and trivial interpretation of divine law; none has been without opposition from within the churches themselves; all of them have been complicated by the intrusion of non-Christian interests. Nevertheless, the history of Protestant concern for social melioration—from anti-dueling agitation through anti-slavery movement to municipal reform, prohibition, and peace crusades—betokens the presence of an independent and critical spirit rather than one of compliant conformity to the social culture.

Throughout their history under the conditions of freedom, the Protestant churches in America have directed their major evangelistic efforts toward individuals. The concentration on selves in their solitariness has been in part the consequence of the Protestant view of life, in part the result of the challenge modern conditions of existence have posed to the churches. But whatever the reasons for it, concern for the religious, moral conversion and education of individuals has taken precedence in American Protestantism over interest in changing the fundamental assumptions of the common mind, the habitual actions of the whole society. The limitations imposed on Protestantism by this approach have been widely recognized in recent decades. What has not been acknowledged, and can probably never be measured, is the effectiveness of this concentration on the individual. Still, from the point of view of democratic society, it remains pertinent to ask what contribution has been made to its viability by the pervasiveness and constancy of Protestant proclamation, exhortation, admonition, call to repentance; by the prayer, preaching, and Biblical instruction that undertook to write the promises and the law of God upon the inward parts and to make men loyal and obedient citizens of an eternal, universal kingdom in the midst of all their exercise of democratic rights and duties. From the point of view of the Protestant principle it is, of course, not of fundamental importance to ask whether this work of the churches has lengthened the life of democratic society or helped to counteract the vices that attend democratic virtues. For an independent Protestantism cannot entertain a utilitarian valuation of God, of faith in Him, or of religion, as though their worth depended on the service they render to the high god of social faith—society itself, or democracy.

In themselves and in their relations, Protestantism and democracy in America present a strange picture of dynamic forces of movement and counter-movement. Not without order, the orders that are visible are those of process rather than those of status. The Protestant democrat or democratic Protestant finds the mixed picture intelligible only as he views it in the light of his fundamental faith, hope, and hunger for righteousness.

CATHOLICISM IN THE UNITED STATES

HENRY J. BROWNE

No PRIEST writes of anything so close to him as the Church with complete impartiality. Nor can an American Catholic be expected to be completely clinical about the place of his Church in the life of his country. An even more basic difficulty would seem to be that there hardly exists what can be considered an American Catholicism. The backgrounds, traditions, personnel, strengths, and weaknesses in dioceses across the broad stretches of the United States are as varied as the topography of the regions they comprise. The lines in the multiple faces of American Catholicity have been etched by strains that are English, Irish, German, Polish, Italian, Portuguese, and Spanish, to mention only the major ones. The sometimes ancient and often foreign usages and outlooks of communities and orders of men and women consecrated to the service of the Church by vows provide another variation to the same theme. The oneness of this nation-wide segment of the world-wide society of Catholic believers is in its profession of the same faith and morals. But even in that respect, emphasis on one doctrine or another may differ from place to place and from time to time. Certainly there is nothing like uniformity of religious devotional practices or artistic and intellectual taste. Accordingly it would seem necessary to sound a warning—even with regard to the author's background—and then to proceed with generalizations.

It has become quite customary to regard the Catholic Church in America as sprung from English origins which were very quickly and almost totally inundated by the Irish immigration of the early nineteenth century. The fact remains, of course, that the first contacts of the religion of Rome came rather from the Catholicism of Spain and France. But neither of these streams left a deep-rooted or strongly organized church that endured into the period of the new national life. They were for the most part but weak extremities branching out from sees in Cuba, Mexico, and Quebec. The Indian missions of Florida, New Mexico, Arizona, and California conducted by Franciscans and Jesuits survived only in relic form, leaving such remnants as the parish church of San Xavier near Tucson or the Santa Barbara mission in California. By the end of the colonial period on the East coast, the French efforts in the Great Lakes and Mississippi Valley areas were even less in evidence. The once-flourishing missions among the Indians of the western end of the lakes region had come to an end by the early eighteenth century and had to be renewed by the mid-nineteenth. The new missionaries often had to divide their time between white men and Indians. St. Mary's Church in the Illinois country survived to acquire the status of a national monument, and similar marks of French and Spanish Catholicism endured in the old quarter of New Orleans.

But the touch of the Catholic faith of Spanish and French origin left other traces. As the nation grew peacefully or otherwise according to its manifest destiny, this faith was to be blended with the life of the Church advancing across the frontier. The Spanish Catholic names strewn like a litany of the saints across the Southwest and California were gratefully assumed as designations of American episcopal sees. The faith planted among Spanish and French families gave a tone of respectability to the Yankee Church when it reached areas where the nucleus of the oldest social elite in a community were Catholic. Similarly, in settlements like St. Louis, frontiersmen could find in their simple cathedrals art objects that French kings had sent to their fellow religionists. Just what organic influence on American frontier life came from the presence of old Spanish and French communities is hard to say,[1] but certainly the traditions of the Old World were

[1] No serious over-all study has yet been made of the Catholic Church on the American frontier.

73

found best preserved in the Catholic Church of the area, in the remnants of a foreign-language clergy, in the shell of Indian missions, and most importantly in the circle of well-established lay members who held to the ancient faith. At Santa Barbara, for example, even today the friars and their mission continue to be one of the most respected elements in the life of the area, where they embody its oldest tradition.

The major organizational activities of the American Catholic Church originated in Maryland. From the superiors of the Maryland missions, and later from the bishops and archbishops of Baltimore, there spread across the continent the network that would in the nineteenth century embrace the French Old Northwest and Mississippi Valley, as well as the Spanish Southeast and Southwest. The English Catholic experience in the New World would therefore be the most important in forming the American Catholic tradition and in pointing its directions for the future. It was under English sanction that the Maryland colony was established in 1634, and it was designed principally to provide a place of religious freedom for Catholics. Since it was predominantly Catholic only in leadership and not in membership, it was interesting and indicative of the whole future emphasis of English Catholic leadership on the new continent that the Catholics were instructed to be careful lest they offend their Protestant neighbors, even by the ostentatious practice of their religion. Several cases were actually adjudicated wherein Catholic colonists were penalized on this basis. Maryland Catholicism was therefore a practical application of the principle of tolerance for the consciences of all its members. It is interesting for the history of freedom of conscience to note than when the Puritan ascendancy began to endanger this early-planted precedent and made it necessary to pass an Act of Toleration in 1639, tolerance required only submission to a Trinitarian formula. Catholics did not conceive of tolerance with the complete theoretical dedication of a Roger Williams in Rhode Island. Yet when they asserted the legal respecting of the individual conscience for the sake of serving the common good, there would seem to have been philosophical commitment as well as political expediency involved.[2]

Meanwhile the Catholic colonial minority—the plantation elite of the Maryland tidewater area, the ordinary English or German craftsman or farmer of the Pennsylvania settlements, the occasional Irish indentured servant found in scattered numbers throughout the colonies—none of these nor all of them together were very influential and it would be absurd to attribute the growth of the notion of freedom of religion to that element in early American society.[3] Nonetheless, its first planting was Catholic, and it enjoyed Catholic favor thereafter, whether in the votes of Daniel Carroll and Thomas Fitzsimons at the constitutional convention, or in the hearty endorsements of the new American way that began with John Carroll, first bishop of Baltimore. From the outset the Catholic Church in America was adapting itself to a world far different from the Christendom of western Europe, or even from that of a primitive missionary country. The first Maryland Jesuits found they were not protected by their traditional rights in ecclesiastical courts, nor was their jurisdiction over marriage as a sacrament so complete as to exclude it from the state's concern. The Church as an institution-in-law in Europe had to become in the new nation merely another private corporation, a society that had to conform with first colonial and then state laws simply to exist. In a sense, the whole history of the Church in the United States has been the gracious accepting of that change, a constant adaptation to that life in a new and secular environment.

The movements and comings-to-life of the Church in colonial America were to see other positive and lasting consequences. But they were also to have their negative side.

[2] Thomas O'Brien Hanley, "Church and State in the Maryland Ordinance of 1639," *Church History*, XXVI, December, 1957, pp. 325–341.

[3] Consequently such studies as Riley's and Ray's on American Catholicism of the eighteenth century are for the most part investigations of reactions to it rather than positive approaches.

The missions among the Indians were not very long-lived in the Tidewater or in the Great Lakes posts. Part of the reason was that hostile Protestant neighbors in Virginia saw them as part of a papist plot. Penal days were actually experienced in Maryland in the eighteenth century with laws putting prices on priests' heads and outlawing the Mass. Hence a fear of American Catholicism, not completely but at least partly political, took firm root in the American colonial mind. Spain and France were nearby enemies and every Romanist a potential fifth columnist. Despite all economic, social, or psychological factors explaining this xenophobia in the later history of the United States, there seems to have been planted an anti-Catholicism which still had Elizabethan roots nourished by the frontier storms of competing empires.

In other ways, nonetheless, colonial Catholics were very much a part of the society in which they lived. They accepted slavery as part of the system of first the tobacco and later the cotton country. Even the Jesuit "gentlemen of Maryland," as they came to be incorporated, held men in bondage on their plantations. Such "priests' slaves" enjoyed a better situation than many of their fellows. Kindly treatment and manumission were rather common. Yet the system was not considered something intrinsically wrong, and was defended as an institution found in St. Paul. American Catholics as a group did not repudiate it into the nineteenth century, except for expressing disapproval of its traffic and some of its other abuses. They were for a gradual change at most, and sometimes propounded the notion of compensation for the owners.[4]

This ability to conform to current modes of social and political thought was shown particularly in the revolution.[5] There was, for example, a whole colony of Catholic Tories who felt their political alliance so strongly that under the

[4] Cf. Madeleine Hooke Rice, *American Catholic Opinion in the Slavery Controversy*, New York, 1944.
[5] Charles Metzger's scholarly articles will soon be superseded by his book which will contain the fruits of years of research on Catholics in the Revolutionary period.

leadership of a priest they removed themselves in a body to Canada from the Mohawk Valley. In general, however, the Catholic record in support of a rebellion that had about a third of the people actively supporting it was as good as that of other segments of the population. It is no longer fashionable in American Catholic circles to try to prove that Irish Catholics won the Revolution by counting names which were mostly Scotch-Irish Presbyterians. Nevertheless, the fact remains that Catholics did military duty in positions as high as aide-de-camp to Washington, and for this the Commander-in-Chief publicly thanked them as a group. His sensitivity to Catholic support, and more particularly to French and Spanish allies, was also demonstrated in his outlawing Guy Fawkes Day anti-Papal celebrations in the Continental army.

An interesting aspect of the subject of Catholic support on the home front was that the Catholics had almost less reason for enthusiasm than anyone. On the positive side was only a vague hope that a political change might mean the gaining of more religious freedom. It has been well established that the revolutionists did not hesitate to draw on the anti-Papal feelings of the colonists in order to sell them on the break from England.[6] In addresses meant to win over the English people, and particularly in the propaganda of such men as Sam Adams after the Quebec Act in 1774 (which saved the Ohio Valley for French Canadian Catholics while respecting their religious institutions), a rabid anti-Catholicism was employed. Catholic support, such as it was, continued despite this and despite the solid hierarchical freeze from the north when Father John Carroll accompanied Franklin and others to seek a Canadian alliance. Certainly the tradition of patriotism in wartime—notwithstanding in recent times a growing fringe of conscientious objectors—has been a hallmark of the American Catholic community. It has been manifest even

---

[6] Metzger, *The Quebec Act. A Primary Cause of the American Revolution*, New York, 1936.

when, before war, the pro-intervention side was not popular with them, and it has remained one of the most frequently used, if not logical, retorts to answer any aspersions on Catholic loyalty to American principles.

As the new republic was unified around the figure of George Washington, so the new American Church was drawn together around John Carroll, its first bishop.[7] Carroll came to personify the desire for complete compatibility of the ancient Church with the new state. As a young priest just returned from continental education and ordination, he had many friendly allegiances in England. Yet he never failed to let them know how righteous he felt the American cause. He did not participate actively in the war for independence, nor risk as much as his cousin Charles, the richest of the signers of the declaration of 1776. But his friendship to the cause did not go unnoticed, as Franklin from Paris endorsed the Roman project of making him the first bishop. A constant theme of his episcopate thereafter was the consonance of American political institutions with Catholic theology. Today no one regards seriously a mildly advanced claim of a Catholic historian of two score years ago that Jefferson depended literally on Bellarmine in preparing the Declaration of Independence.[8] Still, in American Catholic circles and among students of political science, it has become increasingly evident and accepted that the papistical principles of polity stemming from medieval theory were in the political atmosphere of that

[7] The writer collected from archives in Europe and America the writings of Carroll for eventual publication by a committee of the American Catholic Historical Association as one in the series endorsed by the Historical Publications Commission.

[8] Gaillard Hunt, "The Virginia Declaration of Rights and Cardinal Bellarmine," *Catholic Historical Review*, III, October, 1917, pp. 276–289, and the Protestant answer of David S. Schaff, "The Bellarmine-Jefferson Legend and the Declaration of Independence," *Papers of the American Society of Church History*, 1934. An unusual Catholic disavowal of an awareness among supporters of the revolution of any consonance of their religious principles and political philosophy is in the pamphlet of John M. Lenhart, *Catholics and the American Declaration of Independence* (*1774–1776*), St. Louis, 1934.

day. They were found especially in the writings of the Jesuit theologians Bellarmine and Suárez, who opposed the notion of the divine right of kings. They emphasized that authority came to rulers from God but through the people, and resided in the hands of its chosen ministers for as long as it was exercised for the common good.[9] Tory preacher Jonathan Boucher was attacking this concept as much as the democratic notions of Calvinist origin.

"This visionary idea of government by compact was as Filmer says, 'first hatched in the schools; and hath, ever since, been fostered by the Papists, for good divinity.' For some time, the world seemed to regard it merely as another Utopian fiction; and it was long confined to the disciples of Rome and Geneva who, agreeing in nothing else, yet agree in this." [10]

An increasing awareness of these ideological roots of American democracy, even in the face of the official neutrality of the Church toward all forms of just government, has given educated Catholics comforting support for their democratic loyalties. Yet a century ago the lay convert editor, Orestes Brownson, was claiming that American democracy was logically Catholic and that only in the doctrines of the Church could it find solid foundation. At that time also there were clerical exponents of the perfect harmony of Catholic teaching and the American way. These literary priests were as varied in background and field of labors as Isaac Thomas Hecker of German Protestant origin in New York, Adrien-Emmanuel Rouquette of French descent in Louisiana, and Samuel Charles Mazzucchelli, of the Italian Dominicans, in the Midwest. But by that time the rank and file of the Church's

[9] Henrich Rommen, "Catholicism and American Democracy," *Catholicism in American Culture*, New Rochelle College, 1955, pp. 61–70. This symposium is the only recently published attempt to deal with the subject of its title. Cf. Currin Shields, *Democracy and Catholicism in America*, New York, 1958.

[10] Quoted from *View of the Causes and Consequences of the American Revolution* (*1775*) in Richard J. Purcell, "Background of the Declaration of Independence," *Democracy: Should It Survive?*, Milwaukee, 1943, p. 25.

membership were being reassured by the freedom and opportunity they experienced even more than by the Catholic press.

Those who formed the oldest family nucleus of American Catholic society, like the Carrolls and the Brents, were very much a part of their environment.[11] They were mostly federalist in sympathy and close to the English in social connections. They were a respected and respectable element, many with continental educations which had often been forced on them by the earlier penal laws of Maryland. They were indeed a minority, but by the period after independence they were far from despised and not influential beyond their numbers. To this community, and especially to the priesthood, the French Revolution and the subsequent European wars were adding a French flavor in the form of *émigrés*. Meanwhile, the Acadian exiles who were settling in the Baltimore and other coastal areas after 1755 increased the French names in the ranks of the faithful in the East. Among the first priests who came directly from France were the Sulpicians, who began the first seminary for training native clerics. One of these *émigrés* was Simon Gabriel Bruté, who, through the College of Mount St. Mary's at Emmitsburg, exerted a powerful influence. He guided Elizabeth Bayley Seton, who came from the best New York native American background to found the first native sisterhood, and he was influential in the intellectual and spiritual formation of John Hughes, an Irish immigrant lad who later came to dominate the mid-century Catholic scene from his position as Archbishop of New York. Bruté became first bishop of Vincennes, and with others of these cultivated Frenchmen helped to advance Catholic life on the trans-Appalachian frontier. They were the builders of cathedrals in the wilderness whose libraries, art objects, and religious cult were strange and sophisticated representations of the Old World on the primitive frontier of the New.

[11] C. Joseph Nuesse, *The Social Thought of American Catholics, 1634–1829*, Washington, 1945.

In the more cultivated South, where Charleston was the chief center, Roman Catholicism was at home. From that city in fact came the most American-minded leadership of the third and fourth decades of the nineteenth century. John England, from the city of Cork, Ireland, was the leading exponent of non-doctrinal accommodation of Catholic ways to the America of the period. He and other Irish clerics such as John Power, Vicar General of New York, sometimes expressed this mentality by strong opposition to the French element, which in those days was personified by men like John Maréchal, Archbishop of Baltimore (d.1828). In more positive ways Bishop England promoted the development of an American ecclesiastical viewpoint in drawing up a constitution for the governing of his diocese, as well as in successfully advocating a legislative gathering of all the American bishops in 1829. Although sanctioned by canon law and ecclesiastical usage, this first provincial council had to be fought for against French opposition. It became, however, the prototype of meetings for the purpose of taking united stands on issues of doctrine and discipline. Owing to the organization of other ecclesiastical provinces, such meetings grew to national or plenary scope in 1851. This latter council was followed by others in 1866 and 1884, and then the council idea was adapted once again into that of annual non-canonical gatherings of the whole American hierarchy beginning in 1919. These meetings perpetuate the tradition of discussing active problems common to the Church in the United States, although now without making any formal legislation. The published statements issued from these gatherings are an outstanding source on the mind of American bishops as they attempt to apply an age-old ethical system to problems ranging in scope from the national to the family.[12]

The period of England's influence was marked by a de-

---

[12] Peter Guilday, ed., *The National Pastorals of the American Hierarchy, 1792–1919*, Washington, 1923, and for the later period, Raphael M. Huber, ed., *Our Bishops Speak*, Washington, 1952.

velopment along lines that were characteristically American. This may be seen in his advocacy of the press. Newspapers were growing in those decades with unprecedented pace in numbers, circulation, and partisan heat. The bishop's Charleston *Catholic Miscellany* began in 1822 and became the first really Catholic paper of any significant duration in the United States. The devouring of the printed word in newspaper form had become a national mania, and over the next two decades Catholics themselves were finding that being informed in the history and doctrine of the Church was an effective means of counteracting charges against them. The editorial amenities of the age of Jacksonian democracy were not always softened by Christian charity. The Protestant papers rehashed the ancient yet ever-new charges, from idolatry to enmity to American republicanism, while the Catholics as often simply rejoiced that the end of American Protestantism would come as it was sucked dry of doctrinal content. Born from such controversy were the *Freeman's Journal* of New York, the *Catholic Telegraph* of Cincinnati, and the *Catholic Standard* of Philadelphia, to mention but a few of what would become dozens of Catholic weeklies in English by the end of the century. Some few of them, like the *Pilot* of Boston, achieved a national circulation, but all reflected and interpreted American life to an increasing number of Catholics while linking them with the duly-reported affairs in Europe. Over the years that followed, many of their editors were laymen who exercised to the full all the freedom that one associates with personal journalism in the nineteenth century.[13]

The *Wahrheitsfreund* of Cincinnati was the first of the German language weeklies and its very existence indicated the change in the basic makeup of the Catholic element.

---

[13] The richest depositories of American Catholic newspapers for the nineteenth century are, for the pre-Civil War years, the library at Georgetown University and, for the later period, the collection of the American Catholic Historical Society of Philadelphia. The library of the Catholic University of America has been preparing a union list of all such items and has a program of gathering them together in microfilm form.

Beginning in the 1830's the new immigrant came to bring both problems and strength to American Catholicism. The position of a respectable minority status wherein Bishop England was invited to address Congress in 1826 (and did so for two hours on the chief teachings of his church) was henceforth to be more difficult to maintain.

The strange ways of Catholics had already made some impression on their America. In 1813, legal action in New York City tested a priest's right to maintain the seal of confession under all circumstances.[14] This resulted when Anthony Kohlmann, S.J. refused to reveal the penitent in an affair involving the restoration of stolen goods. The court handed down a precedent-setting decision in the priest's favor on the matter of professional secrecy, which was shortly afterwards written into the state laws. Not so quick in finding acceptance in law was the Catholic system of holding and administering church property. The laws of various states, after the disestablishment of favored religious groups, usually recognized only a group of the members of each congregation as the legal owners of church properties. This situation was not really incompatible with Catholic discipline until it led to insubordination among some trustee groups. These groups advanced from the concern with parish temporalities to a desire to designate their spiritual leaders. Such inroads on the canonical power of the bishop led to scandalous public litigation and even to brief schisms in places like Baltimore, Norfolk, New York, Philadelphia, Buffalo, and New Orleans. Complications, created at times by the introduction of a nationality conflict in French or German parishes, were multiplied by maneuvering Irish clerics who led warring factions. The spirit of the age of the common man and the example to Catholics of their Protestant neighbors undoubt-

---

[14] A report of the case and an appendix explaining the doctrine of confession was published: William Sampson, *The Catholic Question in America,* New York, 1813. Cf. Henry J. Browne, *The Diocesan Clergy of New York: an Historical Sketch,* New York, 1951.

edly hurried the movement of trusteeism. It was not till the 1860's that state laws began to be reshaped to meet the situation and to allow various devices acceptable to Catholics. Usually it became possible for the bishop to hold church properties as a corporation sole or through a board of trustees that was predominantly clerical in makeup. For the American Church this meant a greater legal security for its properties, but it concentrated the "business" work in the hands of the shepherds of souls. For all in the United States it meant the interpretation of religious freedom was growing to include the concept of allowing religious groups to govern themselves according to their own individual constitutions.[15]

The strangeness of such Catholic behavior in predominantly and still strongly dogmatically Protestant surroundings was further exaggerated by the increasingly foreign makeup of the Church's membership. The unusual lack of concern shown by the Irish and Germans for observing a Puritan Sabbath was more shocking than public papist processions on the occasion of councils in Baltimore. Anti-Catholicism in America was never purely religious, not even in the pre-Civil War period, for social and economic factors added greatly to the new fear of the stranger. The recent arrivals were somewhat less than orderly neighbors and crowded the labor market. Yet this hardly justified some of the extremes of nativist venom. Salacious stories, which followed a formula that has never died in American Protestant folklore, led to the burning of the Charlestown, Massachusetts convent in 1836. The chartering of St. Louis University by the State of Missouri produced a great fear of a Roman winning of the new west.[16] Catholic churches were burned in Philadelphia in 1844, while in New York a show of armed defense by Catholic congregations

[15] There is no single study of trusteeism but much has been done on it in articles and biographies. In the historiography of an archdiocese like Philadelphia the flood of source materials produced by such controversies would seem to have resulted in a lack of balance in the total presentation of the past.

[16] Cf. Lyman Beecher, *A Plea for the West*, Cincinnati, 1835.

frightened off would-be torch-bearers there. This latter episode was about the only belligerent note sounded by Catholics, whose patient endurance was constantly encouraged by a hierarchy who believed for the most part in the ultimate prevalence of the American sense of fairness. Many times in the 1850's the faithful were admonished to stay away from street-corner meetings where their Church was being attacked. It was not always a quiet suffering, for the Catholic press joined battle—not with vitriol to match the Protestant journals'—but with the smugness of truth-holders opposing a weakening stronghold of error. Catholic-baiting on a wide scale even became political practice by the mid-1850's, but the slavery controversy and subsequent war (even as the Mexican War before it) served to slow up this process. If this period marked the beginning of Catholic determination to prove they belonged on the American scene by bragging about the military achievements of their co-religionists, it may be remembered that they noticed how much more welcomed they were as soldiers than civilians. A tradition of forbearance with Protestant excesses was established, even if not accompanied on either side by moves to close the gap of misunderstanding. At times Protestants had used their political predominance to enforce theological positions, as in the public schools, drawing the complaints of Catholics. But in some cities in the East the rising Catholic population indicated that they might soon have to contend with a strong Catholic constituency, and have a chance to do their own complaining on the score of religious pressure in public life.

It was of the nature of religious groups in American society that they should remain in a certain kind of isolation from one another. The process of growth of Catholic parochial education was a clear example. At first, it was the churches and not the common school societies that gathered together the children of the cities for the purposes of education. By mid-century, however, it had become increasingly difficult to maintain church schools because state funds in aid of this work were going only to public schools. From the 1840's Catholics were practically the only ones to decide to continue fostering church-connected schools.[17] Meanwhile, the common schools on the elementary level had become officially "public" and little by little began to gather not just the residue of children left untutored by the various religious bodies, but the bulk of the youth. These schools used the Protestant version of the Bible and sometimes employed text books that left little doubt about the obnoxious character of Catholicism. It was then that the Catholic decision to provide "literary" as well as religious instruction began to be a far-reaching one. It was necessary to augment the laymen's teaching activities which, in places like Philadelphia, in basements and in side rooms of churches, had already extended beyond the Sunday school. Help came first through the American-founded Sisters of Charity. After the 1830's more strength was brought to the new system with the growing number of nuns and brothers from Ireland, Germany, and France. Bit by bit the hope of state funds for conducting Catholic schools was given up, the pace of acquiescence to the political reality differing from one part of the country to another. Some money was still forthcoming in New York as late as the 1870's.[18] Two decades later a compromise with the parochial school idea, which had proven successful in Poughkeepsie, New York, was tried more widely in Minnesota. It consisted of renting parish schools to local education boards at a nominal price, making them part of the public system, but retaining the right to teach religion after hours. This won Roman toleration after a great domestic squabble among the bishops, but foundered on the shoals of American secular opinion.[19] Actually about a quarter

---

[17] H. J. Browne, "Public Support of Catholic Education in New York, 1825–1842: Some New Aspects," *Catholic Historical Review*, XXXIX, April, 1953, pp. 1–27.

[18] Edward M. Connors, *Church-State Relationships in Education in the State of New York*, Washington, 1951, pp. 109–123, gives the best account of the Poughkeepsie Plan.

[19] Daniel F. Reilly, *The School Controversy (1891–1893)*, Washington, 1943, is pro-Archbishop Ireland not only in emphasis but even in the choice of documentation.

of a century ago, despite the continuing economic pressure created by the expense of their own system, a large segment of Catholic educators was thinking of state aid as a mess of pottage for which they might be selling their birthright of private control. Under their pastors, meanwhile, the faithful had built up a system of primary schools in a spirit which often made the school the first building item in the parish. This phenomenon has often been referred to as one of the great religious marvels of the last century. It was partly motivated by the negative and unhappy thought that the "Godlessness" of the public schools made them a menace to the welfare of their youthful charges. The peculiar outcome was that, in insisting that no Protestant-minded religious instruction be allowed in tax-supported schools, Catholics were aiding in their secularization. At the same time some few American Catholics were keeping alive another attitude, that anyone teaching gave life and light and willy-nilly did Godly work. This was the defense of the public school, put forth by men like Bishop John Lancaster Spalding in the last decade of the nineteenth century. This latter and once weaker tradition has not only survived but is today much the stronger of the two, and nearer to the official attitude of organized Catholic educators who want the parochial school to have an equally important place alongside the public one as cooperator in the service of the community's children.[20]

The mission of the Church in the United States was almost from the outset conceived of as a social one. In the period of freedom's ferment, of course, Catholic thought had no public recognition and could not have been responsible for reforms in the conduct of prisons or asylums. Nonetheless, from its long European tradition there already flowed certain expressions of organized charity. The history of diocese after diocese repeats a pattern of the search abroad for men and women with religious vows to perform these multiple labors.

[20] H. J. Browne, "The American Parish School in the Last Half Century," *Bulletin of the National Catholic Education Association*, L, August, 1953, pp. 323–334.

Among these was the creation of the first homes for the protection of the many orphans left behind by the epidemics so common to early nineteenth-century America. The women of various sisterhoods served as mothers to the girls who fell victim later in life to the moral disease found in every society. Also, owing mostly to the efforts of nuns, hospitals were opened, particularly in the larger Catholic centers like New York and St. Louis, to dispense the charity of Christ in healing. This early start may account in part for the constant high proportion of Catholics in the medical profession in relation to other professional categories. A full century ago a chain of charities was already forming in most of the country's dioceses. In New York some Catholics felt they were being paid the compliment of imitation when Protestants began to add to the number of orphanages and hospitals conducted by humanitarian groups others that were to be directly under church auspices.[21] At any rate, American Catholics' efforts to save through service helped to build up self-supporting organizations of social welfare which would run over another half century without even the aid of centralized diocesan supervision. By then it had been well confirmed that the American way would exclude complete dependence on the state for support and direction of such necessary institutions in society. The ante-bellum humanitarian movement for social reform had had some important effects and declined, while the quiet day-to-day service flowing from Christian conviction continued.[22]

Catholic insistence helped to accelerate another kind of basic reform in hospitals, asylums, prisons, poor houses, and such institutions. Freedom of religious conscience in that

[21] H. J. Browne, ed., "The Archdiocese of New York a Century Ago: a Memoir of Archbishop Hughes, 1838–1858," *Historical Records and Studies*, XXXIX–XL, New York, 1952, pp. 165–168.

[22] The history of Catholic social work remains a vast unresearched area. Cf. John O'Grady, *Catholic Charities in the United States*, Washington, 1930, and the only scientific study, Marguerite T. Boylan, *Social Welfare in the Catholic Church. Organization and Planning through Diocesan Bureaus*, New York, 1941.

period was sometimes hampered not only for soldiers and sailors, but also for patients and inmates in city and county charitable institutions. Occasionally there was forced attendance at the Protestant services, or at least difficulty in getting permission for Catholic ones. Even the visit of a priest to a hospital bed, today so common for all ministers of religion, oftentimes had to be won by a combination of persuasiveness and pressure. If any one religious group was the "nuisance" one a hundred years ago, it was undoubtedly the Catholics, especially in the built-up areas of the East. The fact remains that in winning recognition of certain rights for themselves they were doing a service for all Americans.

Yet, in spite of all this, the Church in the United States was straining to be American. By the 1850's the native-born priest had a distinct factor in his favor when it came to choosing the new head of a vacant episcopal see. This often meant the American hierarchy would contain converts to the American reflection of the Oxford Movement toward Rome that had arisen in England during the previous decade. The distinguished example of a man who combined two old American traditions of Dutch and English origins was James Roosevelt Bayley. He was converted in New York, educated for the priesthood in France, consecrated for Newark, and moved thence to Baltimore as its archbishop. The "American" emphasis, however, was perhaps an unsophisticated reaction to nativist feelings, and it may not be unrelated to that almost jingoist patriotism which showed itself in later expressions of American Catholicism. The effort to prove that Catholics belonged never seemed to die, but rather to remain submerged, now and then reappearing on the surface of national events.

The Civil War was accordingly a great opportunity for American Catholics.[23] Although in considering the country as a whole their reactions were not notably different from

[23] There is nothing adequate on the subject, only the essays of Benjamin J. Blied, *Catholics and the Civil War*, Milwaukee, 1945.

those of their compatriots of other religious beliefs, on a few counts they might be said to have followed distinct trends. Catholics were practically unheard of in abolitionist ranks; their ministers rarely preached of the war as a righteous cause. But they served a purpose, even if that purpose was merely passive, for part of the nativist concern with the threat of the Church was a diversionary tactic to keep the real problem of slavery in the background of political discussion.[24] Catholics took sides, but they alone among national religious groups did not split organizationally. The Holy See stood by neutral, refusing to accept John Lynch, Bishop of Charleston, who arrived in Rome with Confederate diplomatic credentials, as anything more than a bishop. Yet the loyalist northern leader of the hierarchy, John Hughes, Archbishop of New York, operated on the continent freely and quasi-officially for the Union cause as an *ad hoc* salesman of the northern position.[25] In the North flags of regiments were blessed, nun-nurses worked on battlefields and in military hospitals, chaplains functioned officially, if at times free-wheelingly. But they seemed to run to opposites. One Catholic editor in the North, James McMaster of New York, went to jail for attacks on the Union cause, while a Southern bishop, Martin J. Spalding of Louisville, Kentucky, expressed the opinion that the emancipationists bracketed together slavery and popery as outmoded institutions, and that Yankee soldiers burned Catholic churches in the South with extra enthusiasm.[26] And this was at the same time that practically whole regiments of solders were Catholic, al-

[24] Cf. W. Darrell Overdyke, *The Know-Nothing Party in the South*, Baton Rouge, 1950.

[25] His reports from abroad are included in the microcard publication, "Mission Abroad, 1861–1862: a Selection of Letters from Archbishop Hughes, Bishop McIlvaine, W. H. Seward and Thurlow Weed," Rochester, 1954.

[26] Archives of the Congregation Propaganda Fide, Rome, Scritture riferite nei congressi, America Centrale, Volume 20, pages 1–12 v., Martin J. Spalding, Bishop of Louisville, "Dissertazione sulla Guerra Civile Americana," 1863.

though the only argument which had any appeal for them as a reason for fighting was saving the Union, not the emancipation of the slaves.

Out of the war came the great problem of the freed Negro, which created an additional challenge to be faced by the Church. The council of 1866 spoke of it, but happily for the future avoided a suggested procedure of setting up a separate ecclesiastical jurisdiction for the freed slaves in the South.[27] Apart from the more Catholic areas like Southern Maryland and Louisiana, the Negro was not often Catholic, and in the immediately subsequent years the problems of growth by immigration in the North would not permit much promotion of missionary or educational work among them. The sword of war had laid waste much of the Catholic institutional life which might have made a better beginning possible. A few religious orders of women worked especially for them, but for the most part the Negro missions had to be a procrastinated, pious possibility. The council of 1884 centralized an effort to support this endeavor in a board for Indian and Negro missions. Only in the 1890's did the often expressed concern for the freedman become more of a reality through the missions of a priest group known as the Josephites, which sprang from English roots, and the work of a special order of sisters founded by Katherine Drexel, a Philadelphia socialite, for the Indian and Negro apostolate.

A hint of the future came as early as 1903, when the Holy See reacted to complaints of the secondary position given to Catholic Negroes in parishes in the United States with an inquiry. Under James Cardinal Gibbons the hierarchy prepared an answer which was hardly to the point. It avoided the issue by speaking of the special churches for Negroes and of the dedicated missionaries who were working for them

[27] Vincent de Paul McMurray, "The Catholic Church during Reconstruction, 1865–1877." This is an excellent unpublished master's thesis in history, Catholic University of America, 1950, which restricted itself to the Southeast.

in the South.[28] But it was evident that the age-old unprejudiced tradition of the Church was going to make itself felt, even across the sea. The neutrality that they had maintained in the slavery controversy, combined with the unfriendliness which much of the pro-Negro white elements in American society felt for Catholics, was not the most auspicious background against which to begin promoting either justice for the Negro or his spiritual welfare. Moreover, such episodes as the lynching of freed slaves by Irishmen in the draft riots of New York in 1863 helped to build up an almost innate hostility on both sides. Such bad beginnings might almost be obscured by surprising subsequent developments wherein, as early as the 1880's, a Boston editor like John Boyle O'Reilly became a leader of the Catholic apostolate for racial justice. The change in ratio of Catholics among Negroes from probably about one in every forty of the 750,000 emancipated to about one out of every twenty-nine of the approximately 16,000,000 in the United States today would indicate that the Church's primary and ultimate soul-saving objective had advanced little by comparison to its successful achievements in the realm of racial justice.

The area in which the Church would at least hold its own would be the new industrial North. The tendency for most of the Catholic immigrants to settle in the cities continued throughout the 1870's. Even Midwestern colonization projects for the Irish, which were more successful and long-enduring than those of two decades earlier, would not make an appreciable dent on this urban character.[29] The pattern seemed to have been set from the days when bishops of the East under Archbishop Hughes opposed the project of the

---

[28] Jos. Anciaux, *De miserabili conditione Catholicorum Nigrorum in America*, Namur, [1903]. Cf. John Tracy Ellis, *Life of James Cardinal Gibbons*, II, Milwaukee, 1952, pp. 401–404, for some light on this and similar promptings from Rome.

[29] For the story of the greatest success, that in Minnesota between 1876 and 1881, James P. Shannon, *Catholic Colonization on the Western Frontier*, New Haven, 1957.

Buffalo Convention of 1856 which planned to settle colonies on the western frontier systematically.[30] The city parishes were regarded, however short the vision, as havens that the sparsely populated farm lands could not give. The eastern churches were built large and even ostentatiously, the urban parishioners supporting many charitable works, the busy pastors guiding with a short rein their crowded flocks. As the new industrial city grew, Protestant churches began to stand empty where the onrush of Catholic immigrants had driven the congregations out of the neighborhoods. Their buildings were sometimes bought and adapted for Catholic use. Despite the lament of a later day that the rural life supply of population to the nation contained so few Catholics, the Church's early position of strength in the city made a school system even on the secondary and collegiate levels more feasible, and a network of charitable, social, and cultural organizations became an achievable necessity.[31] Next to immigration, urbanization has been the secular phenomenon of American history which has been most responsible for fashioning the peculiar character of American Catholicism. Into the cities flowed the Catholic immigrants of the late seventies. But between this immigration and what it had been before, there was a significant difference. The Catholics of the seventies, eighties, and nineties began to come in increasing numbers from southern and southeastern Europe. Observers in that period and students of the later one would conclude that the Catholic Church was maintaining the loyalties of the common man among the faithful with greater effectiveness than any other religious organization. What they have not as often observed, but what was just as real a goal, was the assistance given to the new arrivals in the difficult process of adjustment to American life.

[30] H. J. Browne, "Archbishop Hughes and Western Colonization," *Catholic Historical Review*, XXXVI, October, 1950, pp. 257–285.
[31] H. J. Browne, "New York City, 1857: Gateway for the Catholic Immigrant," *Catholic Life Annual*, Milwaukee, 1958, pp. 33–40, 95–96.

A jarring note in this process was sounded in the 1870's by a small group of Irish in the anthracite region of Pennsylvania. These miners, who reacted to their depressing lot with violence against their English and Welsh overseers and the property of their companies, were known as the Molly Maguires. Their mysterious story of plots, sabotage, and murders in the coal fields was climaxed by a series of trials which resulted in death penalties and jail sentences. Although much still remains very uncertain about their operations and organization (all of them were members of the Ancient Order of Hibernians and of the hard coal miners' union of that day), enough was revealed, particularly through the evidence of the informer-spy and Pinkerton agent James McKenna, to show the Church's hostility to this means of redress of workers' grievances. It is known that Bishop James Wood of Philadelphia had foreknowledge of the spying means that were used to eliminate the Mollies by bringing them to justice for their criminal acts.[32] The priests of the mining area and the Catholic press began at the same time to show a budding awareness of the socio-economic conditions which were responsible for pushing these workers to such extreme outbursts against law and order. Only perhaps in Brownson's writings had much of an earlier and consistent protest been heard from Catholics against the evils of the laissez-faire system of American capitalism. With this upsetting, almost anarchical reaction to the industrial problem —one which remains unique in American Catholic history— there was implanted in Catholic minds an awareness of an area of American life that demanded their attention.

This development was extended almost immediately by the panic and hard days after 1873. The depression was made more real for Catholics by litigation in the Archdiocese of Cincinnati which by 1879 had reached the Supreme Court of

[32] Fragmentary but friendly correspondence between Wood and Franklin B. Gowen, railroad president and prosecuting attorney, is preserved among the manuscript collections of the American Catholic Historical Society of Philadelphia.

the nation. A private bank conducted by the priest brother of the archbishop for the poor immigrants (despite many conciliar warnings against such activity) had failed. Although there were never charges of fraudulency, the creditors clamored nonetheless for their two and one-half millions of dollars. The affair had repercussions outside Ohio just as the Mollies' had had outside Pennsylvania. Both events occasioned the new awareness that opened a period of great intensity of Catholic social protest. This movement was aided by the circumstance that, unlike some countries on the continent, the owners-and-management class was practically devoid of Catholics. Even by the end of the first decade of the twentieth century, Catholic leaders of industry, according to available studies, still accounted for less than ten per cent of the men of that higher social level. Consequently the trimming of doctrine or ethics to suit the cushioned pews was not often charged against Catholic clergymen, and the loss of the lower classes from the ranks of the faithful was not as marked as among Protestants. For the Catholic group the other-side-of-the-tracks character was becoming more rather than less obvious.

The story of the American workingman was in the 1880's to become intimately connected with that of the Catholic Church. Catholics had always been found among farmers and farm workers, as well as in the commercial and building class, but the highest percentage of them were the hired millworkers, miners, and "mechanics" who made up the rising labor class. The Church's first concern was merely on the local level where pastors saw their worker parishioners being ground down in the new process of industrializing America, and these religious leaders had only the dubious satisfaction of knowing that they would not have to answer for the actions of the factory-owners since they were not Catholics. By the 1850's national unionism had begun to take on greater and greater importance, after the brief ineffectual flight to utopian schemes for the betterment of the worker's lot. Catholic workers were joining such trade unions as the iron molders, the carpenters, or the typographical workers, even though at times with some misgivings. Their pastors were occasionally asked about the legitimacy of their action, and the usual answer seems to have been that as long as they needed to be members for their job security it was all right.[33] This permission, however, was usually accompanied by a pastoral warning to be on guard against any union that was too radical in opposing civil or religious authority or which betrayed any signs of being another offshoot of free-masonry.

The first official Catholic approach to unions in the United States was a hesitant and suspicious one. They were often, after all, secret organizations for the purpose of surviving the strong tactics used against them by business. Their members many times were required to swear an oath, something which for a Catholic was not to be done lightly. Their suspect character was further evident in names like the Sovereigns of Industry and was enhanced by rituals based on the Masonic one, with pantheistic and deistic prayers. They stated their aim as benevolence and mutual help for the worker members, and the sincerity of this claim was apparently accepted by the American hierarchy as a whole in 1866. During the council of that year, legitimate labor unions were explicitly exempted from the prohibition of joining Masonic-like secret societies contained in the legislation of that national meeting. In the interval until the next gathering in Baltimore in 1884, several bishops grew to think of labor unions as socialistic and therefore to be condemned as subversive of the Church and society. Yet general opinion and the earlier legislation stood unchanged, and that Baltimore council merely appointed a committee of the twelve archbishops of the country to examine the specific suspected societies in question, such as the Odd Fellows, the Ancient Order of

---

[33] The continuity of this tradition in the important mother see of Baltimore from the period of the 1840's is attested to in a letter, William McCloskey to John B. Purcell, Louisville, March 17, 1873, found in the Cincinnati Papers in the manuscript collections at the University of Notre Dame.

Hibernians, and the Grand Army of the Republic, whenever the question should be raised. In the fall of 1886 they met to discuss the Knights of Labor, in some ways the first noteworthy national labor organization in American history. Only two prelates—and they came from the strike areas of St. Louis and Santa Fe which had just witnessed violence and bloodshed—favored condemnation, and the case went to Rome for adjudication.[34]

This move created an impact that might have had very bad consequences for the Church and American society. For several years the Knights of Labor had suffered at the hands of confessors as a dangerous secret society, especially in Pennsylvania where the Mollies were well-remembered. An attempt was made to meet the difficulty under Terence V. Powderly, who was still a loyal Catholic at the time, when they modified the requirement of the oath of secrecy that had forbidden even making the name of the group known. But this did not prove to be enough. In the mid-1880's, on the inquiry of the Archbishop of Quebec, Rome twice classified the Knights as condemned. It was February, 1887 when Archbishop Gibbons, then in Rome for the ceremonies of being made cardinal, asserted that great harm would come from extending the prohibition of Catholic membership in the labor organization from Canada to the United States. A "memorial" on this question was prepared for the officials of the Congregation of the Propaganda by Archbishop John Ireland of St. Paul and Bishop John J. Keane, first rector of the projected university in Washington, D.C., but Gibbons alone signed and submitted it. This document used every available argument, from the lofty one that defended the right of the workers to protect themselves through organization, to the pointed one that claimed condemnation would mean the end of the Peter's Pence collection for the Holy

---

[34] For the background and a detailed account of the whole chapter, cf. H. J. Browne, *The Catholic Church and the Knights of Labor*, Washington, 1949.

97

See in the United States. It showed remarkable awareness of the passing character of the Knights' kind of catch-all reformist unionism. Interestingly, if hardly accurately for that age, it contended also that a harsh stand against Catholic participation in the organization would make the Church seem un-American. It was the American contention in Rome that half of the 600,000 members of the Knights of Labor were Catholic, and that it was just as strongly Catholic in leadership. Powderly had promised the archbishops to do all in his power to make the organization acceptable to the Church by amending whatever might be offensive.

Most of the important results in this case were achieved by publicity. A mangled version of the defense made in Rome was broadcast throughout the United States. As a result the Catholic Church was hailed more than the facts warranted, and officially put on the side of organized labor. Forever after, individual Catholics had an official stand of their Church to strengthen their unionism. The final decision of the Holy Office actually was a toleration of Catholic membership provided that certain phrases in the constitutional documents of the Knights of Labor which smacked of socialism and communism were altered. They were, in fact, never altered, but the organization was already on its way into obscurity along the road of agrarian reform. Cardinal Gibbons' stand had not been more than a protest against an imprudent condemnation, but he became thereby a champion of labor, and played that part rather well for the next thirty years despite his conservative fright at socialist strength in the union movement. *Puck* said in cartoons what the conservative press said in scathing words to protest the new alliance, but for better or for worse, and forever after, it seemed consummated. The outcome was that some Catholic members of organized labor were saved for the Church when they did not have to make a choice between earthly and heavenly bread. But from labor's own point of view the strength of unionism was augmented considerably by the fact that a faithful fifty per cent of the membership felt they had their Church's backing in belonging and in fighting for their legitimate claims. This Catholic percentage in the personnel of trade unionism seems to have continued through its subsequent history.

The Catholic lay unionists, however, still did most of the pathfinding for the Church. The American Federation of Labor, with its practical approach of improving wages, hours, and working conditions, and without all the trimmings of land and monetary reform which had marked its fancily named competitor, also had large Catholic membership and leadership. Pope Leo XIII, in his encyclical *Rerum novarum* of 1891, gave a degree of official Church sanction to what was primarily an activity of self-preservation. The certain amount of confusion that followed this and other papal references led to several unsuccessful experiments with Catholic unions. Hence, as some Catholic trade unionists continued supporting their non-religious American unions, Church clarification was requested.[35] As early as 1912 an interested group asked Gibbons to seek a specific endorsement of their policy, but this did not actually come until 1931, when the *Quadragesimo anno* of Pius XI gave explicit permission for what American Catholic workers had instinctively permitted themselves, the affiliation with non-religious (but not anti-religious) or neutral labor unions.

The Catholic support of the A.F. of L. may have affected the progress of that type of unionism. Left-wingers have claimed it played a part in holding back the one-big-union concept and committing the American labor movement to a conservative course. Some Catholics wonder if it did not have some effect in keeping down the socialistic influence in the federation, which, contrary to its ever-prevailing philosophy, would have politicized it to the point of producing something like the ideological unionism of Europe. The voting on key questions in the higher councils of the A.F. of

[35] H. J. Browne, "Peter E. Dietz, Pioneer Planner of Catholic Social Action," *Catholic Historical Review*, XXXIII, January, 1948, pp. 448–456.

L. does not seem to prove that Catholic labor leaders were aligned on the matter of socialism.[36] The fact remains that anti-socialism was the prevailing social doctrine preached by Catholics in the period between the two social encyclicals. We may suppose that Sam Gompers' struggle within the organization was more helped than hindered by those dyed-in-the-wool unionists under him who happened also to be Catholic.

Apparently, American Catholics began to find some guidance for their social thinking in the papal pronouncements. Leo's defense of private property, however, had also been in part stimulated by events in America. The confusion of the Henry George controversy, in which Roman-trained Dr. Edward McGlynn, a pastor in New York, became involved on the side of the reformer, led the bishops in the late 1880's to petition for some enlightenment on the doctrine of private property. They were told that the writings of George on the doctrine of the single tax were to be condemned, but as a concession to the liberal side of the hierarchy this action was to be kept secret. Hence, when the *Rerum novarum* appeared in 1891 it was seized upon by both sides as a defense of their positions. Private property was upheld against the socialist doctrine, but there was no specific reference to the debated modification of that economic creed concerning the taxing of the land by taking only the unearned increment for which society had been responsible. George completed the picture by an open letter to the pontiff against the encyclical. McGlynn in the meantime had broken with the reformer on other economic matters, and in 1893 was reconciled with the Church by accepting the teaching of Leo explicitly and promising to go to Rome, for his refusal to make this trip five years earlier had, as much as anything else, put him outside the Church. He died as pastor of St. Mary's, Newburgh, where he served

[36] Philip Taft, *The A.F. of L. in the Time of Gompers*, New York, 1957, p. 336, rejects the somewhat attenuated argument in favor of strong and direct Catholic influence made by Marc Karson, *American Labor Unions and Politics, 1900–1918*, Carbondale, 1958.

from 1895 to 1900. It is hard to see any other long-range results of McGlynn's work, except perhaps that it served as a
warning that thereafter priests interested in social reform
might achieve more by taking the buffeting of slow-moving
or less progress-minded ecclesiastical authorities more grace-
fully.

The decade of the nineties and the period of progressivism
that followed saw American Catholics generally approaching
the socio-political center from the right. A great terror of
socialism was fixed in their minds by the strikes of the period;
nevertheless an advocacy of industrial arbitration and social
legislation was registered in some of the states. The necessity
of defending the inviolability of private property against the
socialists and the even more radical Industrial Workers of the
World became, after the turn of the century, a constant theme.
But a few more positive voices were heard. John A. Ryan, a
priest who even as a seminarian in St. Paul had shown real
Midwestern Populist sympathies, published his application of
ethics to economics in 1906 in the *Living Wage* and thereby
began a distinguished career.[37] Another clergyman, Peter
Dietz, established his unhappily named Militia of Christ for
Social Service in 1910 to bring together Catholics interested in
permeating the labor movement with Catholic social thought.
It remained pretty much a one-man paper-and-propaganda
organization, and Dietz began to tend more to the burgeoning
field of social welfare.

For the most part, however, the campaign was directed
against socialism, and it was based on the philosophical considerations and condemnations found in ethics and theological
manuals, as well as in modern papal teachings. This necessarily
gave a deeply negative character to much of Catholic concern
with the American social scene even up to the 1930's. Positive
and constructive criticism was to increase, but this negativism
on socio-economic and political problems seems to have lasted

[37] Patrick W. Gearty, *The Economic Thought of Monsignor John A.
Ryan*, Washington, 1953.

into a later period, finding expression through other heavily Catholic-supported phenomena like Coughlinism and Mc-Carthyism.

The pre-World War period was a time of blending for the diverse ethnic groups in American Catholicism. Organized lay activity on a wide scale was found in the Germans' Central Verein which had begun in the 1850's and in the Irish National Benevolent Union which had begun in the 1870's. But into the United States a great flow of people of other nationalities had begun what was so long and with such overtones called the "new" immigration. They, too, followed the natural instinct to organize among themselves. Accordingly, from 1901 to 1917, for the first time there were organizations of many different nationalities working on a national level in the Federation of Catholic Societies. Especially numerous, and important for Catholic strength and future development among later arrivals, were the Italians and the Poles, who are now estimated to contribute to the Catholic body in the United States about six million members each. In lesser proportions were (and are, in their descendants) Catholic Czechs, Jugoslavian Croatians and Slovenes, Magyars, Portuguese, Lithuanians, and Ukrainians and Ruthenians of the Byzantine rite. They found in their own churches both a link with Europe and a bond with America. In the parishes and religious or benevolent societies they found needed help in getting used to the new life. But in another sense the Church did not hasten Americanization and helped instead to preserve, particularly in the language, the diverse cultures brought to American shores in immigrant baggage. After the Great War, for example, the National Catholic War Council, which had under the bishops directed and coordinated Catholic organizational efforts, undertook a program of civic education intended to teach newcomers something of democracy. The effort was explicitly geared not to force the use of English too hastily, or to insist on the too rapid assimilation of American ways by the immigrants. The German Catholic reaction in the 1880's and

1890's to what they had considered Americanizing by, paradoxically enough, a "Hibernarchy" of liberal prelates had provided the experience of a much-publicized controversy on both sides of the Atlantic which no one wanted to repeat. Hence in many parish services, and in their press as well, immigrant tongues were preserved. Priests were sought who spoke them; hymns and pious customs of Europe were preserved. Today in small cities and towns the cultural pluralism of America is graphically enough demonstrated by a series of Catholic churches of different nationality groups. In some cities of upstate New York, for example, one may find as many as five different churches—German, Polish, French-Canadian, Italian, and "Irish" (in the sense that English is used exclusively apart from the Latin liturgy common to all). In the larger centers the separating lines have grown dim, except around the Italian and Polish parishes. Parochial as well as public schools have made Americans of the children of these immigrants as of those before them. At the same time, under Catholic auspices, their cultural heritage from abroad has not been despised. For many of these new citizens, as they worked in the degradation of sweat shops or the danger of railroads or mines and, generally speaking, on the lowest level of hard labor, their religion closed their ears to siren-songs of radicalism or revolt. Sometimes their Church's social doctrine, remaining unknown to them, gave them no incentive to fight for their rights.

A combination of such a conservative influence with some very progressive attitudes prompted Catholic concern with American society. In 1910 there came the first unifying organization of the charitable work of the Church (apart from the St. Vincent de Paul work of laymen, which was over a half-century old already) with the formation of the National Conference of Catholic Charities. Within about ten years thirty centers had been established on a diocesan level, similarly coordinating the individual undertakings of homes and hospitals of various kinds. A great model for such an enterprise in the social welfare field was the organization developed in the Archdiocese of New York.[38] With social-work training under Catholic auspices undertaken in about six schools, the Church's present well-established role in community welfare work was initiated. These multiple programs have grown with the demands of the decades which followed, until today many new areas such as youth work, guidance, and psychiatric care are covered. Many American communities have benefited from this early and firmly rooted Catholic social concern. In recent years, with the swelling of direct and indirect aid from government on all levels, Catholic welfare services have taken on an ever-widening program for all the needy in the communities they serve.

An important event took place in February, 1919, affecting the theory that might guide the social movement, when the Bishops' Program of Social Reconstruction was issued. It was the work of Father Ryan, then of the faculty of the Catholic University of America, but was signed by four bishops who made up the administrative committee of the NCWC (it was still the War Council, was to become the Welfare Council in September, 1919, but to be renamed Welfare Conference in June, 1922, on Rome's direction, to avoid canonical confusion). Their putting the whole American hierarchy on record is more applauded by its members now than it was then. Of all the post-war documents that presented the reform plans of social-minded groups, this Catholic one seems to have been attacked with the greatest hostility. For ten years and more it was labeled socialistic and considered by many as expressing the mentality of only a leftist clique in the American Church.[39]

The program reads like a blueprint of much New Deal social legislation. Other than a greater part for labor in management and profit sharing, all that it advocated was to be-

[38] The publication of Aaron I. Abell's study of this social movement in American Catholicism is awaited by all students of the field who know his articles.

[39] A 1950 NCWC reprint, *Bishops' Program of Social Reconstruction*, showed its vindication by history.

come an accepted part of the American scene. It claimed to be putting forward only what could be achieved within a reasonable period of time. Hence it favored government loans to help settle veterans, as well as the continuance of the federal employment service. The wartime labor board was strongly endorsed, and it was recommended that it be perpetuated. That last specification was eventually carried out when, only a score of years later, the National Labor Relations Board was set up. It was at that late date, too, that labor's right to organize and to bargain collectively was given legal recognition, something the bishops had hoped would never again be questioned by any considerable number of American employers. According to the program, help from government was needed in American life for public housing, unemployment, sickness and old age insurance, as well as for the regulation of utility rates. Today, when almost all of these aims are respectable and acceptable to both major political parties, the prophetic and stimulant role of the 1919 statement is one of the proud boasts of American Catholicism. It helps to explain more basically, and independently of the proletarian origins of priests and bishops, the ideological closeness of the Church and American labor on social questions.

In the 1930's after *Quadragesimo anno* the Catholic social movement picked up momentum. Through the known excesses of individualism and the pending threat of collectivism a path was cut by papal teachings. In the Catholic Worker movement (1933), which arose from the depression, many Catholics found a focus for their new zeal. Much of its policy, its back-to-the-land emphasis, personalist philosophy, distrust of legislative action, and, most of all, its pacifism, caused it to lose much of its following, and yet in spite of this it sowed strong seeds of Catholic social thought and action over the next twenty-five years. Out of a completely "unscientific" house-of-hospitality, serving the most outcast of the poor, came other and more respectable activities and organizations for social justice. One of these was the Association of Catholic

Trade Unionists which, through its schools, began to train leaders of unions and to educate the rank and file to a democratic interest. It ran the danger of being considered a Catholic bloc in the labor movement—a charge of divisiveness that went back half a century. Such criticism usually originated with the racketeers and Communists against whom the ACTU often took decisive action. The waterfront of New York and the electrical workers union were two typical battle areas where this twofold war for decent democratic unionism was waged with some success. The "labor priest" had his day, whether in teaching ethics to unionists or consulting with legislators or serving on government boards when American labor needed him most. Today the labor schools, social action institutes, and the various other local groups seeking an ethical solution for the industrial problem, are organized under the auspices of the Social Action Department of the National Catholic Welfare Conference. This office, since its creation, has been the most consistent spokesman of the American Church in the field. It has interested itself in the whole range of social problems and has often spoken out publicly, even in Washington hearings, on matters like public housing and labor legislation. Often heard, too, in a lobbying position for social betterment has been the National Conference of Catholic Charities, represented by its pioneering director, Monsignor John O'Grady.

Naturally, the state and federal social legislation of the last quarter century cannot be traced solely to Catholic influence. Nonetheless, some of its essential phrases sound a great deal like those which appear in Catholic writings on social justice. Certainly Catholic politicians of the liberal Rooseveltian persuasion have found solace and support in this stream of Catholic thought. The liberal voting record of Catholic representatives in Washington has, in fact, been shown more than once to be proportionally very high. An occasional "encyclical Catholic"—that is, a man, usually young, who is steeped in the social teaching of the Church from his collegiate experience—has made his mark both in Congress and in state government. It would seem, however, that, whereas the articulate Catholic clergyman has been found more often on the liberal side than his Protestant or Jewish counterpart, the Catholic layman himself has probably shown less zeal and activity in social reform than at least his particular counterpart among the Jews. The fact remains that, despite evidence of effective liberalism among Catholics, within the doctrinal unity of the Church in America can be found two journals as vastly differing in social philosophy as the conservative Brooklyn *Tablet* and the liberal *Commonweal,* or two writers as far apart as William Buckley and John Cogley. By any numerical consideration made on a national scale, the Buckley conservatism would most likely have the backing of the rank and file, and the less articulate of the clergy, who, nonetheless, only rarely say anything that smacks of politicking from the pulpit.

The liberal attitude seems certainly to have won out in one area of American Catholicism, that of interracial justice. Rome's well-known color-blind interpretation of the gospels has often echoed in the United States, especially through the Apostolic Delegate of the last quarter century, Archbishop Amleto Cicognani. That Washington voice played a very special role, but over the same period of time there have been organized groups working for the same cause, such as the Catholic Interracial Councils under the leadership of John LaFarge, a Jesuit of an old and distinguished American family. In the early 1930's the Catholic University of America in the nation's capital revived a policy of integration which it had begun in the 1890's. It was thereby much ahead of its five sister institutions of university status in that important locale.[40] In religious communities there were a few martyrs to the cause of equal opportunities for Negroes in their schools, colleges, and novitiates. The new Archdiocese of Washington integrated its school system quietly after 1947. But Raleigh,

[40] *To Secure These Rights. The Report of the President's Committee on Civil Rights,* New York, 1947, p. 91.

St. Louis, and New Orleans became scenes of some resistance, necessitating episcopal edicts which sought to outlaw the discrimination of separate facilities for religion and education for Negro Catholics. Catholic rank-and-file opinion on the racial question has not usually been much different from the prevailing neighborhood outlook, yet right-minded leadership has been widely acknowledged, even when lamented as too authoritarian—but then, no doctrinally connected Catholic opinion is decided by membership vote.

The social thinking of American Catholics has been and is being affected more by the formation of the child's mind than of the adult's. The work of curriculum makers for the parochial and secondary schools, such as the citizenship commission which has operated for twenty years out of the Catholic University of America, has had tremendous if unostentatious effect. The social doctrine of the Church has been incorporated into reading and other textbooks so as to inculcate a sense of community in the children of even elementary school grades. The fostered objective of preparing the young for Christian social living in the American democratic environment has become a common one throughout the states for Catholic educators on these lower levels.[41] The development of a truly Catholic mind in children on such matters as civic obligations, racial justice, labor unions, or international cooperation, has surpassed any work done among their elders, who not only rarely hear such topics in Sunday sermons, but even seldom find them in the more usual Catholic weekly newspaper. Perhaps in recent years only in certain popular Catholic periodicals, such as *Commonweal*, *America*, and *Sign*, has the school enthusiasm for a positive social viewpoint been matched.

In other ways, too, American Catholic educational endeavors have grown significantly in their contribution to American life—in the enlargement of parochial schools them-

[41] Commission of American Citizenship, *Guiding Growth in Christian Social Living*, Washington, 1946, I, 5.

selves, for one, although a constantly increasing population has never allowed more than half the Catholic children to be accommodated in the grade schools. They have generally, that is in most locales, ceased to be regarded as inferior to the public schools. In fact, that selective process demanded by their smaller capacities when enrolling students has often enhanced their academic reputation at the expense of the public schools. In the public schools as well, student overcrowding, aging facilities, underpaid and overworked teachers, and downward curriculum adjustments have perhaps worked more havoc than in the Catholic schools. But it was not until about twenty years ago—apart from an early and extensive development in Philadelphia—that the central Catholic high school began to move into a position to help in the country's burden-bearing at that secondary level. They have filled a gap that the more exclusive college preparatory high schools conducted by religious orders were not able to cope with. The growth and assimilation of Catholic high schools have filled the sports pages of America with strange combat as the names of their saintly patrons, followed by scores, have been spread across the headlines. Today the number of Catholic primary schools connected with parishes or institutions, or privately conducted, has reached over 10,000, while the enrollment climbs toward the four million mark. Meanwhile the high school totals show 1,589 conducted by dioceses or parishes, and 845 under other auspices, usually religious orders of men or women. In all, close to 800,000 students are enrolled on the secondary level. These two types of lower schools have become more centrally supervised under trained priest superintendents in most American dioceses. This has meant a raising of standards both in the training of teachers and in the educational facilities.

The parental demands for such schools have never been so strong as now. Principals are plagued by requests for admission and registration lines are formed early in the morning. The institutions are built and maintained by the personal sacrifices of the congregations. They are an expression of their freedom to educate their children as they see fit, so long as state requirements are lived up to. The Church has fought for the security of this right since the days of the proposed Blaine Amendment of 1876 which would have outlawed parochial schools. Legal recognition of this fundamental parental prerogative was won in 1925 in the Oregon School case (Pierce vs. Society of Sisters). Naturally Catholic educators think they are accomplishing much for their country by their labors and many by the complete dedication of their lives through the religious vows. A commonplace Catholic statistic in many communities shows how much in buildings, equipment, and salaries is saved every year for the general taxpayer by their system of schools. If the local Catholic schools have been late in entering community life in some areas, they have paid in part for this by the consequent ignorance of their work which leads some outside the Church to classify them as nothing more than elaborate Sunday schools.

The Catholic educational role on the college and university level is perhaps better known. A few colleges like Georgetown, the oldest, dating from 1789, have long been integral parts of their communities, while most are developments of the late nineteenth and twentieth centuries. Only one, the pontifical, national, hierarchy-directed Catholic University of America, began as a university with graduate level studies. Some thirty have since taken on that work or at least the title of university. The managers of these institutions, of which another sixty are purely collegiate schools for men or coeducational, are usually members of religious orders, predominantly Jesuits, followed by Holy Cross Fathers, Benedictines, Franciscans, and Augustinians, although a few are diocesan and conducted by secular priests. Then there are well over a hundred women's colleges under the supervision of orders of nuns, commonly with the assistance of some priests and lay people. Some few of these last institutions have achieved high academic reputation. About 300,000 students a year are being educated in these colleges and universities. While observers within the system worry about the thin spread of resources already apparent, Church leaders are concerned about the needs that will be brought on by future demands.

Casting a somewhat jaundiced eye on these institutions, some American Catholics at present are busy disclaiming much of their own cultural or intellectual contribution to American life. The first lament raised appeared in a sketch of the historical reasons why Catholics in the United States had made a relatively poor contribution to American scholarship.[42] It made the usual recall of the immigrant origins of the Church, its very necessary preoccupations for many years with brick and mortar more than books, and added reflections on the anti-Catholicism of the American scene, which Catholics resented, and on the anti-intellectualism which they embraced. The poverty of results in producing scholars from Catholic graduate schools and the general poor showing in scholarship was a commonplace to those in the various fields of study, scientific or humane, who ever surveyed the literature or attended a scholarly convention. The main thesis found wide agreement in subsequent discussions, although no attempt has yet been made to check the facts with scientific and statistical thoroughness.[43] The question has been clouded by use of the term "intellectual life." At this point there are enough devotees of literature and the arts among the American Catholic college graduates who feel as a group that they are intellectuals and who know they are as advanced in education as any of their

[42] John Tracy Ellis, "American Catholics and the Intellectual Life," *Thought*, XXX, Autumn, 1955, pp. 351–388. Actually the eventual breast-beating has gone beyond the scope of that first paper. It is interesting that the cry took hold so strongly since it had been raised thirty years earlier and at least once in practically every decade afterwards. Cf. John A. O'Brien, ed., *Catholics and Scholarship. A Symposium on the Development of Scholars*, Huntington, 1939. Perhaps the post-war organization of the Catholic Commission on Intellectual and Cultural Affairs has done the most in encouraging realistic appraisal.

[43] An interesting analysis more pertinent to the present than Ellis' but likewise in need of more empirical data, is Thomas F. O'Dea, *American Catholic Dilemma: an Inquiry into the Intellectual Life*, New York, 1958.

secularly trained counterparts. One group of laymen, for example, gathers up from all over the world and publishes in *Cross Currents* what they consider the best articles appearing on Catholic thought or in related philosophies. Such Catholics (and there are even what might be called "bohemians" among them) are not unknown these days in urban centers. They preserve their loyalty to their Church and its moral code even when much publicized applications of the latter to movies, plays, or books sometimes disturbs them. Indeed, some basic realities of Catholic scholarly life have not even been alluded to in the many recent discussions. Young and promising lay scholars have regularly left the Catholic academic circle, and possible future reputations in scholarship, for business or government. Many have done so pressed by the fundamental economic problems of feeding growing families on less than the highest wage scale, a difficulty which their professional colleagues outside the Church meet in other ways. From that point of view, however, one might then expect clerics in their celibate seclusion to produce more scholarship. The fact that there is a dearth even there might open an interesting area of study on the dichotomy between ecclesiastical and academic values. But some sign of an advance may be seen in the fact that sermons that used to touch only on intellectual pride are now being supplemented by a few on intellectual sloth. American Catholics are dissatisfied with their small role in the leadership of American intellectual pursuits and in general with their lack of impact on American society. As they have climbed in greater numbers into the middle class, their ghettoism would seem to be crumbling a little. For the most part, they are mature enough to blame themselves and to find little consolation in the old reassuring habit, popular thirty years ago, of counting up Catholic explorers, military men, and famous converts in American history. Yet this attitude is only moderately diffused. With some few notable exceptions, the weekly Catholic newspaper—and perhaps the Sunday sermon—continue to reflect that past day

when the flock was made up of uneducated peasant immigrants, rather than to speak to the present where the educated
sons, grandsons, and great-grandsons of these immigrants
have taken their places. The original immigrant in many parts
of the country is further in the past than is usually taken for
granted.

At present, the cultural contribution of American Catholicism is not a matter of boast.[44] Foreign visitors of the same
faith have often been amused by such features of Catholicism
in the States as its over-all cultural immaturity, its sensitivity
to criticism, its hundred per cent Americanism, and its self-
conscious pride in its prominent members—anyone from pu-
gilist to violinist—especially if the celebrity were a convert.
On the credit side, however, taking into account the omnipresent heavy dead hand of tradition—which at its imitative
best is found in the nineteenth-century Gothic churches of
Patrick C. Keely—all officially sponsored ecclesiastical art and
architecture have not been bad. Catholic artists are appalled
by the lack of backing for their work, but at least enough exists
to keep one review, *Liturgical Arts,* busy reporting it. In
architecture especially, outside the more conservative northeast, Catholics have at least kept up with their Protestant
neighbors in church and school buildings that employ contemporary design and techniques. In liturgical or church music
the advance has been almost exclusively in the revival of the
Gregorian chant rather than in notable original composition.

Perhaps American Catholics have even influenced their
countrymen a little in other and lesser ways. A post-war
emphasis on the contemplative, always a part of the Catholic

[44] For the contrast of an earlier mentality examine the five volume *Catholic
Builders of the Nation: a Symposium of the Catholic Contribution to the
Civilization of the United States,* New York, 1935. There seems to have
been nothing in Catholic periodical literature like M. J. Ahern, "The
Catholic Church and American Culture," *The Catholic Mind,* XXIV,
September, 1936, pp. 345–350, in the subsequent two decades and it took
a Harvard Divinity School tercentenary to bring that lyrical lecture about.
(The writer wishes to thank his summer session graduate students of 1957
for making it possible to make the above statement with great certainty.)

way of life but never before very strong in activist America, has seen a few struggling Trappist monasteries grow into a dozen thriving ones. The example of laymen who have taken advantage of such retreats and other islands of silence throughout the country has also moved some Protestants to participation, if not at times to imitation. The Catholic liturgical celebrations of Christmas and of Holy Week—particularly of Good Friday—are no longer reserved to the Catholic community. Even the use of the crib, an Italian Franciscan tradition, has become widespread. It is more difficult to say what, if any, Catholic liturgical practices may have had influence outside the Church. Occasionally one hears of the Protestant military chaplain trying to borrow the Catholic chaplain's vestments! Evidently the taste for ceremony has increased in America, a high degree of respect being shown for theatrical pageantry with a spiritual significance. Religious medals, including the star of David, are no longer the symbols of idolatry they once were to many, but now are an accepted area for the American jeweler's art. It is interesting to note that American Catholics are commonly thought of as too Protestant by their Latin coreligionists, but the real interrelationship and inter-influence remain to be studied.

American Catholics—including some of the teaching orders of religious—are exhorted on occasion to renew their European-based intellectual traditions. These should make them among the least susceptible to American anti-intellectualism. The facts so far have proven otherwise. Even the tradition kept alive in terms of scholastic philosophy has often been fostered more by non-Catholic scholars and institutions, such as the Medieval Academy of America, than by the Catholics themselves. On the other hand, no one will deny that the Catholic-sponsored emphasis on a natural-law philosophy of law has worked to make it a school of legal thought of some increasing consequence in America. In areas like art, drama, or literary criticism, some voices of Aristotelian-Thomistic approach have been listened to with respect. Still, probably for most Americans the Catholic approach remains one of censorship, centered only in protest, concerned only with morality, and ignorant of esthetics.[45]

Those who think that in cultural and intellectual matters American Catholics have done little are acutely aware that one of their major criteria is the presence or absence of outside recognition. This test gives very evident negative results in the case of the scholarly efforts of their theologians. But, more than by any innate deficiency, an undistinguished reception may be accounted for by a disinterest in communication— a lack of outside dialogue on their part. In the last decade perhaps only the writings of the Jesuit theologian John Courtney Murray, on the question of church and state, have attracted much attention.[46] The Catholic position as traditionally presented by theologians and canon lawyers holds that the one true Church is to be recognized and treated as such by the state. The American Catholic hierarchy, on the other hand, has constantly and consistently, from Carroll through Hughes and Gibbons up to Archbishop John McNicholas, O.P. of Cincinnati, and as late as 1948, expressed satisfaction with the American mode of separation, and evidenced no desire to change it, even should Catholics ever become an overwhelming majority of the population. But two Catholic authorities, John A. Ryan and Moorhouse F. X. Millar, S.J., once pondered the very remote possibility of a Catholic state in America wherein non-Catholics would be a numerically insignificant minority.[47] They allowed on that basis that certain restrictions should be suffered by the minority groups, such as loss of exemption from taxes and restriction of their propaganda. This essay has become to non-Catholics one of the most often-

---

[45] Cf. Walter Kerr, *Criticism and Censorship*, Milwaukee, 1954.

[46] John Courtney Murray, "On the Structure of the Church-State Problem," W. Gurian and M. A. Fitzsimons, eds., *The Catholic Church in World Affairs*, Notre Dame, 1954, pp. 11–32.

[47] Cf. John A. Ryan and Francis J. Boland, *Catholic Principles of Politics*, New York, 1947, revised edition of *The State and the Church*, New York, 1924.

employed and certainly one of the most scare-inciting passages ever penned by American Catholics. Murray's efforts to re-examine the matter of Church and State, however, have reassured and continue to reassure many Americans. His writings have tended to show how the statements of Leo XIII, and papal pronouncements since his time, can be understood to emphasize first and foremost the common good of all in a society, even over any special privilege for the Church. The nature of the state has changed, and in its completely lay character in modern times it cannot be expected to take any position on religious claims. Perhaps the working out of this school of thought, so world-wide in its possible application, may one day be not only a contribution to Catholic theology, but a doctrine pacifying of American Protestant, Jewish, and secularist fears. Meanwhile these fears might well be allayed, too, by an awareness of the teachings of the American bishops who, rather than the theologians by themselves, are to be considered the official teaching voice of the Church in America.[48]

While Catholics in the United States make few claims in speculative matters, they do contend that in the field of ethics or morality they have had significant influence. They usually point with pride to the Catholic family and its strong moral fiber as an essential to the well-being of the whole country, upon which they have always insisted. The challenges of the times are being met with such new techniques as special programs in girls' schools aimed at preparing them for Christian family living. Often given in colleges are "marriage courses," and for the engaged and married there are "Cana Conferences" conducted in dioceses throughout the country, underscoring the importance of a healthy family life and fostering this principle through group education as preparation for marriage and as a means of facing problems that arise in married

---

[48] Their constant and unswerving adherence to the American way is documented in John Tracy Ellis, "Church and State: an American Catholic Tradition," *Harper's Magazine*, CCVII, November, 1953, pp. 63–67.

life. Through other lay activities and "Catholic Action" groups (such as the Young Christian Workers and more than a dozen lay institutes of religious in secular dress) an effort is being made to bring Catholic principles to bear on the moral aspects of labor, politics, education, or whatever area of society in which the Catholic may find himself. More efforts using organizational methods of an older type are found in various fields from rural life to television. One hears very little claim of a Catholic moralizing influence in certain other aspects of American life, since the names that people stories of gangsters or corrupt politicians too often prove too great an embarrassment. Yet, in the realm of national security, Catholics are gratified to find no one in treason cases whose immorality might bring shame upon them. It is probably not so well known what a large percentage of Catholics—and Southern Protestants—the Federal Bureau of Investigation is glad to have as employees in work that requires a certain high moral stability.

In a society of shifting moral standards, both public and private, American Catholics feel secure that, if not they themselves, at least their Church is a bulwark of morality in national life. They see their Church stand firm while from their perspective other religious groups seem to bend to the demands of their members. They condemn legalized divorce, birth control information at the public expense, and public pornography (as others do the sale of alcoholic beverages, bingo-playing, or horse-betting) as contrary to their moral code and harmful to society as a whole. They have tried to advance these points of view to the public, as well as to the law-makers and administrators. However, in doing so, their performances most of the time have not given much evidence of employing more than a minimum of good selling or public relations techniques. Their often awkward efforts have left them open to a charge of pressuring more than any other religious group. This hostile reaction may be owing in part to what is sometimes feared as too great an institutional or material growth of American Catholicism and its isolation, particularly through its schools, from what is paradoxically considered a pluralistic society. Sometimes grounds for annoyance are found in the very sureness of Catholics. Their doctrinal position as the one true Church is still often taken to mean that they deny salvation for those outside the Church, and this despite the fact that a group of fanatics in Boston have been excommunicated for the expounding of a perversion of that doctrine. But the protest of Catholic isolationism holds true in many areas. Catholic feet have dragged in interfaith ventures for the common good like the National Conference of Christians and Jews. In this regard they are sometimes "holier than the Pope," who himself has often called for men of good will to work together to seek solutions to the problems of society where it did not mean yielding to notions of indifferentism regarding creed.

Catholics might also explain their slowness to collaborate in such endeavors by the continued domination of a certain Protestant tradition in the United States. The American position is very unlike that often found in continental European circles. In Germany, for example, Catholics even seek to achieve religious unity through prayer and conference together with Protestants. In the United States, Catholics pray for the unity of all in the Church, pretty much by themselves, and non-Catholic suspicion of the Church has always seemed to make these prayers even more necessary. In the last decade of the nineteenth century the American Protective Association reacted to the Catholic rise to greater social prominence in the same way that the Ku Klux Klan reacted to a similar Catholic rise to political importance three decades later. Today, through Protestants and Other Americans United, a more sophisticated approach is used by certain elements in American Protestantism, but Catholics still feel that the concern over the supposed political machinations of the hierarchy is still greatly motivated by the same deep-rooted nativism of which every generation has had a sample. Meanwhile, on the community level, Catholics are becoming more and more aware that personal social cooperation and improved public relations are necessary to remove the bogey stigma.

American Catholics like to think they have strengthened their country in the ideological warfare against Communism. They are strangely modest about proclaiming how in the days of the fight against fascism they, almost alone in American society, foresaw which was the greater ultimate menace. Perhaps their anti-Communism has not often taken a very positive tack, neglecting to offer programs of social betterment in addition to polemics of speeches and editorials turning on Communism's Godless character and protesting its attacks on the Church in other parts of the world. Nonetheless, the furthering of positive encyclical teachings such as that on industry councils—which the old C.I.O., under Philip Murray, virtually copied in one of its proposals—was a force for social responsibility in democratic capitalism. And as a kind of Catholic stockpile in the material war against Communism, work for better housing might be cited, along with agrarian reform and racial justice, plus successful accomplishments in providing overseas relief after the war and in resettling refugees in America.

In drawing to a conclusion, it would be interesting to have available on real evidence the picture that American Catholicism presents to the rest of the nation. The day when a Roman Catholic was taken as synonymous with an ignorant, brawling Irishman has passed, and there has probably been some advance from the less distant past in the United States when it was admitted that to most Protestants Roman Catholicism meant traffic tie-ups outside city churches on Sunday mornings, birth control controversies in the public press, and priests at baseball games.[49] Now, at any rate, to this mental image there might be added that of a famous prelate as television star. And the picture might be additionally revised, perhaps, to include priests at theatres and concerts. The traveling Ameri-

[49] Willard Sperry, *Religion in America*, Cambridge, 1946, pp. 199–224.

can's contact with the gentle, ascetic Pope Pius XII might have a kindly influence on his mental image of Catholics. The reading of *The Cardinal* will have confused others with a picture of giant corporative efficiency. For the rest, it is undoubtedly a picture made from personal contacts with business or professional associates. The local pastor, the teaching brother, the nursing sister only very seldom have their chance to make their faith felt outside their own little circle of cobelievers.

But over and above this general attempt at seeing Catholics as others see them, it is next to impossible to say in more than relative terms what thirty-six million Catholics—and maybe ten million more, according to less official estimates—contribute to American life. Most interestingly of all, they themselves would never claim to have a great effect on American culture or values.[50] They know that they and their predecessors have to some extent carried their beliefs into education and industry and other avenues of life, even into the field of entertainment. But they have much more often conformed to values than changed them. Where those before them found a Protestant society, they find today a more secular one maintaining only the vaguest of religious standards. The American Catholic, like his Church, is not the same throughout the United States. In a position of great strength in the Northeast,

[50] The last decade has produced a new kind of literature in American Catholic circles, the self-analysis. There seem to be three principal broad categories. There is the *descriptive*, for example, Leo R. Ward, ed., *The American Apostolate: American Catholicism in the Twentieth Century*, Westminster, 1952, the Commonweal's *Catholicism in America*, New York, 1954, Louis Putz, ed., *The Catholic Church, U.S.A.*, Chicago, 1956. There is the *sociological*; first, dealing with the whole Catholic community like John Kane's articles and book, *Catholic-Protestant Conflicts in America*, Chicago, 1955; (this over-all approach, but with concentration on Chicago, is that also of François Houtart, *Aspects sociologiques du Catholicisme Américaine*, Paris, 1957); secondly, dealing with the parish, for example, Joseph H. Fichter, *Southern Parish*, Chicago, 1951. There is a final group of writings that might be called the *philosophical* and these include particularly Walter Ong, *Frontiers in American Catholicism*, New York, 1957, *American Catholic Crossroads*, New York, 1959 and Gustave Weigel, *Faith and Understanding in America*, New York, 1959.

he is apt to be aloof from the rest of the community and tempted to the use of political pressure. Though strong, too, in the central Midwest, he blends in the fashion of frontier society and shows a greater independence of clerical domination. In the South, where he partakes of the lot of a real and practically ineffective minority, though he has less to say about its ultimate values, he shares more in community life. In the Far West he hustles with the rest and tries to strengthen an old hold while the Church faces the challenge of a membership growing quickly by the thousands.

Thus the American Catholic is not one thing in all parts of a very diversified America. He may be French-Canadian in background or Spanish-Mexican; he may be public school or parochial school educated; he may be a Catholic college product (and as different, consequently, as Jesuit and Benedictine), or the alumnus of a state college or one in the Ivy League; he may be a new immigrant or a half-dozen generations removed; he may be in good standing with his Church or halfway outside of it through, perhaps, an ecclesiastically invalid marriage. Nonetheless, his distinct experience as a Catholic living among the political, social, and economic institutions of the United States is turning him into something unique in the history of Christianity—an American Catholic. He is different from an Irish or an Italian member of the Church. His Church, too, is always adapting and adjusting in non-essentials in order that it may better serve him and fulfill its larger mission. In so doing, its institutions may gradually come to affect his life in such a way that his Catholic outlook will further bless his fellow countrymen by providing for American society standards of public morality, social betterment, and cultural and intellectual achievements worthy of the ancient Mother Church.

JUDAISM IN THE UNITED STATES

OSCAR HANDLIN

I N MODERN TIMES, Judaism has involved less a system of
ideas or a formulated creed than a way of life. Formal
theology has never played a very important role in its development; indeed, some religious thinkers have denied the
existence of a Jewish theology at all. Judaism can, therefore,
be described only as a body of assumptions founded upon tradition and imbedded in popular customs, habits, and recognized rules of behavior. The transfer of those assumptions,
with Jewish immigration, to America called for a difficult
adaptation to new circumstances under conditions that were
themselves changing very rapidly.

An analysis of that transfer must take account of a variety
of complex forces. The tradition of Judaism was itself the
product of a long history within many different environments.
In the United States, it was transplanted into a society radically different from any in which it had formerly flourished,
and one which was itself in process of continual transformation. Within that society Jews acquired a status unlike that
which they occupied anywhere else in their history. Finally,
after the middle of the nineteenth century, they encountered
a challenging new intellectual milieu that made unprecedented
demands upon them. All these factors entered into the shaping
of American Judaism.

The complex tradition by which Jews long governed their
lives was the product of two thousand years of exile.[1] Its
foundation was the faith that there was a divine purpose to
their banishment from the Holy Land that had been the land
of their fathers. The Jews were therefore obligated to retain
their identity amidst the nations until that moment at the end
of days when God would choose to send among them a Re-

---

[1] The best general history of the Jews is Salo W. Baron, *Social and Religious History of the Jews*, 1st ed., 3 vols., New York, 1937; 2nd ed., 5
vols., Philadelphia, 1952–57 carries the revision to 1200.

deemer from the house of David to lead them out of exile. Meanwhile tradition—*masoret*, that which was handed down, or *kabbalah*, that which was received—safeguarded their character as a chosen people, preserved them in righteousness and holiness and prepared them for the eventual Messianic return.

At the heart of the tradition was the Torah, a body of law, both written and oral, which enjoined upon the Jews the obligations of piety and the performance of *mitzvoth*, deeds pleasing to a God immanent in the universe. The Torah was a work of direct divine inspiration, both that which was written down to begin with and that which remained oral. The former included the five books of Moses and the rest of the canon of the Old Testament. The oral law was embodied in a vast body of commentary and judicial opinions delivered by rabbis over very long periods. By the end of the second century A.D., much of that material had been codified in the *Mishnah*; and that in turn was thereafter added to in the academies of Babylonia and Palestine to form the Talmud. But to the Talmud there were assimilated the glosses and interpretations of later rabbis as well as the less formal *responsa* or collections of opinions on specific new questions. This immense collection of learning in which Jews continually immersed themselves formed the *halakhah*, the course within which they were expected to guide their lives.

The process of restating the law was thus continuous, with frequent changes as new conditions demanded new interpretations. But that process operated within the limits of the tradition, for alterations were made within a defined pattern of hermeneutics and understood in the light of *haggadah*, an accumulation of stories, parables, and aphorisms that gave depth and meaning to the law.[2]

This tradition was transmitted to the United States through

[2] For a general survey of religious practices see Louis Finkelstein, *The Jews*, 2nd ed., Philadelphia, 1949, II, 1327ff.; also Solomon Schechter, "The Talmud," *Studies in Judaism Third Series*, Philadelphia, 1924, pp. 194ff.

two channels. That of lesser importance emanated from the centers of Jewish life that had developed for five hundred years (A.D. 700–1200) in the lands under Islamic hegemony. Under relatively favorable conditions there, a distinctive way of life, ritual, and form of worship, the Sephardic custom or *minhag*, became defined. With the dispersal of the Jewish communities from Spain, where they had thrived under Moorish and Spanish rule, the exiles carried the influence of these practices northward to England and the Netherlands, and across the ocean to America.

At the point of its highest flourishing, Sephardic Jewry made an intellectual adjustment to Aristotelian ideas that would long remain important. The permanent monument of that adjustment was the work of Maimonides (1135–1204). He was born in Cordova, but misfortune compelled him to move first to Fez and then to Cairo. Thoroughly trained in traditional Jewish learning, he also absorbed the Arabic philosophy and science of his day and, through it, that of the Greek master. His *Moreh Nebukim*, or *Guide to the Perplexed*, attempted to synthesize within an Aristotelian framework the dominant assumptions of the Jews of his time. Denying that there was a conflict between religion and philosophy, Maimonides pictured Judaism as an expression of human intelligence; and his arguments thereafter supplied a point of departure for those who wished to describe Judaism in rational terms. The conviction that religious practice could be reasonably explained was also the basis for Maimonides' effort to codify the whole Talmudic law in *Yad Hakhazaka*, and in a commentary largely within the original categories, upon the *Mishnah*.

The effort to codify and simplify the tradition continued after Maimonides' death, stimulated by the general decline in the level of Jewish intellectual life. In the sixteenth century it produced the most influential Jewish book of modern times. Joseph Karo (b. 1488), who spent most of his life in Turkey, was a mystic and a visionary, but at the same time commanded enormous respect as a legal authority. His *responsa* were influential throughout Jewry. In 1550 he compiled an elaborate code, *Beth Yosef*, which he simplified five years later in an elementary handbook, *Shulkhan Arukh*. The latter work was to be widely republished and its clear, unambiguous statement of the rules of Jewish life would for centuries have binding force in many parts of the world.

All this time another pattern of Jewish life was developing in northwestern Europe, in Christian territory. Its first centers were in France and the Rhineland but it tended to spread eastward through Germany and on into the Polish lands. Later, in the nineteenth century, the descendants of those Jews would undertake a reverse migration westward and would add millions to the population of the United States.

The Northern Jews differed from the Southern in ritual; the *ashkenazim* had their own distinctive *minhag* or customs. They differed significantly also in intellectual development. Lacking the stimulus of exposure to Islamic and Greek thought, the rabbis of France and Germany were hardly interested in philosophy or theology. Their concerns were more legalistic and they were more bound to tradition. Characteristically the outstanding figures among them, like Rashi, were commentators, concerned primarily with the explication of texts.[3]

Through the centuries this community suffered many vicissitudes in alternating periods of persecution and toleration. Its era of greatest achievement came in the sixteenth century in the domains of the Polish kingdom that reached from the Baltic almost to the Black Sea and that included Estonia, Lithuania, White Russia, and the Ukraine. There a distinctive way of life produced a civilization peculiarly oriented toward religious values.

Located among people who were either peasants or noble-

---

[3] See H. L. Ginsberg, ed., *Rashi Anniversary Volume*, Philadelphia, 1941; S. M. Blumenfeld, *Master of Troyes*, New York, 1946; also Solomon Schechter, "Jewish Saints," *Studies in Judaism*, pp. 1ff.; Alexander Marx, *Essays in Jewish Biography*, Philadelphia, 1947.

men, the Jews performed important mercantile and commercial services for their society. Their life was centered in a homogeneous, unified community, the *shtetl* or little village. There religion was interwoven in all the affairs of life. It supplied answers to every question a man could raise, and it provided him with spiritual and aesthetic nurture as well. The life of study was assigned a high order of eminence and occupied the best talent of the community.

Study, however, had a rigorously defined character. In the *Yeshiva,* or academy, as well as in the synagogue, the learning process operated within completely closed assumptions. The authorities existed in the tradition; and when the works of Maimonides and Karo were accepted, it was as summaries of the tradition. All the ultimate answers were therefore known; only the details of application and interpretation needed investigation. Hence the total lack of interest in philosophy or theology, and hence the definition of study as the mastery of texts the validity of which remained constant in an unchanging world.

This order was mortally wounded at the end of the seventeenth century by the series of social disturbances and wars that swept across eastern Europe. There followed a long period of misery that, in historical retrospect, seems not finally to have ended until the total liquidation of these communities by the Nazis in the 1940's. In the long interim there were a number of striking readjustments.[4]

In the eighteenth century the miserable conditions of the Jewish masses, the resentment against the control of the communities by the aristocratic few, and their discontent with the aridity of formal religious life nurtured a movement of protest. Hasidism enlisted wide support. Like contemporary Christian pietism, it sought to restore some sense of emotional content to worship and to compensate for the legalism of the dominant groups. The *mitnagdim,* the traditional leaders en-

[4] See S. M. Dubnow, *History of the Jews in Russia and Poland,* 3 vols., Philadelphia, 1916–20.

trenched in the academies and in the organized communities, fought back in a long-drawn-out conflict that reached down into the nineteenth century. Time obscured the original issues. The *Hasidhim* developed entrenched rabbinic dynasties of their own, while their opponents were diverted by other more portentous challenges.

By then the ideas of the enlightenment had begun to penetrate to the *shtetl*. Rationalism, progress, humanitarianism, and the prospect of equal citizenship eroded elements of the ancient faith. Toward the end of the nineteenth century, even in eastern Europe, secular influences were destroying the traditional communities, as socialism became ever more attractive to the laborers, and assimilation more attractive to the middle classes.

Furthermore, under the pressure of unfavorable economic conditions a steadily growing stream of immigrants moved westward, to central Europe, to France and England, and ultimately to the United States. Weakened from within and battered from without, the old order was collapsing, and its failure conditioned the religious life in the United States of the Jews who fled from it.

The earliest period of Jewish settlement in the New World was the longest.[5] The first Jews landed in the American colonies at New York in 1654, and the conditions of their life did not seriously change until the 1820's.

From the point of view of religious thought, these years were but of slight importance. Life in America then presented no serious intellectual challenges to the Jews. Their number was small, reaching a maximum of perhaps 5,000. Most of them were merchants who lived in the great commercial seaports. The trade that supplied them with a livelihood was largely an extension of European trade, and their mode of existence was not radically different from that in other centers

[5] For a general history of the Jews in the United States, see Oscar Handlin, *Adventure in Freedom*, New York, 1954.

of Jewish life. The earliest arrivals were *Sephardim* of Spanish and Portuguese origin who came from South America or from the Netherlands and England. But by the middle of the eighteenth century they had been joined by large numbers of *Ashkenazic* Jews from Germany and central Europe. The Sephardic ritual nevertheless retained its primacy in the handful of congregations along the coast, strengthened by the connections of the colonies with England.[6]

The elements of instability in the religious life of these Jews stemmed from two novel elements in the American situation. They quickly acquired political and civic rights more extensive than they had elsewhere enjoyed. Religious equality and high social and economic status enabled the Jews to visualize themselves as simply another of the many religious denominations already characteristic of America. Thus the barriers of inequality that had long separated Jews from the people among whom they lived were now breached.

The problems created by such contacts were not readily solved. Indeed the Jewish communities were singularly unprepared to deal with them. The forms of synagogue organization, like the ritual, were transplanted intact and could only be preserved by rigid orthodoxy. No learned men crossed the ocean in these years; in the whole period there was not a single rabbi on the North American mainland. Disputes and uncertainties therefore had to be referred back to England and that made adjustment to local conditions difficult. Nor was there any disposition to deal with religious problems on an intellectual level; these merchants had neither the knowledge nor the interest for speculation in ideas. As a result, adherence to the traditional forms was largely a matter of habit or of family loyalty. The weakness of the community was evident in the high rate of intermarriage, in widespread apathy or conversion, as well as in the lack of any striking contributions to religious thought.

[6] On early American Jewry, see Hyman B. Grinstein, *Rise of the Jewish Community of New York 1654–1860*, Philadelphia, 1947.

The situation changed totally in the sixty years after 1820. The number of Jews rose rapidly as a new wave of immigration brought thousands from every part of Europe. By 1880 there were almost half a million in the United States. Many of the newcomers were Germans and many more spoke Yiddish, a Germanic dialect. In any case there was a tendency to identify them with Germany both by contrast with the earlier Sephardim and because the cultural influences emanating from Germany were important throughout central and eastern Europe.

The country into which the new arrivals came was also changing. Independence was now an accomplished fact, and the United States was entering upon a period of extremely rapid territorial and economic expansion which made room for ambitious and enterprising men. Many Jews now found places in retail trade. As pedlars and shopkeepers they scattered throughout the country, often in the small towns and villages of the interior, and many advanced quickly in wealth and position. The number of congregations grew correspondingly.

The adjustment of the newcomers was facilitated by continued improvement in their civic status. The last vestiges of inferiority disappeared as the nation achieved complete religious equality, and in the generally friendly environment Jews increasingly identified themselves with American conditions and American trends.[7]

As earlier, however, that identification exposed them to the social problems raised by their separateness as a group. Only now that was to be complicated by serious intellectual dilemmas. Against the developing scientific challenges to traditional faith, it was ever more difficult to maintain an unwavering orthodoxy. To the questions raised by the Deists and the rationalists of the eighteenth century, there were now joined

[7] Oscar and Mary F. Handlin, "Acquisition of Political and Social Rights by the Jews in the United States," *American Jewish Year Book*, LVI, 1955, pp. 54ff.

the problems created by historical criticism of the authenticity of the sacred texts upon which the whole Jewish tradition rested. Geology upset the accepted Biblical chronology and ultimately the doctrines of evolution destroyed the orderly picture of a created universe. Buttressed by the prestige of science, these sources of doubt could not simply be rejected as external and Gentile. Like other Americans, the Jews were driven to reassess their inherited beliefs in the light of the new-ideas.[8]

Yet the Jews were in an exceptionally weak condition to deal with these problems. At the start there were still no learned men among the immigrants. The rabbis of central and eastern Europe, secure in their own social status, felt no compulsion to emigrate. Their academies were self-contained, isolated from the external world, and identified with specific localities. American Jews long had to seek at home the intellectual resources for dealing with their own problems.

By the nature of the case, these efforts were feeble. Ignorance of traditional and of secular learning was widespread. The new arrivals were restless men, precisely those who in Europe had been least deeply immersed in study. Once in America, the struggle to succeed in business totally absorbed their attention. Many could hardly spell out the Hebrew of the prayer book. But then, there were not in any case many books for them to read. Their orthodoxy was largely a matter of habit, of ancestral piety, and of emotional recollections of Old World ways.

Such men were not likely of their own accord to devote much thought to religious matters, until goaded into doing so by attacks from outside. The effort of Christian missionaries to induce conversions among the Jews thus evoked a defensive reaction. Solomon H. Jackson, for instance, published his little magazine *The Jew* in 1824 and 1825 as a means of refuting

[8] An aspect of the development of science is treated in Oscar Handlin, *Race and Nationality in American Life*, Boston, 1957, pp. 71ff.

the arguments of the American Society for Ameliorating the Condition of the Jews.

A similar provocation first led Isaac Leeser to take up his pen. Born in Germany, he had come to Richmond in 1824 at the age of eighteen to enter his uncle's business. In a series of articles in the Richmond *Whig* he undertook to refute the missionary claims, and the attention he attracted led him to the post of cantor in Congregation Mikve Israel of Philadelphia. Not a rabbi nor yet a deeply learned man, he had an intensity that gave his work great conviction. In his book, *Jews and the Mosaic Law* (1833), and in his articles in his newspaper *The Occident,* he formulated a simple problem—how to resist the proselytizing efforts of those who wished to convert the Jews. His writing therefore was primarily a system of apologetics and a stolid reaffirmation of tradition. He accepted, as if no argument were needed, the validity of revelation and miracles and took for granted the direct transmission of the oral law down the generations from Moses.[9]

Such statements were directed at those who were already convinced, but who needed elementary instruction in doctrine and ritual. Leeser could not, however, meet the challenge of men who wondered why, as modern Jews, they were bound to the forms of the past. And dissatisfaction on this account had already been displayed in many communities.

The easiest way to reject Orthodoxy was simply to break one's ties with the synagogue; in America it did not even take formal conversion to cut oneself off from the group. But there were also Jews anxious to preserve their heritage, who nevertheless wished to bring Judaism into accord with contemporary ideas and with actual conditions in the United States. The American Reform Movement grew out of that desire.

[9] J. Johlson, *Instruction in the Mosaic Religion.* Translated from the German by Isaac Leeser, Philadelphia, 1830. See also H. S. Morais, *Jews of Philadelphia,* Philadelphia, 1894, pp. 45ff.; Simon Wolf, *Selected Addresses and Papers,* Cincinnati, 1926, pp. 97ff.

The first impulses toward reform were indigenous and grew out of dissatisfaction with the traditional modes of worship. Jews who considered themselves like other Americans were uncomfortable during the long disorderly service conducted in a language few of them understood. They demanded adjustments that would make it more respectable in terms of the dominant Protestant standards of the period. The urgency for change became the greater as they confronted the problem of holding their American-born children to Judaism.

Since each congregation was completely autonomous, there was no consistent pattern to these changes. Some evoked no opposition. Leeser, who in other matters was quite intransigent, thus helped to introduce the English sermon and the Sunday school in Philadelphia. But there were also occasions when the suggestion of change was countered with the demand for explanation and justification. Proposed modifications of a ritual held sacred in its every jot and tittle for centuries led to earnest soul-searching and to serious conflict. The process of innovation thus raised questions about which American Jews had not earlier reflected. The very earliest reformers in Charleston, South Carolina, for instance, found it necessary to defend their actions by rejecting the authority of the Talmud and by asserting the right to derive from the laws of Moses in the Bible those principles most appropriate to the society in which they lived.[10]

These justifications were simple appeals to the spirit of the times. Their authors lacked the knowledge to treat the deeper philosophical and theological problems adequately. Hence the growing desire for an educated clergy competent to discuss these matters. So long as their Judaism rested within its familiar Orthodox patterns, Jews had been content to have the cantor officiate in the synagogue, and to accept the law as

---

[10] Charles Reznikoff and U. Z. Engelman, *Jews of Charleston*, Philadelphia, 1950, pp. 113ff.; B. A. Elzas, *Jews of South Carolina*, Philadelphia, 1905, pp. 160ff.

given. Now they were more likely to seek a learned rabbi who, like the Protestant minister, could deliver sermons to help them to a more sophisticated understanding of what they should believe.

The rabbis who would fill the need were then being trained in Germany. Influenced by the Enlightenment and by the general stirrings of mid-century liberalism, they often enjoyed university as well as theological educations. They could therefore interpret the changes in which they participated in broad terms. Moreover, they were attracted by the liberalism and democracy of the United States and were willing to immigrate. The result was a fruitful collaboration between them and congregations made attentive by American conditions.

In the half-century after 1840, reform was the most creative force in American Jewish life. This was not a carefully organized or coherent movement. No synod or authoritative body defined its doctrines or gave uniformity to its practices. Rather, scattered individuals and congregations proceeded by their own paths. To the extent that they aimed toward a common goal, it was less the result of planning than of their common situation.

The outstanding figure in this development was Isaac M. Wise. Born in Hungary and raised in central Europe, he was educated both in secular and in traditional Jewish learning and had already been ordained as a rabbi when discontent with the Old World induced him to migrate to the United States. America had become his country even before he left Europe; his attachment to its free institutions impelled him to devote his life to the task of reconciling the spirit of Judaism with the spirit of American democracy. After a brief interlude in Albany, Wise settled in Cincinnati where he enjoyed the support of an enthusiastic, wealthy, and powerful congregation. From that center his influence radiated through the rest of the nation.

Wise controlled significant media of communication that magnified his influence. He edited widely read newspapers in both English and German; he established and long guided the destinies of the Hebrew Union College which trained the first generation of American religious leaders; and he brought into being and dominated a union of congregations that he thought would be the instrument of orderly and progressive change.

Through these channels he diffused a consistent set of ideas that long shaped American Reform Judaism. Wise accepted the validity of *halakhah*, of the oral as well as the written tradition, and considered its obligations still binding. But the continuity of tradition had two aspects for him: it involved the extension into the present of the heritage of the past, and also the progressive improvement of that heritage by successive generations.

Looking backward, from the earliest revelations, Wise interpreted history as the progressive unfolding of the divine spirit to man. The earliest act of revelation at Sinai had been direct and immanent; thereafter the process had been indirect. The instrument through which God made himself known to man was human reason. Man's understanding, growing ever more powerful with the improvement of society, was constantly arriving at a fuller knowledge of religious truth. Therefore it was ever necessary to keep adjusting ritual and forms of worship to the advance of knowledge.

That was true of the Jews as of other people. Through the millenniums of their existence they had adjusted their ideas and practices to the conditions of time and place, and in doing so had arrived at ever higher syntheses. Continuity and progress were therefore related aspects of a single process. The cumulative power of reason and learning enabled each generation to improve upon what its predecessors handed on to it.

Wise, however, insisted that the position of the Jews was unique. They were a chosen people because God had endowed them with a special mission, one that was not narrow or particular, but universal and general. That mission was to diffuse through the world the divine spirit and the ideals of social justice of which God had made it custodian. Israel's uniqueness was evidence of that mission. It was not like the other nations, limited to a particular time or place, but rather a world people, carrying to all times and places its message of social redemption.

On that basis, Wise saw a growing identification between Judaism and Americanism, for the United States supplied Jews with a social context altogether hospitable to their ideas. In this democratic society, ancient ideals could actually be realized in practice. And as American liberty spread through the world, it prepared the ground for the universal recognition of the Fatherhood of God and the brotherhood of man which, for Wise, constituted the messianic end of days.[11]

In the last three decades of the century Wise could count on the support of powerful intellectual allies, some of them indeed more radical than he. Excited religious stirrings in Germany had produced an incisive group of reformers whose command of secular and traditional scholarship made them persuasive advocates of change. By mid-century, Abraham Geiger had established the "science of Judaism" as a subject of serious study by modern historical and philological methods; and his view of the evolutionary character of religious beliefs was widely influential. Some of these ideas had been brought to the United States in the 1850's by David Einhorn who had developed a systematic reform theology before his arrival and who was willing to discard much of the letter to arrive at the spirit of the law. But down to the 1870's Wise's restraining influence held these tendencies in check.[12]

Thereafter, the growing pre-eminence of Einhorn's son-in-law, Kaufmann Kohler, reflected the rising intensity of reform sentiment in the New World. Born in Bavaria in 1834,

[11] These ideas may be traced in Isaac M. Wise, *Reminiscences*, Cincinnati, 1901; *Selected Writings*, Cincinnati, 1900; and *Judaism, Its Doctrines and Duties*, Cincinnati, 1872. See also Israel Knox, *Rabbi in America: the Story of Isaac M. Wise*, Boston, 1957.

[12] K. Kohler, *Studies, Addresses, and Personal Papers*, New York, 1931, pp. 522ff.

Kohler had had a thorough Talmudic training, but broke with Orthodoxy in the course of his university studies in philosophy. He came to the United States in 1896 and served as rabbi in Detroit, Chicago, and New York before he went on to become Wise's successor as president of the Hebrew Union College in 1903. An able scholar and a vigorous polemicist, Kohler did not hesitate to push to extreme conclusions ideas that Wise had stated only tentatively, partly because he was the more systematic thinker of the two and partly because he represented a generation more responsive to scientific thought.

Impressed by the conceptions of comparative religion, Kohler did not hesitate to re-examine the articles of his own faith in the light of the development of the ideas of other peoples. His studies convinced him that Judaism was a historic growth. In the course of its long evolution it had developed features of enduring validity, stimulated by contact with what was best in other religions. But Judaism had also acquired from the transient influence of particular social environments accretions of no permanent value. It was the task of the reformer to modernize his faith by excising the latter elements and by strengthening that which was eternal in Judaism with the support of fresh knowledge. The instrument for doing so was the reason with which God had equipped man, made in His image.

Kohler thus discarded every suggestion of the supernatural in Jewish history and cut loose from the conceptions of miracles and direct revelation. The practices based on *halakhah* and those elements of the oral tradition unsupported by reason, had no binding force for him. Rather, he discovered the essence of Judaism in its ethics, in the tradition of prophetic righteousness nurtured by its monotheism. The prophets in one era and the Pharisees in another had "embodied the progressive spirit of the people." [13]

[13] K. Kohler, *Jewish Theology Systematically and Historically Considered*, New York, 1923, pp. 283, 439. See also J. G. Lauterbach, "The Sadducees and Pharisees," *Studies in Jewish Literature Issued in Honor of*

The Reform Movement was taking up the task of the prophets and the Pharisees in the modern world. In furtherance of their priestly mission, the Jews had still to retain their identity as a group; hence the disapproval of intermarriage. But the survival of the group was a means toward an end. "The aim and end of Judaism is not so much the salvation of the soul in the hereafter as the salvation of humanity in history." [14] Kohler had thus arrived, by a somewhat different route, at the same conception as Wise of Israel's mission of moral redemption among the nations.[15]

A declaration of principles adopted by a group of reform rabbis at Pittsburgh in 1885 showed the extent to which these ideas had become formalized and articulated into a system. The declaration began with the recognition that every religion attempted to grasp "the Infinite One." Judaism, however, had preserved the God-idea as the central religious truth for the human race. The Bible and the holy Scriptures were the record of the consecration of the Jews to that idea, but they reflected the primitive conceptions of the ages in which they were written, at times clothing the principles of divine providence and justice "in miraculous narratives." So, too, Mosaic legislation, adequate to ancient Palestine, was not "adapted to the views and habits of modern civilization." Their observance in the present was "apt rather to obstruct than to further modern spiritual elevation." Only the enduring moral laws were still binding.

The modern era was hastening the "realization of Israel's great Messianic hope for the establishment of the Kingdom of truth, justice and peace among all men." Therefore Jews were "no longer a nation but a religious community," expecting "neither a return to Palestine, nor" the restoration of a Jewish

---

Professor Kaufmann Kohler, Berlin, 1913; Samuel S. Cohon, "Kaufmann Kohler the Reformer," *Mordecai M. Kaplan Jubilee Volume*, New York, 1953, pp. 137ff.

[14] Kohler, *Jewish Theology*, pp. 6, 354ff.; Kohler, *Studies, Addresses, and Papers*, passim.

[15] *Studies in Honor of Kohler*, pp. 1–38.

state. Instead, Israel was to labor in the world for a solution "on the basis of justice and righteousness" of the problems presented "by the contrasts and evils of the present organization of society." [16]

The Pittsburgh declaration showed the extent to which the influence of Wise and Kohler had become dominant in American Jewish intellectual life. Supported by Samuel Hirsch and other colleagues trained in Europe, as well as by the graduates of the Hebrew Union College, they encountered little opposition they considered worthy of respect. Above all, they were sustained by the confidence that they moved in accord with the spirit of the times and with the imperatives of the American situation.

The beliefs thus defined were strong enough to survive the shocks of the next fifty years. There were modifications in the interpretation of the place of Israel in the world. But the essential core of Reform Judaism remained unchanged until the 1930's. Moreover its prestige was such as to establish a norm toward which other Jews moved steadily through most of that half-century. Even the agonizing difficulties to which the development of science, the increase in immigration, and the appearance of anti-Semitism subjected the American Jewish community did not diminish its optimism.

The further invasions of secular science in areas in which religion had formerly supplied authoritative answers were accepted with equanimity. The Biblical chronology, the direct Sinaitic revelation, miracles, along with traditional practices of every sort, were swept away as outmoded or, at most, assigned a symbolic quality. There were few fundamentalists among the Jews, partly because of the intellectual weakness of Orthodoxy and partly because of the absence of firm creedal commitments.[17]

[16] Central Conference of American Rabbis, *Yearbook*, XLV, 1935, pp. 198ff.
[17] See Ira Eisenstein and Eugene Kohn, *Mordecai Kaplan: an Evaluation*, New York, 1952, pp. 9ff., 289ff.

The expectation of orderly adjustment to American life survived the new problems created by the tidal wave of immigration from eastern Europe that swept across the Atlantic between 1880 and 1920. Some two million poverty-stricken fugitives from religious persecution and economic degradation now congregated in the metropolitan slums urgently in need of spiritual as well as material aid. Yet the Reformers had faith that the newcomers could be shown a way between the unenlightened Orthodoxy of the Old Country and the atheistic socialism of the radicals.

Even the development of anti-Semitism did not undermine the certitude that progress was the condition of mankind. It was sad, of course, to encounter hatred and prejudice, to see discrimination buttressed by the appearance of support from science, and to learn about outbreaks of violence against one's co-religionists. But those were not grounds for the abandonment of hope. The Dreyfus Case was, despite its prolonged bitterness, a victory for enlightenment; the situation was at its worst in backward, generally unprogressive, countries like Rumania and Russia. The decent opinion of civilized men would in time redeem the situation there as elsewhere.

Efforts in the United States to exclude Jews from desirable occupations, the intense dislike that spilled over in the Frank Case, in the rise of the Ku Klux Klan, and in the accusations of *The International Jew*—all these were explicable and remediable.[18] They were the products of ignorance and of depressed economic and social conditions. The cure was therefore education and social amelioration. In fact, these signs of retrogression could be interpreted as reminders to the Jews of their special mission. They were not a people who could be safe in a world of backwardness and oppression. It was their task as suffering servants of the Lord to struggle for knowledge and justice against the great and powerful majority. They were by their very situation wedded to the cause of religious and social reform.[19]

[18] See Handlin, *Adventure in Freedom*, pp. 174ff.
[19] Kohler, *Jewish Theology*, p. 425.

139

Social reform, it was true, took on new radical aspects as the nineteenth century drew to a close and then turned into the twentieth. The Protestant ministers imbued with zeal for the social gospel were an important element in the liberal movement, and progressive rabbis could readily associate themselves with them. But more extreme doctrines were also finding spokesmen as other critics joined in the attack. Proposals for reform were directed at the government, the currency, medicine, and the family. An aggressive labor movement began to struggle for its rights, sometimes not hesitating to use violence in the process. Meanwhile anarchists, socialists, and communists at various times demanded an end to capitalism as a whole.

In the midst of these confused demands for change, the reform rabbinate kept its equanimity. In common with other American progressives, it tended to regard liberalism as a spectrum of beliefs shading from moderation to extreme, but with its element somehow related to a common striving for human improvement.[20] From this point of view it made sense to consider education, philanthropy, and social justice the primary concerns of religion. The rabbi was thus a teacher of morals and a commentator on the affairs of the day. Emil G. Hirsch in Chicago and David Philipson in Cincinnati thus year after year devotedly and courageously labored to clarify the social obligations of their well-to-do congregations.[21]

On the whole, Jewish laymen accepted this view of religion and religious duties. They threw themselves into charitable and educational endeavors and, for their pains, were rewarded not only with the satisfaction of a worthy task accomplished, but also with control of the Jewish communities in which they lived and which now focused ever more of their attention

[20] For illustrations of the attractiveness of liberalism for the "rebel soul of the Jew" see Lewis Browne, *Stranger than Fiction. A Short History of the Jews*, New York, 1925, pp. 137, 320.

[21] See E. G. Hirsch, "The Philosophy of the Reform Movement," Central Conference of American Rabbis, *Yearbook, 1895*, pp. 90ff.; E. G. Hirsch, "Ethics," *Jewish Encyclopedia*, New York, 1903, V, 245ff.; David Philipson, *Reform Movement in Judaism*, New York, 1931.

upon philanthropy and upon defense against anti-Semitism.

But some rabbis were less at ease in the face of these developments. Their own situation seemed to deteriorate as social service threatened to crowd worship out of the synagogue. If charitable acts were the chief concern of religion, what was the proper role of the rabbi?

Solomon Schindler, for instance, had come to Boston as a young man from Germany and occupied the pulpit of its leading reform congregation, Temple Israel. He busied himself in a variety of communal affairs and established friendly relations with the city's leading progressives. Taken with Bellamy's ideas, Schindler became a nationalist and wrote an epilogue to *Looking Backward*. But the pulpit was inadequate to do what he really wished and his congregants were unresponsive. He found it easier to work directly in philanthropy and by the end of his life had reached the reluctant conclusion that the whole trend toward reform had been a mistake.[22]

A nagging doubt troubled such rabbis. If, as a Day of Atonement Address pointed out in 1893, "there is, practically, very little difference in the various faiths among intelligent people," why linger on the petty peculiarities of Judaism? [23] The larger obligation of the religious spirit was rather to approach the task of reform directly and to address the widest possible audience. Such considerations moved Charles Fleischer who was Schindler's successor at Temple Israel. Convinced that Judaism had to yield to more universal forms, he left the rabbinate to establish a community church from which he could preach to men of all denominations. The same logic had already drawn away Felix Adler and had been responsible for the establishment and spread of the Ethical Culture movement. Wholehearted dedication to the conceptions of progress, of social improvement, of science, and

[22] See Arthur Mann, *Yankee Reformers in the Urban Age*, Cambridge, 1954, pp. 52ff.; Arthur Mann, ed., *Growth and Achievement: Temple Israel, 1854–1954*, Cambridge, 1954, pp. 45ff.

[23] Wolf, *Selected Addresses*, p. 247.

of humanitarianism might thus lead away from the synagogue.[24]

Yet the Reform rabbis were determined to maintain some links with tradition although they often found it difficult to explain why. An undefined sense that ancient values might otherwise be imperiled, the religious pluralism of American society, reluctance to seem to yield to anti-Semitism, and simple stubbornness all contributed to that determination.

Furthermore, there was a peculiar social situation inside the Reform movement. The members of the temples were well-to-do German Jews of the first or second generation. Such people did not aspire to have their own children enter the rabbinate; the clergy lacked the status and failed to receive the rewards to attract to its ranks young people from this level of society. Reform rabbis after 1890 therefore were less often drawn from American Reform families than from the European-born, or from among the children of Orthodox immigrant parents. Such men carried into their mature years unrecognized memories of childhood ritual and unconscious attachments to the ways of their fathers. They were troubled by the fact that God now seemed to recede into a supernumerary role in the temple. They sought earnestly for greater inwardness and dedication.[25] Yet their commitment to rationalism and their situation in advanced congregations inhibited the adoption of practices that smacked of the superstitions of the past. The emotional desire for continuity with the Judaism of their parents among such men found expression in indirect ways; it was touching to find one of them, at the opening of the century, requesting his fiancée to have "some things reasonably Jewish in their gastronomic affiliations" at their wedding reception.[26]

[24] For Fleischer, see Mann, *Growth and Achievement*, pp. 63ff. There is a mature exposition of Adler's views in Felix Adler, *Reconstruction of the Spiritual Ideal*, New York, 1924.

[25] H. G. Enelow, "Kawwana, the Struggle for Inwardness in Judaism," *Studies in Honor of Kohler*, pp. 82ff.; Samuel Schulman, "Israel," Central Conference of American Rabbis, *Yearbook*, XLV, 1935, pp. 26ff.

[26] J. W. Polier and J. W. Wise, eds., *Personal Letters of Stephen Wise*, Boston, 1956, pp. 33, 59.

Such pulls led a few Reform rabbis into Zionism. Through the nineteenth century an extensive stream of Christian literature had envisaged the restoration of the Jews to the Holy Land. Most of it had been animated by millennialist thinking and by the hope for the promised conversion of Israel. But from the novels of George Eliot and Benjamin Disraeli it had also acquired a romantic, mysterious glow. Zionism thus offered a progressive mode for expressing sentimental attachments to Judaism.[27]

The connection was strikingly evident in the career of Stephen S. Wise. A magnetic speaker and founder of the influential Free Synagogue of New York and also of the Jewish Institute of Religion, Wise never developed a systematic theology and rarely touched on purely theological subjects in his speaking and writing. But in practical religious affairs he was thoroughly radical and totally rationalistic. He revered Theodore Parker and respected Felix Adler, conducted services on Sundays, revised the ritual and prayer book, and sought a place in Jewish life for Jesus as a prophet. Wise also threw himself wholeheartedly into the secular reform movements, laboring eloquently on behalf of labor, good government, democracy, and peace.

His nationalism therefore looked forward rather than backward. Zionism for him was progressive, in the sense that it was a means of furthering the advanced social ideals of his times. A homeland for the Jews in Palestine would not only be a haven for the persecuted. It would also be a laboratory in which the spiritual heritage of Israel would be applied to the problems of modern life. The whole world would then profit by such fulfillment of the ancient prophecies.[28]

A similar conviction animated Judah L. Magnes who went to Jerusalem to found the Hebrew University after the collapse of his effort to establish a *kehillah* or unified communal authority in New York. Zionism for such men was not narrow

<hr/>

[27] Moshe Davis, *Israel: Its Role in Civilization*, New York, 1956, pp. 255ff., 234ff.

[28] Stephen S. Wise, *Challenging Years*, New York, 1949.

but universal in objective. It would help the Jews by ending anti-Semitism, but it would help other peoples as well, for it would involve not a restoration of ancient customs and tribal loyalties, but the opening of an era of experimentation and pioneering. "Palestine Americanized," still another Reform rabbi described it.[29]

One branch of the reform movement had thus moved significantly away from the position of the Pittsburgh conference of 1885. While still adhering to universal ideals, such men as Stephen Wise had been drawn by the desire to preserve the group's distinctiveness toward a renewal of national consciousness.

Through this whole period the reformers held the intellectual initiative. Their Orthodox opponents were consistently on the defensive and, on the whole, ineffectual. The number of Orthodox rabbis in the United States remained small. Men trained in the traditional *yeshivoth* were still reluctant to migrate. Sensitive to the dangers to faith concealed in a rapidly changing society, they were not as attracted by America as were the liberals: Not until the end of the century were there effective means for educating a native Orthodox rabbinate. Maimonides College in Philadelphia led but a brief existence, and the Jewish Theological Seminary, founded in 1886, survived with the greatest difficulty.

What few rabbis there were, were overwhelmed with a multitude of practical duties, and often found themselves embroiled in countless petty disputes. The problems, for instance, that Rabbi Jacob Joseph of Vilna encountered when he came to be chief rabbi of New York City in 1888 were hardly of a sort to encourage quiet thought or creative writing.[30] Men

[29] Clifton Harky Levy, "Palestine Americanized," *Independent*, LXXIV, 1913, 622ff. See also N. D. Bentwich, *For Zion's Sake, A Biography of Judah L. Magnes*, Philadelphia, 1954; Browne, *Stranger Than Fiction*, pp. 341ff. On the Kehillah, see Norman Bentwich, "The Kehillah of New York," *Kaplan Jubilee Volume*, pp. 73ff.

[30] Abraham J. Karp, "New York Chooses a Chief Rabbi," American Jewish Historical Society, *Publications*, XLIV, 1955, pp. 129ff.

like Sabato Morais who came to Philadelphia from Italy in 1851 served their congregations with devotion and they could, when the occasion required, deliver sensible sermons. But they could not meet the champions of reform in dispute on even terms.[31]

In part that was due to the fact that the Jews to whom they ministered did not value learning highly. Absorbed in the struggle to establish themselves, they preferred to accept religion as a matter of passive habit rather than to find themselves involved in its troublesome questions. Arnold B. Ehrlich, the most original Biblical scholar of this generation, came to the United States in 1878 and, through most of his lifetime, earned his livelihood by rolling barrels and by other forms of manual labor. He composed his monumental works of exegesis in his leisure time and without the least recognition from the community. Significantly it took a Christian scholar, George Foote Moore, to awaken Americans to the meaning of the Pharisaic tradition.[32]

Moreover, Orthodox habits of thought did not equip even the learned rabbi for disputation. The whole pattern of Talmudic training encouraged intense argument from accepted premises and by reference to accepted authorities, but it supplied no preparation for a challenge to the premises or the authorities themselves. For the brief period of his sojourn in America (1885–1894), Alexander Kohut was able forcefully to deny that there could be any religious progress outside the rabbinic tradition. But he had been educated in Breslau and Leipzig and knew the work of Samson Raphael

[31] Cyrus Adler, ed., *Jewish Theological Seminary of America*, New York, 1939, pp. 5ff.; H. S. Morais, "Sabato Morais," Jewish Theological Seminary Association, *Sixth Biennial Report*, New York, 1898, pp. 61ff.

[32] A. B. Ehrlich, *Randglossen zur hebräischen Bibel*, 7 vols., Leipzig, 1908–14. To the traditional rabbi, Ehrlich was a man "of somewhat whimsical thought." See Bernard Drachman, "Neo-Hebraic Literature in America," Jewish Theological Seminary Association, *Seventh Biennial Report*, New York, 1900, p. 76. For Moore, see G. F. Moore, *Judaism*, 3 vols., Cambridge, Mass., 1927–30; W. W. Fenn, "George Foot Moore," Massachusetts Historical Society, *Proceedings*, LXIV, 1932, p. 429.

Hirsch, the European exponent of a philosophy of modern Orthodoxy. And even Kohut devoted most of his energy to a great Talmudic dictionary, the revision of an eleventh-century work which, whatever its merits, was unlikely to exert wide influence in the United States.[33]

Even the vast addition to the number of the Orthodox through immigration from Poland and Russia had little religious influence. A few *yeshivoth* after the European fashion were established, but they were not well supported, trained but few rabbis, and had no intellectual influence whatever. The number of synagogues grew as each group of new arrivals attempted to reconstruct the local forms of its old home. But each group quickly discovered the difficulty of leading the way of life of the east European *shtetl* in metropolitan America. And, lacking direction as to what could change and what could not, the great majority while remaining nominally Orthodox slipped into the ranks of the non-observant and the apathetic. Meanwhile the growing labor movement was producing a communal leadership that was preponderantly socialist, secular, and agnostic in attitudes.[34]

The presence of the immigrants was as much a challenge to the Reform as to the Orthodox Jews. The American-born felt a sense of responsibility for the newcomers and wished to aid in their adjustment to the New World. In the long run, there was faith that the immigrants would become fully Americanized. But for the moment, it was hopeless to imagine that Jews fresh from the lanes of a Polish village would feel comfortable in the pews of a temple or make much of the English sermon of its rabbi. Yet without help or guidance, they might drift away from their faith entirely.

[33] See Alexander Kohut, *Ethics of the Fathers*, New York, 1920. For a summary of some of the traditional writing of this period, see Drachman, "New-Hebraic Literature," pp. 77ff.

[34] See the radical works of Solomon J. Silberstein, *The Disclosures of the Universal Mysteries*, New York, 1896, and *The Jewish Problem*, New York, 1904. For his Hebrew writings, see Drachman, "Neo-Hebraic Literature," p. 74.

Significantly, the Reform leaders—lay and clerical—were reluctant to see that happen. Although they personally considered Orthodoxy outmoded, they sensed a warmth and inner meaning in the traditional practices, which perhaps touched unconscious memories of their own youth or that of their parents; and they did not wish all that lost until it could progress in an orderly fashion toward the higher forms of the future.

It seemed best, therefore, to encourage the development of a separate immigrant community, with its own institutions and its own leadership. That consideration induced some Reform Jews to come to the aid of the Jewish Theological Seminary, which seemed about to founder after the death of Sabato Morais in 1897. Jacob Schiff and Louis Marshall, among others, supported that institution in the hope that it would develop means by which traditional Judaism could adjust to American conditions. Out of that hope grew the Conservative Movement.[35]

The sponsors of the revived seminary called to its presidency a distinguished scholar, Solomon Schechter. Born in Rumania just before 1850, he had received a rabbinic education in Lemberg, Vienna, and Berlin. He had, however, never actually accepted the charge of a congregation. Preferring the life of study, he had moved to England in 1882 and eight years later became lecturer at the University of Cambridge. In 1901, attracted by its opportunities, he accepted the call to come to the United States.

A man of genuine intellectual gifts, Schechter was above all a scholar, having made his reputation by the discovery of the Cairo Genizah treasures in 1896. He succeeded in drawing a distinguished faculty to the Seminary, and contact with them was stimulating. Israel Friedlander, for instance, a student

---

[35] On the Seminary, see Charles Reznikoff, ed., *Louis Marshall*, Philadelphia, 1957, I, xix, II, 859ff.; Adler, *Jewish Theological Seminary*, pp. 6ff., 135ff., 163ff. On the origins of the Conservative Movement, see Moshe Davis, *Yahadut Amerika Be-Hitpathutah* [Shaping of American Judaism], New York, 1951.

of Islamic Jewry, was arriving at a conception of cultural nationalism and Louis Ginzberg was examining the evolution of the Talmud against its social background. Schechter also was familiar with the European conceptions of historical Judaism. But he was not a rigorous theologian, and his view of Judaism was necessarily colored by the peculiar situation of the Seminary.[36]

Schechter wished to preserve the continuity of Judaism with its traditional past. He would not play fast and loose with *halakhah* as he thought the reformers did. But he also realized not only that some accommodation was essential to meet the conditions of modern America, but also that such accommodations were themselves fully in accord with tradition.

The problem then was how to keep change orderly and regular, to be certain that the essential was never discarded along with the transitory. No authoritative body in modern times had the capacity to do so—neither a Sanhedrin nor a rabbinic academy as in ancient times. Schechter found a personal solution in his concept of catholic Israel. He had faith that there was among Jews an inner unity, the character of which he could not quite define. Faced by a common problem, therefore, all those who were loyal, that is who accepted the basic premises of Judaism, would in time arrive at a common answer. No vote would be necessary; a consensus would appear. Thus Schechter was unconsciously establishing an analogy with the process by which ideas were revised in the world of scholarship, a process that had little meaning to his co-religionists.[37]

[36] Israel Friedlander, "Can Judaism Survive in Free America," 1908, *Commentary*, II, July, 1946, pp. 73 ff.; Robert Gordis, *Conservative Judaism*, New York, 1945.

[37] Schechter's views may be traced in the following of his works: *Seminary Addresses*, Cincinnati, 1915; *Selected Writings*, Oxford, 1946; *Some Aspects of Rabbinic Theology*, New York, 1923; *Studies in Judaism, Third Series*, pp. 47 ff. See also Cyrus Adler, "Solomon Schechter," *American Jewish Year Book*, XIX, 1916, pp. 25 ff.; Adler, *Jewish Theological Seminary*, pp. 49 ff.; N. D. Bentwich, *Solomon Schechter*, Philadelphia, 1938.

The Conservative Movement grew, not through the persuasiveness of Schechter's ideas, but because it supplied a medium through which men brought up under Orthodoxy could hold to parts of their tradition and yet make gradual changes in ritual and belief without shock. The number of rabbis trained in the Seminary grew, and by 1913 their congregations had formed the United Synagogue of America.

For the American Jews who formed the following of the Conservative Movement, Schechter's question—how to introduce gradual change without doing violence to tradition—was less interesting than the problem of why to preserve a sense of separateness at all. The answer certainly did not lie in distinctive common religious beliefs; it was usual in the 1920's to refer to Spinoza, Marx, Bergson, Einstein, and Freud as the great modern Jewish thinkers. Nor were many Jews content with the answer that they preserved their identity through pressure from the Christian world which either rejected them by anti-Semitism or needed them as a challenge and a witness.[38]

Jews had, for the most part, to remain content with the pragmatic answer that they were Jews simply through the circumstance of historical descent. As Morris R. Cohen stated it, that position recognized a heritage, religious in derivation, but involved no commitment as to faith.[39]

This frame of mind lent significance to the experience of Rabbi Mordecai M. Kaplan who, in 1908, had envisaged a new role for the synagogue as a complete center of Jewish social life. Religion, he felt, existed for the people, not the people for religion, hence creed ought to follow upon practice. Shortly Kaplan took up a post in the Teachers Institute of

---

[38] Lewis Browne, *How Odd of God*, New York, 1934; Morris R. Cohen, *Reflections of a Wondering Jew*, Boston, 1950; Morris R. Cohen, *The Faith of a Liberal*, New York, 1946, pp. 13ff., 46ff. See also Waldo Frank, *The Jew in Our Day*, New York, 1944, pp. 73ff.

[39] Cohen, *Faith of a Liberal*, pp. 5ff., 78ff., 307ff.; Morris R. Cohen, *A Dreamer's Journey*, Boston, 1949.

the Seminary where he could think through the implications of these departures.[40]

His own resolution which drew on the cultural nationalism of Ahad Ha-Am, the sociology of Durkheim, and the pragmatism of William James and John Dewey was not fully to be worked out until 1934. Meanwhile he felt an affinity, as did many contemporary American Jews, for Horace Kallen's conception of cultural pluralism. America did not dissolve the cultures of the peoples who settled in the New World but allowed each to retain its identity and was enriched by their variety. The Jews were thus not unique, but one among many groups which retained their cultural identity while politically unified.[41]

Kallen himself extended his analysis to religion. Maintaining that religion was subject to scientific analysis, he divorced it entirely from the question of belief and regarded it purely from the point of view of its function in the individual and in society. In that context all religions were equal, as anthropological and sociological evidence showed, and therefore all could not be identical. Each acquired its validity from the "concrete and historical" circumstances of the people it served. Only through variety could they continue to play their role.[42]

From this perspective, it was possible optimistically and rationally to define the whole religious problem in terms of adjustment. Since large-scale Jewish immigration ended after 1924, it was also possible to foresee a rapid speeding up of the process. The experience of the past century had thus pointed a clear and hopeful road for the future. In these five decades—

[40] Mordecai M. Kaplan, *A New Approach to the Problem of Judaism*, New York, 1924. See also Mordecai M. Kaplan, *Judaism as a Civilization*, New York, 1934; enlarged ed. 1957, p. xii; Eisenstein and Kohn, *Kaplan*, pp. 19, 48.

[41] Horace M. Kallen, "Democracy Versus the Melting Pot," *Nation*, C, February 18, 25, 1915, pp. 190ff., 217ff. This essay was republished in *Culture and Democracy in the United States*, New York, 1924, and its ideas restated in *Americanism and Its Makers*, Buffalo, 1944, and *Cultural Pluralism and the American Idea*, Philadelphia, 1956.

[42] Horace M. Kallen, *Why Religion?*, New York, 1927.

which despite their difficulties were decades of great achievement—few Jews were aware of that change in their religion which was most momentous of all, the disappearance of the immanent God directly concerned with the affairs of man in the world. There survived an idea, a symbol, a metaphor, a figure of speech, a first cause, a principle. But the God of Abraham, Isaac, and Jacob, who for thousands of years had really known and really cared about the acts of piety and righteousness of the individual Jews, had vanished almost without trace.[43]

The twenty-five years after 1930, however, were to be a period of abrupt and shattering disillusionment. Earlier disappointments could be explained away with relative ease. But the cataclysmic disturbances of the 1930's and 1940's raised doubts that could not readily be dispelled and called into question the assumptions of the past hundred years.

The long economic depression, from which Jews suffered as did other Americans, led men to wonder whether the institutions of the United States were really adequate to the needs of modern society. The rise of anti-Semitism was more troubling still; for Nazism took hold, not in some backward corner of Europe but in the nation that had theretofore been considered intellectually the most enlightened and the most advanced in the world. "Our 'progress' is back to hell!" wrote Stephen S. Wise in 1933.[44] And few Jews, watching the advance of these ugly hatreds on both sides of the Atlantic, could refrain from reexamining their beliefs in the inevitability of progress or in the essential goodness of man.

The war put an end to any sense of complacency that might have survived to 1939. Its unthinkable savagery, its perversion of science to destructive ends, and the climactic revelations that 6,000,000 Jews and their communities had been totally

---

[43] Kaplan, *Judaism as a Civilization*, pp. 36ff.

[44] Polier and Wise, *Personal Letters*, p. 225; also Stephen S. Wise, *As I See It*, New York, 1944; Milton Steinberg, *Making of the Modern Jew*, Indianapolis, 1933, pp. 228ff.

liquidated made a hollow mockery of the hopes of the past. The ultimate product of all the cherished advances of modern times had been the crematoria of Maidenek. It seemed almost anticlimactic after the peace to discover that anti-Semitism was at home in the Soviet Union too. If the hatred of the Jew was not simply a relic of the medieval past, nor yet only an illness of capitalism, but endemic to every gentile society, did that not call for a total reconsideration of the place of Israel in history?

These qualms persisted, although the end of the war brought a restoration of prosperity. In the boom of the decade after 1945 the social character of the group changed markedly. It became overwhelmingly native-born in composition. The number of working men declined, while the proportion of professional and business people increased. Finally, the general move out of the metropolitan centers spread the Jews in the great suburbs. They thus came increasingly to conform to the general pattern of American middle class life at mid-century.[45]

Like other segments of the American middle class, the Jews shared in the post-war revival of religious interest.[46] That revival, of course, conformed to their peculiar circumstances. It was clearly not a return to forms that had existed earlier. There was no restoration of the synagogue of the *shtetl* or even of the East Side. Nor was there an explicit rejection of the rationalism and science of the previous century; Marx, no doubt, suffered a loss in esteem, but Freud and Einstein were still the great Jewish thinkers of modern times.

The growth of religious affiliations was not, properly speaking, a revival at all but rather the product of quite new impulses. On the one hand, it was the response to the social needs of Jews deprived by the move to the suburbs of the anonymity

[45] Handlin, *Adventure in Freedom*, pp. 248ff.

[46] Oscar Handlin, *American People in the Twentieth Century*, Cambridge, 1954, pp. 222ff.; Herbert W. Schneider, *Religion in the Twentieth Century*, Cambridge, 1952; Will Herberg, *Protestant—Catholic—Jew*, New York, 1955.

of the metropolis and eager to find modes of association acceptable by middle-class standards. Such people, anxious to buttress their family life by external standards and concerned about the problems of raising their children, wished particularly to fit the new associations into an ethnic pattern, and the most acceptable form of ethnic activity by mid-century was that which focused upon religion. The synagogue and the temple thus became the center of a variegated round of social activities in which men and women made friends, worked for worthy causes, assured some measure of education for the young, and arranged that their children should establish the kind of associations that would lead to desirable marriages in the future.[47]

Religious affiliations also offered now a kind of release from the tensions of modern life. Back in 1939, a rabbi had noted, with chagrin, the size of the following attracted by Emmet Fox. "He puts people at ease, makes all sorts of quieting, soothing, reassuring promises." [48] As the need for reassurance grew greater, Jews more often turned for it to their synagogues and got it from their rabbis.

Although the formal differences among the three major Jewish groups—Reform, Orthodox, Conservative—remained as prominent as ever and, indeed, became more institutionalized, the actual substantive differences among them tended to diminish. All were subject to the same intellectual and social forces and within limited terms were able to cooperate in the Synagogue Council of America.[49]

With the German experience still fresh, the Reform movement could hardly cling to its earlier optimistic expectations. The problems of assimilation and survival absorbed more attention than ever before. Emphasis shifted from the universal mission of the group to its preservation. There followed also

[47] Albert I. Gordon, *Jews in Transition*, Minneapolis, 1949; Evelyn N. Rossman, "Judaism in Northrup," *Commentary*, XXIV, November, 1957, p. 383.
[48] Polier and Wise, *Personal Letters*, p. 253.
[49] Jacob B. Agus, *Guideposts in Modern Judaism*, New York, 1954, p. 138.

a shift in attitude toward Zionism. In 1937 a meeting of Reform rabbis modified the extreme position taken in Pittsburgh in 1885; thereafter the preponderant sentiment was that nationalism was compatible with, if not essential to, Judaism. Meanwhile, efforts were also made to strengthen group cohesiveness by restoring portions of the old ritual and by preserving some elements of tradition.[50]

Orthodoxy was greatly strengthened. The calamities for which Hitler had been responsible caused the first large-scale migration of European Orthodox rabbis and rabbinical students, and they added strength of numbers and zeal to their American colleagues. More important, the disasters of the last quarter century seemed to rebuke those who had put their trust in the unaided power of science and secular knowledge to elevate man. This was a moment for the reaffirmation of the authority of the Torah as the divine and perfect authority sufficient for all time.

Orthodoxy therefore grew in self-confidence and assertiveness. The largest American *yeshiva* had trained only one hundred rabbis in the forty years to 1940; in the next fourteen, it produced four hundred and fifty, capable of entering into vigorous intellectual contests with their Reform and Conservative rivals and venturing to issue decrees of excommunication against those who questioned the essentials of the law.

Nonetheless, while insisting upon spiritual distinctiveness, the main body of Orthodoxy was, in practice and in ideology, approaching a norm common to the other branches of American Judaism. Some rabbis were indeed anxious to shed the designation Orthodox and to be known as Traditional. They emphasized the necessity of integration into the larger Ameri-

[50] There is a revealing statement of attitudes in D. L. Davis, "Why I Joined a Reform Temple," *American Judaism*, VI, no. 2, 1956, p. 17. See also Samuel S. Cohon, *Jewish Idea of God*, Cincinnati, 1936; *Judaism: A Way of Life*, Cincinnati, 1948; Julian Morgenstern, *Nation, People, Religion. What Are We?*, Cincinnati, October 16, 1943; Abba Hillel Silver, *Zionism. Two Addresses at the Temple*, Cleveland, 1944; see above, pp. 134–135.

can community and explained that the forms and rituals of the past were not fossils to be preserved without contact with the environment, but living growths to be nurtured in new ways by the new soil of the United States to which they had been transplanted. "Take the beard off the rabbi and put him into a sports coat," urged an Orthodox spokesman in 1959.[51] While genuine differences remained, these conceptions tended to narrow the distance between Orthodox and non-Orthodox Jews.[52]

The Conservatives, however, were in the most strategic position to profit from the new trend. They offered a refuge for those dissatisfied with the thinness in ritual and tradition of Reform and also for those for whom Orthodoxy was too ritualistic and too traditional. A "modern interpretation of traditional Judaism," one susceptible to change, permitted Jews who felt the pressure toward Americanization to make an adjustment that did not altogether wipe out emotional ties to the memories of the observances of their childhood.[53]

For those concerned mostly with "rites and symbols," it hardly mattered that there had been no further progress in dealing with the crucial question of how change was to be kept within traditional bounds.[54] It was vain to ask for an authoritative statement and it was almost extraneous to wonder about God in this context. Robert Gordis, for instance, a scholarly and eloquent spokesman of Conservatism, and a liberal in theology, in grappling with this problem did little more than restate Schechter's conception of catholic Israel; somehow a voluntary organic community would use scholarship to arrive

[51] John Wicklein, "Judaism on Rise in the Suburbs," *New York Times*, April 5, 1959, Section 1, pp. 1, 80.
[52] See Samuel Belkin, *Essays in Traditional Jewish Thought*, New York, 1956, passim.
[53] Gordis, *Conservative Judaism*, p. 36; Adler, *Jewish Theological Seminary*, pp. 22ff. See also Marshall Sklare, *Conservative Judaism, An American Religious Movement*, Glencoe, 1955; W. Lloyd Warner and Leo Srole, *Social Systems of American Ethnic Groups*, New Haven, 1945, pp. 192ff.
[54] Jay I. Goldin, "Rabbi 1938," *Reconstructionist*, IV, 1938, pp. 13ff.

at a consensus. Others added to that a vague hope, for which there was little empirical evidence, that the State of Israel would supply Americans with a set of guiding norms.[55]

The problem of change within tradition was somewhat easier for those Conservatives and Reformers who enlisted in the Reconstructionist Movement after 1934 and drew their inspiration from Mordecai Kaplan. Kaplan, a radical in theology, wished to transform Judaism "from an other-worldly religion offering to conduct the individual to life eternal through the agency of the traditional Torah which is regarded as supernaturally revealed, into a religion which can help Jews attain this-worldly salvation." Judaism was thus a civilization of the Jewish people which expressed itself through evolving folkways and culture stimulated and protected by an organic community. It was quite compatible with a general American civic religion that expressed universal values. To be a Jew called for no explicit beliefs; one could participate meaningfully in traditional customs and ceremonies without inquiry into their theological meanings.[56]

Kaplan's formulation was attractive because it located the standard for religious judgment in the practices of the community and in the emotional satisfactions of the individual. While that tended to shift the focus from God to man, it capitalized upon the desire of middle-class Jews for stability and security. That accounted for their eagerness to grasp at Rabbi Joshua L. Liebman's assurance that religion was the

---

[55] Gordis, *Conservative Judaism*, pp. 71, 72; Robert Gordis, *Judaism for the Modern Age*, New York, 1956, pp. 25ff., 53ff., 87ff., 175ff. See also Agus, *Guideposts*, pp. 307ff.; Kaplan, *Judaism as Civilization*, pp. 126ff., 160ff.

[56] The quotation is from Mordecai M. Kaplan, *The Meaning of God in Modern Jewish Religion*, New York, 1937, p. viii. The ideas of Reconstruction were fully set forth in Kaplan's *Judaism as Civilization* and summarized in "Judaism as a Modern Civilization," Harry Schneiderman, ed., *Two Generations in Perspective*, New York, 1957, pp. 193ff. See also Eisenstein and Kohn, *Kaplan*, pp. 138ff., 319ff.; Mordecai M. Kaplan, *The Future of the American Jew*, New York, 1948, pp. 34ff., 96; Milton Steinberg, *Partisan Guide to the Jewish Problem*, New York, 1946; Milton Steinberg, *Basic Judaism*, New York, 1947; Agus, *Guideposts*, pp. 382ff.

way to peace of mind.[57] Adherence to the synagogue, as an enormously popular novel assured Jews, was a way of putting order into disordered lives, of establishing roots, and of approaching normality and adjustment. It was thus, in a sense, a painless substitute for psychoanalysis.[58]

A tiny handful of Jews continued to insist that religion—and particularly Judaism—was other than nationalism, custom, and adjustment, that it depended upon the acceptance of the authority of an Immanent God who had prescribed holiness as a way of life for his chosen people, Israel. A few intellectuals had arrived at this position through their interest in existentialism and in crisis theology, particularly in the form developed by Martin Buber in Germany. Often these were men who had passed through several trials of faith—in Marxism or total assimilation—and who now welcomed "a core of intellectual conviction" that was both sophisticated and yet located firmly within a Jewish context.[59]

The response of Abraham Heschel was more deeply rooted in Jewish sources. Himself the descendant of a long line of Hasidic rabbis, Heschel, who arrived in the United States in 1940, was repelled by the soft view of religion as merely an instrument of human accommodation. *"Religion is not expediency,"* he exclaimed. Looking about him he found that the edifices were growing but that worship was decaying. He attacked the emphasis upon symbol and ceremonies—"the homage which disbelief pays to faith"—and he attacked also the notion that religion was merely a form of self-expression. Surely more was needed. Never before had the world been

[57] Joshua Loth Liebman, *Peace of Mind*, New York, 1946; and *Psychiatry and Religion*, Boston, 1948, pp. 26ff.

[58] Herman Wouk, *Marjorie Morningstar*, New York, 1955.

[59] Will Herberg, "Assimilation in Militant Dress," *Commentary*, IV, July, 1947, p. 16, and "Has Judaism Still Power to Speak?", *ibid.*, VII, May, 1949, p. 447; and *Judaism and Modern Man. An Interpretation of Jewish Religion*, New York, 1951; Emil L. Fackenheim, "Can We Believe in Judaism Religiously?", *Commentary*, VI, December, 1948, p. 521; Irving Kristol, "How Basic Is 'Basic Judaism,'" *ibid.*, V, January, 1948, p. 27; Ludwig Lewisohn, *The Answer*, New York, 1939.

assailed with "so much guilt and distress, agony and terror." The conspicuousness of evil on earth was a sign and a token— to teach man his own guilt so that he might learn and repent.

What was lacking was the very essence of faith—the sense of mystery and awe, the categorical imperative toward the reverence of that which was ineffable, the mystical conscious- ness and inner devotion to God that made worship "a way of living." To pray, man had to have "faith in his own ability to accost the infinite, merciful, eternal God"; and to make the observance of ritual meaningful, man had to treat each *mitz- vah* literally as "a prayer in the form of a deed." [60]

Heschel's criticisms and his austere and demanding concep- tion of what faith involved were respectfully received. But they had little measurable influence upon American Judaism in thought or in practice. In the same way, even the most rationalistic Reformed Jews felt a warm response in contact with the absolute, intransigent devotion of the *hassidic* fol- lowers of the Lubovitcher and other rabbis who came to the United States after the war.[61] These sects existed in total isolation from American life and out of contact with its domi- nant forces. They could be observed respectfully but they offered no model relevant to the needs of outsiders.

However convincing Heschel's mysticism may have been as a personal response, it offered no pattern susceptible to emu- lation. His faith was whole and entire; it held forth, and needed, no answers to questions that troubled other Jews who lived fully in the world. Without the shield of that faith, they continued to wonder about the purpose of their survival as a group; they still found it difficult to draw a line between the culture they shared with other Americans and that which was peculiar to them alone; and they remained

[60] See Abraham J. Heschel, *Man Is Not Alone*, New York, 1951, and *Man's Quest for God*, New York, 1954, passim. For Orthodox mysticism, see Agus, *Guideposts*, pp. 37ff.

[61] See, e.g., Nathan Glazer, *American Judaism*, Chicago, 1957, p. 143; Herbert Weiner, "The Lubovitcher Movement," *Commentary*, XXIII, March, April, 1957, pp. 231ff., 316ff.

unclear as to the degree to which tradition was binding and change inevitable.

Therefore the rabbinate was awkward in its response to mysticism. Some attacked "the rootless Jewish intellectual" as a type that created needless discomfort.[62] After all, the traditional Jewish writings were "singularly down to earth and practical. One finds no mysticism in them, no other-worldliness, no metaphysics. Their doctrine is in the main hardheaded, at moments even hard-boiled." [63]

In its essential pragmatism and latitudinarianism American Judaism showed the effects of the New World experience. Without minimizing the differences, it became usual to point to the common elements in Christianity and to recognize the ethical values of the New Testament. The term "Judaeo-Christian tradition" became commonplace.[64] Furthermore, despite all manner of reservations and hedging about, there was ultimately no surrender of reason. The urge to believe that archaeology might confirm tradition did not often weaken the respect of scientific, scholarly knowledge in the sphere of religion.[65] And there remained broad marginal areas in which individual Jews continued their religious speculations quite outside organization lines.[66]

---

[62] Milton Steinberg, "Commentary Magazine," Park Avenue Synagogue, November 18, 1949; reprinted in *A Believing Jew*, New York, 1951, pp. 136ff.

[63] Lewis Browne, *Wisdom of Israel*, New York, 1945, p. xii.

[64] See the exchange touched off by John Cournos, "Epistle to the Jews," *Atlantic Monthly*, CLX, December, 1937, pp. 723ff.; also Robert Gordis, "Jesus and His Modern Kinsmen," *Reconstructionist*, IV, 1938, pp. 5ff.; M. J. Cohen, "Observations on the Nazarene," *ibid.*, V, 1939, pp. 12ff. Contrast in this regard the earlier attitude of Schechter, *Studies in Judaism*, pp. 163ff. For the attitude toward the New Testament, see, e.g., Browne, *Wisdom of Israel*, pp. 147ff. In general, see also Sholem Asch, *One Destiny: An Epistle to the Christians*, New York, 1945, and his novels: *The Nazarene*, New York, 1939, and *The Apostle*, New York, 1943.

[65] See Mordecai M. Kaplan, *Judaism in Transition*, New York, 1936, p. 175. For the assumption that archaeology confirms the Biblical accounts, see Israel Goldberg [Rufus Learsi], *Israel*, Cleveland, 1949, p. 3.

[66] See, e.g., Irwin Edman, *The Contemporary and His Soul*, New York, 1931; and "Religion Without Tears," *Commentary*, I, April, 1946, pp. 1ff.; Paul Weiss, "The True, the Good, and the Jew," *ibid.*, II, October,

Indeed, the absence of authentic authority in American Judaism accounted, in part, for the continuing attractiveness of Zionism as an ideal. The hope of an actual return to Palestine had never been universally held by American Zionists, and it faded completely once the state was established. But the desire that Israel supply American Jews with spiritual inspiration and with religious norms grew in intensity. Earlier in the century the traditionally inclined rabbis like Schechter had been suspicious of the prominence of secular influences in the Zionist Movement. Now those qualms subsided, and to the extent that American Jews grew more adjusted to their environment they grew more determined that Israel should preserve in a Hebraic context a center for traditional life. "Judaism as a religion is colorless and without personality unless it is informed by Zionist content," said Rabbi Israel Goldstein in 1943.[67] The Reconstructionists were representative in this respect. The Holy Land was to maintain communal and cultural standards that they suspected themselves not to be able to maintain in the United States. "Only in Palestine can Jewish creativeness find its proper Hebraic idiom."[68]

The emphasis on Israel as a counterweight to drift at home thus reflected a loss of confidence in the independent creativity of Judaism in the United States. American Jewry, wrote the President of the Jewish Theological Seminary, would not be "one of the foci of a great ellipse of Judaism nor the center of a circle, with only mystic connections with a similar circle surrounding Jerusalem. We recognize that we stand on the periphery of Jewish inspiration." Always it would be necessary to "turn to Zion not only in prayer but also in the hope of instruction."[69] Few joined the rather small group in the American Council for Judaism, hostile to Zionism and at-

1946, pp. 310ff.; Israel Knox, "A Humanist Religion for Modern Man," *ibid.*, IX, January, 1950, pp. 18ff.; Waldo Frank, *The Jew in Our Day.*
[67] Schneiderman, *Two Generations*, p. 167.
[68] Kaplan, *Judaism in Transition*, p. 50.
[69] Davis, *Israel*, p. 16, also Kaplan, *Future of American Jew*, p. 141.

tached to the ideas of classical reform, in dissent from this view.[70]

The willingness to accept this dependent status was understandable in view of the persistence of a pragmatic cast to Judaism within the social circumstances of the 1950's. American Jews retained the nineteenth-century faith in the essential goodness of man, and in the power of his reason progressively to transform the world. Yet in the world of nuclear power and atomic missiles, few were bold enough to stand openly by that faith. A sheltering tradition was more comforting than the unrelenting imperative to change, and, given the difficulty of finding such a tradition at home, it was tempting to seek it abroad. The question was, however, whether such an external source could supply the vitalizing force to sustain the religious life of the group in the future.

[70] The Council point of view is given in Elmer Berger, *Judaism or Jewish Nationalism*, New York, 1957, pp. 117ff. The view of the Jews as a "creative minority" supplies a different basis for the argument of Jacob Agus (see his *Guideposts*, pp. 161ff., 213ff., and *Modern Philosophies of Judaism*, New York, 1941).

RELIGIONS ON THE CHRISTIAN PERIMETER

A. LELAND JAMISON

I

IT may well be the case that few areas of the earth have been so productive of religious proliferation as has America during the past three centuries. The successive waves of exploration and settlement at the outset, augmented by steady streams of immigration down to the present, in conjunction with the characteristic freedom and mobility of American society, have fostered a ceaseless diversification of religious ideologies and institutions. The latest edition of the *Yearbook of American Churches* reports a total of no fewer than 258 autonomous religious bodies in the United States. This number, of course, includes only those groups which can be reached by the statisticians of the National Council of Churches of Christ. Elmer T. Clark estimates that a really accurate enumeration would swell the total to more than 400 more or less definitely organized bodies, and even then no account would be taken of the multitude of store-front churches, local sects, cults, and unclassifiable quasi-religious associations which operate ephemerally but often vigorously in the American scene.[1] There is no way at all of gaining a fully reliable estimate of the number of separate movements and groups which have arisen in the course of our national history. A fair number have existed briefly, perished, and are now unmentioned in available sources. Although every advanced and reasonably open society is characterized by some degree of religious heterogeneity, it would seem, on the surface at least, that the pluralistic pattern obtains more distinctively and extensively in America than elsewhere in Western culture. Any evaluation of this phenomenon must depend

[1] Elmer T. Clark, *The Small Sects in America*, rev. ed., New York and Nashville, 1949, p. 9. Cf. the "Index of Religious Bodies in the United States," pp. 241–246.

on the historical, sociological, and theological stance of the particular observer. It may be regarded as the inevitable consequence of religious freedom; it may be viewed as a symptom of cultural malaise and socio-religious anarchy; some may hail it as an indication of desirable religious vitality. All such judgments may contain elements of truth. What is incontrovertible and significant, in any case, is the *fact* of religious pluralism. There is no indication that the pattern will be altered in any foreseeable future.

This state of affairs has been the constant theme of those who have written from whatever point of view about American religion. Foreign observers in the nineteenth century were impressed by the variety, as well as by the often undisciplined vigor, of religious expression on this continent.[2] The comprehensive histories of American religion, from Baird to Sweet,[3] have in considerable measure been written in terms of the rise and growth of the numerous separate groups. The outstanding illustration of this characteristic diversity is, perhaps, to be seen in the monumental *American Church History Series*, comprising twelve volumes. More recent descriptive studies, such as those by Ferguson, Atkins, Bach, Braden, Clark, Mead, and Mayer (to mention only the most reliable and accessible), suggest that several dozen volumes would be required for anything like a comprehensive account of our religious history. Accordingly, it is difficult to use the terms "church" or even "religion" in proposing generalizations about religious activity and influence in American culture.

[2] Cf. Max Berger, *The British Traveller in America, 1836–1860*, New York, 1943, ch. VI; Alexis DeTocqueville, *Democracy in America*, ed. Phillips Bradley, New York, 1945, I, ch. V; Frances Trollope, *Domestic Manners of the Americans*, ed. Donald Smalley, New York, 1949. Mrs. Trollope frequently commented on "the almost endless variety of religious factions" and "the fanciful variations upon the ancient creeds of the Christian church with which trans-atlantic religionists amuse themselves" (p. 111). However, she came reluctantly to the opinion that "national and authorized indifference in matters of religious belief" might be "less productive of moral evil" than "the unauthorized secessions from the national worship" of her native England (p. 126).

[3] Cf. Vol. IV, Part One, sect. VI, c, d.

One needs always to specify which church and which type of religion are under consideration.

Nevertheless, the picture is by no means as chaotic as it may at first seem. The religious heterogeneity of American life is, in significant respects, far more apparent than real. The broad base of all American religious groups is, of course, Christian or, more accurately, Judaeo-Christian. The three major religious "sub-communities" [4] have a very great deal in common, looking as they do to the Bible, in whole or in part, as the normative source of faith and practice. Each of these sub-communities, in turn, possesses its own variations, but within each broad category are shared significant common assumptions. For example, the gulf between the several segments of Judaism, or between those churches which jealously retain the label of "Catholic" (including the "Orthodox"), is by no means as wide as the gap between Jewish and Catholic or Protestant, or between Catholic and Protestant. To be sure, efforts in the direction of ecumenical rapprochement between the non-Roman Catholic communions and other non-Roman churches have enjoyed a modest success during the past few decades in the activities of the World Council of Churches and its subsidiaries. It remains to be determined, however, whether or not the ethos of Catholicity (with a capital "C") will find more than casual affiliations with those who claim the Protestant Reformation as an integral element of their common heritage.

The designation "Protestant" covers the largest number of American religious bodies. The adjective is obviously misleading and inexact, both historically and theologically, since it must embrace such widely differing groups as the Anglo-Catholic wing of the Protestant Episcopal Church and the Two-Seed-in-the-Spirit Predestinarian Baptists. In the strict sense, "Protestant" can only denote "non-Catholic," Roman or other, and even in this sense the word is unsatisfactorily ambiguous. The vast majority of the approximately 250 identi-

[4] This term is suggested by Will Herberg, *Catholic—Protestant—Jew, An Essay in Religious Sociology*, Garden City, N.Y., 1955.

fiable bodies, nevertheless, must for convenience' sake be subsumed under the Protestant heading. Here, again, chaos is not quite complete. The membership of the so-called Protestant denominations is concentrated in a relatively few great families: Baptist, Methodist, Lutheran, Presbyterian, Episcopalian, Congregational (now the United Church of Christ, since the union with the Evangelical and Reformed Church), and a few independent bodies, such as the Disciples of Christ. Professor Mayer comments that each of these families possesses "the same basic historic background, the same creedal position, and the same church practices." [5] If this statement is valid, the organizational pluralism of American denominations is seen as a less heterogeneous pattern than a first reading of the religious census would indicate. Thus, of approximately 103 million church members in the United States, nearly 35 million are claimed by the Roman Catholic Church, and the two score branches of the Eastern Orthodox Church report more than two and a half million. Jewish congregations account for slightly more than 5 million members. The total of these groups is, accordingly, some 42 million, leaving about 61 million religiously affiliated persons distributed among the various Protestant denominations. Of this number, no fewer than 50 million belong to the seven great ecclesiastical families mentioned above. Moreover, many of the denominations which are not so readily classifiable into family relationships have historically sprung from the major divisions of Protestantism and in some cases are scarcely distinguishable from their parent bodies. The statistics can be variously analyzed, but the conclusion seems to be that the great mass of American Protestants adhere to fewer than ten denominational families.

It is further obvious that the larger Protestant families manage to exist side by side in friendship. This is not the place to describe the numerous centripetal movements among the American churches, but they reflect the character of American Protantism in important respects. Such movements include cooperative efforts at every level, from local minis-

[5] F. E. Mayer, *The Religious Bodies of America*, St. Louis, 1956, p. 3.

terial associations and church councils to the National Council of Churches and several conservative and evangelical counterparts of the latter. Certain denominations, such as the Southern Baptist Convention and the Missouri Synod Lutheran Church, which do not formally support ecumenical movements, still are able to communicate cordially with other churches. Virtually every denomination professes itself open to organic union with some other related group, and several such mergers of real consequence have been achieved within recent years. Meanwhile, the 258 or more independent groups carry on their activities with a minimum of friction. Although religious prejudice and theological exclusiveness undoubtedly persist, sectarian malice has seldom in American history been effectively organized, nor has it, except in sporadic and quite local instances, erupted into persecution and violence. It is probable that discriminatory movements similar to the Know-Nothing Party, the American Protestant Association, the Ku Klux Klan, the Silver Shirts, and the like will periodically arise, but it is fortunately improbable that any such agitation will ever gain mass allegiance. Indeed, theologians and ecclesiasts often lament over the pervasive neutrality and undogmatic nature of the American religious consciousness. Will Herberg writes caustically about the amorphous mood of "American religion," which, he claims, is a creedless surrogate for a vital and defined faith in the God of the Bible.[6] Whatever the deficiencies of this common-denominator American religion may be, it has at least immunized the nation against the plague of overt religious strife.

II

The major families or denominational groupings of American Protestantism are discussed elsewhere in the present volume,[7] supplementing the analyses of Roman Catholicism

[6] Herberg, pp. 85–104; cf. his discussion of the "syncretistic religion of religionized American democracy" in Vol. II of this series.
[7] H. R. Niebuhr's essay, pp. 25 f.

and of Judaism. There remain for some consideration, accordingly, the dozens of disparate groups which are not so easily classified in consistent genealogies. These are the "sects" and "cults," but the assignment of any particular religious body to either category may involve a highly subjective judgment. The conventional categories of "church" and "sect" simply do not apply with precision to American religious bodies. In the legal sense, certainly, all enjoy equal status. The First Amendment to the Constitution explicitly prohibits the "establishment of religion," a provision of quite elastic ambiguity, which yet clearly forbids preferential treatment of any specific religious body. Further, although the autonomous churches differ greatly in respect to size—from the Roman Catholic communion claiming more than 35 million members down to the Church of Jesus Christ (Cutler) with a single congregation of sixteen members—no group or closely related family of groups can muster a majority of the population. Every church is a minority group, and so far as the law is concerned all conform to Sidney Mead's definition of the "denomination" as "a voluntary association of like-hearted and like-minded individuals . . . united on the basis of common beliefs for the purpose of accomplishing tangible and defined objectives." [8] Social and psychological pressures may be employed by various groups in order to recruit and discipline adherents, but such pressures receive no support from the coercive power of the state.[9] Church, denomination, sect, and even "cult" stand on the same plane of legal recognition. Distinctions among these types must be formulated in sociological and theological, rather than legal, terms.

Although legal equality obtains, the differences between religious bodies are of real importance for an analysis of Amer-

[8] Sidney Mead, "Denominationalism: The Shape of Protestantism in America," *Church History*, XXIII, 1954, p. 3.

[9] A partial exception to this is the procedure governing the placement of children for adoption only in families holding the same religious affiliation as the parents of such children. This procedure does not, however, provide for measures to compel the child to join the particular religious group.

ican culture. Sociologists, in particular, have long sought to classify and explain the characteristics of the various types of religious association. The influential studies of Max Weber and Ernst Troeltsch have provided the basic categories followed by most subsequent students, although the proposals of the two Germans were more applicable to the European situation than to America. In this country the most acute interpretation has been offered by H. Richard Niebuhr, whose *Social Sources of Denominationalism* (1929) has attained popular recognition even beyond academic circles. Niebuhr emphasizes the socio-economic factors which gave rise to sectarianism in Europe, and which promoted the further extension of that pattern in America. He makes a primary distinction between church and sect, defining each in a series of cleanly drawn contrasts:

"The difference has been well described as lying primarily in the fact that members are born into the church, while they must join the sect. Churches are inclusive institutions, frequently are national in scope, and emphasize the universalism of the gospel; while sects are exclusive in character, appeal to the individualistic element in Christianity, and emphasize its ethical demands. Membership in a church is socially obligatory, the necessary consequence of birth into a family or nation, and no special requirements condition its privileges; the sect, on the other hand, is likely to demand some definite type of religious experience as a pre-requisite of membership." [10]

Niebuhr goes on to demonstrate that differences in structure are accompanied by no less marked differences in ethics and doctrine. But the really distinctive feature of the church type is seen in the fact that "as an inclusive social group . . . [it] is closely allied with national, economic and cultural interests; by the very nature of its constitution it is committed to the

[10] H. Richard Niebuhr, *The Social Sources of Denominationalism,* New York, 1929, reprinted 1957, pp. 17–18.

accommodation of its ethics to the ethic of civilization." [11]
The sect, on the contrary, represents rebellious, frustrated,
or rejected minorities; it emphasizes, in place of accommodation, sharp discontinuity, between the converted and the unconverted, the religious fellowship and the political state,
the present age of sin and the future age of salvation. In its
organized life the sect is usually critical of, hostile, or indifferent toward the secular concerns of society. Niebuhr
concedes that few sects remain purely sectarian for longer
than a generation. Often they vanish with the death of an
inspiring leader or the quenching, by disappointment or
persecution, of an initial fervor; in many cases prosperity and
parenthood conspire to turn the sectarians toward a stronger
sense of social responsibility and more churchly attitudes in
general. In America the genetic tendency has been for the
sect to evolve into a denomination, a sociological entity rather
more stable and world-accepting than the sect, yet less
comprehensively inclusive than a church of the ideal type.
It is to be observed that Niebuhr makes the principle of
differentiation between churches, denominations, and sects
to be the degree of "their conformity to the order of social
classes and castes." [12] In the volume from which these remarks
are drawn he does, indeed, grant that the religious factor is
not at all negligible: "religion supplies the energy, the goal,
and the motive of sectarian movements." [13] But social factors
must be prominently regarded, since they "supply the
occasion, and determine the form the religious dynamic will
take." [14] In a later book, *Christ and Culture*, Niebuhr makes
a more exclusively theological analysis of the different possible Christian attitudes toward the values and activities of
human society, leaving us to suppose, it may be, that sectarianism may have religious and intellectual roots reaching far
below economic circumstances.

[11] *ibid.*, p. 18.
[12] *ibid.*, p. 25.
[13] *ibid.*, p. 27.
[14] *ibid.*

A considerable weight of evidence, however, seems to support the contention that particular formulations of church polity, ethics, and even theological beliefs "have their roots in the relationship of the religious life to the cultural and political conditions prevailing in any group of Christians." [15] Accordingly, Niebuhr has insisted that the sect type, with its peculiarities of belief, practice, and attitudes toward society, "has ever been the child of an outcast minority, taking its rise in the religious revolts of the poor." The latter "fashion a new type of Christianity which corresponds to their distinctive needs." [16] The Christian faith, we know, was first accepted by the "proletariat," the socially disinherited, of the Roman Empire. St. Paul frankly admitted concerning his converts that "not many of you were wise according to worldly standards, not many were powerful, not many were of noble birth." [17] In time the early church attracted rich, educated, and well-born people, and the discipline of Christian virtue often served to raise the economic status of poorer members. With social acceptance and prosperity came identification with the interests of secular society—and the church itself became a great *imperium*, rivaling and finally outlasting the Empire. But from within the church were constantly generated new religious movements, some of which can only be interpreted as "efforts of the religiously disinherited to discover again the sources of effective faith," [18] that is, of a faith which would satisfy the needs of the classless poor. The Montanists of the second century, the Franciscans, Waldensians, and Lollards originated, in part certainly, in this sort of religious protest. The Right Wing Protestant Reformation in large measure served other interests than those of the poor, being rather, sociologically viewed, a revolt of the rising middle classes. Thus, in independence of and often in opposition to Lutheran-

---

[15] *ibid.*, p. 21.
[16] *ibid.*, p. 19.
[17] I Cor. 1:26 (RSV).
[18] Niebuhr, p. 33.

ism, Calvinism, and conservative Puritanism, there arose the multiplicity of radical reformations—Anabaptists, Millenarians, Antinomians, Seekers, Ranters, Quakers, and the like— among the classes to whose social condition the new orthodoxy of Protestantism offered little apparent relief. Movements of this sort have continued to emerge among comparable social classes throughout the intervening four centuries. Niebuhr says that "the last great revival of the disinherited in Christendom" [19] was the Methodist upsurge in the eighteenth century. While Methodism has long since ceased to be a community of the disinherited, in America it has spawned any number of rebels against its own bourgeois compromises with the world of social success and religious routinization.

It would be presumptuous to dispute the validity of Niebuhr's thesis, at least in its application to the origins of European and English radical sectarianism. This view has been so extensively documented, both before and after Niebuhr's classic study, that it has become a commonplace. Troeltsch earlier commented that certain religious types tend to belong to certain strata of society, and that the sectarian type is most characteristic of the lower social strata.[20] Quite evidently the conventional churches or denominations do tend to become formalized and secularized, leaving too little room for religious spontaneity, and too readily disposed to justify the existing order of society. They do tend to place a premium on worldly success and to adopt a paternalistic attitude toward the unsuccessful and misfits. Small wonder, then, that the latter are frequently prompted to withdraw from religious associations which verbalize fellowship instead of practicing it, and which do not minister adequately to the acute needs of the less fortunate. Whether or not they find better solutions to their problems is another matter.

It is obvious, however, that the Niebuhrean term "dis-

[19] ibid., p. 72.
[20] Ernst Troeltsch, *The Social Teaching of the Christian Churches*, New York, 1931, II, 798.

inherited" must refer to more than economic poverty. It must be stretched to include the educationally deprived, the geographically uprooted, the psychologically disturbed. The fact that many of the latter are economically insecure is significant but not wholly determinative. In America, at any rate, the poor as such have had no monopoly over the creation of new religions. It has not been poverty so much as a general cultural malaise—termed *anomie* by Durkheim—which has produced religious extravagance here.[21] *Anomie* connotes a state of material insecurity, to be sure, but also the lack of spiritual cohesion in society, and the loss of confidence in the normal methods of solving problems. These elements, especially the last two, have existed in varying degrees of intensity for different individuals throughout American history, from the days of pioneer settlement through the expansion of the frontier and into the modern era of urbanization and industrialization. Whenever and wherever "cultural shock" occurs, whether in the wilderness, the slum, or the New Eden of California, the sect and cult find their ripe opportunity. As Yinger says, "When a satisfactory definition of critical life events is destroyed [or has never been found!], religious movements arise to re-establish a sense of security." [22] This statement applies cogently, no doubt, to the entire revival of religious interest in post-World War II America, but it is especially relevant to the motley assortment of movements which are commonly labeled sectarian or cultic.

American sociologists have been prolific of monographs and books which pursue further the kind of analysis which Niebuhr supported so brilliantly with historical data and theological sensitivity. In a recent schematization of religious typology J. Milton Yinger summarizes previous analyses and proposes a six-step classification of religious institutions:

[21] See Werner Cohn, "Jehovah's Witnesses as a Proletarian Movement," *American Scholar*, 24, no. 3, 1955, p. 297.
[22] J. Milton Yinger, "Present Status of the Sociology of Religion," *Journal of Religion*, 31, July 1951, p. 206.

1) the universal church; 2) the "ecclesia"; 3) the class church or denomination; 4) the established sect; 5) the sect; 6) the cult.[23] This typology is based on "typical relationships between religion and society," and two criteria of arrangement are employed. The first is "the degree of inclusiveness of the members of society," that is, the extent to which the group considers itself as coextensive with the entire community. The other criterion concerns "the degree of attention to the function of personal need," measured presumably against the particular group's interest in the institutions and policies of secular society. On the extreme right, as it were, the universal-church type of religious association theoretically represents a maximum degree of inclusiveness, combined with a maximum attention to the function of social integration—the ideal exemplified in the theory of medieval European society as a *corpus Christianum*. At the other end of the hypothetical continuum stands the cult, with its exaggerated exclusiveness and almost total disregard of the operations of economic systems and political governments. Along the line between lie less precisely defined types, representing various degrees of modification of the extreme attitudes toward membership and social integration. If the theological pretensions of particular groups are ignored, it is apparent that America contains neither a church nor an ecclesia. Various groups exhibit characteristics of both types and perhaps aspire to the status of complete religious inclusiveness and dominance. For example, the Roman Catholic Church has been, in other times and places, a universal church blanketing entire societies. In its theological self-consciousness it never ceases to be such, and the achievement of monopolistic status is its goal everywhere.[24] Here, however, it actually functions as a denomina-

---

[23] J. M. Yinger, *Religion, Society, and the Individual*, New York, 1957, pp. 142–155.

[24] It is noteworthy that many American Roman Catholics vigorously maintain the view that religious pluralism is an acceptable and even desirable feature of American society. This opinion, it may be conjectured, is held rather more on practical than on theological grounds.

tion among denominations, compelled to compete with all others for members and to give other groups respectful consideration in public affairs. The same may be said about other ideologically totalitarian groups, including such diverse types as the Eastern Orthodox churches and the Mormons. In practice, if not in theology, all American religious bodies are "free" churches. Further, while such bodies vary greatly in their degrees of pragmatic concern with the welfare of the whole society, only those at the extreme left fringe (e.g., Jehovah's Witnesses, some metaphysical cults) disclaim all social interest.

It appears, then, that it is by no means easy to classify American religious groups according to sociological formulae. The dominant form is that of the denomination, which frankly accepts its status as a voluntary association, aspires to no monopolistic jurisdiction, and directs its attention to both individual salvation and social welfare. Nevertheless, such terms as sect and cult continue to be used, evidently with some meaning for large numbers of people. Another term in common usage is "deviation," although it is not always made clear what is deviated from. This essay is focused on such deviant groups, with full admission that the adjective is unfortunate inasmuch as it bears pejorative connotations which have no place in a non-polemical, objective study. The fact remains, however, that outside the circle of the major families of churches lie numerous religious groups whose tenets and activities vary noticeably from those of the majority of American Christians. They titillate the conventional religious curiosity and provide material for many fascinating studies, both scholarly and in a journalistic vein. Various categorizations of these disparate movements have been suggested. Charles Braden, who is perhaps the most careful observer of contemporary religious eccentricities, arranges the sects in seven main types: 1) non-Christian bodies; 2) offshoots from larger denominations; 3) groups which give exaggerated emphasis to some more or less "orthodox" doctrine or practice;

4) transplanted European sects; 5) sects which center on a personal (modern) founder; 6) syncretistic cults; 7) humanistic or ethicocentric groups.[25] Another scheme, which presents dominant motifs in a clear form, has been used by Elmer T. Clark: 1) pessimistic or adventist sects; 2) perfectionist or subjectivistic; 3) charismatic or pentecostal; 4) communistic; 5) legalistic or objectivistic; 6) egocentric; 7) esoteric or mystical.[26] The concept of the religious motif is perceptively applied by Peter L. Berger, following the lead of some Swedish theologians.[27] The religious motif refers to "a specific pattern or gestalt of religious experience that can be traced in a historical development." This is not an exact instrument of phenomenological analysis, but it is quite helpful in distinguishing between central and peripheral elements in any particular sectarian type, although it must be recognized that a given sect may embody more than one motif. Berger proposes three major motifs, which are primarily experiential and only secondarily expressed in theological terms. These are: 1) Enthusiastic ("an experience to be lived"), which embraces both the revivalist and the pentecostal emphases in religion; 2) Prophetic ("a message to be proclaimed"), including chiliasts and legalists; 3) Gnostic ("a secret to be divulged"), covering Oriental, New Thought, and spiritist movements. Each type has its particular view toward "the world," growing out of the particular view of reality and divine purpose. Most of them incline to stress the personal needs of the individual and his "salvation," rather than social reconstruction, unless that reconstruction is to be wrought by supernatural intervention into the secular order.

Joachim Wach, the late German-American historian and sociologist of religion, has probed rather more deeply into

[25] Charles S. Braden, *These Also Believe*, New York, 1949.
[26] Elmer T. Clark, pp. 22–24.
[27] Peter L. Berger, "The Sociological Study of Sectarianism," *Social Research*, 21:4, Winter 1954, pp. 467–485.

the essence of sectarianism: "Ultimately it is the spirit and not any clear cut manifestation which distinguishes the sect." [28] By "spirit" Wach means "characteristic attitudes rather than specific theological and philosophical doctrines [which] determine the sociological type of the sect or, in instances, of the independent group." [29] He approvingly quotes Troeltsch in this connection, pointing out that a sect "is marked by its selective character ('religious elite'), places intensity above universality, and tends to maintain uncompromising radical attitudes, demanding the maximum from its members in their relations to God, the world, and men." [30] From this stance sectarianism is seen as the expression of a narrow, dogmatic, passionately committed response to the ultimate. Berger also uses the word "spirit" to indicate the differential of sectarianism, but in a somewhat different sense. He takes "spirit" to refer to "the religious object as such, that object which will always, of course, appear to faith as a subject in action." He further specifies that "the spirit may be said, then, to create the religious experience in which man encounters that which is sacred—the *numen,* to use (Rudolf) Otto's term." [31] The difference between the sect and the church (or denomination) is that the former is "an order of spirit," whereas the latter is "an order of law." Sectarians strive for—and claim to attain—an *immediacy* of relation with the numinous object, whether through fresh revelation, emotional conversion and exaltation, mystical union with the divine, or the operation of supernatural power in the natural order (miracles). Traditional modes of mediation between the divine and the human are discounted or totally abandoned—the sect claims that it can existentially accomplish what the churches merely talk about! The sectarian ideal usually involves a return to the fancied immediacy and perfection of some normative

---

[28] Joachim Wach, *The Sociology of Religion,* Chicago, 1944, p. 199.
[29] *ibid.,* p. 202.
[30] *ibid.,* p. 198.
[31] Berger, p. 474.

moment in the particular religious movement, such as the Apostolic Age of Christianity. Cults not related to one of the historical traditions profess, of course, to produce their own normative moments, often in the experience of a founding religious genius. The concept of spiritual immediacy does not, however, apply to certain legalistic and eschatological groups (e.g., the Jehovah's Witnesses) which deal little in mystical experience.

III

If we turn from more or less abstract generalizations to the American scene as it has historically developed, one quite simple—and doubtless quite "unscientific"—benchmark may be used to measure the sect-ness or cult-ness of particular religious groups. That measure is this: what does the group do with—or without—the Bible and the major traditions of Christian orthodoxy? This is admittedly an enterprise which runs the risk of subjectivity, yet no other device seems to do sufficient justice to the complexities of the American milieu. The selection of this principle rests on the historically and statistically verifiable assumption that the overwhelming preponderance of American religious activity has in some manner and degree looked to the Bible for inspiration and validation. Judaism, of course, appeals to only a part of what Christians know as the Bible. A venerable supplementary tradition, based upon but extending far beyond the limits of the Old Testament, exerts weighty authority in the Jewish community. The several forms of Catholicism, too, not only acknowledge a more extensive Bible than do Protestants, but they also attach an equal normativeness to a cumulative tradition which reaches back at least into the second century of the common era. However, since radical sectarianism and religious deviation have been so nearly exclusively Protestant in orientation, the peculiar circumstances of Judaism and Catholicism may for the moment be ignored. And it surely cannot be disputed that the single factor which more than any others gives non-Catholic Christians any semblance of identification is their common acceptance of the Bible as somehow regulative in religion. The development of Protestant churches, denominations, sects—call them what we will—has, without question, been the product of secular as well as theological factors, some direct, some indirect in operation, as sociologists and social historians demonstrate. Nevertheless, some eclectic interpretation of the Bible has, in the final analysis, been the bedrock on which every dissident movement has sought to justify its own separate existence. We may exclude from this assertion the denominations of primarily national origin, such as some of the Lutheran and Reformed churches. Yet it is interesting that even these perpetuate their divisions, not on the basis of ethnic incompatibility or superiority, but instead on the ground of theological disagreement, nearly always based on the Bible. Various cults, too, elude classification according to a Biblical norm, inasmuch as they simply ignore the Bible as a source of revelation. No such difficulty obtains in a consideration of the most numerous types of sects.

It cannot be denied that a group's attitude toward the Bible is something less than a precise instrument by which to identify sects. Variations in interpretation cover so wide a range and often turn on such subtle discriminations that the secular inquirer may despair of identifying significant lines of differentiation. On the empirical level, however, it should be evident that such ecumenical associations as the World Council of Churches or the National Council of Churches are able to exist at all because their constituents share a common approach to the Bible and what it means. Admittedly there are other principles which induce some churches of considerable size to stand apart from cooperative ventures, and it would not be reasonable to classify these (e.g., the Missouri Synod Lutheran Church or the Southern Baptist Convention) as sects in the special sense intended by this essay. But beyond the latter there appear various types of attitude toward the

Bible which clearly deviate from the approach of the majority of organized Christians. Although in the Protestant ethos appeal cannot be made authoritatively to any single interpretative standard which has been accepted *semper, ubique, et ab omnibus,* various deviations from the center are not impossible to identify.

What we may call the principle of selective emphasis has accounted for the most extensive proliferation of American religious groups. This principle involves a virtually monolithic concentration upon some limited aspect of Biblical teaching, making it the touchstone of right belief and religious acceptability. The point of exaggerated emphasis may be doctrinal, ethical, liturgical, dietary, sacramental, or what not. Extreme millennial sects, for example, theoretically base themselves upon the entire Bible, but in practice they could dispense with most of it aside from the books of Daniel and Revelation, plus a few apocalyptic passages from the prophets, the Synoptic gospels, and the letters of Paul. In any event, the whole Bible is rigorously interpreted in the light of its more lurid eschatological passages. Similarly, the modern pentecostal and holiness sects find their distinctive mark in the effort to reproduce the "inspired" behavior described in Acts 2. Again, some ethical perfectionists—as certain pacifistic and communal groups—view the Sermon on the Mount and a few miscellaneous perfectionist demands of Jesus as the sum of Christianity. Other sectarians stress such particularities as the mode of baptism, the rejection of musical instruments or modern hymns in worship, archaism in dress and rejection of modern mechanical devices, and the cultivation of charismatic behavior. Each such emphasis has been literalistically derived from a Biblical precept or custom. Little or no account of the relativity of social customs and religious world-views is taken: the eating habits of the Hebrew patriarchs, or Paul's notions about feminine coiffure are treated as of eternally binding authority. All these emphases—apocalyptic, legalistic, pentecostal, and others of doctrinal emphasis—are supposed to represent what is most important in Biblical religion. The sectarian may argue that the churches and denominations also define themselves according to quite particular details of interpretation—the precise meaning and number of the sacraments, the credentials of a valid ministry, and various divergences in theological emphasis (justification by faith, predestination, etc.). The difference, if any, must lie in *proportion;* the distinction between church and sect here must somewhat subjectively turn on the *weight* of the matter at issue. The major Christian traditions have, implicitly at least, recognized the diversity within the Bible, but they have also sought to maintain a balance between the parts and the whole. It is the characteristic of sectarian deviation to focus so exclusively on one or a few trees, as it were, that the image of the total forest of the Bible is blurred. However, the fact that the favored trees of most sectarian groups still stand in the normative forest is of great importance for the underlying unity of American religion and culture.

A second category includes those groups which stress some esoteric principle or method of interpretation of the Bible. The esoteric element is usually derived from metaphysical and epistemological views which can be read into—or out of —the Bible only by resort to tortuous allegory. From the appearance of the Gnostics and Docetists in the second century, and throughout Christian history until the present, various self-acknowledged Christians have claimed that the Bible must be read entirely in terms of one or the other philosophical position, most frequently of either a radically dualistic or a radically idealistic sort. The church of the center has repeatedly disciplined such endeavors and declared them heretical. The latter indictment, it must be conceded, has meaning chiefly from within some recognized system of orthodoxy, and every branch of Christianity has on occasion judged every other branch as heretical on some major or minor point. Here, however, the word is used to designate those opinions which a clear and overwhelming majority of Christian interpreters have deemed seriously deviant. At whatever cost in philosophical consistency, the dominant Christian consensus has been that the Bible should not be interpreted according to either a thoroughgoing dualism or an idealistic monism. Therefore Gnosticism, extreme forms of neo-Platonism, Manichaeism, Catharism, and Christian Science, to mention only a few, must be located somewhere toward the periphery of the Christian community, if not outside the circle altogether.

A third cluster of groups is characterized by the introduction of a supplementary source of revelation and religious sanction in addition to the Bible. The supplement may take the form of the oral pronouncements of an inspired leader, or it may be embodied in a second book of revealed scripture. In either case, the Bible itself is not merely interpreted; it is added to, with an authority and novelty which exceed the limits of sober, scholarly interpretation. Admittedly, this line between interpretation and fresh revelation cannot always be fairly drawn. Lutherans and Calvinists, by way of example, seem often to ascribe to the writings of their respective patrons an almost Biblical authority. But the qualifying "almost" invariably obtains, as it must also in regard to competing theological symbols—the respective treatises and creeds are thus highly valued "as containing the system of doctrine taught in the Holy Scriptures." The situation was quite otherwise when Ann Lee offered herself as an incarnation of the Christ, or when Joseph Smith deciphered the Book of Mormon and continued to issue inspired pronouncements to his followers, or when Father Divine is worshiped as God in person. The revelational status of *Science and Health* is less sharply defined—after all, its complete title does include the phrase "With Key to the Scriptures." Not many new Bibles have been written in America, but there has seldom been a shortage of prophets, able and willing to communicate divine revelations which the original edition of the Bible neglected to publish.

A fourth type of deviant religious attitude moves quite outside the Judaeo-Christian orbit. This position either dispenses with a holy book altogether or accepts the scriptures of a non-Biblical religion. In this category we may count the pseudo-Islamic cults and those which draw their inspiration from the sacred writings of the Orient. A disparate array of associations is subsumed in this type: New Thought, Theosophy, I Am, Spiritualism, the Bahai Faith, Rosicrucianism, the Moorish Science Temple of America, and the Ahmadiyya Movement, among others. Many of these foster mystical practices and are based on philosophical idealism. They represent a protest against a "materialistic" world, with all its limitations and frustrations, and purport to demonstrate how mind can transcend the imperfections and illusions of matter. Another subtype is racially oriented and attempts to create a new cultural status for Negroes, in particular, by divorcing them from the Christianity of their Caucasian fellow citizens and offering a socially "elite" role through adherence to a different religion.

IV

It goes without saying that reference to the Bible as a criterion of sectarian definition and classification raises many problems. One of the more puzzling difficulties is the status of the so-called "modernists" and "liberals," who have been numerous in American Protestantism especially since the second half of the nineteenth century. Already in the eighteenth century, actually, "critical" views concerning the Bible began to be expressed by men of rationalistic and deistic tendencies. This development is traced in some detail in Volume IV of this work.[32] It is sufficient here to note that the Scriptures

[32] See Vol. IV, Part Two, sect III, B.

were subjected to philosophical and scientific scrutiny, with the result that the whole concept of Biblical infallibility was increasingly challenged. Thomas Jefferson went so far as to prepare an expurgated version of the New Testament, from which he had removed those supernatural and miraculous elements which were unacceptable to the mind of an enlightened, reasonable man of the eighteenth century. Although Jefferson valued Jesus highly as a moral teacher, he deemed the supernaturalistic theology of the Bible and the Christian tradition to be irrelevant and untrue. This manner of approach, which regards the Bible, not as autonomously and a priori authoritative for Christian belief and practice, but as itself subject to verification by reason, scientific knowledge, and immediate religious experience, gained increasing currency in the nineteenth century. Whereas the earliest rebels against Calvinistic orthodoxy imagined that they could support their case by appeal to Scripture, it soon became evident that the Bible, strictly and consistently interpreted, stood decisively on the side of traditional orthodoxy. Therefore, courageous minds —such as Theodore Parker, who studied deeply in German higher criticism, and Emerson, who sought religious certitude in his intuition of the Transcendent—quite openly abandoned the Bible as the sole and incontrovertible measure of truth. Most Unitarians were not willing to follow the extreme course of Parker and Emerson but continued to locate themselves, albeit uneasily, within the Biblical and Christian perimeter. The logical conclusions of the more radical position were drawn by the Free Religious Association, Ethical Culture, and other numerically minor secessions from the Christian camp. Still today a debate is carried on inside Unitarian-Universalist circles as to whether or not the general movement should acknowledge itself as "Christian." The ecumenical bodies have answered this question in the negative.

The large, orthodox denominations continued to be plagued by the problem of Biblical authority throughout the nineteenth century into the twentieth, and the battle has by

183

no means ceased. The steadily growing influence of German criticism, coupled with the intellectual revolution occasioned by the Darwinian hypothesis and the general impact of scientific method, infected large areas of American religion, especially among the better educated clergy and theological scholars. The great theological controversies which agitated several denominations in the late nineteenth century and following turned basically on issues of Biblical interpretation.[33] The climax was reached in the bitter Fundamentalist-Modernist struggles of the first quarter of the present century. The Fundamentalists argued that the Modernists manipulated the Biblical text in accordance with their own predilections, using it, opportunistically, as a peg on which to hang religious ideas derived from other sources. The less extreme Modernists (who might better be called "Liberals") replied that the Bible must somehow be harmonized with the reasonably assured conclusions of modern thought and experience. The most eloquent statement of this position was made by Harry E. Fosdick in his *The Modern Use of the Bible*, in which he viewed the sacred book as a record of "abiding experiences in changing categories." Although the vehemence of the older Fundamentalist warfare has worn itself out, echoes of the conflict are still heard in every church. Indeed, on a highly sophisticated level, the present debate among Protestant scholars over Rudolf Bultmann's method of "demythologizing" the Bible represents a continuation of the fight. The authority and interpretation of the Bible are still the decisive issues in the Protestant scheme of things.

An interesting result emerged from the Fundamentalist-Conservative versus Modernist-Liberal controversies: by and large, it was partisans of the Fundamentalist-Conservative wing who seceded to form new sects.[34] A few liberal ministers have transferred into the Unitarian Church, and others have

[33] See the discussion of this struggle among Presbyterians in Lefferts A. Loetscher, *The Broadening Church*, Philadelphia, 1954.
[34] The formation of "The Orthodox Presbyterian Church" is an example.

broken all formal religious connections. But most liberals have chosen to remain inside the established denominations. This came about, partly because of the liberals' genuine attachment to the Bible and the Christian tradition as a whole, and partly because the theological consensus of many denominations had been powerfully leavened by the liberal attitude toward the Bible. The fact that Protestantism's discussion of scriptural authority has moved away from the narrow limits of dogmatic literalism marks the triumph of the critical methodology in Biblical study, patiently pursued by honest and reverent scholars in the modern age. There are important "neo-orthodox" tendencies at work within contemporary Protestantism but, with a few exceptions, they do not represent a return to anti-scientific Biblical literalism. Moreover, the really effective movements in the direction of church unity are being supported by the resurgence of interest in Biblical theology, since on no other basis can the segments of Protestantism reach a common understanding. But the newer approach to Biblical thought is frankly "critical," and may be described as "post-liberal" rather than "anti-liberal."

V

The story of native American deviation begins with a woman, Anne Hutchinson, the first of a long and interesting line of radical spiritual rebels against the various established orders on this continent. Most of the earliest settlers, Virginia Anglicans excepted, were, of course, dissenters from the national church of their English homeland, but they quickly formed a new establishment, intended to maintain a religious uniformity of the same kind, if not of identical substance, as that from which they had taken refuge in the New World. The description of the Puritan theocracy, with all its assets and debits, has been too frequently and extensively told to demand elaboration here. We merely note that, at least according to Mrs. Hutchinson herself, the Holy Spirit resisted regimentation in a Puritan system no less than in the Anglican structure of old England. Mrs. Hutchinson claimed, in short, that the Spirit of God spoke directly to her and to others of genuine faith, communicating new divine truth or new insight into the meaning of Biblical revelation. She raised again the theological problem which has plagued Christianity from the beginning, namely, the proper relationship between faith and works in the Christian economy.

The mystical, individualistic, and perfectionistic impulses, which can with sufficient validity be derived from New Testament formulations of the divine-human encounter, have perennially disturbed the placidity of institutional Christianity and doubtless shall continue to do so *in saecula saeculorum.* At the outset, the Pauline exaggeration of faith was challenged in the New Testament itself, by the compiler of the Gospel of Matthew and the author of the Epistle of James. Although Christian orthodoxy has always sought to hold the two aspects of religious response in a viable equilibrium, the dilemma has been repeatedly put to the fore by believers of the extreme Pauline type. The two major forms of Catholicism have historically managed to absorb and discipline such impulses, through the monastic orders, special exercises of devotion, and similar devices. Luther's protest originated in an exaggeration of the principle of *sola fide,* and left-wing Protestants carried the conception to logical conclusions from which Luther himself recoiled in horror. While no single causative factor can account for all the phenomena of the Protestant Reformation, it is evident that in it the impulses of anti-authoritarian religious immediacy erupted on a more massive scale than ever before in Christian history. Even so, the Roman Church was able to recoup its losses in most of Europe, while right-wing Protestantism reconstituted itself on quite "catholic" lines. Within the context of a catholicized sectarianism Anne Hutchinson represented the re-emergence of a sectarian impulse claiming not lightly dismissable Biblical credentials. In the train of most of her heretical predecessors, she was summarily expelled from the Puritan community, and no continuing movement grew out of her rebellion. She is chiefly significant as a symptom and prophecy of much that was to come in American religion.

The early Quakers deserve mention as examples of the radical sectarian spirit, and they had no easy time of it in seventeenth-century colonial America. More than one political, geographical, and religious circumstance contributed to the survival and acceptance of the Quakers, not least of which were their irenic attitude and their positive orientation within the Biblical tradition. The Friends fairly rapidly mitigated their original sectarian intransigence and achieved a moderate rapprochement with the environing society—the gulf between meeting-house and counting-house proving not impassable, as Tolles has demonstrated so well. The latter comments that "the Society of Friends has always tended to produce two distinct types . . . on the one hand, a small body of individuals unreservedly committed to the ideal . . . on the other, a somewhat larger number 'who have held it to be equally imperative to work out their principles of life in the complex affairs of the community and the state, where to gain an end one must yield something . . . where to achieve ultimate triumph one must risk his ideals to the tender mercies of a world not yet ripe for them.' " [35] In a manner quite different from the typical sect, sociologically defined, the Quakers in Pennsylvania undertook a "Holy Experiment," in which they sought, not an escape from, but the transformation of, society. In the words of Troeltsch, they worked for "the creation of a real Christian State upon the joint basis of the freedom of the Spirit and a strict ethic." [36] Such a goal connotes a church or ecclesia, rather than a sect, and the Quakers amply illustrate the difficulty of applying a precise sociological typology to American religious groups:

[35] Frederick B. Tolles, *Meetinghouse and Countinghouse: The Quaker Merchants of Colonial Philadelphia, 1682–1763*, Chapel Hill, 1948, p. vii.
[36] Troeltsch, II, 782.

in England a sect, in Pennsylvania a church! While the Society has moved very far in the direction of denominational status, it has also maintained a high degree of tension between the ideal and the actuality of social existence. The Quakers, it may be ventured, have demonstrated the socially creative potentialities of the sectarian impulse, when that impulse is disciplined and enlightened. Stressing, as they do, the sufficiency of the Inner Light for salvation, Quakers resist uniform theological classification. For them theology is, in general, less important than experience. Nevertheless, it is possible for them to participate as members of the National Council of Churches, which would seem to place them in whatever may be defined as the mainstream of American Protestantism.[37]

The most fertile soil of early sectarianism was provided by the colony of Pennsylvania. The broadly tolerant Penn visited the Continent and made contact with numerous dissidents and sectaries. As a result, as early as 1683, there began the series of migrations of German groups fleeing restriction and even persecution in their homeland. Their origins lay in the "Radical Reformation," which in turn owned spiritual affiliations with religious upheavals which had occurred long before Luther made his classic protest. George H. Williams has given the most lucid analysis of this complex radical eruption in the sixteenth century.[38] He refers to Rufus Jones's metaphor of the left wing as a "banyan tree," whose "roots and branches, parent stock and offshoots, are difficult to distinguish." Williams concludes, however, that there were three main branches of the radical Continental revolt: the

[37] It should be recalled, however, that the "Great Separation" of 1827 arose, in effect, precisely from a divergence concerning the normative authority of Scripture and the further theological implications of such authority. Without abandoning their traditional emphasis on the Inner Light, the larger group of Friends chose to follow "the full stream of Protestant, and indeed of Catholic orthodoxy." Cf. W. W. Comfort, *Quakers in the Modern World*, New York, 1952, p. 53.

[38] George Hunston Williams, *Spiritual and Anabaptist Writers*, "The Library of Christian Classics," Vol. xxv, Philadelphia, 1957, pp. 19–35.

Anabaptist, the Spiritualist, and the Evangelical Rationalist. The German sectarians of Pennsylvania were related, in one way or another, to the two former types. According to Williams, "though Anabaptists, Spiritualists, and Evangelical Rationalists differed among themselves as to what constituted the root of faith and order and the ultimate source of divine authority (the New Testament, the Spirit, reason), all three groupings within the Radical Reformation agreed in cutting back to that root and in freeing church and creed of what they regarded as the suffocating growth of ecclesiastical tradition and magisterial prerogative." He distinguishes several modifications of the major radical types, such as the revolutionary, contemplative, and evangelical divisions within the general Anabaptist framework. The distinction of greatest importance for the American scene would seem to lie between the characteristic Anabaptist emphasis on the Bible as the sole norm of religious and social life, and the Spiritualist stress on the centrality of the Holy Spirit, as "superior to any historic record of the work of the Spirit," whether in the form of the Bible or the visible church and its tradition. Williams says that the Anabaptists "looked steadily into the *past*, finding their own image and ecclesiastical blueprints in the Bible and the martyr church of antiquity." The Spiritualists, on the other hand, were mostly oriented toward the future. Some of the latter were moved to attempt a reconstruction of the present evil world by revolutionary means, but more were content to await, passively and hopefully, the consummation of God's purpose, sustained by continuing fellowship in his Spirit.

Not many American sects can be derived simply from either Anabaptist or Spiritualist sources. The lineage of the various Mennonite groups—of which some, at least, are more fairly described as denominations at present—doubtless places them somewhere on the Anabaptist family tree. It may be more accurate to observe that both the Anabaptist and Spiritualist kinds of impulses have throughout American history been blended in particular individuals in particular circumstances, leading to the creation of new—yet not really new—brotherhoods, sects, and communities, as well as of different theological and ethical formulations. The importation of German Pietism in the eighteenth century represented another wave of Bible-and-Spirit-centered religion, constantly seeking a sure sense of salvation and a supramundane personal perfection. More significantly, the succession of revivals since the Great Awakening has kept winds of the Spirit blowing across the nation, resulting not only in the revitalization of entrenched denominations but also in the recurrent stimulation of secession and new beginnings. It is seldom easy to understand why the numerous new movements have arisen when and where they did—"the Spirit bloweth where it listeth." We do know that they have been able to get a foothold at all because of the favorable conditions of geography and political rule which originally obtained on this continent. We know, too, that the radical sectarians have contributed in a major way to the American acceptance of individualism and voluntarism as basic principles of religious relationship. It is further apparent that some types of sects have tended to survive and usually to develop into denominations, while other types have in general tended to pass into oblivion within a generation or two. It is a thesis of this essay that the survivors have been those types, *exceptis excipiendis,* which have been firmly yet flexibly based on the Biblical tradition, and which have shown concern for an exigent present, as well as for a hallowed past or an idealized future. Unless the sectarian impulses are disciplined and made relevant to the whole range of human needs, they run into triviality and disillusionment. On the other hand, unless the churches are periodically re-energized and purified by sectarian impulses, they lose the vision of authentic religion and become the more or less sacred tools of merely secular interests. The churches or denominations may not be able to live always comfortably with the sects, but they can seldom live in integrity without them.

One is tempted to linger over several of the more exotic forms of German sectarianism which appeared briefly in colonial Pennsylvania. A fascinating footnote in American religious history is provided by Johannes Kelpius, who in 1694 led a few devoted followers to a quasi-monastic settlement on the Wissahickon near Philadelphia. Kelpius professed himself a "true Rosicrucian," who proposed to "put into practical operation the mystic and occult dogmas studied in secret for many previous ages." [39] The community was known variously as "The Contented of the God-Loving Soul" and "The Woman in the Wilderness." Kelpius' curious amalgam of occult mysticism, apocalypticism, and ethical perfectionism did not attract many disciples, and the community became extinct soon after his death. The Ephrata colony, founded by Conrad Beissel in 1728, on only slightly less eccentric principles, enjoyed a somewhat longer life span. It is noteworthy, nevertheless, that movements of the same kind, expressing a rejection of the present corrupt world and an urge for transcendental perfection, have repeatedly sprung up, even in activist, pragmatic, optimistic America. That any neat socio-economic theory of motivation can explain them is highly dubious. They may represent, instead, deep impulses of the human spirit as it undergoes the perennial tension between the ideal and the actual. Most persons are content to deal with this tension by less extreme means, as religious developments in so limited an area as colonial Pennsylvania indicate. Other German and Swiss sectarians, Baptists and Pietists, sought havens of freedom there and found the opportunity of implementing their peculiar tenets. Their peculiarities, however, were clearly Biblical in origin, centering on such items as pacifism, plain dress, ritual foot-washing and love feasts, extreme laicism, and abstention from worldly amusements and technological improvements. In their striving for spiritual and ethical perfection the German sectarians

[39] Julius F. Sachse, *The German Sectarians of Pennsylvania, 1708–1742*, Vol. I, Philadelphia, 1899, I, 6ff.

frequently found themselves at odds with the unregenerate secular society "outside," and accordingly generated separate communities, after the example of Kelpius and Beissel. The succession of such communal experiments reaches into the twentieth century: Peter Lehman and Snowhill, the Rappites, the Separatists of Zoar, the Amana Society, William Keil and his establishments at Bethel and Aurora, and the Bruderhof or Hutterian communities, among others. The Amana Society and the Hutterian brotherhoods still exist, although walking at all times an unsteady tightrope between religious perfection and secular involvement. While maintaining their aloofness from society at large, the Hutterites have become so economically dynamic that at least one state has passed legislation to restrict their land holdings. The major Mennonite, Brethren, and Moravian groups, on the other hand, have more and more made their peace with American society, until they can only with difficulty be distinguished from their more churchly Christian colleagues. Brethren and Moravian groups, indeed, hold membership in the National Council of Churches.

VI

In addition to immigration and the transplantation of European sects, other major forces promoting religious divisiveness in colonial America were the Great Awakening and the comprehensive revivalistic impulse which it set in motion. We may remark, parenthetically, that since the early eighteenth century revivalism has been endemic in American Protestantism. That impulse has been expressed in various degrees of intensity and ubiquity, yet it has never been entirely absent from the American scene, and it has left its mark on the structure and ideas of every Protestant body. The Great Awakening was actually one of several spiritual upheavals which occurred both here and in Germany and England. Nelson Burr demonstrates that the leading revivalists in the Middle Colonies and New England had relations with spokesmen for Pietism, the movement which had earlier roused large sections of the German churches from formalism and spiritual lethargy.[40] Further, simultaneously with the stirrings of the revival spirit on this continent, the Wesleys were prosecuting their mission in England, and George Whitefield became the indefatigable link between the colonies and the mother country.

As in other significant mass movements, the causes and effects of the Great Awakening cannot be simply assessed. History does not support the thesis that the Awakening took its rise among the disinherited of society, or that it was primarily a democratic movement paving the way for a political revolution before the end of the century. The disinherited may have received it gladly, and by it the American mind may have been further prepared for the momentous decisions of 1776, yet the Awakening itself was directly motivated by religious concern. Indirectly, the economic success of the Puritan experiment and the accommodation of original Puritan ideals to the ways of the world did have their effects on religious vitality. Perry Miller has minutely described the "jeremiads" in which the New England clergy berated the indifference and wickedness of their parishioners.[41] But the churches themselves were not unaffected: "as religion became more institutional and less personal, more a product of instruction than of experience, and more an affair of the intellect than of the emotions, piety waned." [42] So it was that "gales of heavenly wind" began to blow over New England, as earlier they had blown with renewing vigor over the Middle Colonies. These winds blew upon all classes of society, in settled areas and on the frontier, on intellectuals and religious primitivists. All of New England was not

[40] Cf. Vol. IV, Part Two, sect. III, A.

[41] Perry Miller, *The New England Mind: From Colony to Province,* Cambridge, 1953, ch. II.

[42] Edwin Scott Gaustad, *The Great Awakening in New England,* New York, 1957, p. 14.

converted, nor did all the clergy regard the Awakening as a true work of God. Its effects were confusingly ambiguous, certainly in respect to theological change. Perhaps we can best summarize those effects by saying that it gave impetus to the accelerated development of tendencies already at work in America. The sect or denominational pattern definitely triumphed in the Awakening and its after-effects; the dominance of Calvinism in New England was seriously challenged, giving opportunity for the free growth of both Arminianism and the philosophy of the Enlightenment; pietism, with its emotional and perfectionist emphases, became a pervasive element of the American religious mentality. In broader cultural terms the Awakening meant, as Perry Miller writes, "the end of the reign over the New England and American mind of a European and scholastical conception of an authority put over men because men were incapable of recognizing their own welfare." [43] From the Awakening the principles of religious individualism and religious voluntarism became ever more solidly entrenched in the American scheme of things, and the transference of these principles to the political order was the inevitable concomitant. The democratization of religion went hand-in-hand with the extension of political responsibility to the masses of Americans.

The pattern of revivalism continued to be the most striking characteristic of American religious development for the next century following the Great Awakening. It was probably inevitable that it should be so, since revivalism is merely a particular mode of evangelism, and free churches in a pluralistic society must rely on evangelistic techniques if they are to survive and grow. To be sure, the eighteenth century witnessed many debates about the legitimacy and usefulness of revivalistic methods in securing religious commitment, and that particular debate has been carried on even until the present. The issue of revivalism has split the

[43] Perry Miller, *Errand into the Wilderness*, Cambridge, 1957, p. 166.

Presbyterians at least twice, although in each instance problems of deeper theological import were at stake. Attitudes and ideas brought to expression by revivalism have caused schisms in other denominations, as well, and the general religious atmosphere fostered by revivalistic enthusiasm has encouraged the emergence of a few radical movements sharply at variance with traditional Christianity. Let us look at these matters in order.

Not much needs to be said here about the effects of the successive waves of revivalism prior to the Civil War on the conservative churches of Calvinistic leanings. It has been noted that the grip of strict Calvinism was loosened among Congregationalists and Presbyterians. This trend, begun in the Great Awakening, was carried further in subsequent periods of revivalism, causing many bitter theological battles along the way. In theological terms, revivalism implies a more Arminian than Calvinistic doctrine of human nature, not in any minimizing of human sinfulness, but in a recognition of man's capacity to respond freely to God's grace. The thrust of revivalism is away from deterministic views of the human will, in the direction of both man's freedom and his perfectibility. A paradox is seen in the fact that the Calvinistic churches were seedbeds of the Great Awakening and figured prominently in subsequent revivalism, furnishing some of the most successful preachers of revival, from Jonathan Edwards through Charles Finney to Billy Sunday. However, Calvinists have agonized in their efforts to retain a degree of theological consistency and at the same time to utilize the method of mass appeal. As Sweet points out, the Calvinists characteristically addressed themselves to "those well grounded in the correct doctrines of Christianity," a strategy which was not calculated to reach large numbers of probably unpredestined sinners.[44] By contrast, Baptists, Methodists, Disciples, and Cumberland Presbyterians directed their gospel to the "great mass of

[44] William Warren Sweet, *Religion in the Development of American Culture, 1765–1840*, New York, 1952, p. 148.

religious illiterates," who always are more numerous than the educated, not least so in rural and frontier America of the eighteenth and nineteenth century. Further, the Calvinism of the spectacular revivalist Presbyterian and Congregational preachers, after Edwards at any rate, was suspect, if not non-existent. In spite of the Presbyterian origins or affiliations of Finney, Moody and Sunday, these men were not Calvinistic by any reasonable definition of the word. In any event, by the middle of the nineteenth century those churches which had been dominant a century earlier—Congregationalists, Presbyterians, Episcopalians, Lutherans, and Reformed—had quantitatively lagged far behind the denominations which could employ the revivalistic method without theological, liturgical, ethnic, educational, or temperamental reservations. Nevertheless, the revival impulse was one of the forces making for a "loosening" in the theological structure of the Calvinist churches, so that even the Presbyterians, by the middle of the nineteenth century, had been strongly permeated by more lenient ideas of man's role in the process of salvation.

Baptists and Methodists, on the contrary, were the chief gainers from the surges of revivalism. Other factors helped these groups in their remarkable growth: theological simplicity, lack of emotional inhibition, an optimistic view of the possibilities of man and society, and minimal institutional rigidity. As the frontier pushed steadily westward, preachers of the revivalistic type were able to follow the settlers and to provide the religious excitement, unsophisticated confrontation, and emotional release which uprooted migrants seem so often to need. It is estimated that by 1855 the Methodists and Baptists accounted for nearly 70 per cent of the total number of Protestant church members in the country.[45] There were nearly twice as many Methodists as the combined

[45] Timothy L. Smith, *Revivalism and Social Reform*, New York and Nashville, 1957, p. 22.

number of Presbyterians, Congregationalists, and Episcopalians. Although the Methodists were distributed among ten separate bodies, all groups were identifiably Methodist. Baptists were about two thirds as numerous as Methodists, being at that time divided among seven bodies. In 1955 the relative position of Methodists and Baptists was the reverse, with Baptists claiming half again as many members as the other group. The two families together, however, include approximately half of all Protestants in the United States. And it is significant that both these groups have kept the revivalistic tradition vigorously alive throughout their history. On the debit side, that tradition has continued to cause numerous fragmentations of both families. Nevertheless, it has never ceased to be a dynamic means of propagating Christianity, and the present statistical superiority of Baptists over Methodists may be due to their more consistent and enthusiastic practice of the method, especially in the South. In any case, while revivalism brought new currents into the main stream of American Protestantism, it remained reasonably well within the existing channels of religious grouping. Only one sect which grew to be a major denomination was born during the flurry of revivals. That is the Disciples of Christ, and from the start it was about as distinctively "American" as any religious group can be. Certainly it was never in any serious respect a deviant from the Biblical norm, nor has it ever sought to separate itself from either the American society or the community of Protestant orthodoxy.

VII

The real impact of revivalism is not to be measured in membership statistics or the number of new religious groups which it has historically brought into being. Rather, its significance lies in what Stow Persons has called "the spirit of evangelical revivalism," the ideas, attitudes, feelings, dreams, and hopes which revivalism helped to disseminate and to be expressed among the American people.[46] No new ideas, in the absolute sense of newness, were generated by the revivalists, but the movement helped to produce climates of opinion differing in important ways from what had previously been characteristic of the American mind. This it did in connection with other elements in America, such as the existence of a frontier with apparently unlimited possibilities of geographical expansion, and conditions of religious and political freedom, coupled with a high degree of economic and social mobility. Here, as probably nowhere else or ever in Christendom, people had the opportunity of implementing and institutionalizing various particular religious emphases, most of which were as ancient as the Bible itself.

We may identify at least four such emphases which revivalism tended to express and encourage. First, there was the emphasis on direct inspiration and religious emotionalism. The aim of the revivalist preacher was always to stimulate an immediate confrontation of the sinner by God. Such confrontation could have various results: the warmed heart of a Wesley, oddly ecstatic speech and movement, the conviction of mystical illumination or even of new revelation. These are the experiences of the Spiritualist, the Quaker, the Pietist, but revivalism made them common currency among the masses. Another emphasis which figured prominently concerned perfect sanctification as a possible, even necessary state of the converted individual. This, too, is a very ancient notion, with support in the teachings of Jesus and the Johannine letters of the New Testament, and is a haunting theme in all Christian history. There have always been Christians with an intense "hunger for a higher, holier life" and, what is more, who believe that a life free from sin

---

[46] Donald Drew Egbert and Stow Persons, eds., *Socialism and American Life*, 2 vols., Princeton, 1952, I, 128. Persons' essay is entitled "Christian Communitarianism in America."

can be achieved, with God's help, here and now. This was a persuasive element in the religion of John Wesley, and the theme was elaborated with variations in most of the great revivals. A third emphasis lay on universalism, the possibility and perhaps also the probability of salvation for all. The immediate reference of this conception in the eighteenth- and early nineteenth-century setting was anti-Calvinistic, but it had positive implications, also, in the context of the openness and expansiveness of American society. The fourth emphasis which contributed to a characteristic climate of opinion was the millenarian expectation of the return of Christ and thereby the resolution of all evil and conflict. This, again, is a basic Christian doctrine, confessed by all the orthodox, yet capable of divergent interpretations, and frequently disruptive of religious and social unity.

The most illuminating study of the manner in which the spirit of evangelical revivalism, with its distinctive emphases, affected the subsequent development of religion in America has been made by Whitney R. Cross. In his exhaustive investigation of the "Burned-Over District" of western New York State during the period 1800–1850, Cross shows that the area was a microcosm of virtually every religious excess which arose in the United States prior to the Civil War. After 1850 industrialization and accelerated urbanization provided new conditions for social and religious development, yet the tendencies observable in the earlier period carried on into the later. With careful documentation Cross demonstrates how the social, economic, and political conditions of the area and the period, in combination with the peculiar temperaments of the inhabitants and the campaigns of enthusiastic preachers, combined to generate some of the most spectacular forms of religious radicalism ever seen in this country: "Upon this broad belt of land congregated a people extraordinarily given to unusual beliefs, peculiarly devoted to crusades aimed at the perfection of mankind and the attainment of millennial happiness. Few of the enthusiasms or eccentricities of this generation failed to find exponents here." [47] The characteristic attitude permeating the period has been called "ultraism," which connotes a passionate idealism, usually concentrated on some particular reforming cause as the panacea for all human ills.[48] The ultraistic attitude produced a multitude of crusades—abolition, temperance, women's rights, and the like. For the most, perhaps, ultraism took an individualistic turn, so that the existing denominations were able to absorb it, although their theologies and objectives were greatly modified in the process. On the other hand, erratic movements did arise and found air to breathe in the climate of the period. From a neutral perspective, the radical movements seem to have deviated from normative Christianity by carrying to quite logical extremes the particular emphases nourished by evangelical revivalism. It will not do to place all excesses and eccentricities at the door of revivalism, yet it is significant that as the vigor of the Second Awakening was gradually dissipated, the more radical religious movements tended also to wither away. Mormonism, of course, offers the exception, but by 1850 the Mormons had withdrawn themselves, temporarily, from the mainstream of American culture.

Although particular radical sects and cults may be analyzed in terms of some dominating motif or idea, it is also true that historically each has been characterized by a blending of such motifs. In the case of some of the most deviant types, however, one basic causal factor is usually present: an inspired leader whose personality and teaching provide the core of adherence. This statement is a truism, no doubt, since every movement, religious or secular, must be initiated by someone, and usually a single dominating personality furnishes the requisite guidance and élan. In religious movements the problem of the leader or founder may be an

[47] Whitney R. Cross, *The Burned-Over District*, Ithaca, 1950, p. 3.
[48] A less scholarly but more entertaining account of ultraist extravagances is given by Gilbert Seldes, *The Stammering Century*, New York, 1927.

especially delicate one, because the temptation to personal idolization is always strong. In the atmosphere of evangelical revivalism, with its encouragement not only of uninhibited emotionalism but also of direct communication with Deity, this temptation was especially strong. As Thomas O'Dea suggests, the progression "from such inner guides of truth understood in terms of the general framework of the Christian tradition to idiosyncratic interpretation outside that tradition" was all too easily made under the conditions of revivalistic freedom in America.[49] Such a departure is observed clearly in the career of Mother Ann Lee. However objectionable to Christian orthodoxy may be Shaker theology in general, the line between Shakerism and traditional Christianity was drawn most decisively in the strange doctrine which identified Ann Lee as the female Christ, to whom is due the same honor hitherto accorded Jesus. A claim of this magnitude has been made for few other persons in America. A contemporary counterpart to Mother Ann is Father Divine, who is acclaimed by his followers as "King of the Universe, God Almighty, Source of Salvation, King of Peace, Power House of Redemption, the Almighty, the Holy Magnetic Body of God," and many other equally grandiose appellations.[50]

Less drastic claims were made by and for Joseph Smith, Jr. While no aura of divinity as such was attached to him, he was and is regarded by the Mormons as a unique recipient of revelation, a revelation that both interprets and supplements the canonical Bible, and without which the Biblical exposition of salvation is incomplete. Insofar, Mormonism resembles Islam, in which Mohammed is venerated as a prophet and not as a divinity. Mormonism, to be sure, contains polytheistic doctrines which further widen the breach between it and the historic churches, but the Book of Mormon alone was sufficient to raise an unscalable wall between the

[49] Thomas F. O'Dea, *The Mormons*, Chicago, 1957, p. 12.
[50] Mayer, p. 545.

Mormons and the religion of the American majority. Other prophets and visionaries have announced themselves in America, pretending to offer new revelations of the truth and purpose of God. Soon after Mother Ann set the style, Jemima Wilkinson, inaugurator of the Community of the Universal Friend, was accredited with prophetic powers, although the records do not clearly indicate that she herself made the claim. Cross lists several minor prophets of his chosen period —an anonymous ex-officer of the British army who gathered a following in Vermont and Massachusetts in the 1790's; a man named Winchell and his disciple, Oliver Cowdery, in Vermont before the War of 1812; Matthias, who enjoyed a brief notoriety in New York in the 1830's. All spiritualist and mystical movements verge in the direction of extra-Biblical revelation, but usually the new revelations are kept in spoken form rather than in a written canon. A curious aberration of the late nineteenth century was the Shalam group in New Mexico, which was supposed to base itself on a mysterious scripture called "Oahopee." [51] In general, however, it may be said that the radical sectarian leaders who have adhered to the Bible at all have been characteristically distinguished by their vagaries of interpretation of that book, vagaries arising either from a peculiar approach to the Bible or from mystical illumination concerning its meaning. The Book of Mormon remains the only important second Bible produced in this country.

VIII

Any survey of revivalism and its effects must recognize that the two emphases which it most dynamically stimulated were the desire for absolute perfection and the millenarian view of divine-human history. The first aim of the revivalist preacher is to bring about the conversion of sinners. In the

[51] William A. Hinds, *American Communities and Co-operative Colonies*, 2nd rev. ed., Chicago, 1908, pp. 452–455.

usual context of revivalism "conversion" means vastly more than a change of intellectual conviction; what is demanded is a metamorphosis of the whole personality, so that the sinner becomes truly sanctified, freed from the power of sin. This is an altogether orthodox view of things, justified by countless Biblical texts. Difficulty often arises, nevertheless, when this conception of spiritual transformation is understood apart from certain qualifications which the New Testament makes. The writers of the New Testament have, for the most, no illusions about the possibility of any particular human being's (regenerated or not) living an absolutely perfect life in the present world order. The summons to perfection is set in the context of Biblical eschatology: the achievement of perfect sanctification belongs to the Kingdom which is already present in some manner, yet whose consummation lies beyond history. The Biblical doctrine of perfection implies the paradox of "is" and "is yet to be." Post-Biblical perfectionists have characteristically stressed the "is" at the expense of the "is yet to be," striving immediately to close the gap between the actual and the ideal. Christian history has been sprinkled with sincere zealots who have wished to enter the Kingdom without delay, and with the rise of the revivalist spirit America acquired its share of similar zealots. All who put great emphasis on the direct and immediate work of the Holy Spirit in the regenerated incline toward perfectionism. This was true of the early Quakers and of the Wesleyan movement at its inception. Methodism as a whole has kept the perfectionist impulse under control, sometimes to the point where it seemed to be lost. Thus, of the more than fifty extant bodies which E. T. Clark calls perfectionist, a majority rose from Methodism, in many instances retaining the Methodist name. Allied in spirit with perfectionist groups are the Pentecostal movements, which cultivate the charismatic "gifts" of the Spirit, such as speaking with tongues and healing. This emphasis in religion, probably more than any other, seems to have had attraction for the socially and economically disinherited, as studies by

J. B. Holt and Walter Muelder have shown.[52] In any case, both perfectionism and pentecostalism have given birth to radical religious movements throughout American history, from the ecstatic phenomena of the Great Awakening to the latest outbreak of snake-handling in some mountain hinterland of the South.

From the Puritan period to the present, millenarian ideas have exerted powerful influence on American religious and social thought. I. V. Brown has referred to millenarianism as "part of the cultural baggage which the Puritan brought from England to America." [53] It is surely much more than that, however, since eschatology stands at the heart of the message of the New Testament. The Apostles' Creed, the most widely accepted formulation of Biblical faith, states that Christ "will come to judge the quick and the dead." This is terse shorthand for a complex of hopes which the Bible expresses in vivid, often fantastic, symbols. The common meaning of the hopes is plain: the present evil world must be purged and transformed according to God's purpose and through his intervention; human history cannot fulfill itself but must await a decisive and final deliverance by God; Jesus Christ will return to complete his work of salvation, begun in Palestine so many centuries ago. This has not been an easy faith for Christians to hold, yet it has been a persistent one, especially in times of social collapse. Moreover, the myths of the End in the Bible are sufficiently ambiguous that no single, universally received interpretation has been attainable. The very ambiguity of the Biblical presentation of the matter has made it possible for Christians with a sense of responsibility for society to subordi-

---

[52] J. B. Holt, "Holiness Religion: Cultural Shock and Social Reorganization," *American Sociological Review*, 5, no. 5, October 1940, pp. 740–747; Walter Muelder, "From Sect to Church," *Christendom*, Autumn, 1945, pp. 450–462.

[53] I. V. Brown, "Watchers for the Second Coming: The Millennial Tradition in America," *Mississippi Valley Historical Review*, 39, December 1952, p. 444.

nate the apocalyptic hope to other less catastrophic conceptions of human duty and destiny. Nevertheless, the eschatological element, particularly as articulated in the Book of Revelation, has appealed to religious extremists in every age, providing materials for the most bizarre speculations.

Biblical millenarianism can be viewed in several ways. The premillenarian position assumes that the world must grow (by divine intention) steadily worse, until God's patience is exhausted, and Christ comes to defeat his enemies, human and supernatural, as a prelude to the start of the new and perfect age. This was, in effect, the belief of William Miller and his numerous followers, and it has survived in the Adventist groups and among the Jehovah's Witnesses, as well as among many other fundamentalists, some of whom remain in the denominations of the center. Wherever such a belief may be found, it is essentially a counsel of despair, so far as the amelioration of evils in the present world is concerned. Fortunately for the stability of society, not many premillenarians go to the quite logical extreme of Miller and his more credulous disciples, who reportedly sold their property and awaited the coming of the Lord on a specific day, October 22, 1844.

The most consistently apocalyptical of contemporary millenarian groups is the Watchtower Society of the Jehovah's Witnesses, which traces its lineage more or less directly from the Millerites through "Pastor" Charles T. Russell and "Judge" Joseph F. Rutherford. The Society—which militantly eschews the label of "church" and claims to be the only authentic "Christianity" in contrast with the mere "religion" of all other Christian bodies—is a real sect, in both the theological and the sociological meanings of the word. Intransigently Biblical in their formulation of doctrine (and doctrine is all-important; there is little of emotion in the Witness assemblies), the Witnesses believe that Christ "came" spiritually and invisibly in 1914, to inaugurate the final act of the cosmic drama. The millennial kingdom already exists for those who know the truth; within two decades, at the most, the predicted (Revelation 16:16) Battle of Armageddon will be fought and the absolute theocracy will be established "on earth as it is in heaven," publicly and irresistibly. The Witnesses reject the trappings of ecclesiasticism and regard all post-Biblical developments of Christianity as sinful repudiations of Jehovah's sovereignty. They have no concern for political action or social amelioration. Although they have made no effort to form isolated communities, they have a class conflict view of present society and foresee the violent overthrow, under Satan's leadership, of every human government. While refusing to salute the flag or to participate in the pointless wars between doomed nations, they are in other respects law-abiding citizens. Few other groups have so neatly solved the problem of remaining "in" secular society without also being "of" it. In 1958 some 200,000 Witnesses from every continent gathered in New York to reaffirm their loyalty to Jehovah, offering a demonstration of strength which only the Mormons among American sects could hope to equal. The astounding growth of the sect, together with the obvious prosperity of its members, leads some observers to surmise that it has already begun the evolution into denominational status. If the confidently voiced predictions of the climactic struggle at Armageddon within the next two decades are disappointed, the process of accommodation to the orthodox pattern may be accelerated. If one may look to the past for a model, the primitive Christian community, ardently apocalyptic at the outset, almost unconsciously developed the modus vivendi of the Catholic cultus, theology, and discipline in response to the frustration of millennial hopes. It is not inconceivable that the Witnesses will follow suit. The several Adventist denominations, certainly, have so far compromised the logic of their millenarianism that they engage in programs of medical missions and humanitarian relief, support a growing educational system, and in general share in the life of the whole community. Meanwhile, the global wars and other social catastrophes of the twentieth century have stimulated a new interest in the premillennial view of history, and the doctrine is being discussed even in the ecumenical councils. The most ardent and literalistic espousal of the view, nevertheless, continues to remain in the pentecostal and adventist sects, which flourish in greater number at mid-century than ever before in American history.

Whereas premillennialism, strictly construed, implies a proximate pessimism about the world and human society, other modes of millennial thinking take a more optimistic attitude toward the human enterprise. The postmillennial view assumes that an era of perfect peace, justice, and goodness must occur *before* the return of Christ. This variation on the millenarian theme attracted many in the eighteenth century and accorded well with ideas of human progress toward perfection. Timothy Dwight of Yale anticipated that the millennium would begin around A.D. 2000, and that it would come to pass "not by miracles, but by means." [54] The major denominations of America, even though their official creedal statements may sometimes seem to give support to a premillennial theology, have by and large functioned on postmillennial or non-millennial assumptions. The visible return of Christ in judgment remains a "far-off divine event" for them, and during the interim they move actively into the world, not only to convert individual souls, but also to reorder society according to the will of God. In point of fact, millennialism of any sort does not figure prominently in the thought of the socially adjusted churches of the present. The case was somewhat different in the revival upheavals of the early nineteenth century. Timothy L. Smith writes that "revivalism and perfectionism became socially volatile only when combined with the doctrine of Christ's imminent conquest of the earth." [55] This explosive amalgam of *idées fixes* resulted in part in

[54] Brown, p. 449.
[55] Smith, p. 228.

moral crusades, and Smith, indeed, finds the origins of the Social Gospel movement in the revivals which occurred before the Civil War.[56]

IX

The most radical effects, however, of the blending of perfectionism and the millennial hope are to be seen in several communitarian movements which flourished for a time in the age of the frontier and the revivals. Religious communism has a long history in Christianity. The Acts of the Apostles relates that the earliest apostolic community in Jerusalem "had all things in common," and this has provided precedent for subsequent experiments in communal living. Further, the ideal of absolute perfection is difficult to sustain by individual effort within a non-perfect society, so that extreme perfectionists have often sought to create favorable conditions by withdrawal into separate communities. A. T. Mollegen relates the American religious communitarians to a venerable tradition, stretching back at least to Plato, which has sought to transcend "the particularity [of human existence] which in the Bible is accepted as a divinely willed creaturehood, the limits of which only sin oversteps." [57] This particularity has characteristically been located in human sexuality and in private property. The transcendence of sexual particularity has been attempted in two very different ways, the one approach emphasizing rigorous celibacy, while the other road has led in the direction of some kind of promiscuity. Both approaches have been employed in the quasi-monastic expressions of American radical perfectionism.

Previously noted were some relatively short-lived experiments in communitarian isolation made by the Dutch Laba-

[56] Smith's point is disputed by Bernard Weisberger, *They Gathered at the River*, Boston, 1958, p. 308. The latter says that "the benevolent associations of revivalism were aimed entirely at the conversion of individuals, after which it was expected that social improvement would be automatic."

[57] Egbert and Persons, eds., I, 113.

dists, Johannes Kelpius, and the Ephrata community. Sporadic immigration of such communal groups from Germany, in particular, continued into the nineteenth century, and the Amana Society and the Hutterite Brotherhoods survive as examples of this type of imported sectarianism. Revivalism, however, began to create the appropriately receptive climate of opinion for more indigenous movements in the late eighteenth century. It was in 1774 that Ann Lee and her eight companions reached New York and within a few years set about building their own version of the Kingdom of God on earth, in preparation for the comprehensive Kingdom yet to be fully realized. Although Ann Lee was an import, her following was drawn from among native Americans and became the outstanding example of religious communitarianism based solidly on perfectionist and millennial ideas. As we have remarked, certain theological extravagances of the Shakers,[58] as well as their perfectionist repudiation of the normal sexual relationship, were sufficient to debar them from the main stream of American religion. Their peculiar version of millennialism, however, had strong affinities with the burgeoning self-consciousness of the American people and the fervent expectation of future progress toward a perfect society on this continent. Ann Lee herself had said, "I knew that God had a chosen people in America." Her followers were confident that the appearance of Mother Ann was the Second Coming of Christ, so that his kingdom on earth had actually been inaugurated in their Society. This was altogether in the mood of American "Manifest Destiny," although the Shaker movement itself was fated to die as a result of its theological oddities and its social separateness. With other theological premises it might have survived as a monastic vestigium within a larger, more world-affirming church. In its chosen role of autonomous church, however, it was unable to stay

---

[58] Mayer, p. 445, comments: "They deny every specific Christian doctrine —the deity of Christ, the authority of the Scriptures, the Trinity, the vicarious atonement, and the resurrection of the body."

alive in a dynamic society. Nevertheless, it is noteworthy that the Shakers attracted new members so long as the fervor of rural revivalism reigned, down to the beginning of the Civil War. By 1874 the few remaining "families" of Shakers were driven to advertise for new members, and at present Shakerism is remembered more for its distinctive handicraft than for its religious ideology.

Of the scores of communitarian experiments, both religious and secular, which sprouted in the nineteenth century none was more typically "American" than the Oneida Community headed by John Humphrey Noyes. Noyes himself was a product of the Finney revivals and embraced the characteristic emphases of revivalistic fervor. Regeneration, perfection, inspiration, and millennialism all figure prominently in his thought. But he passed beyond the atomistic individualism of most revivalists and perceived the inescapably social nature of religion. As he wrote in retrospect: "The Revivalists had for their great idea the regeneration of the soul. The great idea of the Socialists was the regeneration of society, which is the soul's environment." [59] His theology was a potpourri of ideas relating to the possibility of human sinlessness, the superiority of Spirit-inspired love over static moral law, and the progressive realization of the Kingdom of God in this world. Coupled with his religious zeal was a Yankee shrewdness in mundane affairs, which was reflected in the economic productivity of the Oneida Community. Recognizing clearly the difficulty of achieving a balance between freedom and order in communal experiments, he sought to resolve the persistent Christian dilemma of being both "in" and "out of" the world by creating conditions favorable to individual perfection without rejecting participation in normal human concerns. Life at Oneida was world-affirming, and not a repressive asceticism.

Although the pragmatic and non-esoteric character of Noyes's project was more congenial to the American temper than were the mystical, ascetic forms of religious communism,

[59] J. H. Noyes, *History of American Socialisms*, Philadelphia, 1870, p. 24.

the nation was not receptive to his tampering with sex and family mores—perhaps he affirmed too much in regard to natural human impulses! Whereas the naïve celibacy of the Shakers could be dismissed as a socially innocuous eccentricity, the apparent—and partly misconstrued—encouragement to promiscuity by Noyes stirred up violent hostility among "respectable" Americans. By 1879 Noyes, who had already withdrawn from active leadership of Oneida, felt compelled to defer to public sentiment, and the system of complex marriage was abandoned. Within two years the principle of economic communism was similarly repudiated, and the colony became a joint-stock company. It is an ironic turn of fate that a brand of silver-plated cutlery remains as the chief monument to a high-minded dream of sinlessness and of an actualized Kingdom of God on earth. This was due not so much to specific failures of Noyes and his coterie of Christian socialists as to the general abatement of revivalist and millennial enthusiasm in post-Civil War America. As urban and industrial expansion was accelerated, popular revivalism accommodated itself ever more individualistically to the prevailing patterns of society, while ardent religious idealists found more relevance in the Social Gospel than in the isolated regenerate community awaiting either the beginning or the end of the millennium.

X

The revivalist impulse stimulated a wide variety of curious movements, but none was more curious in its origin than the new faith "revealed" to the world by Joseph Smith, Jr. This semi-literate son of unstable New England parents passed his formative years in the Burned-over region of New York State and, as it later appeared, absorbed much from the maelstrom of religious excitement which swirled through that area. No merely naturalistic explanation of his religious achievements is wholly satisfactory: neither neurosis nor avarice nor sensuality suffices to account for the book he produced or for the loyalty which he inspired in great numbers of people, not all of them simpletons by any means. His was indeed a "grandiose illusion," comparable (from the point of view of "normal" folk) to the pretensions of Ann Lee or Father Divine. But, as Gilbert Seldes has suggested,[60] the abnormalities of Smith were relevantly connected with normal life, so that a powerful religious community could base itself on his message, a community which after more than a century shows no signs of serious disintegration.

The precise place of Mormonism in the American religious spectrum is not, however, easily assessed. In origin it was a sectarian deviation of the most radical kind. In its mature development, on the other hand, it embodies the ideological and sociological characteristics of a church.[61] One may reasonably maintain that no other sizable religious group in this country, not even Roman Catholicism or Orthodox Judaism, has so effectively blended religious and secular elements of life into a coherent ethos. The Mormon scheme of values is still culturally potent, despite the encroachments of secular and "gentile" influences. The Mormons early drew a boundary between themselves and the American community as a whole, and this was a prime cause of their recurrent difficulties at Kirtland, Independence, Far West, Nauvoo, and in Utah. Nevertheless, as has so often happened in religious history, they thrived on persecution and were able finally to establish a more enduring society than were the intransigently utopian enclaves of the German communitarians, the Shakers, or even of the mellower Oneida perfectionists. The Saints built a church which was—and to a significant degree still is—also a "regional culture area." In O'Dea's apt phrase, they avoided "sectarian stagnation," partly by deliberate plan, it may be, but partly by what the Mormons themselves can only describe

---

[60] Seldes, pp. xiii–xvi.

[61] Thomas F. O'Dea, "Mormonism and the Avoidance of Sectarian Stagnation: A Study of Church, Sect, and Incipient Nationality," *American Journal of Sociology*, LX, no. 3, November 1954, pp. 285–293.

as the "providential" aid of favoring historical circumstances. Social ferment, revivalistic enthusiasm, and an open frontier collaborated to make success possible for people with the Mormon kind of faith, courage, and practical ingenuity. No other nineteenth-century group, orthodox or deviant, was able to discipline the peculiar vitalities of that century in so comprehensive a religio-social structure.

The historical evolution of the Mormons furnishes the most thrilling chapter in the whole chronicle of American religion. By comparison, the adventures of the settlers in New England seem tame. It is noteworthy, however, that Puritans and Mormons followed the same star of hope and aspiration: both aimed to build the Kingdom of God in America, to establish Zion in the wilderness. Of the two groups, the Mormons more nearly attained the ideal, at least in terms of their own conception of what the Kingdom could and should be. The brigades fired by Smith's faith and guided by Brigham Young's iron will outstripped their foes, mastered hostile nature, and fashioned a genuine theocracy which ruled a numerous multitude for nearly half a century, certainly down to the acquisition of statehood. It required no outlandish stretching of the pious imagination to find the telling analogy to their saga in the Hebrew Exodus: out of bondage they were led by a Moses and a Joshua through wilderness and war into a Promised Land; they were a Chosen People, in possession of a new Law, and commissioned by Almighty God himself to create the perfect society in a recalcitrant world—and ultimately to convert that world to their own scheme of things. In the Mormon perspective, Palmyra was no less numinous than Sinai, and Deseret came to rival Jerusalem in splendor. Joseph Smith had not been an utter madman when he revealed that the locale of the Biblical *Heilsgeschichte* had been transferred from Palestine to America. The events of nineteenth-century Mormon history seemed to give very tangible corroboration of the prophecy.

From the theological point of view, the Mormon system

of thought is at once an irreconcilable Christian heresy and the most typically American theology yet formulated on this continent. It probably never occurred to Joseph Smith that he was anything but a Christian, just as Paul of Tarsus never considered himself an apostate from the form of religion which God intended that Israel should embrace. In both instances, however, were present factors which irresistibly caused separation from the parent group. The analogy between early Christianity and Mormonism is indeed striking: each claimed to offer, not simply a variant interpretation of an existing canon, but a new revelation and a new series of crucially redemptive events. Thus, even as the New Testament both presupposes the Old Testament and fulfills it, so the Book of Mormon and its subsidiary documents present a revelation *beyond* the Christian Bible. To be sure, the Bible (especially certain portions of the Old Testament) is the point of departure for the Mormon revelation, yet the latter embodies a different faith, with related but demonstrably incongruous conceptions of God, man, history, the *ordo salutis,* and final human destiny.

Bernard DeVoto has remarked that Mormon theology was "a great catch basin of evangelical doctrine. Everything ever preached by any Protestant heresy in America, celibacy excepted, was at one time or another preached if not adopted in Mormonry." [62] By whatever process he may have absorbed them, Joseph Smith certainly did manage to give expression to various common themes of Protestant revivalism—millennialism, perfectionism, synergism, among others—and insofar his message had immediate appeal for people who were already conditioned to respond to such themes. But certain of Smith's basic points of doctrine—the polytheizing of deity, the prospective deification of man, the total repudiation of the historic church, above all, the interposition of a new organ of revelation—served to raise an apparently permanent wall of separation between Mormon thought and the central Chris-

[62] Bernard DeVoto, *The Year of Decision: 1846,* Boston, 1943, p. 80.

tian tradition. The issue of polygamy, which most conspicuously provoked hostility against the Mormons, was only a minor excrescence of a more serious theological incompatibility. It is interesting, nevertheless, that the Mormon church seems never to have cultivated the science of theology as such. The interpretation of doctrine has been carried on by laymen, rather than by professional theologians, with the result that the full implications of the distinctive ideas of the Mormon scriptures are seldom drawn in a consistent and careful manner. For this reason the musically excellent radio program from the Mormon Tabernacle has for several decades been a favorite among listeners of all faiths. The program is thus acceptable precisely because its homilies are couched in the abstract language of general piety and ethics, with few if any allusions to peculiar Mormon doctrines. What the Mormon house-to-house missionaries propagate may be quite of another order. The radio approach, however, reflects the common blurring of theological distinctiveness in the American situation of pluralistic interaction. A similar observation, to be sure, may be made in regard to programs sponsored by both Catholic and Protestant groups at the national level. But in its professed creed Mormonism remains theologically apart from ecumenical Christianity, and the breach cannot be healed unless the Book of Mormon is abandoned as a source of doctrine.

Whatever its theological status may be, Mormonism was from the outset authentically "American." This may be said, not only because its major prophet and its architects were native born, but more especially because it brought together various impulses and ideas of the emerging American *Weltanschauung*. In the Mormon mythology the Old World has become obsolete: the American Indians are descendants of the so-called Lost Tribes of Israel, and the millennial kingdom will be established in the American West. Of greater significance is the pervasion of the Mormon scripture by ideas which were altogether congenial to the spirit of the nineteenth-century frontier: the emphasis on human freedom and rationality, the view of the universe as an infinite frontier which man may conquer and use for his own benefit, the confidence in man's capacity to progress and to master his environment, the hope for a perfect society on this earth.[63] Such optimism, expansiveness, and self-reliance, so characteristic of westward-moving America, was given theological moorings by Joseph Smith and made organic to Mormon piety. Further, despite all the vagaries of Mormon eschatological speculation, it is bewitched by no ethereal spirituality or denial of human wholeness, but gives major attention to the worthfulness of a quite "materialistic" here-and-now. Smith's vision of a kingdom of God upon earth was "saturated with Yankee enthusiasm for material blesings." [64] The continuing prosperity of the Mormon people has been no accident: their theology sanctifies productivity and prosperity. As DeVoto has written: "Mormonism is a wholly American religion, and it contrived to satisfy needs which are basic with a good many Americans and which none of its competitors managed to supply." [65] Although the first generations of Mormons were compelled to implement their faith in relative isolation from the rest of the nation—a circumstance which surely enabled them to consolidate their peculiar ethos—they learned also how to live *with* the nation. Once the inane polygamy phobia of those who opposed statehood for Utah ended, there have been no serious doubts of the Americanism of this religiously unique people and their church.

XI

At farthest remove from the Biblical consensus of historic Christianity stand the cults, properly so-called. In considering these it is necessary, once again, to distinguish between the

[63] O'Dea, *The Mormons*, ch. II and passim.
[64] Fawn M. Brodie, *No Man Knows My History*, New York, 1945, p. ix.
[65] Bernard DeVoto, *Forays and Rebuttals*, Boston, 1936, p. 79.

sociological and theological senses of the term. In the former sense, Yinger has characterized the cult as "small, short-lived, often local, frequently built around a dominant leader . . . relatively unlikely to develop into an established sect or denomination." [66] He further asserts that "pure type cults are not common in Western society; most groups that might be called cults are fairly close to the sect type." By sociological criteria the latter statement is undoubtedly true. It is also true that the two most prominent American cults, theologically defined, have evolved into quite well established denominations: it cannot be claimed that either Mormonism or Christian Science is small, short-lived, or local. Both have spread far beyond Utah and Boston to the far corners of the world; both possess highly efficient and stable organizational structures; there is no indication that either will soon pass out of existence.

Nevertheless, it may be argued—and this opinion is offered descriptively rather than pejoratively—that both these groups represent far more than sectarian exaggerations of elements in normative Biblical Christianity. Each, in its own way, has shifted the religious problem into a context different from that of the Bible, even though both profess adherence to the Bible and continue to use its language, if not its accepted meaning. Although Mormonism has, as we have indicated, marked affinities with the multitude of perfectionist-millenarian-communitarian sects that were spawned by nineteenth-century revivalism, its supplementary canon of scripture and its constitutive theological vagaries set it very definitely apart from the general Christian position. Christian Science, on the other hand, is less closely related to any previous Christian organization or theology; it stands, indeed, as the most successful example of a distinctive cult type which has enjoyed increasing popularity in America since the late nineteenth century. Both Mormonism and Christian Science, however, are altogether "respectable" in American society, being con-

[66] Yinger, *Religion, Society, and the Individual*, pp. 154–155.

sidered by the religiously unsophisticated and by impartial secularists as simply two more instances of Protestant denominationalism, as sociologically both certainly are. But from the point of view of ecumenical theology both are unassimilable deviants, entitled to all respect yet not to be confused with traditional Christianity. A cult may be quite churchly in its polity, ethical norms, and relations with secular culture; its cultness is determined by its attitude toward the Bible and the historic Christian tradition.

A long and tortuous road leads from the hermit Johannes Kelpius, cultivating a syncretism of Rosicrucian lore and Christian piety on the banks of the Wissahickon Creek, to the Mother Church of Christ, Scientist or the latest lecture on divine metaphysics in a metropolitan hotel. Points of interest along the route include a bewildering array of names: the Fox sisters and spiritualism, Mesmerists, Phineas P. Quimby, Mary Baker Eddy and Christian Science, the Theosophical Society, New Thought, Divine Science, the Unity School of Christianity, the Vedanta Society, the Liberal Catholic Church, the Society of Sikh Saviors, the Neological Society, the Lemurian Fellowship, the Infinite Magi, the Agabeg Occult Church, the Ancient Order of Melchisadek, the First Temple of Universal Law, the Great White Motherhood, Self-Realization Fellowship of America, the Purple Mother, Krotana, Psychiana, I AM—the complete list, if it could be assembled, would stretch over several printed pages. Obviously the road in question is not a single, connected highway, but a series of short avenues tending in more or less the same direction. Further, it spans the continent, although its favored terrain lies in the centers of highly mobile population, such as New York, Chicago, and Los Angeles. Carey McWilliams has dubbed Southern California "the breeding place and rendezvous of freak religions." [67] Whether or not the adjective "freak" is justified, it remains that the area offers a most

[67] Carey McWilliams, *Southern California Country*, New York, 1946, p. 249.

exciting laboratory for the study of religious pluralism and deviation. This circumstance may be attributed to various factors—a climate conducive to contemplation; proximity to the desert, comparable to the situation of the religion-generating Near and Middle East; the pervasive influence of the Orient; the cultural instability of migrants. However, the slums of Harlem and of Chicago's South Side have also sheltered new religions, so that not too much should be made of the geographical factor.

The one label which seems most inclusively to cover such a disparate conglomeration of movements is that proposed by Peter L. Berger: "Gnostic." [68] Most look to a single leader claiming special inspiration or illumination; if they use the Bible at all, it is interpreted by some a priori esoteric principle or allegorical exegesis; the majority look entirely outside the Bible for ultimate truth. The common denominator linking nearly all is their preoccupation with a certain kind of truth and with the attainment of religious welfare by the acquisition of a peculiar knowledge. But knowledge, as understood by the cults, does not refer to the inductive discoveries of the modern natural and social sciences, or to the critical wisdom of humanistic research, or to the logically argued proposals of academic philosophy. Rather, it consists in the intuitive apprehension of the "spiritual" order and processes of the universe, which are beyond the reach of conventional epistemological activity. Reality is Mind or Spirit; matter—the whole realm of ordinary sense experience—is either unreal or of inferior worth and potency; by appropriate mental insights and disciplines man can adjust himself to the ultimate spiritual order and even manipulate its energies for his own benefit. Thus, the human mind is the point of contact with the divine Mind, and correct knowledge is the sole means of grace. He who learns the secrets of the Infinite and thinks rightly can transcend all the limitations and frustrations—sin, disease, pain, sorrow, poverty, death itself—of natural existence. This may or may

[68] Berger, p. 478.

not be a true reading of the human situation; it certainly is at sharp variance with the Bible. The Bible has no doubt of either the reality or the potential worth of the created physical world. It also locates the basic tragedy of man, not in his creatureliness and ignorance, but in the perversion and rebellion of his will against a sovereign, personal God.

The Gnostic way of regarding reality was not, of course, original in America. It is actually a variation—some might call it a perversion—of the "perennial philosophy," which in the nineteenth century received fresh expression in Transcendentalism. James Leuba refers to the "psychotherapic cults" as "popularized and distorted formularizations, on the one hand, of important truths regarding the 'power of thought' over body to which psychology has recently given added significance, and, on the other, of a non-theistic philosophy allied to the absolute idealism of modern metaphysics." [69] William James traced the immediate literary sources of the various "mind-cure" groups to the Four Gospels, Emersonianism, Berkeleyan idealism, spiritism, optimistic popular science, evolutionism, and Hinduism. But, he said, "the most characteristic feature of the mind-cure movement is an inspiration much more direct. The leaders in this faith have had an intuitive belief in the all-saving power of healthy-minded attitudes as such, in the conquering efficacy of courage, hope, and trust, and a correlative contempt for doubt, fear, worry, and all nervously precautionary states of mind." [70] Although the numerous mind cults and movements have differed widely in their particular mythologies and theologies, all have shared a basically pantheistic view of the divine and a characteristically optimistic view of man. Compulsive in their search for certainty, they have devised short cuts to salvation in the here and now. Turned inward to the needs and desires of the self, they have shown colossal indifference to the problems of

[69] James L. Leuba, *The Psychological Study of Religion*, New York, 1912, p. 296.
[70] William James, *The Varieties of Religious Experience*, London, New York, Toronto, 1929, pp. 94–95.

history and society. They reflect a radical individualizing and subjectivizing of religious experience, but also a radical universalizing, which rejects the scandal of particularity in historic Christianity. In such cults the world-view of the ancient mystery religions, Gnosticism, Manichaeism, neo-Platonism, medieval cabalism, and every variety of Oriental mysticism has been revived and is offered as the panacea for modern ills.

The sub- and non-Christian cults do not fall neatly into place in the main stream of American religion. Somehow they seem incongruous in a nation which has so vigorously exploited its material abundance and which has been so "common-sense" in its approach to reality. Insofar as the cults have been oriented toward purely mystical experience, no wholly satisfactory explanation of their popularity may be possible: some persons, in all cultures, are strongly mystical by temperament while others are not, and it is not clear that either type is the product of cultural factors. Further, the appeal of the unusual and occult has been constant in religious history. It has engaged the interests of people who find themselves, for whatever cause, unresponsive to the generally accepted media of religious authority, and who consequently turn to exotic philosophies and subjective personal experience for enlightenment and assurance. In a study of "transient cults" Robert P. Casey has described "the cosmic sweep of sectarian philosophies, their intimations of immense power newly discovered and cunningly applied, the sense of 'being in' with the universe and enjoying, as a small minority, altogether extraordinary privilege and the reward of possessing unrecognized but unique penetration into the mysteries of the cosmos. . . ." [71] There are always the ontological do-it-yourself adepts, looking for a rapid and certain short cut to health, prosperity, and salvation. Perhaps the cults belong, in Max Lerner's words, among "the defensive strategies and ruses by which the neurotic personality tries to bolster itself." [72] When the problems

[71] Robert P. Casey, "Transient Cults," *Psychiatry*, IV, 1941, pp. 525ff.
[72] Max Lerner, *America as a Civilization*, New York, 1957, p. 697.

of culture become too complex and intimidating; when the old sources of ultimate authority seem to crumble beneath the impact of materialistic science or higher Biblical criticism or the hard knocks of human existence, then some persons seek new centers of meaning apart from the "culture-sanctioned patterns of ideas, conduct, and feelings." [73] Although, as a matter of history, rural, revival-singed America before the Civil War dabbled along the fringes of occult religion, in spiritualism, mesmerism, and Swedenborgianism, the real vogue of mind-over-matter, "scientific" religion began later in an industrialized, urbanized, increasingly impersonal society. What may have begun as a reaction against the pessimistic anxieties of classical Calvinism became, in the appropriate circumstances, a protest, via evasion, against those forces of modern scientific and technological culture which seem to threaten the autonomy and security of every human self.

It is significant that the cults of mental transcendence have by and large attracted their adherents from among the moderately well-to-do. The low income groups have turned more frequently to emotional and millennial theologies to find the religious reinterpretation of their poverty. Writing in October, 1929, H. R. Niebuhr viewed the popularity of mind-cults as "the victory of the bourgeoisie over Calvinism." His comment offers a suggestive interpretation of American religious development:

"It remained for America to carry the accommodation of the [Christian, Puritan] faith to bourgeois psychology to its extremes. A single line of development leads from Jonathan Edwards and his great system of God-centered faith through the Arminianism of the Evangelical revival, the Unitarianism of Channing and Parker, and the humanism of transcendental philosophy, to the man-centered, this-worldly, lift-yourself-by-your-own-bootstraps doctrine of New Thought and Christian Science. . . . Here the comfortable circumstances of an es-

[73] *ibid.*

tablished economic class have simplified out of existence the problem of evil and have made possible the substitution for the mysterious will of the Sovereign of life and death and sin and salvation, the sweet benevolence of a Father-Mother God or the vague goodness of the All. Here the concern for self has been secularized to its last degree; the conflicts of sick souls have been replaced by the struggles of sick minds and bodies; the Puritan passion for perfection has become a seeking after the kingdom of health and mental peace and its comforts." [74]

Niebuhr concluded that the mind-and-self-centered type of faith was the real, if not always openly professed, religion of "a bourgeoisie whose conflicts are over and which has passed into the quiet waters of assured income and established standing." The economic chain-reaction which exploded in the very month when those words were sent to the publisher violently roiled the quiet waters and precipitated serious dislocations of established social standing. The same religious approach, however, has continued to furnish psychological compensations to a now fearful and insecure bourgeoisie. In the contemporary nuclear age of anxiety it has penetrated deeply into American religious life, as the spectacular success of "peace of mind" books and the renewed interest in faith healing attest. The former complacency and sentimental optimism of the bourgeoisie (and the majority of Americans share the bourgeois psychology—there are relatively few self-conscious proletarians) have given way to a "new failure of nerve," reflected in a "flight from [social] responsibility," an assault against scientific method (as distinct from mere technology), and a widespread "metaphysical hunger." [75] The quasi-scientific philosophical cults are, at worst, only pathological expressions of a neurosis which pervades all the institutions of mass religion in our society.

[74] Niebuhr, pp. 104–105.
[75] Sidney Hook, "The New Failure of Nerve," *Partisan Review*, x, no. 1, January–February 1943, pp. 2ff.

XII

A widespread but superficial assumption concerns the supposed predilection of American Negroes for religious cultism. The grotesqueries of a Father Divine or a Bishop ("Daddy") Grace have provided exciting material for popular evaluations of American religion, far in excess of the real significance of such movements. The fact is that extremely deviant cultism has at no time captured the Negro masses. From the time when the slaves were progressively converted to the Protestant Christian faith of their masters, American Negroes have reproduced, in their own manner, the general religious situation obtaining in American society. They have shown a decided preference for the Baptist and Methodist forms of church organization and worship. Other denominations have fared indifferently in their attempts to proselytize among Negroes. In any case, the basic and most distinctive fact of Negro Protestantism has been its segregated character: as H. R. Niebuhr says, "The dogma which divides the racial churches is anthropological, not theological, in content." [76] The non-segregated church is still the exception rather than the rule, even north of the Mason-Dixon Line. The Roman Catholic Church has more adequately absorbed its relatively few Negro members into inclusive parishes than has any Protestant denomination—not, we may venture, as the consequence of any superiority of doctrine, but rather by the force of hierarchical control. Outside the South, at least, the Protestant pattern seems to be slowly turning in the direction of interracialism. Nevertheless, a considerable gap continues to stand between the official pronouncements of national ecclesiastical agencies and the practice of local congregations in respect to the full acceptance of Negro members by historically "white" churches. The segregated, autonomous Negro denominations will doubtless maintain their numerical strength and distinctive characteristics for a long time to come.

[76] Niebuhr, p. 236.

Many observers, foreign and domestic, have described the modes of worship and religious behavior which are supposed to be typical among Negroes: their tendency toward overt emotionalism, the theological naïveté and otherworldly escapism of Negro preaching, the prevalence of primitivistic superstition among them. Such features cannot, of course, be ignored, yet the more important perception is this: the old "spirit of evangelical revivalism" has remained powerfully alive in Negro Christianity. In their churches that spirit has been often exaggerated and, no doubt, distorted. But they have constantly cultivated the central emphases of the revivalistic movement: the sense of divine immediacy, spontaneity of individual response, the urge toward personal holiness, the vision of universal transformation and the redress of present injustice. Above all, with whatever disregard of theological subtleties, the Negro churches have unswervingly looked to the Bible as the sole source of religious certitude—their leaders and ministers have known little and cared less about creedal subtleties, alien philosophies, or the conflicting claims of science. Insofar they have remained anchored in the framework of ecumenical Christianity. Their heresies and religious eccentricities have resulted from temperamental exuberance, ill-informed exegesis, and general cultural lag, rather than from any programmatic theological speculation. Moreover, their deviations from the norms of orthodoxy have, for the most part, been exactly parallel with the vagaries of non-Negro Christians at comparable cultural levels. Religious response seems to be only minimally, if at all, conditioned by so-called racial factors—there is no Negro religious mentality, as such. On the contrary, the way in which all people behave religiously is determined by such factors as native intelligence, educational achievement, social and economic status, and the total cultural heritage of particular persons and groups. As individual Negroes (and non-Negroes!) gain more education, become more prosperous, and are increasingly recognized as "first-class" citizens, their religious behavior grows more intellectually sophisticated and emotionally disciplined. The store-front churches (which are largely of the pentecostal, mille-narian, faith-healing type) continue to mushroom in urban slums—just as the "holy rollers" and snake-handlers continue to infest certain rural slums—simply because ignorance, pov-erty, and social discrimination prevail in such places.

Nevertheless, despite the basically orthodox intention of the overwhelming majority of American Negroes, some inter-esting footnotes to our religious history are provided by a few cults which have exploited the racial theme, with little or no adherence to the Bible and traditional Christianity. Al-though the theological bases of these cults are altogether heterogeneous, all share the common purpose of bringing to the Negro a new status of dignity and equality with other races, if not indeed an aggressive consciousness of superiority. They may be described as "nativistic" in the sense that they pridefully resist acculturation in the dominant white pattern, in contrast to the usual striving by the Negro for assimilation to that pattern.[77] Each cult forms a "self-contained micro-cosm" in which basic personal and racial needs are satisfied in relative isolation from and defiance of the outside world.[78] The question of ultimate metaphysical validity is irrelevant: the point is that adherents and initiates *believe* that their par-ticular cult possesses the exclusively true account of reality, and within the cultic structure they find meaning and relief from frustration. The Negro cult must bear a heavy load (as do, to be sure, all Negro religious associations). Not only must it offer a remedy, immediate or prospective, for the ordinary limitations of humanity; in addition, it must compensate for the ingrown, institutionalized injustices of a segregated soci-ety. To achieve this end, resources both of eschatological as-surance and of concrete social amelioration must be utilized within the microcosm.

[77] Yinger, p. 177.
[78] Hadley Cantril, *The Psychology of Social Movements*, New York, 1941, p. 126.

The overtly racist cults have been neither numerous nor significant in Negro life. However, they do express certain deep-seated discontents and represent some desperately imaginative efforts to overcome the handicaps which American society has imposed on the race. Sparked by charismatic innovators —some of whom may be opportunistic charlatans, but others are surely sincere in their delusions of grandeur—these cults turn to non-Christian systems in search of support for conceptions of a manifest destiny of the Negro people. None of them ignores the Bible altogether, but each professes to find evidence for Negro superiority in other scriptures and esoteric traditions. Thus, the Black Jews, stemming from Bishop Cherry, claim to be the authentic Jews mentioned in the Bible (one is reminded of the "British-Israel" theme). God is black, they assert: the patriarchs were black, as were their legitimate descendants, including Jesus; in the coming millennial kingdom the Black Jews will occupy the highest places. Although the New Testament is used by this group, the Old Testament and an evidently bowdlerized version of the Talmud provide essential guidance for life and thought.[79] Another cult, the Moorish Science Temple of America, employs a self-styled "Holy Koran," as the authoritative revelation. The appellation "Negro" is rejected, in favor of "Asiatic" or "Moorish American." An inchoate amalgam of Christian, Moslem, and Oriental ideas is set forth as the true religion of all the colored peoples of the world.[80] These two cults are more or less typical of various experiments in non-Biblical articulations of racial religion. They seem to have a connection with the protest movement centering in a supposed Negro messiah, Marcus Garvey, who agitated among American Negroes following World War I. Garvey symbolized the most aggressive racial pretensions, and his brand of Negro

---

[79] Arthur Huff Fauset, *Black Gods of the Metropolis*, Vol. III, "Publications of the Philadelphia Anthropological Society," Philadelphia, 1944, pp. 31–40.
[80] *ibid.*, pp. 41–51.

chauvinism is marginally perpetuated in the more exotic cults.

Of all the recent Negro cult figures, the most interesting and successful has been Major J. "Father" Divine, who has been the subject of several popular books as well as of numerous scholarly investigations. This unprepossessing little man, of uncertain origin and apparently uneducated in a formal way, claims to be no less than God in the flesh. He stands in a charismatic succession which includes such intriguing personalities as Father Jehovia (Samuel Morris) and St. John the Vine Hickerson. Although his activities can be traced to the early years of the present century, Father Divine first began to acquire a substantial following during the Great Depression of the 1930's. Harlemites, chiefly, who had plumbed the depths of economic deprivation flocked to him in increasing numbers, and they were soon followed by not a few white persons. Branches of his movement were established in many cities, particularly on the West Coast. The theological aspects of his Peace Mission movement are too confused to permit orderly analysis: he has somewhere drunk at the fountain of New Thought; the Bible still figures prominently in the cult ideology, but the binding revelations are contained in the torrential pronouncements of Father himself—the new Bible is to be read in the verbatim transcripts of his every public address, published in *The New Day*, a periodical. His cult has been described as "the only indigenous Negro religion . . . a part of Negro protest with all its illusory and contradictory trends." [81]

It is a practical cult, however, promising and implementing a "formula for Heaven on Earth." His followers do not wistfully look forward to "pie in the sky"; here and now they participate in a communal life of marvelous abundance; they enjoy freedom from economic want and physical suffering; they experience emotional rapture in the tangible presence of

[81] Abram Kardiner and Lionel Ovesey, *The Mark of Oppression*, New York, 1951, p. 358.

Deity; in their "heavens," if not in the outside world, all racial distinctions are abolished, and true brotherhood is the order of things. From his transcendental eminence Father is even able to wield influence in the political affairs of the external community. In his abolition of sexual relations and private property, as in his perfectionistic view of love and his Utopian hope for human society, Father Divine is strongly reminiscent of both the Shakers and John Humphrey Noyes. It has been charged, however, that his movement functions mainly as a fantasy-retreat for the psychopathic proletariat and for unbalanced idealists, and that, in any case, "it is to discrimination what a cough medicine is to pneumonia; it tries to alleviate a symptom, but leaves the underlying disease untouched." [82] That may or may not be a just estimate. What is indubitable is that the Peace Mission movement and other erratic cults point toward a multitude of needs which neither traditional religion nor American society has been able to satisfy. It may be that such satisfaction is not attainable this side of the millennium or heaven or whatever goal lies ahead of humanity. If so, all the varieties of religious and political short cuts will continue to gain disciples among the impatient and the frustrated.

XIII

We have attempted to view some typical deviations from the soberer, more stable strands of traditional Christianity. Such deviations have been so numerous and heterogeneous that only a few could be mentioned, and none could be presented in the detail which each deserves. We have touched only superficially on the apparent causes of the proliferation of sects and cults in America—social unrest, psychological instability, changing intellectual climates, or whatever it may be that leads people to break away from established religious

[82] *ibid.*, pp. 358–359.

institutions and ideologies. It cannot be doubted that social dysfunction and psychological maladjustment operate as catalysts of religious change. Nevertheless, the process of any single person's "conversion" to a different religious scheme may always elude naturalistic causal explanation. In religion, no less than in other areas of human involvement, people may embrace new ideas and modes of expression simply because they become somehow convinced that these are more true than any available alternatives. Not all who experience conversion and alter their theological beliefs are psychopaths or social malcontents, although some kind of dissatisfaction with things-as-they-are is usually the precondition of radical religious change. The dissatisfaction may be quite sanely and rationally based, and the consequent shift to a new understanding may be sought by respectable intellectual effort. Neither poverty nor psychosis, for example, can adequately explain why a Jehovah's Witness accepts the curious eschatology of that group; he may do so because he believes that it is a true interpretation of the Bible, respect for whose authority is deeply entrenched in the American mind. It may be the case that such a person is in some respect maladjusted within the total culture—but the same may be said of virtually everyone in America. When any man confronts the ultimate questions of human and cosmic destiny, it is still true that, to paraphrase Luther's observation, every man must do his own believing no less than his own dying. The decision between religion and no religion, or among the various brands of supernaturalism, can never be reached through absolutely coercive demonstration. The facts are too numerous, the possibilities too various; beyond a certain point even the mechanist must walk by faith.

Is the "chaos of cults" a desirable or undesirable aspect of American culture? An evaluation depends on one's stance. A bishop of Durham once asserted: "When all allowances have been made, it cannot be denied that American sectarianism presents a spectacle equally perplexing, repulsive, and, to the student of Christianity, humiliating." [83] From an opposite point of view, Charles W. Ferguson has said: "It is in the babble of isms that religious life best expresses itself, for here the people have expressed their discontent with the standard forms of religion and taken the reins in their own hands. . . . The cults stand for creative religion in the hands of the people." [84] The sects and cults—and the deliberate rejection of all religious observance, too—belong to the very substance of democracy. They reflect the insecurities and neuroses of a society fumbling with freedom; they serve as escape valves for explosive passions, and as fantasy retreats from the burden of personal responsibility for a recalcitrant world. But they also stand in judgment over the failures and complacencies of both society and the great churches.

[83] Quoted by Ray Strachey, *Group Movements of the Past and Experiments in Guidance*, London, 1934; rev. ed. of *Religious Fanaticism*, London, 1928, p. 8.

[84] Charles W. Ferguson, *The Confusion of Tongues*, Grand Rapids, 1936, p. 8.

THEOLOGY IN AMERICA:
A HISTORICAL SURVEY

SYDNEY E. AHLSTROM

R ELIGIOUS and theological debate has always flourished in the luxuriant pluralism of the American environment. Scholars and theologians have regarded contention as a birthright. But almost everyone has so far agreed on at least one point: that a comprehensive historical account of American theology is unnecessary. European interpreters have habitually considered the very term "American theology" to be self-contradictory and Americans have made only very feeble efforts to correct the picture, with academic historians doing little better than the journalists. The conception of the World Council of Churches as a meeting place for "activists" from America and other-worldly theologues from across the waters is generally accepted. A recent book-length interpretation of *The Spirit of American Christianity* states the same view almost eloquently:

"The 'simple gospel' proclaimed by the American churches is not essentially a matter of rationalism or liberalism, but of grace for all. Nearly all the factors . . . contributing to the non-theological spirit of our faith are much older and run much deeper than the liberal tendency to discount the importance of dogma. The emphasis on simplicity is in part a Christian application of democracy. Our preachers have often quoted a saying attributed to Abraham Lincoln: 'God must have loved the common people, he made so many of them.' " [1]

This commonly drawn picture of American theology is essentially defective. By way of contrast, therefore, let me begin with Horace Bushnell's description of the little country

---

[1] Ronald E. Osborn, *The Spirit of American Christianity*, New York, 1958, p. 115. The many works of William W. Sweet show the same tendency. In both, the influence of Frederick Jackson Turner's frontier hypothesis is very marked.

church in western Connecticut where he, as a youth of nine-
teen, had "owned the covenant" in 1821.

"The dress of the assembly is mostly homespun. . . . They
are seated according to age, the older in front near the pulpit
. . . only the deacons sitting close under the pulpit, by themselves, to receive as their distinctive honor the more perpen-
dicular droppings of the word. . . . There is no affectation
of seriousness in the assembly, no mannerism of worship;
some would say, too little of the manner of worship. They
think of nothing, in fact, save what meets their intelligence
and enters into them by that method. They appear like men
who have digestion for strong meat, and have no conception
that trifles more delicate can be of any account to feed the
system. Nothing is dull that has the matter in it, nothing long
that has not exhausted the matter. If the minister speaks in
his great-coat and thick gloves or mittens, if the howling blasts
of winter blow in across the assembly fresh streams of ventila-
tion that move the hair upon their heads, they are none the
less content if only he gives them good, strong exercize.
Under their hard and . . . stolid faces, great thoughts are
brewing, and these keep them warm. Free-will, fixed fate,
foreknowledge absolute, Trinity, redemption, special grace,
eternity—give them anything high enough, and the tough
muscle of their inward man will be climbing sturdily into it;
and if they go away having something to think of, they have
had a good day. A perceptible glow will kindle in their hard
faces only when some one of their chief apostles—a Day, a
Smith, or a Bellamy—has come to lead them up some higher
pinnacle of thought, or pile upon their sturdy mind some
heavier weight of argument." [2]

In such a milieu theology could and did flourish. But New
England is not alone as a center of theological concern. At
least a half-dozen other traditions besides the Puritan have

[2] "The Age of Homespun" in *Work and Play; or, Literary Varieties,*
New York, 1864, pp. 387ff.

long, rich, and continuous theological histories. The basic mistake of those who radically discount the American churches' intellectual tradition or who create the image of the American minister as an empty-minded frontiersman in the pulpit is that they look for theology where it could not possibly be and then generalize their findings.

This essay will attempt to correct or amend these generalizations, but at the outset three general observations may be in order. The first points to the *diversity* of the American theological tradition. The Puritanism which informed and structured New England's Congregational thinking was chiefly English in derivation. The Presbyterian tradition, strongest in the mid-Atlantic region, relied heavily on Scottish thought and the great Reformed scholastics of the Continent. Lutheran theology was oriented chiefly on German developments. And so on. Sometimes these traditions became closely interrelated, but they were often substantially autonomous. The total effect, in any event, is that it is difficult to speak of a single American tradition.

My second observation to a degree stems from the first: American theology is far more *derivative* than is German, or French, or English theology. Because the history of the United States virtually *is* the history of immigration, the American people have necessarily looked to the cultures, thought-ways, university traditions, and philosophical tendencies of their respective homelands. Strong intellectual traditions made the ties necessarily closer, and institutional ties made them closer still. On the other hand, because America is relatively new, conceived as a nation in the bright noonday of the *Aufklärung,* it obviously cannot have a tradition that springs from some immemorial folk-tradition or from centuries of cohesifying historical experience. The very fact of its multiple derivations, on the other hand, helps to explain the broad catholicity of American theology.

My third generalization is but a refinement of the second,

namely, that the first quarter of the nineteenth century constitutes something of a *watershed* in the flow of theological
influences. Before those years, British sources were by far the
most important. After 1815, however, German influences
became increasingly strong, this being no less the case for
their being mediated by English and Scottish thinkers like
Coleridge and Carlyle.[3]

In the historical essay which follows these generalizations
will be given some decent vesture, though we shall first of all
come to see that the large fields of religious scholarship and
philosophy of religion have generally had to give place to
more systematic thinking about the Church's message.[4] Second, our concentration here is upon a few prominent and
creative theologians rather than broad social, institutional,
and intellectual trends. Christian theology is not the product
of solitary activity. Like the great confessions of the faith
and like the great liturgies, it has arisen in the historical context of corporate church life. The theologians considered in
this essay, therefore, are to some extent "representative men."
They are revelatory of their particular traditions. But they are
also "heroes" who in most cases put their stamp on their community. A certain amount of historical connective tissue is
here provided, but I have sought to preclude the impression
that theological movements and traditions come into being
and transform themselves due to immanent, impersonal
forces. Needless to say, not every important development can
be touched upon in this one essay, nor is detailed exposition
possible, yet something of the scope and spirit of America's
theological history is at least suggested.

[3] See Henry A. Pochmann, *German Culture in America*, Madison, 1957,
and H. A. Pochmann and Arthur R. Schultz, *Bibliography of German Culture in America to 1940*, Madison, 1953.

[4] Though by no means strictly, I thus tend to stress thinkers who are, if
not dogmaticians, at least much concerned with dogmatics, a discipline
whose task is to clarify the significance and meaning of the Christian faith.
See Gustaf Aulén, *The Faith of the Christian Church*, Philadelphia, 1948,
pp. 3–22; and Karl Barth, *Dogmatics in Outline*, New York, 1949, pp. 9–14.

The Puritan Impulse

Puritanism, for weal or woe, provided the theological foundation and molded the prevailing religious spirit in virtually all the commonwealths which declared their independence in 1776. With lasting effect and hardly less directness it conditioned the people's social and political ideals. In a moderate form it made entry with the Anglicans at Jamestown. Drawn to radical extremes it informed the Quakerism of Philadelphia. In a normative, almost classic form it undergirded the major colonies of New England, and through them wrought great influence on American Presbyterianism. The architects of the "Puritan Way," therefore, were in a very real sense the founders of the American nation. Because the Puritan spirit was also to have a profound effect on the whole course of American theology, here is the logical place to begin the story.

Puritanism as a system of thought or a way of thinking is a product of the great "second phase" of the English Reformation which began during the reign of Queen Elizabeth (1558–1603).[5] Ever since Henry VIII had broken off England's relation to the papacy, incursions from the Continental Reformation had been deflecting the new national church from its course. Under Edward VI (1547–1553) these influences became dominant, only to be overthrown by Queen Mary Tudor's determined efforts to reestablish papal supremacy (1553–1558). With the coming of Elizabeth something like a genuine settlement had been achieved, with the revised Thirty-nine Articles to define the Church's doctrinal position, with the Book of Common Prayer to guide its visible practice, and with the Queen encharged as "Supreme Governor" to steer it along Protestant lines. Despite the widespread desire for peace, however, demands for a still more complete refor-

[5] In view of the accompanying bibliographical volume, footnote references to the general secondary literature or to unquoted primary materials will be strictly limited, but I have often cited works containing especially useful bibliographies.

mation could not be stilled. To the strident voices of the Marian exiles a rising group of "spiritual brethren" were adding their demands for a greater depth of piety. The discontent to be voiced so eloquently in Milton's *Lycidas* was growing. Down into the Cromwellian period it waxed constantly stronger.

When a young man like Thomas Hooker, to be known in America as the "father of Connecticut," arrived at Cambridge University in 1604, James I was king, and the conflict had intensified. At Cambridge, moreover, and particularly at Emmanuel College, the student would feel the force of the Puritan movement in all of its spiritual rigor and intellectual force. These were days when Dr. William Whitaker, author of the forthrightly Reformed "Lambeth Articles" (1595), was Regius Professor of Divinity. William Perkins, whose name figures strongly in any account of the origins of the Federal or Covenant Theology of the Anglo-New England Puritans, was holding forth as Lecturer at Great St. Andrews. Master of Emmanuel was Laurence Chaderton, whose powerful preaching would be remembered by generations of later Puritans. He would be succeeded as Master in 1622 by John Preston, whose *The New Covenant, Or The Saints Portion* (1629) was a magisterial exposition of Covenant doctrine which was to rank with the works of William Ames as a source of New England divinity. This man Ames was at Cambridge, too, though he lost his University appointments for his refusal to wear the surplice and, still later, for more serious deviations from conformity, he had to flee the country altogether.

Facing so mighty a host of God's witnesses, Hooker—like so many other fellow spirits—received his "effectual calling" and "implantation into Christ," and shortly after his conversion entered upon an intensely active ministry that would make him a virtual archetype of the New England church leader during the first generation.

His life expresses almost the total experience and full agony of the Puritan: the university confrontation of Reformed divinity, the searching demands for the soul's humiliation and exaltation, the silencing of an immensely fruitful preaching ministry in England by Laud and the Court of High Commission, the unsettled wandering and contentions of exile in Holland, the corporate movement to the Bay Colony, the daring migration into the still deeper wilderness of Connecticut to undertake anew the tasks of ordering state and church, and finally the need to make intellectual defenses of the Holy Commonwealth. Aside from the cumulative effect of such experiences and adversities, the characteristic theological temper of the New England Puritan is difficult to fathom.[6]

If one looks for the sources of this religious impulse, however, he must go first (as all of New England's founders would have insisted) to the New Testament, perhaps especially to the epistles of St. Paul. More particularly, the Reformation would have to be taken into account, and especially that aspect of this great renewal usually designated "Reformed" to differentiate it from the Anglican, the Lutheran, or the more radical "left-wing" movements. What is usually seen as the beginning of this Reformed movement is Zwingli's revolt in Zurich, which by a swift chain reaction was conveyed to the other cities of German Switzerland and down the Rhine valley to Germany and the Lowlands, and also to the French cantons, above all Geneva, and into France. It already was a well-formed tradition by the time John Calvin published the first edition of his *Institutes* in 1536; it was an established fact in Strassburg when Calvin took refuge there, and in Geneva when he was called back to that city. And from these various Reformed sources comes an influence every bit as direct as that which stems from Calvin. Indeed, the forces that have so much to do with changing the course of the English Reformation under King Edward VI and then more radically

---

[6] The Puritan "fathers" were thus twice winnowed: by persecution in England, and by the challenge of migration. It goes without saying that their unwinnowed descendants would show less intense evangelical ardor.

in the century after the accession of Elizabeth (1558) are more accurately termed "Reformed" than "Calvinistic." [7]

Far more important than the *term* is the realization that we confront a broad movement for the reconstruction of Christian life and thought which is far more radical, sweeping, and total than any account of personal influences can sustain. Based on an enormous surfeit with ecclesiasticism, corruption, and popular impiety, the basic point of view was thought out internationally and spontaneously. Yet the specifically Puritan movement that came to flower in England and then was transplanted to New England, there to flourish in its own way, was a unique product. It was formed into a massive and carefully articulated theology by William Perkins, John Preston, William Ames, Richard Sibbes and other devoted university men. It reached its ultimate dogmatic expression in the Westminster Confession and Catechisms, and the Savoy Declaration.

Beneath all the spiritual turmoil and theological ferment lay three unquestioned Reformed tenets (each in a sense a complex of several tenets) which were almost as essential to the Puritan's religious outlook as width, height, and depth to his conception of a cube. These coordinates were the depravity of man, the sovereignty of God, and the necessity of worshiping God and ordering the Church strictly in accordance with Biblical prescription. Although the third may seem anticlimactical, it was actually the most divisive, as the party-names of the age (Congregational, Presbyterian, Episcopal, and so on) strongly suggest. Aside from problems of church order, there was a remarkable degree of consensus between contending parties.

Faced by the awesome facts of man's sinfulness and God's almightiness, the Puritan found the dead center of spiritual concern in the experience of regeneration, the profoundly felt knowledge of his implantation in Christ, the assurance of elec-

[7] Consider, for example, the continuing influence of Peter Martyr, Martin Butzer, Heinrich Bullinger, and John Oecolampadius.

tion, the certainty that the covenant of grace was for him. This was an event and a state of being to be prepared for and to be instructed for. For the first time in centuries (if not ever) the conversion experience was made normative for church membership on a wide and comprehensive scale. This central concern provided the point of departure for the most characteristic emphases in Puritan preaching, dogmatics, and church order.

Probably no distinguishing mark of the Puritan was more important, or more obvious, than his interest in "practical" preaching, which would be the means of bringing into existence the "sincere convert." This does not mean that Puritans saw human agency replacing the divine in redemption. Their felt need for preparation and the obligation to nourish the smallest seed of faith made that unnecessary. The sermon was a means of grace (almost *the* means) and its purpose was to make God's irresistible grace rational. Yet they were not *quietists*. They would have agreed with Luther: "Heaven is not for geese." They demanded theological concern for the human will. In fact, their determination to avoid a mechanical conception of God's saving acts while yet averting the heretical horrors of Arminianism was one of the chief provocations to their doctrinal thinking. They regarded the inner spiritual struggles of men as intensely meaningful. Without denying the objective, purely gracious character of God's redemptive acts, they wished also to make a place for the willing, knowing, repenting, thanking, loving acts of the human person. Without ever forgetting their responsibilities for the clear "opening" of God's word, or the need to convince the human intellect, and to prevent rather than to encourage a simply emotional "decision for Christ," they yet sought to make a place in the economy of salvation for *subjectivity*, for the acts of human consciousness.

The clue to their understanding of regeneration as well as to their theories for ordering the church and society is the *covenant*. It was around this point that the particular dogmatic interests of the English and later the New England Puritan theologians were oriented. Theirs was a *covenant theology*, based, as Preston put it, on the conviction that the covenant "is the ground of all you hope for, it is that that euery man is built vpon, you haue no other ground but this, God hath made a Couenant with you, and you are in couenant with him." [8] By covenants, they said, God had successively dealt with his children—with Adam, with Noah, with Abraham, with Moses. By the Covenant of Redemption the Persons of the Trinity had contracted as to the mode of man's salvation, and, through the New Covenant of Grace, God now dealt through Christ with individual men. The covenant is thus the means by which the foreordained and saving grace is given to the elect. "It is individual, between God and each of his created elect; it is sure, for God no less than man is bound by the terms of the covenant; it is essential, for in no other way does God convey his salvation or draw men unto himself." [9]

As night follows day, "covenant thinking" carried over into the Puritan's ecclesiastical and social thinking. In fact it was almost constitutive of his theology of the Church, which, they insisted, exists in its true and scriptural form only when "visible saints" who had entered the covenant of grace covenanted one with another to form a congregation, which was then, with Christ as its head and ruler, authorized to call and ordain its ministry and to rule on its membership, as well as discipline, admonish and, if need be, excommunicate these members.[10]

Beyond church affairs the covenant became normative as a means for ordering civil affairs. The Plymouth company in

[8] *The New Covenant, or the Saints Portion* (1629), quoted by Perry Miller, "The Marrow of Puritan Divinity," *Errand into the Wilderness*, Cambridge, 1956, p. 60. An essay of major importance.

[9] Edwin S. Gaustad, *The Great Awakening in New England*, New York, 1957, p. 8.

[10] Invaluable on Congregational polity is John Norton's *Responsio* of 1648, Douglas Horton, ed. and tr., *The Answer*, Cambridge, Mass., 1958. See also, Emil Oberholzer, *Delinquent Saints: Disciplinary Action in the Early Congregational Churches of Massachusetts*, New York, 1956.

its famous Mayflower Compact covenanted together before landing. Aboard the *Arbella* while en route to America, Governor Winthrop of the Bay Colony spoke of his entire group as being in covenant with God. What all this meant in a practical sense was that the Puritans thought about economic, political, and social problems in extraordinarily *corporate* terms. The Church consequently directed its attention not only to the problems of the individual before God but to the *state* before God. The Church assumed a responsibility for society because Puritans thought in terms of a social or national covenant.

Perry Miller has shown how a century of "jeremiads" continued this tradition.[11] The Puritan's systematic theology cannot here be described in detail. Suffice it to say that it sought to be a faithful elaboration of the formularies worked out by the Westminster Assembly of Divines, as they had been amended as to polity at Savoy in 1658. With large consequences for the future, Puritan theologians turned with considerable scholastic rigor to three especially challenging themes: (1) the experience of regeneration, its issue in the covenant of grace, and the preparation for this decisive event; (2) the rationality of God's dealing with men, hence the need to promote an intellectual understanding of God, man, and nature, and to explore the avenues of natural theology and ethics; and (3) the necessity of interlacing personal religious concern with the corporate demands of a visible church-way and a Holy Commonwealth whereby the ecclesiastical and social-political orders were together and alike under the rule of God and to be regulated according to His expressed will.[12]

---

[11] *From Colony to Province*, Cambridge, Mass., 1953, ch. 2; see also H. Richard Niebuhr, *The Kingdom of God in America*, New York, 1937.

[12] On the Westminister Confession, the Savoy amendments made by Independents, and the Cambridge Platform (1648) of the New Englanders, see Williston Walker, *Creeds and Platforms of Congregationalism*, New York, 1893. Three important recent works also provide up-to-date bibliographies on Puritanism: John D. Eusden, *Puritans, Lawyers, and Politics*, New Haven, 1958; Edmund S. Morgan, *The Puritan Dilemma*, Boston, 1958; Alan Simpson, *Puritanism in Old and New England*, Chicago, 1955.

Their principles were to become long-lasting emphases in American church-life and theology not only because they were so effectively institutionalized in a region destined to wield major influence in a growing nation but because, in somewhat modified form, they were also perpetuated by contemporary Anglicans, Presbyterians, Baptists, and even Quakers. They would become part of the westward-surging Methodist tide and make their way, as well, into many communions of Continental heritage. The stage of American theology, in other words, has a Puritan and Reformed backdrop.

Jonathan Edwards, the Enlightenment, and the New Divinity

The Puritan theological impulse was brought to fullest articulation in *The Compleat Body of Divinity* of Samuel Willard, published posthumously in 1726. The largest tome that had ever been published in British America, it consisted chiefly of systematic lectures on the Westminster Confession of Faith. It was an intricate monument to the age of the Mathers, and the theological parallel to Cotton Mather's great historical work, the *Magnalia Christi Americana* of 1702. Both of these works, however, were a legacy to posterity which posterity ignored because they expressed an ideal of the past which became increasingly unpalatable and incredible.

The fact is that two contemporaries of Increase and Cotton Mather had decisively changed the course of European and American theological history and jeopardized such enterprises as the publication of Willard's lectures. One of the two men was Isaac Newton, whose *Principia Mathematica* of 1686 provided the Atlantic community with a new conception of

---

I am, of course, deeply indebted to Perry Miller, *The New England Mind: The Seventeenth Century*, New York, 1939, especially Book II on reason, knowledge, and nature; and to Walter J. Ong's superb treatise on Petrus Ramus, *Ramus; Method, and the Decay of Dialogue*, Cambridge, Mass., 1958.

the cosmos whereby the planets in their majestic orbits, as well as falling apples, were brought into a physical and mathematical synthesis. He proclaimed an orderly world where natural laws were the clue to the world's events. The other man was John Locke (1632–1704), who more successfully than any other translated these new scientific notions into the language of philosophy, psychology, morals, religion, and government. The result of this intellectual revolution was a crisis in the European mind. Its most significant product was that complex phenomenon which we term the Enlightenment.

One theological result of this revolution was the rise of "Enlightened Christianity," according to which the canons of rationalism and "reasonableness" became normative. The more radical, deistic spirits announced that Christianity was not mysterious, that revelation told of nothing that the human reason operating on the evidences provided by the Creation itself could not inductively or deductively infer. The more conservative thinkers would insist, on the contrary, that revelation was necessary and that it conveyed truths otherwise inaccessible; but they hurried on to demonstrate the reasonableness of these truths and exhausted themselves with ingenious demonstrations that Holy Scripture was inspired, that the Evangelists were trustworthy, that St. Paul was not a deceiver, and that God (despite the Lisbon earthquake) was benevolent. The thought of radicals and conservatives alike was characterized by an immense confidence in the workings of the human mind and a determination to make the Christian message as simple and acceptable as possible. The doctrinal implications of this drive for simplicity and reasonableness were clear. Speculation about the Trinity was pushed into the background. Doctrines of man's sinfulness and "spiritual inability" gave way to confidence in his moral freedom and goodness. Conceptions of faith and regeneration that had resulted in a concern for assurance and conversion were replaced by a view that equated "faith" with "intellectual as-

sent." Notions of divine providence were modified or transformed by new ideas of natural law. Jehovah, the personal,
wrathful, and loving God of Israel, became the Great Archi-
tect and Governor of the Universe.[13]

In New England these currents flowed even as they flowed
in England, France, Germany, and the Low Countries. In
the more cosmopolitan society of the maritime towns and
cities they became increasingly pervasive. To no small degree
Cotton Mather himself was swept along by them, and
Harvard College to an even greater degree. A tradition that
its enemies called "broad and catholick" ensconced itself in
the seaboard churches.

Enlightened rationalism, however, was by no means limited
to the maritime regions of New England. Its spirit also
infiltrated Western Massachusetts and Connecticut. There,
too, it encouraged thinking in terms of law and reasonableness. There, too, the old Puritan sense of God's providence
was vitiated. Church membership and the sacraments tended
to become decorous formalities. It was not at Harvard but in
the orthodox sanctuary of Yale that the serious, fourteen-
year-old Jonathan Edwards came upon John Locke's *Essay
on the Human Understanding* and found his pleasures at
the discovery greater "than the most greedy miser finds,
when gathering up handfuls of silver and gold from some
newly-discovered treasure." [14]

This incident is premonitory of a major fact about Jonathan
Edwards: he was not only America's and possibly the Church's
greatest apostle to the Enlightenment, but he was also a
philosophe himself. He was a *Dortian philosophe*, if the term
be allowed; that is, he adopted as his own certain of the most

[13] Other movements naturally contested these rationalistic trends: German
Pietism, the Scottish Evangelicals, the English Methodists. Each had its
American equivalent or representatives.
[14] Edwards was born in East Windsor, Conn., in 1703, graduated from
Yale in 1720, ordained at Northampton in 1726, and settled at Stockbridge
in 1751. He died in 1758 at Princeton. On his life, see Ola E. Winslow,
Jonathan Edwards, New York, 1940.

basic and seminal ideas of the Enlightenment, yet because in the deepest sense his faith was the faith of his fathers, he adapted these ideas to the major principles of Reformed Christianity affirmed by the Synod of Dort in 1619. His major works constitute a powerful apologia for the "Five Points" (each of which was anathema to the characteristic "Enlightened" mind of Europe and America): (1) total depravity, (2) unconditional election, (3) limited atonement, (4) irresistible grace, and (5) perseverance of the saints.[15] That such was or would be the character of Edwards' life work was made clear to those with ears to hear or eyes to read even in his first published utterance, "God Glorified in the Work of Redemption by the Greatness of Man's Dependence upon Him in the Whole of It," a Thursday Lecture which he delivered in Boston in 1731. The same thinking underlay his sermon-series on Justification by Faith—the very sermons which seemed to precipitate the momentous revival that broke out in his Northampton parish during the winter of 1733–1734.

Revivalistic "seasons of harvest" were not new in New England; there had in fact been five of them during the Northampton ministry of Edwards' grandfather and predecessor, Solomon Stoddard. The "Great Awakening" itself had been stirring in the Presbyterian and Dutch Reformed churches of New Jersey and Pennsylvania for several years. As it radiated out from Northampton, however, it developed a characteristic New England coloration for which no one person was more responsible than Edwards. As a defender of the revivals he put his mark on the New England conception of Christian piety for a century and more. By the power of his thought he would also revolutionize the Puritan theological tradition. In view of the scope, subtlety, and

---

[15] On the Synod of Dort, see Philip Schaff, *The Creeds of Christendom,* 3 vols., New York, 1877, III, 550–597. See this great work also with regard to the Augsburg, Heidelberg, Westminster, and Swiss confessions referred to elsewhere in this essay.

significance of this effort, it is an outrage that Edwards should be best known throughout America as a hell-fire revivalist and by a few lines from one imprecatory sermon, delivered outside of his own parish, on "Sinners in the Hands of an Angry God."

Edwards was, of course, interested in defending "experimental" as against merely rational or formal religion. By a kind of inexorable internal logic he was thus led to attack certain common practices that had grown up in the New England churches during the period of Puritan "declension," particularly the watered-down conceptions of church membership that had led to the Half-Way Covenant and the opening of the Communion to the "unconverted." This last assault created the animosities in his parish and among the surrounding ministers that finally contributed much to his expulsion from Northampton. He was thus in virtual exile at Stockbridge, as pastor to a little frontier parish and catechist to the Indians, when he produced the great treatises on the *Freedom of the Will* (1754) and *Original Sin* (1758) which would establish him as the founder of a new school of Reformed divinity. Recognition for his services finally came in the form of a call to be president of the College of New Jersey (Princeton). But in 1758 he was swept to his reward by a smallpox vaccination even before he could properly assume his duties.

As a system of thought in the mind of Jonathan Edwards, Edwardseanism was no doubt a single, unified thing. Certainly the contradictions and disjunctions that appear to the observer were taken up in the higher synthesis of his personal evangelical piety. A description of this "New Divinity," however, must deal in terms of appearances. When this is done, four salient emphases stand out.

First of all, Edwards sought to state in a thorough, untendentious, and scripturally based way the full Christian message as it had been transmitted to him by his Reformed and Puritan forebears. His zeal in this regard is attested not only by frequent professions of faith or by the reading he did but by the manuscripts for over a thousand carefully constructed sermons. Conceived in the form and delivered in the "plain style" of the Puritans, the sermons could, if taken out of the order of their delivery, be arranged either to form a "body of divinity" or a commentary on Holy Scriptures. They are in fact both. But as is perfectly proper for homiletical discourse, they are not, except in the rarest instances, philosophical. They "open the Word" in the fine Puritan tradition: the text is read and put in its Biblical context, the doctrine or doctrines are stated, and their practical "use" is indicated. The scholar can perceive in them the nuances of the theological and philosophical system that he knows to lie behind them, but taken by themselves they would serve simply to put Edwards down as the possessor of an amazingly thorough and cohesive knowledge of the Bible and as a brilliant expounder of accepted Old Puritan theology as it was stated in the Westminster formularies.[16]

Another aspect of Edwards' thought (almost another Edwards!) is exposed by his great argumentative treatises on the *Religious Affections, Freedom of the Will,* and *Original Sin* as well as a good many other writings published during his lifetime and since. Here more than elsewhere we see the *philosophe* who is conversant with the scientific and philosophic thought of his day and is profoundly affected by its meaning and tendency. Above all, we have a man imbued with the new psychology and philosophic starting-point of John Locke. Basic to this view is its concern for proximate causes, its insistence on causal categories, its determination to be deterministic, as it were. These works contain much more than that, to be sure (not least of all are the long completely

---

[16] See Perry Miller, *Images and Shadows of Divine Things,* New Haven, 1948; Ralph G. Turnbull, *Jonathan Edwards as a Preacher,* Grand Rapids, 1958; and Sheldon B. Quincer, ed., *Jonathan Edwards' Sermon Outlines,* Grand Rapids, 1958. There were, of course, variations within "Old Puritan theology."

exegetical arguments), but what stands out is the new "sensational" philosophy and Edwards' enormous competence in turning its arguments back against those who would see in it reason for modifying traditional theology. Above all, these works give us Edwards as the eighteenth-century philosophical apologist for the truths of the Christian religion, a religious thinker in the empirical tradition, who not only accepts Locke but goes beyond him to Berkeley even to an anticipation of Hume.[17]

The third aspect of Edwards was far less known in his day because much of the writing most clearly exhibiting it was published posthumously or still remains hidden from public scrutiny. This is Edwards the speculative theologian, communing with the long and rich tradition of Christian Platonism, dwelling on the ancient metaphysical problems of the faith, pondering the inner mysteries of the Trinity, concerned with the ineffable problems of Being, and ultimately resting his conception of *The End for Which God Created the World* and *The Nature of True Virtue* on an essentialist ontology that unites him with precisely those aspects of St. Augustine's theology which the great Reformers (Luther and Calvin) had found least acceptable and with which John Locke could never have sympathized. Thorough investigation of the implications of this side of Edwards' thought is yet to be made, but one can safely predict that the publication of his vast *Miscellanies* will make possible a more complete integration of his thought than has yet been possible.[18]

The fourth aspect of Edwards' thought must forever remain something hauntingly potential rather than actual. It rests on his conviction that the ultimate mode of expressing the meaning of the Christian faith was through *Heilsge-*

[17] See Perry Miller, *Jonathan Edwards*, New York, 1949; Paul Ramsey's Introduction to Edwards' *Freedom of the Will*, Yale ed., Vol. I, New Haven, 1957; and John E. Smith's Introduction to *The Religious Affections*, Yale ed., Vol. II, New Haven, 1959.

[18] But see the selections from the Miscellanies published by Harvey G. Townsend, ed., *The Philosophy of Jonathan Edwards*, Eugene, 1955.

schichte (salvation history; sacred history). Unexcelled is his own description of this grand aim, which unfortunately he never lived to carry out:

"I have had on my mind and heart . . . a great work, which I call a 'History of the Work of Redemption,' a body of divinity in an entire new method, being thrown into the form of a history; considering the affair of Christian Theology, as the whole of it, in each part, stands in reference to the great work of redemption by Jesus Christ, which I suppose to be, of all others, the grand design of God, and the *summum* and *ultimum* of all the divine operations and decrees; particularly considering all parts of the grand scheme in their historical order, . . . beginning from eternity, and descending from thence to the great work and successive dispensations of the infinitely wise God, in time; considering the chief events coming to pass in the church of God, and revolutions in the world of mankind, affecting the state of the church and the affair of redemption, which we have an account of in history or prophecy, till at last, we come to the general resurrection, last judgment, and consummation of all things; when it shall be said, '*It is done; I am Alpha and Omega, the Beginning and the End.*' Concluding my work, with the consideration of that perfect state of things, which shall be finally settled to last for eternity." [19]

During the year 1739 Edwards did preach a series of thirty sermons on this topic, which were published posthumously in 1777 as *The History of the Work of Redemption;* but the full degree to which his completed work would have rounded out our understanding of his views (perhaps even negating some of his other emphases) will possibly never be known. Certainly it will have to await careful study of the several volumes of yet unpublished exegetical writings. Even now,

[19] Quoted by Sereno E. Dwight in his *Life of President Edwards* in *The Works of President Edwards,* Dwight ed., 10 vols., New York, 1829, I, 569–570.

however, it can be said that this dimension (quite literally the fourth dimension) to his thought makes him stand out against his eighteenth-century Enlightenment background more sharply than his other writings. Herein may lie his most impressive originality.[20]

One can safely insist, in any event, that no man was more concerned than Edwards with the "admirable contexture and harmony of the whole." Historically we may never be able to remove every contradiction, resolve every paradox, or fill all the interstices in Edwards' system. Only his own devout and active intelligence could do that. Despite his abrupt death, however, Edwards' "New Divinity" did much to define the issues for a century of American Reformed theologizing.[21] Even when it ceased to be a living force in the churches, it was kept alive by academic admirers, and at the bicentennial of his death there are signs that a movement from the academy back to the Church is taking place. By negative reaction it had hardly less effect on America's emerging religious liberalism.

William Ellery Channing and "Enlightened" Christianity

The leading figure of the liberal or "Arminian" party [22] in eastern Massachusetts during most of the eighteenth century was Charles Chauncy, minister of the First Church in Boston from 1727 to 1787. Though a descendant and name-

---

[20] Post-millennialism was one very significant and fateful aspect of his understanding of the fourth dimension; see C. C. Goen's article, "Jonathan Edwards: A New Departure in Eschatology," in *Church History*, XXVIII, March, 1959, pp. 25–40.

[21] Edwardsean theology was given its clearest and most faithful systematic expression by Joseph Bellamy who had studied in Edwards' home and whose *True Religion Delineated* (1750) was published with an introduction by the master himself.

[22] "Arminianism" as used in this essay refers not to the specific doctrines of Jacob Arminius, the Dutch theologian, but to the broad tendency to accentuate the human role in redemption. Creeping Arminianism, of course, had provided a major incentive to Edwards' preaching and controversial activities.

sake of one of the first generation's most rigorous conservatives, Chauncy was an outspoken assailant of the Great Awakening, a critic of Edwards, and the intellectual leader of the steady yet barely perceptible process by which "Arianism," Universalism, and more optimistic views of human nature came to dominate the Harvard-educated clergy of the Boston area. Tensions between the contending parties increased until finally, during the two decades from 1805 to 1825, the Massachusetts Standing Order broke in two, with sharp, penetrating controversy becoming the order of the day. By 1830 Unitarianism was a community by itself, a new denomination.[23]

Andrews Norton was the "Pope" of Unitarianism, probably having more to do with its pre-Civil War theological development than any other, especially as it became necessary after 1830 to attack new and more radical Transcendental enemies on the "left." But the soul of the movement, as well as the man who provided its deepest theological inspiration, was William Ellery Channing (1780–1842). Born in Newport in 1780 and reared under mildly Orthodox auspices, he was graduated from Harvard in 1798, a time of spiritual desuetude in the college. For him, however, his college years were a time of spiritual renewal. Led by his reading of the Scottish philosophers, he discovered one day "the glory of the Divine disinterestedness . . . [and] the sublimity of devotedness to the will of Infinite Love." [24] A few years later, while serving as a tutor in Richmond, Virginia, after a deep and moving conversion experience, he determined to enter the ministry. In 1803 before the "Unitarian Controversy" had broken out, he was ordained at the socially

[23] See Conrad Wright, *The Beginnings of Unitarianism in America,* Boston, 1955.

[24] William Henry Channing, *William Ellery Channing,* Boston, 1880, p. 32. See also, *Unitarian Christianity and Other Essays,* Irving H. Bartlett, ed., New York, 1957; Sydney E. Ahlstrom, "The Interpretation of Channing," *New England Quarterly,* xxx, March, 1957, pp. 99–105; Conrad Wright, "The Rediscovery of Channing," *Proceedings of the Unitarian Historical Society,* xii, 1959, pp. 8–25.

prominent Federal Street (now Arlington Street) Church of Boston, where he conducted a distinguished and influential ministry until his death in 1842.

Channing took an active part in the divisive events of 1815, but as an "event maker," the most important thing that he ever did was to preach at the ordination of Jared Sparks in Baltimore in 1819. Published as *Unitarian Christianity*, his sermon became the manifesto of the new liberal movement in theology. If read together with his other controversial writings of the 1815–1820 period, it reveals the basic features of the "Christian Unitarian Mind," though only subsequent controversy with Parker and the extremists would clarify the degree to which this Puritan-based liberalism was a distinctive, unique, and integrated theological synthesis. Its foundation was the inspired Word of God as revealed in Holy Scriptures, which revelation, however, was to be interpreted within the limits of reasonableness. The divine Christ was still the chief cornerstone, sent of the Father, though not God. God was understood in strictly personal terms. His will was wrought in man through the agency of the Holy Spirit. Channing and Norton agreed that by a proper definition of terms they both could be regarded as Trinitarian. The basic issue, thus, was not that which led to the name "Unitarian." It was the question as to the nature of man, and it was on this subject that Channing was most distinctive, even radical, with his doctrine of the "essential sameness" of man and God, and hence of man's perfectibility.[25] This "perfectibilitarianism," in turn, undergirded the strong ethical element in his teaching and buoyed up his confidence in human progress.

Channing's impact on the Unitarian movement through his preaching and personal influence as well as through his sermons and occasional writings was enormous. Yet his influence also flowed far beyond organized Unitarianism. In Europe he became possibly America's most widely known

[25] See Robert Leet Patterson, *The Philosophy of William Ellery Channing*, New York, 1952.

nineteenth-century religious thinker. This larger influence stemmed from the subtle yet profound way in which Channing anticipated and reflected the romantic impulse which reached its culminating American expression in the Transcendentalist movement. Outwardly he remained loyal to the Scottish philosophy and Enlightenment motifs of natural theology, yet for him nature was beginning to suggest more than God's law-governed handiwork; it proclaimed the divine immanence. His doctrine of man's "essential sameness" had the same theological force. He also showed an outspoken individualism that confounded his more orthodox brethren. He asked that "none listen to me for the purpose of learning what others think," and he refused to join the assault on Theodore Parker's self-proclaimed heterodoxy. Not without reason would Ralph Waldo Emerson refer to Channing as "our bishop."

Perhaps in these various but unified tendencies we see the explanation for Channing's failure to complete his long-intended work of systematic divinity. Quite certainly we have the key, or one of the keys, to the secret of his powerful claim on the religious thought of his own and several succeeding generations. Half-consciously but explicitly, he provided a major Christian synthesis of historic New England doctrines, the Enlightenment, the fervor of Pietism, Transcendental romanticism, and American democratic optimism.

Nathaniel William Taylor and the New Haven Theology

New England during the century before the Civil War was the scene of America's most important native flowering of theology. In one area the tradition of Chauncy and Channing established the religious background for the New England renaissance of letters. At the same time, in another area and with controversy as a constant spur to theological creation, the New Divinity became a self-conscious and brilliantly articulated movement. Probably no "school" of American thought, in fact, has been graced by so many men of originality and intellectual power as the New England Theology founded or set in motion by Jonathan Edwards. In the course of a century it enlisted the zeal not only of Jonathan Edwards, Jr., Samuel Hopkins, and Joseph Bellamy, his most faithful successors, but also Nathanael Emmons, Leonard Woods, Timothy Dwight, Bennet Tyler, Edwards Amasa Park, Nathaniel William Taylor, and many other serious thinkers, each one of whom would deserve discussion in the present essay if space permitted. Nor were their efforts simply private preoccupations. Bellamy, Hopkins, Emmons, and the younger Edwards must together have trained over a hundred and fifty other ministers; Woods, Taylor, and Tyler came to personify three separate theological seminaries devoted to the Orthodox cause (Andover, Yale, and Hartford, respectively). Dwight is credited (though not with complete justice) with precipitating an Awakening which far outshone that associated with his grandfather.

Yet none of these men, with the exception of Tyler, were docile Edwardseans. Each was to be remembered for specific and hotly contested innovations. In fact, the determining characteristic of the New Divinity is not so much its specific content as its categories, its vocabulary, and its conception of the problems. From Bellamy on there is a distinct tendency among these successors to formulate a "governmental" rather than a "satisfaction" theory of the atonement, to inveigh against the idea of a "limited atonement" with the insistence that Christ died for all men, to deny the imputation of Adam's sin, to conceive of original sin as privative or dispositional rather than forensic, and to insist that God's permission of sin in the world was essential to a moral (as against a purely mechanical) order. Through this last-mentioned loophole, Edwards' grandson Timothy Dwight marched the legions of "human agency," and to the practical, ethical obligations of the human agent he devoted seventy-two of his four-year cycle of 173 sermons.[26]

Of all the Edwardsean diadochi Samuel Hopkins is undoubtedly the most arresting. No one ever faced the implications of "Consistent Calvinism" more fearlessly than he, with his dramatic insistence that sin was necessary to the world and therefore good, and most infamously, the old doctrine of Thomas Shepard and Thomas Hooker, that one test of a Christian's conversion be his willingness to be damned if it be God's will. Hopkinsian emphasis on "disinterested benevolence" was likewise to be a leaven to New England's humanitarianism, a factor, even, in the life of Channing. Yet the true culmination of the post-Edwardsean tendency is in the theology of Nathaniel William Taylor, who was also the first of the successors to take up the philosophical questions Edwards had posed. In 1880 George Park Fisher could rightly name him as America's greatest metaphysical theologian "since President Edwards." [27] In terms of influence as well, the reach of Taylorism exceeded any other New England system since that of Edwards. He died on the centennial of Edwards' death in 1858, just thirty years after he had startled the Connecticut clergy by setting forth his most distinctive ideas in the annual *Concio ad Clerum* sermon. Between those dates the Yale Divinity School (founded in 1822) had become an exciting center of theological activity with a large and avid student body, a distinguished faculty of kindred spirits, and the *Quarterly Christian Spectator* to carry its views abroad.

In retrospect, two special characteristics of Taylor's the-

---

[26] On Edwards' more important successors see Joseph Haroutunian, *Piety versus Moralism: The Passing of the New England Theology*, New York, 1932, and Frank Hugh Foster, *A Genetic History of the New England Theology*, Chicago, 1907.

[27] *Discussions in History and Theology*, New York, 1880, p. 37. See also Sidney E. Mead, *Nathaniel William Taylor*, Chicago, 1942, and Charles R. Keller, *The Second Great Awakening in Connecticut*, New Haven, 1942.

ological effort loom most prominently. In the first place it was inspired by a highly rationalistic apologetic purpose. As an observer of the Unitarian controversy during the early 1820's, Taylor was convinced that the outmoded arguments of his Orthodox colleagues at Andover were setting the Trinitarian cause back fifty years. His "improvements" on the Edwardsean system, therefore, were those gauged to make the Orthodox case more appealing to the nineteenth-century American mind. For these purposes he drew on the same rationalistic philosophic resources as the Unitarians, but he turned them to Orthodox (or what he considered to be Orthodox) purposes.[28]

Taylorism was at the same time a "revival theology." He himself was "converted" in the Second Great Awakening which his teacher, Timothy Dwight, had done so much to arouse in the Yale and New Haven community. He first gained the public eye as a commanding preacher of spiritual awakening in Center Church, New Haven. And his influence was to be greatest among the men who were to make this Awakening a nation-wide movement of evangelical resurgence.

These purposes or motivations are, of course, very similar to those of Edwards, but beyond this fact the resemblance to a large degree disappears. A good case could be made for the fact that one as much as the other wished to stand under the canopy of Westminster, yet the spirit of their doing so was very different. The basic difference between Edwards and Taylor had to do with their centers of interest. One man lived out his life in a remote part of a colonial dependency during the eighteenth century; the other in the nineteenth-century heyday of a young republic's "Manifest Destiny." The all-consuming concern of Edwards was Almighty God and Being as such; the persistent concern of Taylor was man, above all his freedom and moral agency. In philosophical out-

[28] See Roland H. Bainton, *Yale and the Ministry*, New York, 1957, chs. 7 and 8; H. Shelton Smith, *Changing Conceptions of Original Sin*, New York, 1955, chs. 5 and 6; and Ralph H. Gabriel, *Religion and Learning at Yale*, New Haven, 1958, chs. 7 and 8.

look the two men were equally at variance. What Locke was to Edwards, Thomas Reid was to Taylor, which is to say that Taylor, as a devotee of the "Scottish Philosophy," is part of that large international reaction to the "necessitarian" conclusions seeming to flow so inexorably from the "sensationalist" premises of Locke.

The aspect of Reid and Stewart's Common Sense Realism which attracted Taylor particularly was its argumentation for man's agency, his ability to be a creative first cause, his status outside the causal chain of "nature." Regardless of one's moral choice, Taylor insisted, one had "power to the contrary." Sin, therefore, was in the sinning; man's guilt was actual, not imputed. Nor could God have it otherwise if He wanted "moral government" in the world. Sin was not a necessary good or an "advantage" in the sense of Bellamy or Hopkins; nor did God decree sin, but rather a world in which man made genuine ethical decisions. Taylor argued that it was *certain* that man would sin, but not *necessary*. This distinction between certainty and necessity, therefore, was a crucial link in the chain that held Taylor's system to Orthodox doctrine.[29]

Another contrast between Edwards and Taylor springs from (or ends in) their utterly different approach to ontological and metaphysical questions. Edwards learned from Locke but did not allow his thinking to be circumscribed by him. Edwards would say with Taylor that "guilt was actual, not imputed," but he justified the statement in a vastly different way. From the "moral inability" of the natural man to choose the "good" demonstrated in his *Freedom of the Will*, Edwards leads the reader to his treatises on *Original Sin*, *True Virtue*, and *God's End*, where the argument opens out into a profoundly conceived metaphysics according to which all that is, all that has been, and all that

[29] Of Taylor's works see especially his *Concio ad Clerum* (1828) and *Lectures on the Moral Government of God*, New York, 1859. See also Sydney E. Ahlstrom, "The Scottish Philosophy and American Theology," *Church History*, XXIV, Sept., 1955, pp. 257–272.

happens has God as its immediate cause. If God were not, nought would be. In Edwards' idealism mankind is one with Adam; there was thus no logical difficulty in the phrase from Wigglesworth's primer, "In Adam's fall we sinned all." We did in very fact sin; one need not talk of imputation, or inheritance, or concoct "representative" theories of Adam's significance. Edwards' daring metaphysics, suggesting the Neo-Platonism of Plotinus and at times hovering near to pantheism, solves the problem. At the same time man's dependence becomes an irresistible sub-conclusion and his autonomy a transparent illusion.

All of this is alien to Taylor's Common Sense Realism. Faced with the need for expounding the Pauline paradox in terms of Scottish rationalism and to an audience which had lost contact with Reformation theology, Taylor had no other recourse than to labor a distinction between certainty and necessity.

Taylor's most energetic disciple was his close friend, Lyman Beecher, who carried the revival spirit into Unitarianism's Bostonian heartland and then out to Cincinnati where, as President of Lane Theological Seminary, he was to advance the New Haven Theology among the New School Presbyterians. Taylor's influence would also be strongly (almost embarrassingly) visible in the thinking of that turbulent "Father of Modern Revivalism," Charles Grandison Finney (1792–1875).

Finney was not a product of Yale, though he was born and received his early education in Connecticut. His conversion had come in upstate New York under Presbyterian auspices, but the highly effective "New Measures" that he developed as a rampaging revivalist broke all the old rules and made him unique. Yet after he had more or less settled down as Professor of Theology and then President of Oberlin, the theological system that he developed and expounded to a generation of revivalists bore clear marks of Taylorism, notably in the strong emphasis Finney constantly placed on human agency in the work of an individual's redemption.[30]

The impulse to revivalism, of course, had many sources. In the West, especially, it would be hard to overstate the influence of Methodism. Yet Taylor's impact during the antebellum period was extraordinarily large, among both Congregationalists and Presbyterians, and in the Old Northwest no less than in the East. The American Home Missionary Society and the Plan of Union both served indirectly to extend his influence. In a stricter sense, however, it must be said that Taylor had no true disciples. Nobody of even remotely equivalent intellectual stature carried on his ideas after his death. This can be explained only by the anachronistic character of Taylorism. It was born out of its time. Mid-eighteenth-century Edinburgh could not solve the problems of mid-nineteenth-century America. Horace Bushnell was unconsciously aware of this when he sat in Taylor's classes, and he became symbolic of the new set of presuppositions that were to take over the thinking even of Taylor's successors in the Yale Divinity School. By the time of Taylor's death, moreover, Finney's influence at Oberlin had become an independent phenomenon, while both Congregationalists and Presbyterians had abandoned the Plan of Union and gone their separate ways to seek inspiration at other fountains.

Charles Hodge and the
Princeton Theology

Outwandering New Englanders have from the first been important to the religious and theological development of the middle and southern commonwealths of America. New Ark, New Jersey, a colony of dissatisfied purists who fled the corruptions of New Haven in 1666, may be taken as one instance. Another is provided by the Sandy Creek (N.C.)

[30] On Finney, see George Frederick Wright's *Life*, Boston, 1891; and Charles C. Cole, *Social Ideas of the Northern Evangelists*, New York, 1954.

Baptist Association founded by Shubael Stearns and other New Englanders converted in the Great Awakening. Puritan influence was especially pronounced among Presbyterians, where in conscious opposition to the more dour and dogmatic tradition of that church's Scottish wing, the New England men were enthusiastic champions of the Great Awakening. In 1741 the heated efforts of these revivalistic and anti-hierarchical New Englanders provoked the Old Side–New Side schism of the Presbyterian Church. Largely through their efforts the College of New Jersey (Princeton) was founded, and at the apogee of their influence they called Jonathan Edwards to be its president. His untimely death in 1758, however, coincided with the healing of the schism, and from that time forward the tides of Scottish and Scotch-Irish immigration began to shift the scales. When Princeton turned to John Witherspoon, a prominent Scottish "Evangelical," to be its president (1768), a new balance of power was foreshadowed.[31]

Typical of the new strength to come to the Scottish camp was the Alexander clan, three brothers·of which immigrated from Northern Ireland in 1736. One of them, who was in due course deeply affected by the Great Awakening, led his family westward into the Great Valley of Virginia. There his son prospered as a farmer, electing in turn to see that Archibald, one of *his* sons, should be educated. After long-drawn religious struggles in which his Old School scruples about enthusiasm were finally overthrown by the deeply experienced facts of regeneration, this Archibald Alexander finally ended up as minister to an important Philadelphia congregation. From this position he was leader in the movement to found a general Presbyterian theological seminary at Princeton, N.J. When these labors were crowned by success,

[31] See Leonard J. Trinterud, *The Forming of an American Tradition*, Philadelphia, 1949; Lefferts A. Loetscher, *The Broadening Church: a Study of Theological Issues in the Presbyterian Church since 1869*, Philadelphia, 1954.

he was called by the General Assembly to be its first (and for a time its only) professor.[32]

The works of Jonathan Edwards had contributed their share to the theological education of Alexander, but the new professor set the school in a quite different direction. The Westminster Confession and Catechisms (from which he had been taught as a boy) were of course his starting point; beyond that he turned for his chief support to the great scholastic theologians of the Reformed tradition. Most valuable as a resource were the works of Francisco Turretino of Geneva, whose life had been spent in "Ultra-Orthodox" polemics against Amyraldism in France and all forms of apparent deviations elsewhere.[33] His three-volume, 2,000-page *Institutio Theologiae Elencticae* (1679-1685) remained for half a century the basic text in dogmatics at Princeton. When superseded, its place was taken by the three-volume, 2,000-page *Systematic Theology* (1871–1872) of Alexander's most devoted student, Charles Hodge (1797–1878).

Hodge joined his beloved master on the faculty as a professor of Old Testament in 1822, only three years after graduating. From this eminence and later from the more exalted chair of Exegetical, Didactic, and Polemic Theology, he surveyed the American church-scene like an American Turretine. For fifty years he held forth, with over 3,000 students carrying the Hodge-Alexander tradition throughout Presbyterianism and into other denominations, all across the country and to remote parts of the world. Through the solidly packed pages of the *Princeton Review* innumerable others were reached. Danhof's judgment that Hodge was "the greatest theologian America has ever produced" may be overly fervent; but he is not far wrong in saying that "without

[32] James W. Alexander, *Archibald Alexander*, New York, 1854.
[33] Turretine is the usual English form of his name. See John W. Beardslee's unpublished doctoral dissertation, Yale, 1956, "Theological Development at Geneva under Francis and Jean-Alphonse Turretin 1648–1737."

[Hodge] American Presbyterianism and American Calvinism would have received an entirely different shape." [34]

The cast of Hodge's theology was profoundly different from that of Edwards'. In the first place the passage of a century had wrought a revolution in critical studies of the Biblical literature, a development which Hodge (unlike Taylor) confronted during his two student years in Germany and continued to follow throughout his life. The result of these forces in Princeton was the overt formulation of an almost absolutely rigidified Biblicism. It rested on the unprovable but also irrefutable doctrine that the original manuscripts of the Bible were literally, word for word, inerrant or infallible in every respect.

Next in significance for Hodge's thought was the philosophic allegiance traceable to President Witherspoon. This meant a reliance not on Locke, a fortiori not on Kant, but rather on the Common Sense Realists of Scotland, who were considered the last word in critique of post-Lockean determinism or of utilitarian ethics. This fact notwithstanding, the Princeton Theology as Alexander and Hodge developed it was in no sense a metaphysical system. Notably abandoned was Edwards' rationalization of original sin, instead of which Hodge insisted upon an "imputation theory" drawn very literally from the historic Reformed confessions.

Confessionalism, indeed, is the hallmark of Hodge's theological system. The Reformed confessions constituted for him a Fortress Ehrenbreitstein, and any theologian who challenged them or evaded their literal meaning was to be treated like a foolish knight errant or a traitor. Some measure of his doctrinal rigor is suggested by his suspicion of Edwards,

[34] Ralph J. Danhof, *Charles Hodge as a Dogmatician*, Goes, The Netherlands, n.d. [c. 1928–34], pp. 171–172 and passim. See also John O. Nelson, "Charles Hodge," in *The Lives of Eighteen from Princeton*, Willard Thorp, ed., Princeton, 1946; Nelson's unpublished doctoral dissertation, Yale, 1935, "The Rise of the Princeton Theology"; and Archibald A. Hodge, *Charles Hodge*, New York, 1880.

his deprecation of Hopkins, his forthright attacks on E. A. Park, and his conviction that Taylor was altogether outside the pale. This kind of strictness underlay his oft-quoted and much misunderstood boast that "a new idea never originated" at Princeton Seminary.

Actually many ideas originated in Hodge's Princeton, but they were chiefly in the realm of apologetics and "polemical theology." Hodge was as well-informed a thinker as American Presbyterianism possessed in the mid-nineteenth century, and his erudition ranged widely over the fields of Biblical scholarship, the history of doctrine, and philosophical theology. Probably nobody in the country was so generally well-versed in all the sciences of theology. What makes his *Systematic Theology* memorable, however, is not easily stated. Comprehensiveness, despite its length, is not a notable feature, and it is even said that he projected a fourth volume to round out its discussion of the Church. Nor is orderliness its chief characteristic, for the immense machinery of numbered divisions and subdivisions fails to veil the fact that it stands unsatisfactorily midway between the series of relatively isolated and unrelated "issues" in Turretine and the marvelously integrated, logical discussion of Calvin's *Institutes*. To commend its lucidity would provoke little dissent, though it did contain some serious contradictions. To call it novel or original would be, according to Hodge himself, to condemn it, for fidelity to the Reformed tradition in dogmatics was his ideal. Yet there were innovations, and some typically American ones.

The chief characteristic of his method is his dependence on the dogmas set forth in the Reformed confessions, even though the nature and status of dogma are not defined. Hodge's system is allegedly "inductive" in a manner that can be traced to Witherspoon and the Scottish Realists, but the "facts" of Hodge's inductive science of theology are the propositional units of Scripture as they had been isolated and interpreted in the light of Reformed dogmatics.

The most notable feature of the content (*pars materialis*) of his work is the degree to which he reflects a scholastic rather than an "Old Calvinist" point of view. This tendency is apparent in his clean separation between natural theology and revealed theology, in the powers he assigns to the former, and in his mode of discussing the attributes of God. Yet he also departed from Turretine and the scholastics in the direction of "clemency" on those points where Calvinism had been traditionally regarded as "harsh." He categorically counted infants among the elect; he held that most professed Christians are redeemed; and in other ways he seemed to extend the Covenant of Grace beyond the bounds set by stricter Reformed theologians. Unlike Samuel Hopkins, whom he criticized on many grounds, Hodge preferred not to discuss how God is glorified in his judgment of the reprobate.

If these tendencies and characteristics are borne in mind, the safest quick guide to the spirit and content of Hodge is provided by the Westminster formularies plus the two chief Swiss symbols, which Hodge's son interestingly included in his own *Outlines of Theology*, a vast text in dogmatics which actually preceded Charles Hodge's *Systematic Theology* into print.[35] No nineteenth-century American strove so hard as Hodge to expound faithfully, and then to defend, strict scholastic Reformed confessional theology.

In the Presbyterianism of his day, however, Hodge's role was heavily conditioned by the Church's political controversies, which had continued unresolved since the schism of 1741–1758. The old cleavage was reopened, therefore, after 1801, when the Congregational-Presbyterian "Plan of Union" was hastily adopted to consolidate the work of these denominations in the West. Strict Old School men (and Hodge was that) naturally rallied to the defense of Presbyterian principles on three major fronts: (1) against the alteration of Presbyterian

---

[35] The Consensus Tigurinus of 1549 and the Formula Consensus Helvetica of 1675. See Appendix to Archibald A. Hodge, *Outlines of Theology*, rev. ed., New York, 1878, first published in 1860.

church-polity through concessions to Congregationalism; (2) against the inter-denominational control of mission funds by voluntary associations such as the American Home Missionary Society; and most fundamentally (3) against the doctrinal innovations associated with the New Haven Theology, which seemed to be making large inroads. When New School men, independent of the Assembly, founded Union Theological Seminary in 1836, Princeton became increasingly the intellectual center of the Old School and Hodge its theological leader, though the seminary faculty, including Hodge, sought to steer a course that would avoid schism. Pacific gestures went for nought, however, and in 1837 the Old School-dominated General Assembly cut the denomination almost in half by excising four large western Synods where "Presbygational" organization was most widespread and where the New Haven Theology was most pervasive.

Princeton Seminary, needless to say, stayed with the Old School and remained the center of its theological activity with Hodge, his son, and two sons of Alexander prominent on the faculty. Hodge lived to see the agonizing Civil War schism that later split both divisions of the Church. He also survived to oppose (without avail) the 1869 reunion of the Old and New School branches of the North. After his death the Old School spirit continued substantially intact at Princeton until Professors J. Gresham Machen and Robert Dick Wilson withdrew to found Westminster Seminary (1929). The Hodge tradition continues to be honored by conservative theologians in several Reformed denominations. From his own time to the present, before the Fundamentalist Controversy and after, his learning, his doctrinal rigor, his respect for confessional tradition, and his insistence on intelligible discussion have held large groups of strict conservatives from anti-intellectual and compulsively partisan activities and alignments. Few men did more to prevent emotionalism or sentimentality from submerging theological concern.

John Williamson Nevin and the
Mercersburg Movement

Charles Hodge can be regarded as the assailant par excellence of New School divinity in general and Taylorism in particular under their doctrinal aspect; but John Williamson Nevin led the most inspired movement to repair the havoc which revivalism was working on Reformed church life in America. Outside of a narrow circle he was ignored, but he made, nevertheless, the nineteenth century's most distinguished effort to bring the Reformed churches of America back to a "pre-Puritan" understanding of the Church, the sacraments, and the historic catholic heritage. This effort, it should be added, brought even the mighty Hodge under criticism. As the chief theologian of the Mercersburg Movement, Nevin was also an important means by which the post-Kantian renaissance of German theology and churchly scholarship entered into American religious life.

He was born in 1803 of Scotch-Irish parents in Pennsylvania, attended Union College at Schenectady, N.Y., and then Princeton Seminary, where he also taught for two years while Hodge was abroad. He became professor of Biblical literature in Western Theological Seminary (Presbyterian) in Allegheny, Pa., until his decision in 1840 to accept a call to (of all places) the German Reformed Seminary in Mercersburg, Pa. It appears that diverse readings had already prepared his mind for the change, but he could not possibly have foreseen the eventful new career that lay ahead of him.

When Nevin arrived at his new post, his only real colleague was Frederick A. Rauch, a German-educated philosopher-psychologist of the Hegelian-Right tradition, a man almost certainly destined for a career of great and rich influence. But he died in 1841—to be replaced by another young and promising scholar, Philip Schaff of the University of Berlin, who for a full half-century would play an active role in American church life. That two (or three) of the country's foremost and most brilliant scholar-theologians should be thus set down in mountains of Pennsylvania as professors to a handful of students in a struggling seminary of a very small denomination is almost as ironical as the exile of Jonathan Edwards to Stockbridge. Lacking in the Mercersburg case, however, was the justice that came to Edwards through the widespread acclaim of his writings. The Mercersburg theologians—Nevin above all—have had to wait a century for adequate recognition from beyond their immediate sphere of activity in the German Reformed Church and from a small outside circle of readers.[36]

The first of Nevin's controversial writings was his small but fierce attack on *The Anxious Bench* which appeared in 1843. It was a direct challenge to the "New Measures" in revivalism associated with the name of Charles G. Finney. Nevin minced no words. "The spirit of the Anxious Bench is at war with the spirit of the Catechism. . . . The Bench is against the Catechism, and the Catechism is against the Bench." He condemned high-pressure revivalism as "unfavorable to deep, thorough and intelligent piety . . . absolutely fatal to the true idea of devotion [and] . . . injurious to the worship of God."[37] Nor was he simply hurling epithets; the book consists chiefly of a series of closely knit arguments calculated to demonstrate that the ground principles of this radical experiential emphasis were not only superficial but subversive of the Faith. The book's influence on the "German churches" to which it was primarily directed seems, moreover, to have been very considerable.

Nevin's influence among the German Reformed had been much strengthened by the series of masterly essays he had

---

[36] See Theodore Appel, *John Williamson Nevin*, Philadelphia, Reformed Church Publ. House, 1889; Luther J. Binkley, *The Mercersburg Theology*, Lancester, 1953; Howard J. Ziegler, *Frederick Augustus Rauch, American Hegelian*, Lancaster, 1953; and David S. Schaff, *The Life of Philip Schaff*, New York, 1897.

[37] Nevin, *The Anxious Bench*, Chambersburg, 1843, p. 56.

published during the years 1840–1842 on *The History and Genius of the Heidelberg Catechism,* published as a book in 1847. This work was to some extent an apologia for his own transfer of denominational allegiance, but in a larger sense it was a theological and historical exposition of that great confession and the men and events connected with its creation. It was a thorough reevaluation of the sixteenth-century Reformation witness and a dramatic indication of the degree to which British Puritanism, American revivalism, and rationalistic modernism had drifted away from the profoundly catholic and churchly stand of the Reformers.

Nevin's campaign for a better appreciation of the Church's whole tradition was deepened in 1845 when he brought out an English translation of Schaff's enlarged *Principle of Protestantism.* In his Introduction he showed his thoroughgoing approval of Schaff's historical approach and his conviction that out of it could come a conception of the Church more adequate to the American scene than the attenuated Puritanism of the revivalists. The chief thrust of the argument elaborated by the two men in this book and in countless articles published through the *Mercersburg Review* was in two directions. First, they sought to advance a truly historical understanding of the Church's past, emphasizing especially the need for adequately appreciating pre-Reformation developments and the early Church. Through the same categories they stressed the Church's potentialities for the future and envisioned the reunion of Christendom. In this dual or two-directional historical interest, the formal principle of the Mercersburg Theology could be said to lie.

To continue the scholastic metaphor, one could go on to say that the material principle was expressed in Nevin's *The Mystical Presence: A Vindication of the Reformed or Calvinistic Doctrine of the Holy Eucharist* (1846). This small masterpiece presents the central thesis of the movement: that the heart of any theology or mode of church life lies in its conception of the Eucharist, and that the Reformed churches had lost the high views of church and sacrament which had been held and defended by Calvin.

"The question of the Eucharist is one of the most important belonging to the history of religion. It may be regarded indeed as in some sense central to the whole Christian system. For Christianity is grounded in the living union of the believer with the person of Christ; and this great fact is emphatically concentrated in the mystery of the Lord's Supper. . . .

"The sacramental controversy of the sixteenth century then was no mere war of words; much less the offspring of mere prejudice, passion or blind self-will. . . . It belonged to the inmost sanctuary of theology, and was intertwined particularly with all the arteries of the Christian life. This was *felt* by the spiritual heroes of the Reformation. . . . With the revival of a deeper theology, there cannot fail to be a revival of interest also, on the part of the Church, in the sacramental question; as on the other hand there can be no surer sign than the want of such interest, in the case of any section of the Church at any given time, that its theology is without power and its piety infected with disease." [38]

Nevin then went on to lay out in great detail the sacramental theology of the founders of the Reformed tradition, above all Calvin and the Heidelberg Catechism. From a wide array of sources he marshalled the evidence that these men agreed with Luther as to the *fact* of the Real Presence in the sacrament, but disagreed only as to the *mode* of its presence. He finds this early view held even in that late product of English Puritanism, the Westminster Confession and Catechisms. This is followed by a well-documented section on "The Modern Puritan Theory" in which he arraigns the whole New Divinity tradition—President Edwards, Samuel Hopkins, and President Dwight—as well as nearly every other denominational tradition in the country. They had,

[38] *The Mystical Presence*, Philadelphia, 1846, p. 51.

claimed Nevin, degraded the sacrament into a merely memorial or subjective event. He then goes on in the last half of the book to theological, historical, and Biblical demonstrations that the early Reformers were right in their judgment and that, by the same token, nineteenth-century churchmen should mend their sacramental ways.

What we have in this insistence is an objective instance of the whole drive of the Mercersburg movement: its persistent effort to achieve a Christ-centered theology. The chief purpose of both Nevin and Schaff (as well as their successors in the Seminary) was to make the *person* of Christ the center of theology and church life. In this they were immensely indebted to Schleiermacher and Neander, yet there is a profound difference between the Mercersburg theology and the Liberalism of German academic theology. In part this is because they were also influenced by the conservative reaction to Schleiermacher and by the great mediating theologians such as I. A. Dorner. The English Oxford Movement also played a role. Basically, however, the impulse stemmed from those historical studies that were the constant inspiration of the Mercersburg leaders. Whatever the sources, the result is fairly definite: a movement of church reform based on an objective, catholic, and yet Reformed understanding of Christ and His Church. Both required and implied in this effort was the conviction as to Christ's bodily subsistence in the visible Church and His presence in the Eucharistic sacrament. After Nevin and Schaff had retired, their impulse was carried on by a continuous line of professors. In the German Reformed Church, at least, the movement made a lasting impact not only in theology but through diverse liturgical, catechetical, and even architectural forms.[39]

[39] The "Mercersburg theology" received its full doctrinal expression in Emmanuel V. Gerhart's *Institutes of the Christian Religion*, 2 vols., New York, 1891, 1894 published with an introduction by Philip Schaff.

Carl F. W. Walther, Charles P. Krauth, and Lutheran Theology

Lutheran theology in America poses special difficulties for the historian in that so many issues determining its development are outside of the British-American traditions. This is not to say, however, that the Lutheran Church was spared the experience of adapting itself to America's voluntaristic church ways or to a denominational pluralism in which Reformed theology and radical revivalistic practice predominated. A considerable number of Lutherans responded in a very affirmative way to the impact of "American Evangelical Protestantism." [40] John W. Nevin, indeed, felt obliged to direct much of his attack on the "Anxious Bench" at Lutheran advocates of the revivalistic "New Measures" such as Benjamin Kurtz, editor of *The Lutheran Observer*. Even Samuel S. Schmucker (1799–1873), who more than any one man was responsible for rescuing early American Lutheranism from dissolution through the organization of a national General Synod (1820) and the founding of Gettysburg Seminary (1826), was an exponent of these attitudes, measures, and doctrines. [41]

As the years went by, however, the Lutheran situation in America began to change with increasing rapidity, the first and most obvious cause for change being immigration. After the 1840's, the "Great Atlantic Migration" from Northern Europe brought hundreds of thousands, finally millions, of Lutherans to the United States. These new arrivals, whether German or Scandinavian, often disagreed among themselves

---

[40] On the generalized concept of "American Evangelical Protestantism," see Ralph H. Gabriel, *The Course of American Democratic Thought*, 2nd ed., New York, 1956; Sidney E. Mead, "The Rise of the Evangelical Conception of the Ministry in America: 1607–1850," in H. Richard Niebuhr and Daniel D. Williams, eds., *The Ministry in Historical Perspectives*, New York, 1956, and other essays by Mead therein cited.

[41] See Vergilius Ferm, *The Crisis in American Lutheran Theology*, New York, 1927, and Abdel R. Wentz, *A Basic History of American Lutheranism*, Philadelphia, 1955.

as to the relative merits of Orthodoxy and Pietism, but they were generally far more consciously Lutheran than their co-religionists in this country. As a consequence they tended to organize new churches even when there were ethnic ties to existing bodies.

No man personifies this trend more effectively that Carl Ferdinand Wilhelm Walther (1811–1887) whose biographer does not go far wrong in naming him as "easily the most commanding figure in the Lutheran Church of America during the nineteenth century." [42] Walther was born in Saxony, the son and grandson of pastors, but his education reflected the firm grip the Enlightenment had on the churches and schools of Germany. While pursuing theological studies at the University of Leipzig, however, he was part of a little group of students who were cultivating the Christian life and reading together in the great classics of Pietism. From these associations and his pre-ordination Luther studies it was a short step to the convictions about pure doctrine and experiential preaching that finally made it impossible for him to continue in good conscience as a pastor in the state church. With his brother, therefore, he joined the company of over six hundred Saxons who left their homeland in 1839 to found a pure Lutheran Zion in Missouri. In the New World he soon rose to preeminence as a teacher and theologian. As theology professor in Concordia Seminary, St. Louis, from 1849 to his death in 1887, his private life became literally a part of the Synod's public life, and his thoughts very nearly came to be its thoughts. What these thoughts were, however, cannot be quickly stated, for he ranged over the entire field of Christian dogmatics and brought to his pronouncements a depth of historical erudition and type of theological acumen which no survey can convey. Yet three of his running controversies do light up characteristic emphases in his thought.

[42] D. H. Steffens, *Carl F. W. Walther*, Philadelphia, 1917, p. 10. See also Walter O. Forster, *Zion on the Mississippi*, St. Louis, 1953, and Robert C. Schultz, *Gesetz und Evangelium in der lutherischen Theologie des 19. Jahrhunderts*, Berlin, 1958, pp. 158ff.

First to emerge was a doctrine of the Church that arose out of his own Synod's agonizing need to reestablish itself after the defalcation of its first "bishop." This accent continued in Walther's conflict with Pastor J. A. A. Grabau who had led a group of earnest Lutherans out of Prussia and founded the Buffalo (N.Y.) Synod very much in the spirit of Missouri's Saxon Zion. Grabau was a high churchman who directly challenged Missouri's insistence on rooting the life of the Church in the congregation and on the power of the Word rather than on a hierarchy, ministerial authority, and apostolic ordination. Walther fiercely defended his "transfer theory" of the ministry, according to which the congregation called its ministry and delegated authority to it. In 1867 he had the satisfaction of seeing most of the Buffalo Ministerium join the Missouri Synod; but far more important than this triumph was the strength he gave to a deep-seated characteristic of American Lutheranism: a strong emphasis on Biblical rather than institutional authority, and a concern for questions of doctrine rather than church order.

But how much doctrinal agreement must there be? That was the issue between Walther and the theologians of the Iowa Synod who contended for the legitimacy of "open questions" and a somewhat broader conception of what was adiaphorous.[43] Walther's stand was unequivocal: doctrinal consensus on an extremely wide range of subjects must precede pulpit and altar fellowship. Even within Missouri, however, there was not complete agreement, and around 1880 this disunity finally resulted in the third of Walther's great controversies, which was also one of the most fateful in American Lutheran history.

Because of his forceful statement of man's need for God's grace in redemption, Walther was accused of "crypto-calvin-

[43] The Iowa Synod was founded in 1854 by Germans who were materially aided and profoundly inspired by Wilhelm Loehe (1808–1872), an outstanding missions leader, liturgical reformer, and theologian of Neuendettelsau (Bavaria). J. Michael Reu (1869–1943) was the Iowa Synod's great historical scholar and theologian.

ism," a charge made with special vehemence by those with pronounced Pietistic sympathies and heard with special rancor by those whose chief role was the defense of true doctrine. The justice of these charges is still a sensitive question, but at the time it was positively explosive.[44] Several of Walther's own ministerial brethren withdrew from the Synod; synodical relations with Norwegian Lutheranism and other German groups had to be broken off. Missouri was left in the near isolation in which she remained for nearly half a century. Walther's influence continued, nevertheless, to hold the American Lutheran churches by a kind of invisible tether to the Reformation's Biblical and doctrinal heritage, above all in resisting the tendency of revivalists and liberals to augment the human role in salvation. Walther's influence was especially significant in that he stood almost alone in the nineteenth-century American theological scene as one fully aware of the crucial importance of the problems of Law and Gospel to the Christian faith. In his insistence on their importance he anticipates the emphasis of Karl Barth and the "Luther renaissance" of the next century, but by the same fact he doomed himself to attack and misunderstanding in his own time.

Yet there was another, more indigenous source of the changed temper in American Lutheran theology. As with Nevin's thinking, it arose from a deep-going disenchantment with the prevailing revivalistic modes of American church life and had a spontaneity akin to the rise of Transcendentalism in Massachusetts. At the same time it partook of the large-scale turning of American eyes to the philosophical, theological, and "churchly" ferment of the Lutheran countries of Europe. The response, however, was not unanimous. Many

---

[44] On this controversy, see Wentz, *Basic History*, pp. 212–216. See also C. F. W. Walther, *The Proper Distinction between Law and Gospel*, W. H. T. Dau, tr., St. Louis, 1929; and Franz A. O. Pieper, *Conversion and Election; a Plea for a United Lutheranism in America*, T. Graebner, tr., St. Louis, 1913.

men like Schmucker and Kurtz did not participate in this process but rather rested their program for an "American" Lutheranism on elements drawn from the Enlightenment, the revivals, and the later Puritanism. The long-developing tension was increased in 1855 with the anonymous publication of the *Definite Synodical Platform,* in which Schmucker's proposals for changing the doctrinal position of Lutheranism were made explicit. When the venerable Pennsylvania Ministerium established its own seminary in 1864, disruption of the General Synod shortly followed. In 1867 the conservatives organized the General Council with the hope that it would become the national rallying-point for churches holding to the unaltered Lutheran confessions.

Out of this period of dissension in the Lutheran Church there emerged a great quantity of distinguished theology and scholarship in most of the major branches of the Church. There is little doubt, however, that the most influential American-born leader of this movement was Charles Porterfield Krauth (1823–1883) whose grandfather, an organist and teacher, had come to America just before the War of 1812, and whose father was for a time president of Gettysburg College and later a professor at Gettysburg Seminary. After an education in these institutions, the son held a series of six pastorates in Maryland, Virginia, and Pennsylvania, during which time his convictions about the uncommitted nature of American Lutheranism became a thoroughgoing preoccupation. With increasing concern he devoted himself to scholarship, writing, and translating designed to deepen the general understanding of liturgical and doctrinal matters, above all the meeting-place of these two concerns in the Holy Eucharist. These activities finally culminated in 1860 with his becoming editor of *The Lutheran and Missionary,* a church paper dedicated to the revival of traditional doctrinal interests. In 1864 he was made Professor of Systematic Divinity in the new Philadelphia Seminary of the Pennsylvania Ministerium. From 1868 to 1883 he was Professor of Philosophy in the

University of Pennsylvania and after 1873 Vice-Provost as well. But his most dedicated activity had to do with the theological support of the new General Council and its confessional standards.[45]

Krauth's chief literary labor, a massive treatise on *The Conservative Reformation and Its Theology* (1871), was at once a summary of his life's work and the century's most influential Lutheran doctrinal work of native American authorship. In it he had a dual purpose, the first being to describe the Lutheran Reformation and the events surrounding the origins of the Confessions. He sought to show that the issue was then, as it still remains, "between conservative reformation and revolutionary radicalism." With great felicity and persuasiveness he brought to an English-reading audience his vast erudition and a minute knowledge of an immense body of German scholarship. The second part was a cogent defense of the "Specific Theology of the Conservative Reformation," especially on original sin, Christology, baptism, and above all, the Lord's Supper.

A few brief paragraphs cannot summarize so detailed and wide-ranging a volume, but the essential thrust of Krauth's demand can be suggested. Most notably he directed the attention of men to the Church's confessions, insisting that "they are parts of the Reformation itself." The Church, he insisted, must stand for something more definite than "Protestant hermeneutics." To Krauth a confession was not only a doctrinal norm but a kind of doxology, a witness, a hymn of praise, an affirmation that took on the liturgical quality traditionally evoked in and through the Apostles' and Nicene Creeds. For him ". . . the object of a *Creed* [or Confession] is not to find out what God teaches, (we go to the Bible for that,) but to show what we believe." Part and parcel of this idea was his eloquently expressed conviction that the Church was bound to affirm the faith it held rather than search for a platform

[45] See Adolph Spaeth's excellent biography, *Charles Porterfield Krauth*, 2 vols., New York, 1898.

broad enough to hold everyone whom it was not willing to condemn as certainly lost. "The Church," he insisted, "is not merely designed . . . to bring into outward association, men who are to get to heaven. . . ."

Equally characteristic of Krauth was the way in which he refused to express these doctrinal concerns in simply anti-Roman terms. Over and over again he insists that:

"the overthrow of Romanism was not the primary object [of the Lutheran Reformation]; in a certain sense it was not its object at all. Its object was to establish truth. . . . There was no fear of truth, simply because Rome held it, and no disposition to embrace error, because it might be employed with advantage to Rome's injury." [46]

What was still more unusual in Protestant America, he turned his heavy artillery upon many other aspects of Reformed dogmatics than the much battered and misunderstood doctrine of double predestination. Like John W. Nevin,[47] he also sought with special zeal to reform the Church's liturgical and theological understanding of the Sacrament of the Altar. He knew the central place of this issue in the sixteenth century, and he believed that "well-set bones knit precisely where they broke; and [that when] well knit, the point of breaking becomes the strongest in the bone." [48]

No man could read Krauth's treatise without realizing the extraordinary unity and significance of the "historic moment" that produced the confessional writings. Because he was so thoroughly Americanized in his manner, interests, and occupation (German was an acquired second language for him), he was especially effective in making the Lutheran renaissance relevant for America and American Christianity. In English-speaking circles, therefore, and among those who were for

---

[46] *The Conservative Reformation and Its Theology*, Philadelphia, 1871, pp. 184, 189, 203–205.

[47] For Nevin's opinion of the book see Spaeth, *Krauth*, II, 307ff.

[48] *Conservative Reformation*, p. 829. Theodore E. Schmauk, in effect, supplied a sequel to Krauth with his *The Confessional Principle*, Philadelphia, 1911.

any reason alienated from Professor Walther, Krauth provided an eloquent and persuasive basis for the labors in dogmatics that were carried on in synod after synod.

In any estimate of the structuring and re-formation of
American Lutheranism during the post-Civil War decades,
Krauth's magnum opus must be recognized as a milestone,
just as Walther's persistent hammering must be seen as an
indirect pressure even on men such as Krauth. In the long
run, the influence of both men, no less than the kindred efforts
of theologians and scholars in other synods, has extended far
beyond the borders of the Lutheran Church.

Horace Bushnell and Early Liberalism

During the two decades before the Civil War the "Church
Question" profoundly agitated the American churches—and
far beyond the confines of the German churches where the
historical, liturgical, and theological impact of Nevin and
Krauth was felt. As we have seen, Nevin himself had been
deeply moved by the "Tracts for the Times" of the Oxford
Movement in England. In the Protestant Episcopal Church,
meanwhile, the "Catholic" and "Evangelical" parties became
locked in irreconcilable conflict on the issues raised by the
Tractarians. A major factor in the heightening of tensions
on this issue was the mushrooming Nativist movement directed against the Roman Catholic Church. Already in 1834
a mob had burned the Ursuline Convent in Charlestown,
Mass., and in the 1850's the "Know-Nothing" movement was
to gain vast political proportions.

Yet the drastic contrast between the Catholic tradition and
American revivalism was not the only mode of conceiving the
issue, and it is the special distinction of Horace Bushnell
(1802–1876) to have confronted the church issue in an almost
completely different way.[49] This is not to say that Bushnell's
motivations were utterly removed from those of other Ameri-

[49] The basic *Life and Letters of Horace Bushnell*, New York, 1880, is by
his daughter, Mary Bushnell Cheney, but also see the biographies by Theodore
T. Munger, Boston, 1899, and Barbara Cross, Chicago, 1958.

can church reformers. He was, first of all, immensely distrustful of the mechanisms and philosophy of the revivalism which in his day dominated New England Congregationalism, and this despite his profound concern for religious experience, even conversion, in himself and in others. At the same time he was defiantly anti-Roman. He could be projected into otherworldly ecstasy by the organ music of Santa Croce, but the most permanent and by far the best known result of his travels in Italy was his excoriation of papal despotism in an open "Letter to the Pope."

Bushnell's roots were sunk deep in the church life of rural Connecticut, already described in his own words.[50] After vocational sorties in teaching and journalism, he studied law and was about to enter private practice when a conversion experience in 1831 set his steps to the Yale Divinity School where he became an unimpressed student of Nathaniel William Taylor. The remainder of his active career was spent as minister to the North Church in Hartford. In this position, first as a preacher, then increasingly as a lecturer, and finally as a widely read writer, he defined, elaborated, and defended a new and extremely creative religious outlook. In the end he would deserve the two "titles" frequently conferred on him: the "American Schleiermacher" and the "Father of American Liberalism."

His initial stimulus was akin to Nevin's: what Neander was to the Presbyterian professor of theology, Coleridge was to the Congregational minister. Behind both was the message of German romantic idealism, above all Schleiermacher's immanentistic theology of feeling. The historical situation peculiar to Bushnell was the need to develop a viable conception of Christian church life between the alternatives posed in Hartford by the revivalism of the First Church and the socially gratifying parish life of the Episcopal churches.[51] In a

---

[50] See above, p. 233.
[51] See especially Cross, *Bushnell*, passim. Note also Mrs. Cross's delineation of Bushnell's profound but imperfectly articulated conception of God's sacrificial love (ch. 9).

more theological sense, Bushnell was seeking for a conception of Christian life and thought that would transcend the encroaching materialisms of science and commercial civilization without disappearing into the clouds of romantic pantheism where all contact was lost with the concerns of this world and the realities of revealed Christianity, the incarnate Lord, and the Church. He was, thus, a mediator.

Bushnell was not a systematic theologian, however. Sermons, lectures, addresses, essays, and controversial writings constitute the greater part of his published writing, though three important treatises bulk very large.[52] Yet the unity of his thought is one of its most impressive features. The deepgoing disjunctions that create such problems for the interpreter of Jonathan Edwards do not exist. For the interpreter of Bushnell, in fact, this very unity creates a serious problem. How break into the circle? The answer, I think, lies in seeing the motif for Bushnell's thought in his rigorous emphasis on the contextual nature of reality, the close interrelatedness of all things. In such thinking he was—like Nevin and Ralph Waldo Emerson—much indebted to German idealistic thinkers; yet more than any of these men Bushnell carried the new philosophic and theological tenets into his thinking about human relations, human groups (such as the family), and above all, the Church in both its universal and local manifestations. In his use of this theme lies his chief claim to originality.

The most useful key to Bushnell's method of achieving his purpose is the theory of language which he made public in 1849.[53] To him all words are faded and indistinct metaphors. Except in their simplest and least used sense they can not be transferred from one mind to another like coins. Each word is organically related to its history, its user's history, and the

[52] *Christian Nurture*, New York, 1847; *The Vicarious Sacrifice*, New York, 1866, as augmented and altered by *Forgiveness and Law*, New York, 1874; and *Nature and the Supernatural*, New York, 1858.

[53] "The Preliminary Dissertation on Language" in *God in Christ*, Hartford, 1849; defended and enlarged in "Language and Doctrine" in *Christ in Theology*, Hartford, 1851.

situation—that is, to a context whose only limit is the Logos of the Creation. Creeds, confessions, doctrinal statements, and even the Scriptures must be so understood. They are linguistic and hence poetic efforts to speak the unspeakable, to frame the illimitable Mystery. Paradox and contradiction thus appear as unavoidable aspects of religious discourse. Because of their primarily evocative role, moreover, words and language must be seen as preeminently *social* phenomena. By a logical extension, thought and conceptual knowledge are likewise social, and the "language of Canaan" is no exception.[54]

Working back in the other direction, Bushnell sought to understand the life and work of the Church in this social context. Its status as a *community* of faith came to the fore: it was not the collection of atomic individuals voluntaristically gathered for the better prosecution of revivals. Yet here again, by a logical extension, the boundary lines became indistinct. Thinking contextually of the nurture of the Christian community, Bushnell found it hard to distinguish the "saved" and the "unsaved." Rightfully, he argued, a child is brought into the church by baptism and he should, if rightly nurtured, never remember a time when he had not been a Christian. By so saying, he broke down another boundary, that between family and Church. Beyond the family, moreover, there would be other interlocking group relationships. Spurred on by his unbounded optimism for the future of American democracy, Bushnell could ultimately entertain the idea of a "divine society."

The doctrinal accompaniments of these rich and refreshing views were often adaptations of Schleiermacher's thought, which was already being widely appropriated and adapted on the Continent and which was soon to become important for America's religious liberalism. In this sense they were not new; but they were new, even shocking, to New England

[54] Charles Feidelson discusses Bushnell's language theory perceptively and in a very useful context: *Symbolism in American Literature*, Chicago, 1953, pp. 151–157.

Orthodoxy. Bushnell began by occupying the ground Taylor had cleared: a strict doctrine of election or of the imputation of Adam's sin was nowhere to be seen. In their place was an insistence on man's moral responsibility (not his "moral inability" as Edwards had said). Coupled with this was a characteristically "contextual" conception of human sinfulness as "an organic depravation of humanity" radiating throughout mankind from Adam's fall until it exists as a veritable "kingdom opposite to God." [55]

The redemptive principle in this disordered world is Christ and His atoning work. Unlike so many critics of Unitarianism, however, Bushnell did not sacrifice the human Christ to the divine. Man could not be regenerated without the moral influence of Christ's atoning work, yet the working of the atonement in the world was like the workings of all other spiritual and creative forces. It was outside the mechanistic linkage of material causality, and was therefore supernatural. Precisely here we contact the real radicalism of Bushnell: the "supernatural" to him was consubstantial with but distinguishable from the "natural."

"Nature . . . is that created realm of being or substance which has an acting, a going on or process from within itself, under and by its own laws. . . . That is supernatural . . . that is either not in the chain of natural cause and effect, or which acts on the chain of cause and effect, in nature, from without the chain. . . . There is, however, a constant action and reaction between the two, and, strictly speaking, they are both together, taken as one, the true system of God." [56]

In such a "system" the effect of Christ's "vicarious sacrifice" works as the vicarious sacrifice of any person might work, only more so. By the same argument, the real force of Bushnell's position on the two natures of Christ is exhibited, for in

[55] *Nature and the Supernatural*, p. 135. See also H. Shelton Smith, *Changing Conceptions*, ch. 7.
[56] *Nature and the Supernatural*, pp. 36–38

all persons the natural and the supernatural, the human and the divine, are consubstantial.

From the foregoing discussion it must have become clear that the central purpose of Bushnell's theological effort was apologetic even when its form was constructive. He was overwhelmed by the apparent fact that "a time of jeopardy has come."

"There is a growing multitude in our own churches, and a still larger more heavily insurgent multitude outside, who, in tones that indicate all kinds of tempers, gentle and fierce, candid and contemptuous, join their testimony against all we have been calling Expiation and Legal Atonement. There is the new infidelity: not that rampant, crude-minded, and malignant scoffing which, in a former age, undertook to rid the age of all religion; on the contrary, it puts on the air and speaks in the character of genuine scholarship and philosophy. . . . Whether Christianity can finally survive this deathdamp of naturalism in our political and social ideas, remains to be seen." [57]

That Bushnell would be harshly criticized could be counted upon. Hodge was grateful for *Christian Nurture* as an alternative to revivalism, but he felt that Bushnell's larger theological work misinterpreted or ignored the Church's precious confessional treasure or dissolved it into poetry. When he detected Bushnellian influence at Andover in Professor Edwards Amasa Park's address on "The Theology of the Intellect and That of the Feelings," he no doubt regarded the apostasy of New England as complete. And on this point Nevin agreed with Hodge: Bushnell's theology seemed to him essentially a romanticized naturalism. Taylor, whose doctrinal innovations Bushnell in a fashion absorbed, was more uncomprehending than critical: Scottish rationalism, not German idealism, informed his thinking. But Taylor's archcritic, Bennet Tyler, then President of Hartford Semi-

[57] *ibid.*, pp. 16, 27.

nary, made a full-scale assault. More painful to Bushnell, there proved to be a great many Connecticut Congregationalists who in a general way agreed with Tyler, and finally North Church withdrew from its consociation to forestall a heresy trial of its minister.[58]

Yet references to critics and opposition distort the case because Bushnell's influence was in the long run incalculably large, with even the immediate reception of his ideas often very friendly. Park's inclination was an important sign. In another thirty years Bushnell's ideas would have swept Park out of Andover Seminary. It was little different at Yale. In the meantime important pulpits were occupied by his admirers: Washington Gladden at Springfield and then Columbus; Newman Smyth at Center Church on the New Haven green, where Taylor had made his name; Theodore Munger next door in the church where Jonathan Edwards, Jr. had held stubbornly to his father's views. In 1865 when New England Congregationalism made one of its last corporate utterances on doctrine,[59] Bushnell's impact had not yet been widely registered, but in the next half-century his influence was to become decisive not only in his own denomination but far beyond.

The Changing New Theology

Charles Darwin and Alfred Russell Wallace presented their theory of biological evolution to Britain's Linnaean Society in 1858; a year later Darwin's *Origin of Species* came from the press. As a consequence, the Christian Church was confronted by as troublesome a theological problem as any it had experienced since facing the challenge of Hellenic philosophy. For the time being the slavery problem pre-

[58] Tyler, *Letters to Dr. Bushnell on Christian Nurture*, Hartford, 1848. See also Enoch Pond, *Review of Dr. Bushnell's "God in Christ,"* Bangor, 1849. The chief orthodox objections to Bushnell were his modalism and his "moral influence" theory of atonement.

[59] The Burial-Hill Declaration; see Walker, *Creeds and Platforms*, pp. 553–569.

empted the attention of American thinkers. Then the agonies of the Civil War and Reconstruction staved off the issue another decade. But by 1870 it was being faced on a wide front and during the remainder of the century it provided the leitmotiv for most American thinking—philosophical, religious, political, social, and even literary. For the champions of "progressive orthodoxy," who were committed to keeping theology abreast of public presuppositions, an immense task of reconstruction was involved.

Bushnell lived only to see the problem and not to attack it, but he did have the satisfaction of knowing that, like Nevin, he had responded to those pre-Darwinian preparations for a dynamic historical understanding of civilization, society, and the Church. Time was to prove these foundations very satisfactory for the construction of a comprehensive alternative theory of development which would in a religious way incorporate all that Darwin was to say and nearly all that the "Social Darwinians" were claiming. Not only would the positivistic and mechanistic tendencies of the new science be sublimated and transcendentalized, but the idea of progress and American democratic ideals would be incorporated as well.

In America the "New Theology" is the name often given to this large and extremely creative enterprise of accommodation and incorporation. "Liberalism," as an alternative designation, forges an important link with the earlier efforts of Schleiermacher, Coleridge, Channing, Emerson, and the others. Taken as a whole, the movement would, of course, have to deal with much more than evolution. The nineteenth century threw down a veritable gauntlet for the Church. Yet the "New" theologians produced scholarship and developed an outlook which dealt brilliantly with all of these composite developments. The theological result was a fairly definitely structured religious movement whose major contentions can be summarized even though the emphasis varied from man to man. Most basic was a revised and favorable estimate of human nature, coupled with an optimistic view of human destiny that paralleled the secular idea of progress. To capitalize on the former and advance the latter, the Church's task was seen increasingly in terms of ethical counsel and education. Doctrinal and churchly concern yielded to a man-centered emphasis on moralism and religious experience, while philosophical theology in a complementary fashion moved toward affirmations of the unity or interpenetration of God, man, and nature. Christ and his work were in this manner "naturalized," but nature, including human nature, was seen as instinct with the divine.

H. Richard Niebuhr has described the process by which the Liberal movement in American theology gradually divorced itself from its roots in the Reformation tradition. He points out how the moral emphasis of a Channing or the experiential emphasis of a Bushnell remained in close touch with the ancient piety, but how the next generation, at another remove, showed a loss of vitality, and the next generation a still greater loss. Ultimately the Christian proclamation almost disappeared: "A God without wrath brought men without sin into a kingdom without judgment through the ministrations of a Christ without a cross." [60] In general this estimate of the movement as a whole is true enough, and just. But we must bear in mind that the transmutation of Liberalism would have been far more rapid had it not been for constant infusions of evangelical fervor. Furthermore, it would seem that many of the most creative contributions to Liberalism were made by "first-generation men" with roots in the conservative, and usually the revivalistic, traditions. The fact remains that the real nature of the Liberal enterprise cannot be understood

---

[60] *The Kingdom of God in America*, New York, 1937, p. 193. On the liberal movement see Frank Hugh Foster, *The Modern Movement in American Theology*, New York, 1939; John Dillenberger and Claude Welch, *Protestant Christianity*, New York, 1955; H. Shelton Smith, *Changing Conceptions*, ch. 8; Daniel D. Williams, *The Andover Liberals*, New York, 1941; and Winthrop S. Hudson, *The Great Tradition of the American Churches*, New York, 1953. A generic "liberalism" is to be found in nearly all ages; but the capital "L" used in this essay emphasizes the unique spirit of the nineteenth-century movement.

except in the context of the immense religious problems with which it grappled. Because these problems persist into the twentieth century, moreover, one is justified in considering them at greater length than the actual popular strength of the Liberal movement would seem to justify.

A. Borden Parker Bowne and the Trend to Philosophic Idealism

The foundations of Liberalism were constructed out of those romantic enthusiasms and dissatisfactions so well exemplified in America by Emerson and Bushnell. But as the passing decades laid new problems bare, the crisis deepened. Because greater metaphysical and logical sophistication was required, moreover, the philosophic task of the later nineteenth-century theologian became very great—indeed in certain quarters the "philosophy of religion" was looked upon as the higher form of life into which theology and dogmatics had evolved. As at no other time in American history, philosophy was hewing wood and drawing water for the Church.

Of the many religious and idealistic philosophers engaged in this task, Borden Parker Bowne (1847–1910) was probably the most influential as far as the churches were concerned, but even if his influence had been negligible he would merit study due to his representative character. He began his philosophical career fittingly with a sharp criticism of the materialistic evolutionist, Herbert Spencer. He then went to Germany for advanced study at Göttingen under Rudolph Hermann Lotze, who is remembered for his concern for bringing the facts and methods of science and religion into a unified idealistic philosophical synthesis. Bowne, like Lotze, was to feel this need for refuting naturalism as a constant goad. The single and ideal ground of all reality and the absolute irreducible nature of the self were basic insistences of his system. "The continuity of law," he felt, "is a pure postulate which must either be referred to an abiding purpose in the cosmic intelligence, or else be accepted out of hand as an opaque fact." As for evolution, he accepted it both as an ancient "cosmic formula" and as a recent biological doctrine. The popular forms of naturalistic theory that rested on it, however, he dismissed as "simply a piece of bad metaphysics produced by bad logic." Good logic and good metaphysics, on the other hand, lead to the conclusion that "thought can never recognize anything which is not rooted in thought." [61] The material world is not compounded of atoms and their forces, but is rather a product of one infinite, omnipresent, eternal energy by which it is continually supported, and from which it incessantly proceeds.

The system of "personalistic idealism" which Bowne erected on this basis was by no means strictly Kantian, yet Bowne recalls Kant with his words that "speculation makes room for belief, but for positive faith we must fall back on the demands of our moral and religious nature, or on some word of revelation, or on both together." [62] Much more even than Bushnell, Bowne "fell back" upon our "moral and religious nature." Theology for him was an extrapolation from the facts of religious experience and the interpretation of moral obligation. Revelation, in its traditional meaning, played a very minor role, though he, like all idealists of this period, took a text from St. Paul's sermon in Athens: "In God we live and move and have our being" (Acts 17:28).

Bowne, of course, never pretended to be a theologian. His career was in the Philosophy Department of Boston University.[63] His influence on many generations of seminarians was nevertheless great, with Professor A. C. Knudsen, Edgar S. Brightman, together with many other men in various Methodist seminaries making more specific doctrinal applications. Everywhere in the movement, however, Bowne's characteristic emphases (idealistic, personalist, immanentistic, value-oriented, and ethical) persisted. Some Liberals, like the great

[61] *Metaphysics*, rev. ed., New York, 1898, p. 276.
[62] *ibid.*, p. 379.
[63] On his life, thought, and influence, see Francis J. McConnell, *Borden Parker Bowne*, New York, 1929.

Boston preacher George Angier Gordon, would think in more Hegelian categories. For such men Josiah Royce might seem a safer guide than Bowne. Many more would tend toward the voluntaristic irrationalism of William James and Henri Bergson. Others would take their cue from Albrecht Ritschl and attempt to divorce Christian thinking from metaphysics altogether. Nobody has quantified the strength of these various tendencies. But one thing can be safely affirmed: that down to World War I nearly all Liberals, even when they abjured speculation, tended toward subjectivistic or idealistic modes of thought.

B. William Newton Clarke and Systematic Liberalism

The discomfiture which evolutionary theory brought to the Church was most serious in the long run because of the stimulus given to naturalism. More immediately troublesome, however, was the enormously enlarged timetable demanded and provided by modern geology and biology. Still more provocative was the process which brought the Bible and the whole history of the Church within the scope of critical historical research where the methods of philology, paleography, comparative religion, and many other related disciplines were brought to bear. Textual critics exposed the shortcomings of the "received text" on which most modern translations of the Bible were based. Some celebrated passages, like the Trinitarian affirmation in I John 5, came almost unanimously to be regarded as later interpolations, and many others were rendered suspect.

Meanwhile the so-called "higher criticism" took up a host of problems posed by the sacred literature itself. Because the Old Testament was more complex and less sensitive on doctrinal grounds, it was attacked first, but the New Testament was soon involved. Authorship questions arose: Did Moses write the Pentateuch? Did John write the Fourth Gospel? Did Paul write Ephesians? In their train were much larger questions of interpretation: Was the Creation story derived from Babylonian myth? Did St. Paul transform and distort "the religion of Jesus"? Could the "historical Jesus" be recovered? And beneath all of these searchings lay the real, the basic question: Was the Bible inspired? Could something so historically conditioned truly bear a revelation, and if so, how and in what sense?

William Newton Clarke (1841–1912) was one of the many Liberal theologians who took full cognizance of this entire developmental approach to the world, man, and revelation:

"With respect to the Bible, I am one of the men who have lived through the crisis of the Nineteenth Century, and experienced the change which that century has wrought. I began, as a child must begin, with viewing the Bible in the manner of my father's day, but am ending with a view that was never possible until the large work of the Nineteenth Century upon the Bible had been done. Thus I am entering into the heritage of my generation, which I consider it both my privilege and my duty to accept." [64]

The son of a Baptist minister, Clarke had been born in 1841 in Cazenovia, N.Y., and educated at Colgate University and the Colgate Baptist Theological Seminary. After a brief ministry in Keene, N.H., he was called at the age of twenty-seven to the important Baptist Church of Newton Center, Mass., where the Newton Seminary faculty and students were part of his congregation and where during an eleven-year ministry he came to appreciate Bushnell's theology and the new Biblical criticism. Later he served in Montreal and in Hamilton, N.Y. But in 1890 his life was permanently set on a new course that would have repercussions throughout the country: he was called to the chair of theology at Colgate Seminary. His students during two decades of teaching were many (Harry Emerson Fosdick among them); but those who

[64] *Sixty Years with the Bible: a Record of Experience*, New York, 1912, p. 3. See also Emily S. Clarke, *William Newton Clarke*, New York, 1916.

were to feel the impulse of the New Theology through his many books were numberless.

Clarke's first published work was appropriately Biblical, a *Commentary on the Gospel of Mark* (1881), but it gave only small intimations of changes in approach that were expounded in his last complete book, a bold defense of critical scholarship entitled *The Use of the Scriptures in Theology* (1905). His true vocation, however, lay in another direction; he felt himself one "who has been called to construct a system of theology." The fruit of these systematic labors, the *Outline of Christian Theology*, is unquestionably Clarke's most memorable accomplishment. Lucid and fervently written, conceived against the broad background of evolutionary theory and in full cognizance of the historical criticism, it became virtually the *Dogmatik* of American Liberalism. Published first in 1898, it had passed through twenty editions by 1914.

The special characteristics of the *Outline* are apparent from the first page on. It begins with the assertion that "Theology is preceded by religion," and thus reveals the degree to which the historical approach shaped Clarke's views. In discussing the "sources" of theology, he laid strong emphasis on those sources outside of Christian revelation: science, history, and other religions, but above all—Man. To know man is in a measure to know God, since man bears God's image. "Toward him the great movement [of evolution] has steadily advanced. Man himself is not yet complete, however, for his powers are still unfolding and increasing. . . . Man, the crown of the process, is no mere animal, but a spiritual being." Concerning the spiritual constitution of man, Clarke insisted further that *"man is immortal,*—that is to say, the human personality is undying."[65] Man is also a free moral being, guided by a conscience whose "ground" is God. Sinful and self-willed he is by nature, but along with this inheritance is another "flow" of good tendencies which happily are, with

[65] *Outline*, pp. 224–225; 192.

the passage of time, becoming more and more dominant. "God has certainly endowed humanity with a tendency to rise; which is only another way of saying that *nature is favorable to goodness.*" [66]

What has happened in the past, moreover, will continue in the future and it is in the expounding of this doctrine that, for Clarke, eschatology consists.

"If our Lord will but complete the spiritual coming that he has begun, there will be no need of visible advent to make perfect his glory on the earth. . . . The apostles grasped the spiritual idea of his kingdom but imperfectly. . . . It is plain [furthermore] that one's view of the resurrection must correspond to the companion view of the second coming of Christ. . . . If the coming of Christ is conceived as spiritual, not visible, and as a process, not an event, . . . no simultaneous resurrection of humanity on the earth will be expected. . . . According to this view resurrection is not simultaneous for all, but continuous, or successive. . . ." [67]

In his thinking on the nature and work of Christ, Clarke followed a path marked by Schleiermacher and Bushnell. But at no point does he identify himself so clearly as a Liberal as in the almost total neglect of ecclesiology. Holy Baptism, the Lord's Supper, the nature and authority of the ministry, and the role of preaching are not discussed at all. Only five pages out of nearly five hundred are devoted to the Church, which he defined "as a comprehensive name for the Christian people," or as "the sum of those organizations which have been formed to serve as organs of Christ, for the expression and promotion of his religion." He does not expect or hope for a visible unity of the Church but only that it be "united in some practical order for mutual benefit and common service. . . ." [68] Perhaps reflecting a tendency not uncharacteristic

[66] *ibid.,* p. 245 (italics mine).
[67] *ibid.,* pp. 444–445, 458.
[68] *ibid.,* pp. 381–382.

of Baptists, he even suggests that denominationalism is a blessing.

Another field on which Clarke wrote little or nothing and which he touched upon only in the most general terms was that of ethics, and especially what is now so often called social ethics. He naturally affirmed the ancient counsel of Ignatius of Antioch, "Let us learn to live according to Christianity." [69] But he was not concerned with the application. In this lack of social emphasis, moreover, it is important to realize that we behold a prominent characteristic of Liberalism. Until late in the century the "Social Gospel" was advocated only by a small minority. Winthrop Hudson is entirely right in referring to Walter Rauschenbusch as a "lonely prophet." [70] Yet because Liberalism in the twentieth century was so often to be identified with the Social Gospel, and because the Federal Council of Churches (founded in 1908) was regarded as a monument to the Christian social-actionists, the growth of Christian social concern, especially during the turn-of-century decades (1890–1910), requires passing note. In this regard, Rauschenbusch himself is the obvious point of focus.

C. Walter Rauschenbusch and the Social Gospel

Walter Rauschenbusch (1861–1918), like Clarke, came from an intensely pious family, his father having been a missionary of Lutheran background who became a Baptist because of profound personal religious experiences.[71] The chief clue to his lifetime of social concern, nevertheless, can not be traced to the piety of his parental home, nor to his formal education (in Germany, at Rochester University, or at Roches-

[69] *The Circle of Theology*, Cambridge, Mass., 1897, p. 54.
[70] *The Great Tradition of the American Churches*, ch. 10.
[71] Carl E. Schneider, "The Americanization of Karl August Rauschenbusch," *Church History*, XXIV, March, 1955, pp. 3–14. On Walter Rauschenbusch's life and thought, see Vernon P. Bodein, *The Social Gospel of Walter Rauschenbusch and Its Relation to Religious Education*, New Haven, 1944, and Dores R. Sharpe, *Walter Rauschenbusch*, New York, 1942.

ter Seminary where his father was a professor and where he himself taught for two decades). His crucial experience was an eleven-year ministry to the Second German Baptist Church in New York's "Hell's Kitchen." Here he witnessed the early cruelty and inhumanity of American industrialism and the tragedy of rampant urban expansion. Here his Christian ethical concern was given another dimension and his life a new direction. *Christianity and the Social Crisis* published in 1907 and *Christianizing the Social Order* in 1912 made known his state of mind, his analysis of the problem, and his prescription for Christian action.

The common tendency to make Rauschenbusch a symbol of the Social Gospel, however, distorts the situation. Theologically he stands quite by himself, to be distinguished both from Liberalism in general and from other advocacy of Christian social concern in particular. One important distinction is that which justifies his inclusion in the present essay. Unlike many advocates of social Christianity, he remained in touch with the Church's evangelical tradition and tried to express his demand in doctrinal terms, a task which his formal duties as a professor of church history prepared him to do. Another exceedingly important distinguishing mark—undoubtedly the most important—was his power of prophetic utterance on the social question. Insisting that being a Christian involved one in a social-existential way with one's neighbors, he sought to make men see that evil was something "out there" to be fought, not only an inner demon to be subdued. Closely related to these two efforts, but less commendable, is a third characteristic of Rauschenbusch's thought, namely the tendency to develop his social theories in isolation from doctrines of personal sin and salvation, and to keep these latter considerations in a separate, unintegrated department of his mind or even to disparage them for their sedative effect on men's social consciousness.

Basic to Rauschenbusch's Social Gospel was his doctrine that not only individuals but human institutions were saturated with sinfulness and hence in need of purgative reform. Convinced thus of the "super-personal" nature of evil, he made the "Kingdom of Evil" a key concept of his theology. Yet he was extraordinarily optimistic. All of his early and most influential books are pervaded by a conviction that collective, institutional evil was remediable and transient. He thought the larger victories had already been won—in the evolving human conscience and in the socially conscious Western states. The Kingdom of Righteousness was just around the corner. Even in his far more sober *Theology for the Social Gospel,* written during World War I and published a year before his death, Rauschenbusch dwells upon sin as a reformable social inheritance.

The other key doctrine in Rauschenbusch's Social Gospel was the Kingdom of God. "This doctrine," he said, "is itself the social gospel," and he dwelt on it repeatedly. The novelty, however, did not come from his exegesis of the New Testament, but from the social implications he drew. His definition was simple and direct:

"The Kingdom of God is humanity organized according to the will of God. . . . [It is] the organic union between religion and morality, between theology and ethics. . . . It contains the teleology of the Christian religion. It translates theology from the static to the dynamic. . . . By laboring for it we enter into the joy and peace of the Kingdom as our divine fatherland and habitation." [72]

As for the place of the Church in this program, Rauschenbusch adopted the characteristic Liberal view that it could serve to advance the Kingdom, though its record was one of hindrance. His views, therefore, were substantially those formulated by William Newton Clarke. Nearly all of Rauschen-

---

[72] *A Theology for the Social Gospel,* New York, 1917, pp. 140–142. See also Benson Y. Landis, ed., *The Rauschenbusch Reader,* New York, 1957.

busch's thinking could, in fact, be superimposed upon Clarke's famous *Outline*.

His differences from Clarke, nevertheless, are what make Rauschenbusch a man to remember. Instead of a few highly generalized paragraphs on ethical matters, Rauschenbusch offered a lifetime of passionate concern. He filled books with prophetic declarations about what America and American Christians *must* do if they were to correct the besetting evils and injustices. As he frankly admitted, his own inspiration to this end came not from the Church but from outside it, and by the same token, the content of his reform program came from outside: from Henry George, from sociologists, from economists, or from his own penetrating observations of American society. For this reason, Rauschenbusch must loom very large in any history of American social reform or even of social theory. For his capacity to dramatize the crisis of industrialism he also deserves an important chapter in American church history. But his place in the history of theology is small. Any Liberal in America would have discovered that he had a "theology for the social gospel" much like Rauschenbusch's if once he had become awakened to the moral implications of the social situation.

As has been suggested, Rauschenbusch did have the satisfaction of being heard, or at least of seeing the social movement grow. Yet he died a troubled and dejected man—most obviously, perhaps, because World War I had shattered his hopes for the Kingdom's coming. His final book was a desperate effort to tighten the relationship between his social interests and the Church's theology; but in the end it must be said that this union was achieved in his person, rather than through a logical, systematic theology. This failure may have had something to do with the one-sided nature of his influence. Whatever the cause, it is a fact that American social Christianity (if we judge by its major exponents in the 1890–1930 period) came increasingly to center its interest on man, not God; on social theory, not the Gospel. It grounded its message on little more than certain ethical passages from the Sermon on the Mount, and fastened its hope on the evolutionary process and American politics.

William Porcher DuBose and Anglican Modernism

Liberalism in American theology was, from the first, primarily a Northern phenomenon, and much of its dynamic was received from the Civil War. The full religious effect of that tragic event, our only really national trauma, has never been adequately analyzed, but certainly one result—in the North—was a resurgent faith in moral progress. The total experience was unforgettable for a person like Newman Smyth. He had heard the serialized version of *Uncle Tom's Cabin* read to him as a boy by his militant abolitionist father. He had fought as a soldier and marched home after Appomattox to the accolades of cheering throngs. Evil had at last met the irresistible force: social and moral evolution. "His truth is marching on!" Glory hallelujah! The Battle Hymn of the Republic became the battle hymn of the moral optimists.

In the South such attitudes did not, to put it mildly, spring forth spontaneously. The career of William Porcher DuBose (1836–1918) suggests some reasons. He belonged to that tiny proportion of ante-bellum southerners who had actually known the satisfactions of plantation life. His father was a cultivated university graduate of Huguenot extraction whose large self-sufficient plantation was a model of scientific and diversified southern farming. Though ordained just before the War, he served as a line officer, being several times wounded and narrowly averting death. In the meantime his family's estates were devastated by General Sherman's army. In 1871, after his return to the parish ministry, he was called to the University of the South (Sewanee) as Chaplain and

Professor of Moral Science, with the additional charge soon to be given of founding a Theological Department. Here the Doctor (as he was familiarly called) lived out his days, entering deeply into the life of the college and the seminary, but publishing nothing until he was fifty-seven. Then came a productive burst of literary activity between 1892 and 1911. He died in 1918, loved intensely by his former students and associates, read with some attentiveness in the Church of England, but almost completely unappreciated in America even by his fellow Episcopalians.

There was no reason to expect great theological depth or breadth from DuBose. Educated mainly at a military academy, a state university, and a struggling diocesan seminary, rudely treated by the War, rector in two pleasant but parochial towns, teacher for a lifetime on Sewanee's isolated mountain, he had every excuse for being nothing more than a kindly Arcadian stereotype. In fact, however, he, like so many other men discussed in this essay, defies environmentalist interpretations by having developed a view of the Bible, the Church, history, and the Christian message which vies with any other American effort in originality and insight. Francis J. Hall's vast dogmatic works are more comprehensive, but DuBose nevertheless deserves the tardy encomium of a present-day theologian as "the only important creative theologian that the Episcopal Church in the United States has produced." [73]

DuBose was born and bred, as he said, "in the nurture and admonition of the Lord." But he was converted as a military cadet of sixteen, and he defined what followed as a "life-time process . . . of gradually digesting, assimilating, and converting that faith into [my] own, and finding in it the full food and content of [my] life." [74] What he assimilated was prodigious. It was begun most seriously at the seminary where he was driven to a lifelong concern with St. Paul by confron-

[73] W. Norman Pittenger, "The Significance of DuBose's Theology," in his edition of DuBose's late writings, *The Unity in the Faith*, Greenwich, 1957, p. 21. See also the other works on DuBose therein published and cited.

[74] *Turning Points in My Life*, New York, 1912, pp. 17, 22–24.

tation with the Calvinistic stream of southern Episcopalianism. To this was added in due time a deep sympathy for the Germans who followed after Schleiermacher: the spiritual Neander, whose passion for history made a permanent mark on DuBose, the churchly Olshausen, and above all the great "Christologist," Isaak August Dorner. The Oxford Movement and the Mercersburg Theology also engaged him, for he was from the start a high churchman in the theological sense of that term. The historical categories of these men became controlling in his thought, and they were accentuated by his enthusiastic reception of evolutionary doctrines. Over against these tendencies, as a kind of disciplinary factor, stood Aristotle, whose *Nicomachean Ethics* was from the first his basic guide to "moral science."

Yet genetic accounts cannot do him justice. He was an independent and resourceful Biblical theologian and "church thinker." The heart of his theological endeavor is his effort to capture the apostolic understanding of salvation in the light of the Church's ecumenical witness, especially as that witness was developed by the early "undivided Church." As he put it: "I have . . . become personally convinced that there is a truth of the Scriptures and that there is a mind of the Church." [75] In an age when most men of his temperament and with his interest in making the faith intelligible and credible were going "back to Jesus," he stood fast with the Christ of Paul, who, of course, was as well the Christ of the Synoptic Gospels.[76] Pervading all he wrote is a fervent Incarnation-Resurrection faith.

What, then, it may be asked, makes DuBose significant beyond the fact that he held to traditional views? The answer cannot be easily given. His espousal of Aristotle was one thing, for that was unusual in his time—but the significance of this is diminished by the subordinate place Aristotle actually takes. His real claim to greatness rests on the success with which he

---

[75] *The Gospel According to St. Paul*, New York, 1907, p. 3.
[76] See *The Soteriology of the New Testament*, New York, 1899.

blended his profoundly evangelical theology with a catholic concern for the Church, its life, its mind, and its authority. His commentary on Romans makes the first emphasis clear:

"From the works of law shall no flesh be justified in God's sight; for through law comes knowledge of sin. . . . The Gospel of Jesus Christ was for sinners of every type save the impossible one of self-righteousness. . . . It is impossible to attach too much importance to this turn of thought." [77]

His autobiographical essay reveals the other emphasis:

"I am convinced in my own mind beyond all question, that the evolution of interpretation and expression of the truth of Jesus Christ to the end of the Sixth General Council was in the straight line to the inevitable end. I am standing now for absolutely nothing in the Councils but the simple outcome of expression of faith in the one truth of the union and unity of the divine and the human in the One Person of Jesus Christ. After that Council, thought ceased, and faith receded to its stage even before Chalcedon. Much of what had been gained for the completeness of the humanity of our Lord was lost, and Christianity became too much a one-sided worship of deity made visible for adoration under the eikon or semblance of humanity." [78]

In these two quotations are exhibited the poles of DuBose's thought. But between these poles there is room, so to speak, for him to develop his most characteristic turns of thought and to adapt them to the intellectual idiom of his day.

Preeminent is the fact that DuBose is an "incarnational theologian." His thought centers on the Prologue of the Fourth Gospel: "In the beginning was the Word, and the Word became flesh and dwelt among us." At this point, too, his thought meets the temper of the time. He incorporates the

[77] *The Gospel According to St. Paul*, p. 71.
[78] *Turning Points*, pp. 57-58.

impulse of evolutionary thinking, speaking like Bushnell of the interfusion of the divine and the natural.

"We cannot kick against the pricks; the world has begun to make the discovery, and it will not go backward in it, that the natural is God's way. The natural is the rational and divine. There is no real break between the natural and the supernatural; the one is only the higher or further other. We shall come to see that Adam and Christ are the same Man; that earth and heaven are one continuous life. . . . Under the prevalence of the modern scientific principle of evolution we have discovered that the great primal truth of God creating is neither denied nor obscured. . . . Still more shall we need to learn in Jesus Christ and His Church that the greater truth of God redeeming and saving is neither diminished nor obscured by the fact that it is a truth made visible to us only in the phenomenon of humanity self-redeemed and self-saved. . . . God was in Christ *sub specie hominis,* not *Dei.* He was here to fulfill and manifest Himself in us, and us in Him. . . ." [79]

Over and over again in this manner evolution and incarnation are linked in DuBose's writings. The accent is always Christological, with a comprehensive, almost cosmic, doctrine of incarnation expressing the ultimate fact.

"The incarnation, as we know it, is both a generic and a particular fact. Generically it is the Incarnation of God in man, in humanity; and is still in process, not to be completed until Christ is glorified in His mystical body, the Church. Particularly it was completed in the ascension of our Lord Himself, and is the Incarnation of God in the man Christ Jesus." [80]

In this precise doctrinal statement from his earliest treatise we have the center of DuBose's theology. Almost everything

[79] *The Gospel According to St. Paul,* p. 9. See also, *The Gospel in the Gospels,* New York, 1906, p. 263.

[80] *The Soteriology of the New Testament,* p. 125. For later, more pronounced views, see Pittenger, ed., *Unity in the Faith,* pp. 69, 83.

else he wrote could be related to it as explicative or derivative. The term "modernist" may be too strong, but that DuBose stands basically within the Liberal tradition is apparent. He felt the impact of all the major nineteenth-century difficulties and responded to them with the characteristically dynamic, historical, and optimistic formulations. To a remarkable degree he naturalizes objectively Christian events and dogmas, drawing them into a cosmic process. Yet his effort is distinguished by a remarkable concern for New Testament theology and a consistent effort to be faithful to the witness of the Church catholic.

Edgar Young Mullins and Southern Baptist Orthodoxy

Few men stand out more prominently in the history of the Southern Baptist Convention than Edgar Young Mullins (1860–1928). President of Southern Theological Seminary for nearly forty years, leader in mission endeavors, President of the Baptist World Alliance, founder and editor of the Convention's major theological journal, and the leading philosophical and theological spokesman for conservative Baptists in a difficult time of controversy, he made an indelible mark on his denomination.[81]

For the study of his thought, however, nothing could be more damaging than the preconception of a fire-breathing Fundamentalist. Urbane, conciliatory, and reasonable, Mullins stands far removed from this familiar stereotype. In the Landmark controversy which had torn the Convention since the 1850's and disrupted the administration of his predecessor at the Seminary, he was diplomatic; but ultimately he rested

[81] Mullins (1860–1928) was born in Mississippi and was a graduate of Texas A & M and of Southern Baptist Seminary in Louisville. When called to the seminary presidency he was minister in Newton Center, Mass. See the biography by his wife, Isla May Mullins, Nashville, 1929 and the biographical articles in the *Review and Expositor*, XXII, January, 1925, and XXVI, April, 1929; also William W. Barnes, *The Southern Baptist Convention, 1845–1953*, Nashville, 1954.

the issue with historical scholarship.[82] In theology he was profoundly influenced by the forces which molded Liberalism. Comparative religion was one of the first new courses he instituted at the Seminary; the problems of science and religion, evolution, and the new Biblical criticism were lifelong concerns. In most of his works he is explicitly or tangentially "making the case" for religion, or for faith, or for the idea of revelation. His argumentation and evidence, moreover, leaned heavily on that developed or adduced by prominent Liberals. The critical contributions of William James and F. C. S. Schiller, particularly their assault "upon the absolute systems of philosophy," were greeted with enthusiasm. James's emphasis on the *will* was especially appealing to him. He regarded the effort of Borden Parker Bowne to lift the *self* out of the continuum of nature as "the highest stage in the development of philosophic idealism."

"As we thus take the universe as personal and approach it as person, through Jesus Christ, it does not remain dumb and inarticulate as it does when taken merely as matter, force, and motion. It responds in a personal way, the veil is drawn aside and the hidden mystery suddenly stands revealed before our eyes in all its splendor, and we know where previously we have guessed." [83]

Perhaps most characteristic of Mullins' theology is his extremely high regard for the witness of religious experience, a tendency much clarified by the following lengthy but unabridgeable quotation:

"Positively stated, the best theology of the future will continue to accept the authority of the Scriptures, but it will take as its starting-point, for the interpretation and illumination of

---

[82] The Landmarkers represented a "high church" movement among Baptists. They resolved the problem of authority by postulating a "Baptist succession" from New Testament times to the present and insisting on strict maintenance of this alleged continuity.

[83] *Review & Expositor*, V, October, 1908, pp. 508, 509–510; VII, January, 1911, pp. 29–30.

Scripture, the facts of Christian experience, not in a single aspect, but in their totality. First, because Christian experience, thus employed, conforms to the scientific ideal which above all things seeks to know the facts of nature, life, and religion, and resents theoretical constructions apart from experience in the realm of facts. It conforms, second, to the true philosophical ideal, which also demands a fact basis for all the speculative attempts of the intellect. Thirdly, experience will also restore with greatly increased power the older arguments from the cosmos for the existence of God, transferred in part, however, from the cosmos of nature to the cosmos of the inner life. Fourthly, experience will sustain the cause of the supernatural in its collision with naturalism, because it brings contact with the supernatural in consciousness, the most indubitable of all the spheres of reality. In the fifth place, experience will in increasing measure establish the validity of the vicarious atonement of Christ, and its corresponding doctrines of sin and of Christ's deity and present action upon men. Thus it will indirectly add an important contribution to the doctrine of the Trinity. It will also affirm, and at the same time limit and define, the reality of knowledge of transcendental objects in the religious sphere, and indirectly rejuvenate the weakened convictions of an agnostic science in the realm of material research. Sixth, theological dogma will increasingly become the dogma of conviction as opposed to the dogma of mere authority." [84]

The manner in which these varying influences and tendencies were incorporated and integrated is nowhere better seen than in Mullins' extremely influential work of systematic theology, *The Christian Religion in Its Doctrinal Expression*, first published in 1920 and many times reprinted. This work makes a ringing defense of personal idealism as the only adequate way of construing reality and as an excellent way of

[84] "The Theological Trend," *Review & Expositor*, II, October, 1905, pp. 517–518.

reenlivening the historic proofs for the existence of God. Also along the personalistic lines laid down by Lotze and Bowne, Mullins accommodates the claims of the sciences: psychology, biology (including evolution), comparative religion, and the historical disciplines (including their work on the sacred literature). His view of the Bible as "a book of religion, not of science" shows the same moderation:

"It is a vital and living authority, and not a mechanical and ecclesiastical one. It is our authoritative source of information as to the historical revelation of God in Christ. It is regulative of Christian experience and Christian doctrine. It is the instrument of the Holy Spirit in his regenerative and sanctifying influences. . . . It saves [us] from subjectivism on the one hand and from a bare rationalism on the other. It holds us to the great saving deeds of God in Jesus Christ the Redeemer and Lord. It is final for us in all the matters of our Christian faith and practice." [85]

Moderation, indeed, remains a hallmark of Mullins' system of doctrine. On the nature and origin of sin, on the meaning of human depravity, and on the issue of predestination and human freedom, he constantly strikes a center position among the recognizably Reformed theologies of America. Many of his positions bring Nathaniel William Taylor to mind, others suggest New School Presbyterianism. But invariably he steers away from extremes. He will have nothing of Methodistic Perfectionism. In eschatology he eschews both pre- and post-millennialism, arguing instead that "Christians should cultivate the New Testament attitude of expectancy" and not rest so large a theological burden on the highly symbolic phraseology of Revelations 20:1–10.

With regard to Christian "theology" proper (that is, the doctrine of God, the Trinity, etc.), Mullins is conventionally orthodox. If space permitted, certain interesting nuances could

[85] *The Christian Religion in Its Doctrinal Expression*, Philadelphia, 1917, p. 153. See also *Review & Expositor*, XX, April, 1923, p. 136.

be noted, but basically he presents a fairly perfunctory summary of accepted doctrines. That he meant every word was amply indicated in his criticism of Liberals like Shirley Jackson Case, who were satisfied if they could prove the "microscopic" fact that Jesus once existed.[86] But radically unlike DuBose, Mullins does not dwell in rapture over the Incarnation, or the marvels of Trinitarian theology, or the cosmic glories of Christ's work.

Unlike Rauschenbusch, Mullins shows almost no ethical passion. In fact, he devotes one sentence in his *Christian Religion* to the whole object of Rauschenbusch's career: "It is as clear as day that all forms of social wrong and injustice are opposed to the ends of the gospel and the kingdom of God." [87] In one respect he does resemble both Clarke and Rauschenbusch, however—in his relative disinterest in questions of the Church itself, its ministry, and its "ordinances." In his major doctrinal treatise even a matter so distinctive in his tradition as baptism does not receive a full page of discussion.

Yet Mullins did have his positive enthusiasms, and they go far to explain the remark of one eulogist that he was a "typical Baptist." Above all, of course, was his conception and use of Christian experience. His heart, if one may so speak, lies with the heart. It is on the subject of the Holy Spirit, conversion, and the growth in Christian holiness that he makes clear his place in the lineage of the "spiritual brethren" of early Puritanism.

Through this enthusiasm one is led to his other special concern: the philosophical defense of the faith. The activity which calls forth the most zestful exercise of Mullins' talents is not the expounding of Christian doctrine or special Baptist precepts, but defending the Christian view of life against philosophical materialists, naturalistic advocates of the "principle of continuity," historical critics, or scientists with negative views on theology. Apologetics was the theme of his first

[86] *Review & Expositor*, XII, April, 1915, pp. 174–192.
[87] *Christian Religion*, p. 426.

major book, *Why Is Christianity True?* (1905), his important treatise on *Freedom and Authority in Religion* (1913), and his last book, *Christianity at the Crossroads* (1924).

Taken as a whole Mullins' work was a "free-church theology" par excellence. His allegiance was to Scriptures alone in matters of dogma; he deprecated the significance of councils, creeds, and confessions. This characteristic is especially prominent in his most widely read and most forcefully "denominational" book, *The Axioms of Religion* (1908). Here he writes fervently as a Baptist, bases his argument on the fundamental axiom of "the soul's competency in religion," and expounds a thoroughgoing, integrated rationale in which leading Baptist tenets become "axioms." [88] Yet here as elsewhere he appropriated and preserved the Reformed legacy; the spirit and force of Westminster pervade this work as they do his others.

Notably lacking in Mullins' thinking is the frantic acrimony of Fundamentalism. Mullins' full awareness of the nineteenth-century intellectual tradition and the consequent absence of defensiveness explain this: he faces the issues with equanimity, not with desperation. Also explicative of the absence of this hostility is the fact that the Southern Convention itself was not invaded by the Liberal-Modernist party. There are many explanations for this state of affairs—economic, social, and educational, not least of all the entire Secession and Civil War experience of the South. In any event, the Southern Convention was not so seriously disrupted by the Fundamentalist Controversy as were several other predominantly northern denominations. Later in the century vast economic changes, the growth of higher education in the South, and the expansion of the Southern Convention's program of seminary education might seem to have opened the way for just such a struggle, but by this time the theological

[88] The axioms based on the doctrines of the "soul's competency" are familiar enough (divine sovereignty, equal human access to God, equal privilege in the church, moral freedom, church-and-state separation, and the Great Commandment), but Mullins' argument had an integrated character of its own.

atmosphere of the country as a whole had drastically changed. "Modernism" in the old militant sense was very weak and Fundamentalist belligerency was correspondingly obsolescent. This change of theological climate is our next concern.

The Niebuhrs:
Neo-Orthodoxy and After

By the turn of the century Liberal theology had scored notable advances, but along lines and in ways that submit to no single or simple explanation. Among Congregationalists, Disciples of Christ, and Northern Baptists where congregational autonomy was pronounced, it waxed strong. Yet it grew hardly less luxuriantly in the tightly organized Methodist Church of the North and gained considerable strength among Episcopalians and Presbyterians. Its seed flourished best on soil that had been prepared by revivalism, yet for the most part only in the North, and especially in urban areas. Liberalism was likewise regnant in many important divinity schools—at Oberlin, Chicago, Yale, Union Theological Seminary (N.Y.), and at Harvard where it transformed the older Unitarianism. More strictly denominational seminaries like Bangor, Andover-Newton, Colgate, Rochester, Crozer, Boston University, and the two Episcopal seminaries in New England also came under its influence.

Despite World War I, the movement probably reached its height of general acceptance in the mid-1920's. During the postwar decade, in fact, Liberalism was invigorated by a new school of militant theological "Realists" led by Professor Douglas Clyde Macintosh of Yale (1877–1948), author of *Theology as an Empirical Science* (1919), and Professor Henry Nelson Wieman of Chicago (1884——), author of *Religious Experience and Scientific Method* (1927). As these titles suggest, the Realists were in revolt from the romantic subjectivism of earlier Liberalism. Leaving behind the tradition of Emerson and Bushnell, denying that the object of faith was merely the "God-idea," they took seriously the dictum of William James "that a new era of religion . . . will be ready to begin [when empiricism] is associated with religion as hitherto . . . it has been associated with irreligion." [89] The Realists led a campaign for objectivity, and nobody reveals the lengths to which they went better than Macintosh:

"I will not mince words in this connection. . . . If in proclaiming the Christian gospel we can predict and promise that whosoever will fulfil the prescribed conditions of repentance and faith . . . will experience ethico-religious salvation, then it cannot be denied that there is in the Christian message a nucleus of essentially or potentially scientific generalization." [90]

In 1931 Macintosh was able to edit a composite manifesto on *Religious Realism* which brought a large and distinguished group of men under the Realist banner.

As in so many instances, however, the high water mark was also the turning point. Stresses within American life and influences from the Continent were soon to break the solid front and splinter the movement. As "Realism" began to take on new meanings, Liberal advocacy itself began to lose its force. In this process the War was undoubtedly a factor, though the failures of the peace settlement probably occasioned more sober second thoughts than had "the war to end wars." The uninspiring character of Harding-Coolidge "normalcy" was another factor, especially in the context of the harsh and satirical social criticism issuing from secular and literary quarters. The economic collapse of 1929 and the deepening depression of the succeeding years was more decisive than any of these. The thirties felt the added hammer-

[89] Quoted by Julius Seelye Bixler, "Can Religion Become Empirical?" in *The Nature of Religious Experience: Essays in Honor of Douglas Clyde Macintosh*, New York, 1937, p. 68.
[90] "Empirical Theology and Some of Its Misunderstanders," *Review of Religion*, III, May, 1939, p. 398.

blows of Fascist inhumanity to man and increasingly dis-
illusioning reports from the great Communist experiment
in Russia. When intellectual problems posed by the whole
relativistic thrust of the new psychology, sociology, and
cultural anthropology were added to these woes, Liberalism
began to crack. The intellectual autobiographies gathered in
Vergilius Ferm's two-volume *Contemporary American Theology* (1932) reveal a basically undisturbed exterior, but there
were rumblings from without, within, and below.

Especially provocative to American theology in those years
were the new and incisive evangelical voices being heard
again in Europe, where devastation, tragedy, and intellectual
crisis had come sooner and with more terrifying force.
Sverre Norborg from Norway put it plainly in the American
edition of his *What Is Christianity?*

"This unpretentious book comes across the Atlantic as a
greeting from a continent in fatal crisis and endless fear of
tomorrow. Still, it is not written in panic: Living Christianity
knows no despondency. This is to be a greeting from the *Unknown Europe*, hidden from the shrieking headlines . . . ,
living its rich and victorious life, whatever befalls it. That
Unknown Europe is the living communion of believers
throughout all the nations. . . . They have not been "rethinking" Christianity, or been busy remodelling its message.
They have *heard* a Word, coming from the Other Side of
mere human possibilities. . . ." [91]

Those words were probably written in 1935. But there had
been bells rung long before that. As Norborg well knew,
Kierkegaard had made his protest against complacent Christendom almost a century before. In 1906 had come Albert
Schweitzer's devastating critique of the long liberal *Quest
of the Historical Jesus*. For almost as long, the Lutheran

[91] J. C. K. Preus, tr., Minneapolis, 1936, p. vii. For a more extended
discussion of these forces, see my article, "Continental Influences on American Theology since World War I," *Church History*, XXVII, Sept., 1958,
pp. 256–272.

churches of Scandinavia and Germany had been rediscovering the meaning of Luther and of the Reformation's "theology of the cross." Since the late twenties Germany had been stirred by a new evangelical and existential kind of social-Christian protest. And with the publication of his *Commentary on Romans* in 1918, European Liberalism had heard the commanding "Nein!" of Karl Barth. In the wake of all these movements came a new school of Biblical interpretation led by Dibelius, Schmidt, Eichrodt, and Bultmann. In the 1930's America began to hear all of these voices—and they could no longer be dismissed as Old World "disillusionism," or as a rebirth of Fundamentalism or, in Professor Macintosh's words, as "reactionary irrationalism."

In 1928 Douglas Horton became a disturber of America's theological peace by publishing his English translation of some stirring essays by Karl Barth on *The Word of God and the Word of Man*.[92] In 1931 H. Richard Niebuhr showed himself to be something of a fifth-columnist in the Realist movement by contributing an essay to Professor Macintosh's symposium which was in fact a report on what German realistic theologians like Paul Tillich might well consider inadequate in American realism. In 1932 Walter Lowrie, later to become famous as a chief translator of Kierkegaard, published a book-length demand that Americans heed the "crisis-theologians" of Europe who were calling into question virtually every last premise of American liberal thinking.[93] In the same year Reinhold Niebuhr loosed his bombshell on individualistic and utopian social thinking, *Moral Man and Immoral Society*.

The year 1934 becomes a kind of *annus mirabilis*. Reinhold Niebuhr made the evangelical roots of his protest more explicit in a series of important lectures later published as *An*

[92] Reissued in 1957, with a new foreword, as a Harper Torchbook (paper).
[93] H. Richard Niebuhr, "Religious Realism in the Twentieth Century," in *Religious Realism*, D. C. Macintosh, ed., New York, 1931, ch. 12, and Walter Lowrie, *Our Concern with the Theology of Crisis*, Boston, 1932.

Interpretation of Christian Ethics. The Methodist theologian, Edwin Lewis, followed up an article on "The Fatal Apostasy of the Modern Church" with a book-length *Christian Manifesto*. George W. Richards, from the seminary of Nevin and Schaff, published his *Beyond Fundamentalism and Modernism, The Gospel of God*, and edited a volume of Barth's sermons. Walter Marshall Horton broke from the Macintosh-Wieman axis with his *Realistic Theology*. In the meantime, Joseph Haroutunian had written a crucial re-evaluation of the Edwardsean tradition and Perry Miller had published the first of his massive works reassessing the Puritans. By 1939, therefore, when the *Christian Century* published a series of spiritual autobiographies not unlike those Ferm had published seven years before, a major theological fact was to be laid bare: the general temper of American theology had been fundamentally transformed. One could speak of a broad, many-sided "resurgence of the Gospel." [94]

The transition was emphatically a collective phenomenon which depended on no one man, coterie, or "school." Yet it would be almost impossible to imagine the last three decades of American theology without Reinhold and H. Richard Niebuhr in prominent roles. The action would have gone on without them. Indeed, as both of them have said, it was going on when they began to change their minds. Yet the fact remains—their thirty years of sustained, incisive thinking has, at the very least, provided the best possible means for pointing to the essential issues involved in America's theological *bouleversement*. [95]

At the level of social analysis, each of them made contributions during the period 1929–34. They pointed out how the mind and heart of the Church were in bondage to the social situation—to national claims, ethnic loyalties, and class

[94] See Taito A. Kantonen, *Resurgence of the Gospel*, Philadelphia, 1948.
[95] For critical essays and bibliographies see Robert W. Bretall and Charles W. Kegley, eds., *Reinhold Niebuhr: His Religious, Social and Political Thought*, New York, 1956; and Paul Ramsey, ed., *Faith and Ethics: the Theology of H. Richard Niebuhr*, New York, 1957.

ideologies. Both of them lamented the degree to which the Church had identified itself with the bourgeois ideals of capitalist civilization and its consequent incapacity to understand the depths of the social crisis. The early temper of H. Richard Niebuhr was perhaps best expressed by the book *The Church Against the World* (1935), but his later thinking seems to dwell more on the unresolved and possibly unresolvable problem of the Church's proper relation to the world. Reinhold Niebuhr's most memorable feat has been the adaptation of Rauschenbusch's passion for social justice to a realistic view of man, history, and politics that is neither utopian, cynical, nor pessimistic. Nor has it been an academic or theological feat only; he has been a major factor in whatever renewal of social concern in the churches has come about since 1932.[96]

On the question of human nature Reinhold Niebuhr spoke with especially strong effect. Doctrinally speaking he did no more than take seriously the view of man's sin held by Augustine and the Reformers, but he combined it so effectively with an activist view of social reform and expressed it with such historical and theological depth that he gave new meaningfulness to old doctrines. What did most to impress (and to confuse!) his audience was his dialectical manner of thinking, his insistence on taking the concept of paradox seriously and thus speaking constantly in terms of "both-and" and "yes-and-no." Niebuhr saw man as *both* creature *and* creator; as involved in history, yet transcending it. No less dialectical were his analyses of other problems in theology and ethics.

The philosophy or theology of history has been a major concern of both men. Most characteristic of Reinhold Niebuhr

---

[96] H. Richard Niebuhr's thought on the relation of the Church and the world is best seen in *The Social Sources of Denominationalism*, New York, 1929, reissued as a Meridian paperback; *The Kingdom of God in America*, New York, 1937, reissued as Harper Torchbook; and *Christ and Culture*, New York, 1951, reissued as Harper Torchbook. Reinhold Niebuhr's social advocacy is described and cited in Paul A. Carter, *The Decline and Revival of the Social Gospel*, Ithaca, 1956.

has been his exposition of the process by which the Judaeo-Christian understanding of history was progressively secularized in the West until under the standard Liberal interpretation it could virtually be asserted that "history is the Christ." Probably no American has done so much to dramatize the distinction between a Biblical view of history as against the Hellenic and the "Modern" ideas. With H. Richard Niebuhr, on the other hand, the chief grappling has been with problems of historicism, either to dwell on the rich sociality of man's existence in history or the relativistic obstacles to knowledge. Among the most widely appropriated of his ideas has been the distinction between inner history and external history which he developed in his lectures on *The Meaning of Revelation* (1941). Here, too, are expounded those characteristic themes of community, collective memory, conversation, and mutual correction and confirmation which explain the way the Church confronts and apprehends the revealing Word. Both brothers, needless to say, have delivered forceful attacks on the idea of progress or the inevitable coming of God's kingdom, and both have written books interpreting American history from this vantage point.

Unfortunately, the thought of two men as prolific of books and ideas as these can only be abused by the rude categories required in a brief essay, but even at the risk of further abuse a final category must be indicated. It pertains to a broadly diffused quality that they have imparted to American theological thinking, though it has in no sense been contributed by them alone. It pervades nearly all of the new theological departures of the period of transition here treated. Lacking a better term, I call it "Kierkegaardian," for no other adjective so effectively implies the major features of the movement in question: its critique of group, class, and personal complacency; its demand for personal appropriation of Christian truth; its insistence that man's moral obligation under the Gospel cannot be stated in terms of legalistic precepts; its warning against the dangers of rationalizing the great Biblical paradoxes; its emphasis upon a radically personalistic understanding of the self, of other selves, and of God; above all, the reality, the objectivity, and the sovereignty of God and His judgments. This spirit permeated their thinking, whether practical or speculative, and characterized their impact on individuals, on the churches, and on the course of American thought in general. The new movement, of course, did not literally depend upon Kierkegaard. Yet his voice did reach beyond the grave—and he spoke not only to Barth, or Unamuno, or Heidegger. After translations began to appear during the 1930's, he reached innumerable Americans. The so-called "neo-orthodox" protest was not final, however, or even a completed revolution. It destroyed some illusions, reassessed the meaning of Liberal scholarship, and opened new channels of thought. But theology changes as the times and human needs change, and during the last decades it has changed enough to render obsolete the very term "neo-orthodox." Further continuation of the story in the present essay would be unstrategic, however, because our perspective disappears. Only a few broad lines of development are indicated.[97]

These have been years when the impact of the ecumenical movement came to be felt, especially after the Edinburgh conference on Life and Work and the Oxford conference on Faith and Order, both of 1937. Incident to this has been the growing concern for matters pertaining to the Church, its authority, its ministry, and its sacraments. Biblical scholarship, especially in the Old Testament, has been brought out of its exile in departments of Near-Eastern studies and put back into its place in church thinking. Perhaps most significant of all are the ways in which Biblical theology has helped to reveal the deep, underlying reality of Christian unity and

[97] See Daniel D. Williams, *What Present-Day Theologians Are Thinking*, rev. ed., New York, 1959.

has broken down barriers to communication between traditions which had been deadlocked for centuries. As a result, dogmatics has become a respectable discipline. Ethical thought, too, has been put into an increasingly evangelical focus so that the Christian's moral obligation is seen more in the light of Christian freedom and less in terms of rules and laws. In other circles one notes a new and "chastened" Liberalism; still elsewhere a revived interest in Thomism and natural law. All of these tendencies, however, are open-ended. Events of decisive importance may be hidden from our vision just as the significance of the procuratorship of Pontius Pilate was hidden from Tiberius Caesar. Interpreting the present calls for a seer, not a historian.

Retrospect

The very idea of a retrospective view propels one toward unitive concepts and intimations of homogeneity; with regard to American theology the tendency must be resisted, the temptation forsworn.[98] The contrary directions of America's theological development must be insisted upon. Even in the closely knit confines of eighteenth-century New England, Edwards and Chauncy were moving out of communication with each other, becoming inhabitants of separate intellectual worlds. In the country as a whole and during three centuries of theological history this trend became even more apparent and widespread. The early Puritan-Reformed tincture faded; denominational traditions deepened and diverged. There is no structure, no "cycle," no developing pattern. In contrast with that of, say, Sweden, or even with that of Germany, the American tradition is heterogeneous and unsusceptible to synthetic survey, unless we do what is so often done, snip off a sub-pattern and treat that as the

[98] I tend, in any event, to be skeptical of generalizations on national character. See David M. Potter's discussion of the problem, *People of Plenty: Economic Abundance and the American Character*, Chicago, 1954, Part I.

whole. The wide spectrum of belief, method, and tendency revealed in the present essay, therefore, does not spring from the author's desire for wide representation; it reflects the basic facts of the case.

On the other hand, we must deny the common observation that America reveals a characteristic disinclination to theology, or an activistic satisfaction with theological mediocrity. Theology has had a vigorous life in many of America's numerous church traditions. There are eminences whose grandeur in no way derives from the Lilliputian standards of an observer. Just as Thomas Jefferson, Benjamin Franklin, and John Adams stand in their own right as flowerings of the Enlightenment comparable with any men of their age, in the same manner a long train of American theologians play important roles in the history of Christian thought even though their predicament often makes their work too American in its focus to allow wide international assimilation of it. Jonathan Edwards stands as the chief figure in the Reformed tradition between Calvin and Barth; and though so much may not be said of any other, there is not a man brought under consideration in this essay who was dwarfed by his contemporaries anywhere. Moreover, they were with few exceptions widely heard and read; they had audiences who understood them and took them seriously. The quality of attention that Bushnell remembered in his childhood parish [99] was reproduced over and over again—among Scotch-Irish pioneers in the Shenandoah valley, among Norwegian settlers in Iowa, among the proto-suburbanites who listened in turn to William Newton Clarke and Edgar Young Mullins in Newton Center.

It is not enough, however, to say that America has a respectable theological tradition; nor to say—as in the introduction to this essay—that the peculiar history of the United States has given its theology a highly variegated and very derivative character. We must see that these evaluative and

[99] See above, p. 233.

formal propositions are related and interdependent. What there may be of distinction in American theology stems from the diversity and derivativeness of its heritage.

From the earliest times forceful anti-intellectual currents have been flowing in American church life, as in the country generally.[100] During the nineteenth century, for many reasons, the current became a tide. An emotional, legalistic, and superficial folk-theology prospered; large sections of American Christianity were literally uprooted from the Church's great tradition. In more recent years a kind of "Christianity of Main Street" has come into being, and with it an implicit theology—a farrago of sentimentality, moralism, democracy, free enterprise, laicism, "confident living," and utilitarian concern for success.[101] The spokesmen for this practical, man-centered, and "down-to-earth" spirit have, in turn, given substance to the stereotype of the American churchman as a mere Organization Man and a builder of buildings. In all of this, alas, there may be something typically American, but it has little to do with theology proper. At most it is a widespread and significant *obstacle* to theological endeavor, different in form but not in substance from the obstacles raised in Europe's state-church traditions.[102]

[100] The relation of anti-intellectualism to the churches is a major but inadequately explored subject in itself. See, however, the series of articles on the subject, especially the historical essay by William Leuchtenberg, in the *Journal of Social Issues*, XI, 1955, pp. 3–60; Eugene Burdick, "The Estrangement of the American Intellectual," *Pacific Spectator*, IX, Autumn, 1955, pp. 352–360; Edward A. Shils, *The Torment of Secrecy*, Glencoe, 1956, especially the discussion of nationalism, xenophobia, isolationism, and populism in ch. 4; and Norman F. Furniss, *The Fundamentalist Controversy*, New Haven, 1954.

[101] See Theodore O. Wedel, *The Christianity of Main Street*, New York, 1953. See also my own essays, "The Pieties of Usefulness," *Stetson University Bulletin*, LVII, July, 1957, and "The Levels of Religious Revival," *Confluence*, IV, April, 1955, pp. 32–43; and Louis Schneider and Sanford M. Dornbusch, *Popular Religion: Inspirational Books in America*, Chicago, 1958.

[102] In Europe and Latin America where the residues of medieval social stratification are more significant and where an established church figures strongly in past history or present reality, the "obstacles" are far more sharply defined; anti-clericalism and defiant intellectual opposition to Chris-

Virtually every thinker discussed in this essay was aware of these dangers. He regarded a sustained counter-attack upon them as an integral part of his task as a theologian. In such efforts both America's religious diversity and its intellectual ties with Europe have been vital stimuli to serious and vigorous endeavor. Each factor served to mitigate the inevitable pressure upon the churches to conform themselves to cultural and nationalistic ideals. The second, especially, provided a kind of depth and catholicity that retarded the drift into an unreflective non-denominationalism.

All of these facts notwithstanding, a portentous anomaly underlies the total theological situation in America, namely, that theological individuality has not arisen in a country characterized by an astounding degree of individuality in church organization and parish life. The whole history of Christianity has seen no larger experiment in voluntaristic church life than in the United States. The way in which egalitarian attitudes and democratic procedures have influenced church polity is likewise sensational. The lack of ancient and deeply imbedded forms of social stratification is apparent at almost every level and in virtually all denominations. No less significant is the vitality, expansiveness, and popular basis of the churches at every point in the denominational spectrum, from Pentecostal to Roman Catholic. So far, however, the chief theological accompaniment of this unique situation has been negative rather than positive. It has fostered an anti-theological and anti-doctrinal bias. It has reduced the number of theologically responsive and responsible people, lay and clerical. But it has not altered American theology per se, nor given rise to a specific "American Theology."

In the future it may be that the theologians who face their task in the United States will find themselves converging upon certain presuppositions or common attitudes and approaches that will mark them off as American. So far, how-

tianity have a popular social basis. The issues are less clouded and the faith is not so much subverted as openly abandoned or vigorously attacked.

ever, there is little evidence of such convergence or that American theology has a character of its own. Even the commonly alleged tendency toward "Arminianism" and away from Augustinian modes of thought, and more recently the opposite tendency, were not so much "characteristically American" as they were simply aspects of large-scale Western phenomena.[103] One can be reasonably confident that the American churches will continue to champion their distinctive emphasis on lay-stewardship, democracy in government, individual freedom, and voluntarism. Whether or not will emerge a characteristic American theological tradition which in some way reflects this emphasis and which yet remains catholic rather than national in the scope of its witness—this is a momentous but unanswerable question.

[103] Not even the "Social Gospel," so often cited as "typically American," is an exception to this statement. Aside from the fact of its minority status in the U.S., it was and is deeply indebted to parallel movements in Germany (from Ritschl to Blumhardt, Ragaz, Wünsch, Tillich and Bonhoeffer) and in England (from Maurice, Kingsley, and Fremantle to Archbishop Temple).

FROM THE COVENANT TO THE REVIVAL

PERRY MILLER

I

O N June 12, 1775, the Continental Congress dispatched from Philadelphia to the thirteen colonies (and to insure a hearing, ordered the document to be published in newspapers and in handbills) a "recommendation" that July 20 be universally observed as "a day of publick humiliation, fasting, and prayer." The Congress prefaced the request with a statement of reasons. Because the great "Governor" not only conducts by His Providence the course of nations "but frequently influences the minds of men to serve the wise and gracious purposes of his providential government," and also it being our duty to acknowledge his superintendency, "especially in times of impending danger and publick calamity"—therefore the Congress acts.

What may elude the secular historian—what in fact has eluded him—is the mechanism by which the Congress proposed that the operation be conducted:

". . . that we may with united hearts and voices unfeignedly confess and deplore our many sins, and offer up our joint supplications to the all-wise, omnipotent, and merciful Disposer of all events; humbly beseeching him to forgive our iniquities, to remove our present calamities, to avert those desolating judgments with which we are threatened. . . ."

The essential point is that the Congress asks for, first, a national confession of sin and iniquity, then a promise of repentance, that only *thereafter* may God be moved so to influence Britain as to allow America to behold "a gracious interposition of Heaven for the redress of her many grievances." [1] The subtle emphasis can be detected once it is compared with

[1] B. F. Morris, *Christian Life and Character of the Civil Institutions of the United States*, Philadelphia, 1864, p. 525.

the formula used by the Virginia House of Burgesses in the previous month, on May 14:

"... devoutly to implore the Divine interposition for averting the heavy calamity which threatens destruction to our civil rights, and the evils of civil war, to give us one heart and one mind firmly to oppose, by all just and proper means, every injury to *American* rights. . . ."

Jefferson testifies that in Virginia this measure was efficacious. The people met with alarm in their countenances, "and the effect of the day through the whole colony was like a shock of electricity, arousing every man and placing him erect and solidly on his centre." [2] However gratifying the local results might be, it should be noted that this predominantly Anglican House of Burgesses, confronted with calamity, made no preliminary detour through any confession of their iniquities, but went directly to the throne of God, urging that He enlist on their side. The Virginia delegation in Philadelphia (which, let us remember, included Patrick Henry but *not* Jefferson) concurred in the unanimous adoption of the Congress's much more complicated—some were to say more devious—ritualistic project. Was this merely a diplomatic concession? Or could it be that, once the threatened calamity was confronted on a national scale, the assembled representatives of all the peoples instinctively realized that some deeper, some more atavistic, search of their own souls was indeed the indispensable prologue to exertion?

The question is eminently worth asking, if only because conscientious historians have seen no difference between the two patterns, and have assumed that the Congressional followed the Virginian.[3] And there are other historians, who may or may not be cynical, but who have in either case been corrupted by the twentieth century, who perceive in this and

---

[2] *ibid.*, pp. 526–527.
[3] Cf., for instance, Arthur M. Schlesinger, *Prelude to Independence*, New York, 1958, pp. 31–32.

subsequent summonses to national repentance only a clever device in "propaganda." [4] It was bound, they point out, to cut across class and regional lines, to unite a predominantly Protestant people; wherefore the rationalist or deistical leaders could hold their tongues and silently acquiesce in the stratagem, calculating its pragmatic worth. In this view, the fact that virtually all the "dissenting" clergy, and a fair number of Anglicans, mounted their pulpits on July 20 and preached patriotic self-abnegation, is offered as a proof that they had joined with the upper middle-class in a scheme to bamboozle the lower orders and simple-minded rustics.

This interpretation attributes, in short, a diabolical cunning to the more sophisticated leaders of the Revolution, who, being themselves no believers in divine providence, fastened onto the form of invocation which would most work upon a majority who did believe passionately in it. This reading may, I suggest, be as much a commentary on the mentality of modern sociology as upon the Continental Congress, but there is a further observation that has been more cogently made by a few who have noted the striking differences in phraseology: the Congressional version is substantially the form that for a century and a half had been employed in New England. There, since the first years of Plymouth and the first decade of Massachusetts Bay and Connecticut, the official response in the face of affliction had been to set aside a day for public confession of transgression and a promise of communal repentance as the only method for beseeching the favor of Jehovah.[5] Hence some analysts surmise that the action of the Congress, if it was not quite a Machiavellian ruse for hoodwinking the pious, was at best a Yankee trick foisted on Virginia and New York. Leaving aside the question of whether, should this explanation be true, it might just as well have

[4] Philip Davidson, *Propaganda and the American Revolution*, Chapel Hill, 1941, passim.
[5] Perry Miller, *The New England Mind: From Colony to Province*, Cambridge, Mass., 1953, pp. 19–26.

been a Virginian fraud, one which cost Patrick Henry and Peyton Randolph nothing, perpetrated to keep the New Englanders active, the simple fact is that unprejudiced examination of the records of 1775 and 1776 shows that New England enjoyed no monopoly on the procedure. The House of Burgesses might suppose it enough to petition Almighty God to redress their wrongs; the churches of the dissenters, and indeed most Anglican communities already knew, whether in Georgia, Pennsylvania, or Connecticut, that this was not the proper way to go about obtaining heavenly assistance. The Biblical conception of a people standing in direct daily relation to God, upon covenanted terms and therefore responsible for their moral conduct, was a common possession of the Protestant peoples.

However, there can be no doubt that New England had done much more than the other regions toward articulating colonial experience within the providential dialectic. Because, also, presses were more efficient there than elsewhere, and Boston imprints circulated down the coast, it is probable that the classic utterances of Massachusetts served as models for Presbyterians and Baptists as well as for "low-church" Anglicans. For many decades the Puritan colonies had been geographically set apart; the people had been thoroughly accustomed to conceiving of themselves as a chosen race, entered into specific covenant with God, by the terms of which they would be proportionately punished for their sins. Their afflictions were divine appointments, not the hazards of natural and impersonal forces.[6] Furthermore, the homogeneity of the Puritan communities enabled their parsons to speak in the name of the whole body—even when these were internally riven by strife over land banks, the Great Awakening, or baptism. Finally, this same isolation of the New England colonies encouraged a proliferation of the "federal

[6] Perry Miller, *The New England Mind; The Seventeenth Century*, New York, 1954, pp. 464–484.

theology" to a point where the individual's relation with God, his hope of salvation through a personal covenant, could be explicitly merged with the society's covenant. Hence in New England was most highly elaborated the theorem that the sins of individuals brought calamity upon the commonwealth.

In that sense, then, we may say that the Congressional recommendation of June 12, 1775, virtually took over the New England thesis that these colonial peoples stood in a contractual relation to the "great Governor" over and above that enjoyed by other groups; in effect, Congress added the other nine colonies (about whose status New Englanders had hitherto been dubious) to New England's covenant. Still, for most of the population in these nine, no novelty was being imposed. The federal theology, in general terms, was an integral part of the Westminster Confession and so had long figured in the rhetoric of Presbyterians of New Jersey and Pennsylvania. The covenant doctrine, including that of the society as well as of the individual, had been preached in the founding of Virginia,[7] and still informed the phraseology of ordinary Anglican sermonizing. The Baptists, even into Georgia, were aware of the concept of church covenant, for theirs were essentially "congregational" polities; they could easily rise from that philosophy to the analogous one of the state. Therefore the people had little difficulty reacting to the Congressional appeal. They knew precisely what to do: they were to gather in their assemblies on July 20, inform themselves that the afflictions brought upon them in the dispute with Great Britain were not hardships suffered in some irrational political strife but intelligible ordeals divinely brought about because of their own abominations. This being the situation, they were to resolve, not only separately but in unison, to mend their ways, restore primitive piety, suppress vice, curtail luxury. Then, and only thereafter, if they were sincere, if they proved that they meant their vow, God would

---

[7] Perry Miller, *Errand into the Wilderness*, Cambridge, Mass., 1956, pp. 119–122.

reward them by raising up instruments for the deflection of, or if necessary, destruction of, Lord North.

Since the New Englanders were such old hands at this business—by exactly this method they had been overcoming, from the days of the Pequot War through King Philip's War, such difficulties as the tyranny of Andros, small-pox epidemics, and parching droughts—they went to work at once. For the clergy the task was already clear: beginning with the Stamp Act of 1765, the clerical orator who spoke at every election day, in May, surveyed the respects in which relations with England should be subsumed under the over-all covenant of the people with God. Charles Chauncy's *A Discourse on the good News from a far Country*, delivered upon a day of "thanksgiving" (the logical sequel to several previous days of humiliation) to the General Court in 1766, explained that repeal of the odious Stamp Act was a consequence not of any mercantile resistance but of New England's special position within the Covenant of Grace.[8] As the crisis in Boston grew more and more acute, successive election orators had an annual opportunity to develop in greater detail proof that any vindication of provincial privileges was inextricably dependent upon a moral renovation. Following the "Boston Massacre" of 1773, anniversaries of this atrocity furnished every preacher an occasion for spreading the idea among the people. The form of these discourses was still that of the traditional "jeremiad"—a threatening of further visitation upon the covenanted people until they returned to their bond by confession and reformation—but by the time the Congress issued its wholesale invitation, the New England clergy had so merged the call to repentance with a stiffening of the patriotic spine that no power on earth, least of all the government of George III, could separate the acknowledgment of depravity from the resolution to fight.

Everything the Congress hoped would be said in 1775 had

[8] John Wingate Thornton, *The Pulpit of the American Revolution*, Boston, 1860, pp. 105ff.

already been declared by the Reverend Samuel Cooke of
the Second Church in Boston at the election of 1770.[9] If that
were not precedent enough, the General Court on October
22, 1774, confronting General Gage and the Boston Port Bill,
showed how double-edged was the sword by proclaiming not a
fast day but one of thanksgiving; it was illuminated by the
sermon of William Gordon, from the Third Church in
Roxbury, which was all the more memorable because Gordon
had been English-born.[10] On May 31, 1775, six weeks after
Lexington and Concord, Samuel Langdon, President of Harvard, put the theory of religious revolution so completely before the Court (then obliged to meet in Watertown) that the
doctrine of political resistance yet to be formulated in the
Declaration seems but an afterthought.[11] A few weeks before
that assertion, on May 29, 1776, Samuel West of Dartmouth
made clear to the General Court that what was included
within the divine covenant as a subsidiary but essential portion had been not simply "British liberties" but the whole
social teaching of John Locke.[12] After the evacuation of Boston, both Massachusetts and Connecticut were able to as-
semble as of old, and comfortably listen to a recital of their
shortcomings, secure in the knowledge that as long as jeremiads denounced them, their courage could not fail. The
fluctuations of the conflict called for many days of humiliation
and a few for thanksgiving; in Massachusetts, the framing of
the state constitution in 1780 evoked another spate of clerical
lectures on the direct connection between piety and politics.
Out of the years between the Stamp Act and the Treaty of
Paris emerged a formidable, exhaustive (in general, a repeti-
tious) enunciation of the unique necessity for America to win
her way by reiterated acts of repentance. The jeremiad,
which in origin had been an engine of Jehovah, thus became
temporarily a service department of the Continental army.

[9] *ibid.*, pp. 147–186.
[10] *ibid.*, pp. 187–226.
[11] *ibid.*, pp. 227–258.
[12] *ibid.*, pp. 259–322.

The student of New England's literature is not astonished to find this venerable machine there put to patriotic use; what has not been appreciated is how readily it could be set to work in other sections. On this day of humiliation, July 20, 1775, Thomas Coombe, an Anglican minister at Christ's Church and St. Peter's in Philadelphia, who once had been chaplain to the Marquis of Rockingham, explained, in language which would at once have been recognized in Connecticut, that our fast will prove ineffectual unless we execute a genuine reformation of manners (interestingly enough, the printed text is dedicated to Franklin):

"We must return to that decent simplicity of manners, that sober regard to ordinances, that strict morality of demeanor, which characterized our plain forefathers; and for the decay of which, their sons are but poorly compensated by all the superfluities of commerce. We must *associate* to give a new tone and vigor to the drooping state of religion among ourselves. We must support justice, both public and private, give an open and severe check to vices of every sort, and by our example discourage those luxurious customs and fashions, which serve but to enervate the minds and bodies of our children; drawing them off from such manly studies and attainments, as alone can render them amiable in youth or respectable in age." [13]

This Philadelphia Anglican combined as neatly as any Yankee the call for patriotic resistance and the old cry of Cotton Mather that the people respond to a jeremiad by implementing *Essays To Do Good*. By Coombe's standard, Quaker Philadelphia would appear to be a Babylon, but the opportunity for salvation was at last providentially offered: "Let such persons, however, now be told, that patriotism without piety is mere grimace." [14]

Thus we should not be surprised that Jacob Duché, preach-

[13] Thomas Coombe, *A Sermon*, Philadelphia, 1775, pp. 11–12.
[14] *ibid.*, p. 15.

ing on this same July 20 before not only his Anglican parish
but the assembled Congress, portrayed the whole trouble as
"a national punishment" inflicted on "national guilt." He
surveyed, as did all "Puritan" speakers, the manifest favors
God had shown the colonies, and then diagnosed their present
affliction as centering not on the iniquity of the British Cabinet
(iniquitous as it undoubtedly was) but rather on the infidelity
of Americans:

". . . have we not rather been so far carried away by the
stream of prosperity, as to be forgetful of the source from
whence it was derived? So elevated by the prospect, which
peace and a successful commerce have opened to us, as to
neglect those impressions of goodness, which former affections had left upon our hearts."

Was it not palpably for this reason, and this alone, "that the
Almighty hath bared his arm against us?" If so, the answer
for Duché, as for President Langdon, was clear: by reformation of manners, by a return to primitive piety, we would, as a
united people, win the cause of American liberty. "Go on, ye
chosen band of Christians," he cried to the Congress.[15] The
fact that after the Declaration Duché lost heart and turned
Loyalist does not make his *The American Vine* any less a
spiritual jeremiad of the sort that most invigorated Patriot
courage.

The way the War went, and especially the British occupation of Philadelphia, prevented among the middle states
the copious displays that flowed from the presses of Boston
and Worcester. Even so, there was some sort of printing shop
in Lancaster, and there in 1778 Hugh Henry Brackenridge
brought out *Six Political Discourses Founded on the Scripture.*
Known to fame—such fame as he has—for his picaresque
novel of the 1790's, *Modern Chivalry,* Brackenridge figures
in our histories as a Jeffersonian rationalist. So profound is
the spirit of the Enlightenment displayed in this work that

[15] Jacob Duché, *The American Vine,* Philadelphia, 1775, pp. 24–26.

330

we are convinced that he could not have later imbibed it, but must have learned it at Princeton, where he was classmate and friend of Madison and Freneau. In 1778, however, he was an ordained Presbyterian minister; hence this fugitive publication is of more than passing interest as illustrating the continuation, three years after the first day of national humiliation, of the religious conception of the struggle. George III, declares Brackenridge, was instigated by Satan; divine providence must perforce be on the patriot side. "Heaven hath taken an active part, and waged war for us." This he can say, even when the British hold Philadelphia! However, he can produce Saratoga for evidence. Hence it is clear that "Heaven knows nothing of neutrality," providence is the agency of God, and "there is not one tory to be found amongst the order of the seraphim." For our reverses we must have only our own sins to blame, and the surest way to victory is our conversion: "it becomes every one in the day of storm and sore commotion, to fly swiftly to the rock of Christ Jesus!" Granted that a man like Brackenridge might cleverly play upon these stops to excite a pious auditory, still it is evident that these were the appeals even a rational patriot would need to sound.[16]

To glance for a moment at the other end of the geographical spectrum: the people of Georgia had so far in their brief history found few opportunities to promote themselves into the role of an elected community; certainly the saints of Connecticut would never suppose Georgians equal in standing before the Lord with themselves. Still, when the Provincial Congress of Georgia met in 1775, before proceeding to support the Revolution they first listened to a clerical address— for all the world as though they were in Connecticut—by the Reverend John J. Zubly. It was printed in Philadelphia as *The Law of Liberty*.

Zubly reproduces the pattern of New England argumenta-

[16] H. H. Brackenridge, *Six Political Discourses Founded on the Scripture*, Lancaster, 1778, pp. 50–61.

PERRY MILLER

tion, though perhaps with somewhat less provincial egotism. These Americans are the result of a consecutive unfolding of God's covenant with mankind, now come to a climax on this continent; for Americans, the exercise of liberty becomes simply the one true obedience to God. This is not license, but resistance to sin; those who do not combat depravity will be judged:

"We are not to imagine because the gospel is a law of liberty, therefore men will not be judged; on the contrary judgment will be the more severe against all who have heard and professed the gospel, and yet walked contrary to its precepts and doctrines."

By this logic, once more, patriotic resistance to England is a way—the only way—to avert the wrath of Jehovah.[17]

If anywhere among the states the lineaments of Puritan federal theology would be dim, one might suppose that place to be Charleston, South Carolina. Legend continually obscures for us, however, how profoundly Protestant the culture of that region was at this time and for several decades afterwards. In 1774 William Tennent, son of the great William of Log College, expounded to planters and merchants that they were threatened with slavery because of their transgressions. The first dictate of natural passion is to imprecate vengeance upon the instruments of our torment, to resolve to endure hardships rather than surrender the privileges of our ancestors. But this, Tennent explained, is the wrong procedure. The first duty of good men is to find out and bewail "the Iniquities of our Nation and country," which are the true causes of the dismal catastrophe about to befall us.[18]

[17] John J. Zubly, *The Law of Liberty*, Philadelphia, 1775, p. 6.
[18] William Tennent, *An Address, Occasioned by the Late Invasion of the Liberties of the American Colonies by the British Parliament*, Philadelphia, 1774, p. 11. Tennent must have charmed his Carolinian audience by exclaiming (p. 17) that if these judgments have begun in New England, the bulwark of piety, those awaiting the profane South would be "more dreadful calamities."

332

Though by now the Revolution has been voluminously, and one might suppose exhaustively, studied, we still do not realize how effective were generations of Protestant preaching in evoking patriotic enthusiasm. No interpretation of the religious utterances as being merely sanctimonious window-dressing will do justice to the facts or to the character of the populace. Circumstances and the nature of the dominant opinion in Europe made it necessary for the official statement to be released in primarily "political" terms—the social compact, inalienable rights, the right of revolution. But those terms, in and by themselves, would never have supplied the drive to victory, however mightily they weighed with the literate minority. What carried the ranks of militia and citizens was the universal persuasion that they, by administering to themselves a spiritual purge, acquired the energies God had always, in the manner of the Old Testament, been ready to impart to His repentant children. Their first responsibility was not to shoot redcoats but to cleanse themselves; only thereafter to take aim. Notwithstanding the chastisements we have already received, proclaimed the Congress on March 20, 1779—they no longer limited themselves to mere recommending—"too few have been sufficiently awakened to a sense of their guilt, or warmed with gratitude, or taught to amend their lives and turn from their sins, so He might turn from His wrath." They call for still another fast in April, 1780: "To make us sincerely penitent for our transgressions; to prepare us for deliverance, and to remove the evil with which he hath been pleased to visit us; to banish vice and irreligion from among us, and establish virtue and piety by his Divine grace." And when there did come a cause for rejoicing (almost the only one in four or five years that might justify their using other vestibule, the surrender of Burgoyne), patriots gave little thought to lengthening lines of supply or the physical obstacles of logistics; instead, they beheld Providence at work again, welcomed Louis XVI as their "Christian ally," and congratulated themselves upon that which had really produced victory—their success in remodeling themselves. Now more than ever, asserted the Congress on October 31, 1777, we should "implore the mercy and forgiveness of God, and beseech him that vice, profaneness, extortion and every evil may be done away, and that we may be a reformed and a happy people." [19]

II

Historians of English political thought have reduced to a commonplace of inevitable progression the shift of Puritan political philosophy from the radical extreme of 1649 to the genial universals of 1689. John Locke so codified the later versions as to make the "Glorious Revolution" seem a conservative reaction. As we know, Locke was studied with avidity in the colonies; hence the Congress used consummate strategy in presenting their case to a candid world through the language of Locke.

Nevertheless, we do know that well before the Civil War began in England, Parliamentarians—and these include virtually all Puritans—had asserted that societies are founded upon covenant; that the forms of a particular society, even though dictated by utilitarian factors, are of divine ordination; that rulers who violate the agreed-upon forms are usurpers and so to be legitimately resisted. This complex of doctrine was transported bodily to early Virginia and most explicitly to Puritan New England. The turmoils of Massachusetts Bay—the expulsion of Roger Williams and Anne Hutchinson, the exile of Robert Child, the disciplining of the Hingham militia, and the first trials of the Quakers—whatever other issues were involved in them, were crises in the political creed. Governor Winthrop was not much troubled, though possibly a bit, when he told the men of Hingham that in signing the covenant they had agreed to submit to rulers

[19] Morris, pp. 533–536.

set over them for their own good—unless they could positively prove that their rulers were the violators!

The development of New England, however, steadily encouraged the citizens to deduce that they themselves, in framing the compact, had enumerated the items which made up their good. John Cotton and John Winthrop, having entirely accepted the contractual idea, were still making within it a last-ditch stand for medieval scholasticism by contending that the positive content of the magisterial function had been prescribed by God long before any specific covenant, whether of Israel or of Massachusetts, was drawn up. By the mid-eighteenth century, even in "semi-Presbyterial" Connecticut, good Christians were certain they could designate both the duties and the limitations of magistrates. In basically similar fashion, though not so easily traceable, the same transformation was wrought among the Protestant, or at least among the "Calvinistic," elements of all the communities. To put the matter bluntly, the agitation which resulted in the War for American Independence commenced after an immense change had imperceptibly been wrought in the minds of the people. That they needed from 1765 to 1776 to realize this was not because they had, under stress, to acquire the doctrine from abroad, but because they did have to search their souls in order to discover what actually had happened within themselves.

Consequently, every preacher of patriotism was obliged to complicate his revolutionary jeremiad by careful demonstrations of exactly how the will of almighty God had itself always operated through the voluntary self-imposition of a compact, how it had provided for legitimate, conservative resistance to tyrants. Early in the eighteenth century, John Wise prophesied how this union of concepts would be achieved, but he seems to have had no direct effect on the patriot argument. Jonathan Mayhew was far ahead of his fellows; after his death in 1766 the others required hard work to catch up. In general it may be said that they started off serenely confident that of course the philosophy of the jeremiad, which required abject confession of unworthiness from an afflicted people, and that of the social compact, which called for immediate and vigorous action against an intruding magistrate, were one and the same. Then, discovering that the joining required more carpentry than they had anticipated, they labored for all they were worth at the task. Finally, by 1776, they triumphantly asserted that they had indeed succeeded, that the day of humiliation was demonstrably one with the summons to battle.

Political historians and secular students of theory are apt to extract from the context those paragraphs devoted solely to the social position, to discuss these as comprising the only contribution of the "black regiment" to Revolutionary argument.[20] To read these passages in isolation is to miss the point. They were effective with the masses not as sociological lectures but because, being embedded in the jeremiads, they made comprehensible the otherwise troubling double injunction of humiliation and exertion. In this complicated pattern (which could be offered as the ultimate both in right reason and in true piety), the mentality of American Protestantism became so reconciled to itself, so joyfully convinced that it had at last found its long-sought identity, that for the time being it forgot that it had ever had any other reason for existing.

A few examples out of thousands will suffice. Gordon's *Discourse* of December 15, 1774, runs for page after page in the standardized jeremiad vein: "Is not this people strangely degenerated, so as to possess but a faint resemblance of that godliness for which their forefathers were eminent?" Is it not horrible beyond all imagination that *this* people should de-

---

[20] For example, Alice Baldwin, *The New England Clergy and the American Revolution*, Durham, N.C., 1928, a pioneer work of great value, but upon which later historians have unhappily depended. In this view, I should take Clinton Rossiter, *Seedtime of the Republic*, New York, 1953, as representing the strain of obtuse secularism.

generate, seeing how scrupulously God has befriended them according to the stipulations of their covenant with Him? Yet the ghastly fact is "that while there is much outward show of respect to the Deity, there is but little inward heart conformity to him." And so on and on, until abruptly, with hardly a perceptible shift, we are hearing a recital of the many palpable evidences that Divine Providence is already actively engaged in the work. Only by the direct "inspiration of the Most High" could the unanimity of the colonies have been brought about. From this point Gordon's cheerful jeremiad comes down to the utilitarian calculation that Americans are expert riflemen, wherefore "the waste of amunition will be greatly prevented"; after which he concludes by urging the people to "accept our punishment at his hands without murmuring or complaining"! [21]

The elements woven together in this and other speeches can, of course, be separated one from another in the antiseptic calm of the historian's study, and the whole proved to be an unstable compound of incompatible propositions. What may be left out of account is the impact of the entire argument, the wonderful fusion of political doctrine with the traditional rite of self-abasement which, out of colonial experience, had become not what it might seem on the surface, a failure of will, but a dynamo for generating action.

President Langdon's sermon of May, 1775 played a slight variation on the theme by suggesting that the notorious crimes of England had brought these troubles as a divine visitation on *her!* Other preachers occasionally toyed with this device, but obviously it was not the full-throated note the populace expected and wanted. Langdon returned to the really effective music when he justified the afflictions of America:

"But alas! have not the sins of America, and of New England in particular, had a hand in bringing down upon us the righteous judgments of Heaven? Wherefore is all this evil

<hr>

[21] Thornton, pp. 208, 212, 225.

come upon us? Is it not because we have foresaken the Lord?
Can we say we are innocent of crimes against God? No
surely."

After several pages of such conventional self-accusation, the
moral emerges as easily in 1775 as it used to flow from the
mouth of Cotton Mather: "However unjustly and cruelly
we have been treated by man, we certainly deserve, at the
hand of God, all the calamities in which we are now involved." [22]

Then follows a turn which is indeed novel, which reveals
the subtle yet largely unconscious transformation that the
Revolution was actually working in the hearts of the people.
Langdon concludes his jeremiad by calling upon Americans
to repent and reform, because *if* true religion can be revived,
"we may hope for the direction and blessing of the most High,
while we are using our best endeavors to preserve and restore
the civil government of this colony, and defend America from
slavery." [23]

Here, in exquisite precision, is the logic of the clerical
exhortation which, though it may seem to defy logic, gives a
vivid insight into what had happened to the pious mentality of
the communities. For, Langdon's argument runs, once we
have purged ourselves and recovered our energies in the act
of contrition, how then do we go about proving the sincerity
of our repentance (and insuring that Divine Providence will
assist us)? We hereupon act upon the principles of John
Locke! At this point, and not until after these essential preliminaries, Langdon turns to his exposition of Whig doctrine:

"Thanks be to God that he has given us, as men, natural
rights, independent of all human laws whatever, and that
these rights are recognized by the grand charter of British
liberties. By the law of nature, any body of people, destitute of

[22] *ibid.*, p. 247.
[23] *ibid.*, p. 249.

order and government, may form themselves into a civil society according to their best prudence, and so provide for their common safety and advantage. When one form is found by the majority not to answer the grand purpose in any tolerable degree, they may, by common consent, put an end to it and set up another." [24]

The next year, Samuel West of Dartmouth persuaded the General Court of Massachusetts, not to mention readers elsewhere in the colonies, that the inner coherence of the thesis was maintained by these two combined doctrines: while, because of our abysmally sinful condition, we must obey magistrates for conscience' sake, we also find "that when rulers become oppressive to the subject and injurious to the state, their authority, their respect, their maintenance, and the duty of submitting to them, must immediately cease; they are then to be considered as the ministers of Satan, and as such, it becomes our indispensable duty to resist and oppose them." [25] What we today have to grasp is that for the masses this coalescence of abnegation and assertion, this identification of Protestant self-distrust with confidence in divine aid, erected a frame for the natural-rights philosophy wherein it could work with infinitely more power than if it had been propounded exclusively in the language of political rationalism.

There were, it should be pointed out, a few clerics who could become patriots without having to go through this labyrinth of national humiliation. But in the colonies they were a minority, and they came from a Protestantism which had never been permeated by the federal theology—which is to say, they were generally Anglicans. The most conspicuous was William Smith, later Provost of the College of Philadelphia. When he responded to the Congressional recommendation, on July 20, 1775, at All-Saints in Philadelphia, he emphasized his dissent from the covenantal conception at once:

[24] *ibid.*, p. 250.
[25] *ibid.*, p. 296.

"I would, therefore, cherish these good dispositions; and what may, peradventure, have begun through Fear, I would ripen into maturity by the more cheering beams of Love. Instead of increasing your afflictions, I would convey a dawn of comfort to your souls; rather striving to woo and to win you to Religion and Happiness, from a consideration of what God hath promised to the Virtuous, than of what He hath denounced against the Wicked, both through Time and in Eternity." [26]

A historian not versed in the discriminations of theology may see little difference, considered as propaganda, between Provost Smith's form of Christian exhortation and President Langdon's, since Smith also aligns the Providence of God on the side of resistance. But for men of 1775—that is for most of them—there was a vast gulf between Smith's conception and that of the New Englanders, of Coombe, of Duché, of Zubly. The really effective work of the "black regiment" was not an optimistic appeal to the rising glory of America, but their imparting a sense of crisis by revivifying Old Testament condemnations of a degenerate people.

Smith's method, however, did have one advantage: more readily than the Puritans and Presbyterians, he could promise that God would bless a victorious America with prosperity, with that "happiness" which the Declaration said all men had a natural right to pursue. Smith did note in passing that we must repent and sincerely reform our naughty manners,[27] but his recruiting sermons pay much more attention than do those of New England or of the back-country to the strictly legal contention. These generally conclude, as did one to a battalion of militia on June 25, 1775, with the earthly rewards in prospect:

"Illiberal or mistaken plans of policy may distress us for a while, and perhaps sorely check our growth; but if we main-

[26] *The Works of William Smith, D.D.*, Philadelphia, 1803, II, 119.
[27] *ibid.*, pp. 123, 138.

tain our own virtue; if we cultivate the spirit of Liberty among our children; if we guard against the snares of luxury, venality and corruption; the Genius of America will still rise triumphant, and that with a power at last too mighty for opposition. This country will be free—nay, for ages to come a chosen seat of Freedom, Arts, and Heavenly Knowledge; which are now either drooping or dead in those countries of the old world." [28]

Surely Smith's logic is straightforward. On December 28, 1778, he preached before a Masonic chapter and dedicated the sermon to Washington. There is no mention in it of affliction; hardships, even unto death, are to be borne in a spirit of Christian fortitude, and Christians are simply to fight the good fight, confident that when they die they shall have full scope for the exercise of charity.[29] But, though Smith's form of Christianity, with its piety hardly more than a species of Stoicism, might appeal to Washington and prove unobjectionable even to Jefferson, and though Smith delivered a heartfelt eulogy on Benjamin Franklin,[30] it was neither Smith's genial Anglicanism nor the urbane rationalism of these statesmen which brought the rank and file of American Protestants into the War. What aroused a Christian patriotism that needed staying power was a realization of the vengeance God denounced against the wicked; what fed their hopes was not what God promised as a recompense to virtue, but what dreary fortunes would overwhelm those who persisted in sloth; what kept them going was an assurance that by exerting themselves they were fighting for a victory thus providentially predestined.

To examine the Revolutionary mind from the side of its religious emotion is to gain a perspective that cannot be acquired from the ordinary study of the papers of the Congresses, the letters of Washington, the writings of Dickinson,

[28] *ibid.*, pp. 283–284.
[29] *ibid.*, p. 67.
[30] *ibid.*, I, 44–92.

Paine, Freneau, or John Adams. The "decent respect" that these Founders entertained for the opinion of mankind caused them to put their case before the civilized world in the restricted language of the rational century. A successful revolution, however, requires not only leadership but receptivity. Ideas in the minds of the foremost gentlemen may not be fully shared by their followers, but these followers will accept the ideas, even adopt them, if such abstractions can be presented in an acceptable context. To accommodate the principles of a purely secular social compact and a right to resist taxation—even to the point of declaring political independence to a provincial community where the reigning beliefs were still original sin and the need of grace—this was the immense task performed by the patriotic clergy.

Our mental image of the religious patriot is distorted because modern accounts do treat the political paragraphs as a series of theoretical expositions of Locke, separated from what precedes and follows. When these orations are read as wholes, they immediately reveal that the sociological sections are structural parts of a rhetorical pattern. Embedded in their contexts, these are not abstractions but inherent parts of a theology. It was for this reason that they had so energizing an effect upon their religious auditors. The American situation, as the preachers saw it, was not what Paine presented in *Common Sense*—a community of hard-working, rational creatures being put upon by an irrational tyrant—but was more like the recurrent predicament of the chosen people in the Bible. As Samuel Cooper declared on October 25, 1780, upon the inauguration of the Constitution of Massachusetts, America was a new Israel, selected to be "a theatre for the display of some of the most astonishing dispensations of his Providence." The Jews originally were a free republic founded on a covenant over which God "in peculiar favor to that people, was pleased to preside." When they offended Him, He punished them by destroying their republic, subjecting them to a king. Thus while we today need no revelation to inform us that we are all born free and equal and that sovereignty resides in the people—"these are the plain dictates of that reason and common sense with which the common parent has informed the human bosom"—still Scripture also makes these truths explicit. Hence when we angered our God, a king was also inflicted upon us; happily, Americans have succeeded, where the Jews did not, in recovering something of pristine virtue, whereupon Heaven redressed America's earthly grievances. Only as we today appreciate the formal unity of the two cosmologies, the rational and the Biblical, do we take in the full import of Cooper's closing salute to the new Constitution: "How nicely it poises the powers of government, in order to render them as far as human foresight can, what God ever designed they should be, power only to do good." [31]

Once this light is allowed to play on the scene, we perceive the shallowness of that view which would treat the religious appeal as a calculated propaganda maneuver. The ministers did not have to "sell" the Revolution to a public sluggish to "buy." They were spelling out what both they and the people sincerely believed, nor were they distracted by worries about the probability that Jefferson held all their constructions to be nonsense. A pure rationalism such as his might have declared the independence of these folk, but it could never have inspired them to fight for it.

This assertion may seem too sweeping, but without our making it we can hardly comprehend the state in which American Protestantism found itself when the victory was won. A theology which for almost two centuries had assumed that men would persistently sin, and so would have to be recurrently summoned to communal repentance, had for the first time identified its basic conception with a specific political action. Then, for the first time in the life of the conception, the cause was totally gained. Did not a startling inference follow:

[31] Samuel Cooper, *A Sermon Preached . . . October 25, 1780,* Boston, 1780, pp. 2, 8, 11, 14, 15, 29.

these people must have reformed themselves completely, must now dwell on a pinnacle of virtuousness? But there was no place in the theology of the covenant for a people to congratulate themselves. There was a station only for degenerates in need of regeneration, who occasionally might thank God for this or that mercy He granted them, forgiving their imperfections. Where could Protestantism turn, what could it employ, in order still to hold the religious respect of this now victorious society?

III

An Anglican rationalist, as we have seen with William Smith, would have no difficulty about the sequence of statements which said that by resisting England we would assure the future prosperity of the republic. The patriotic Jeremiahs also employed the argument, but they had to be more circumspect. Protestant political thinking had never doubted, of course, that God instituted government among men as a means toward their temporal felicity—or, at least toward their "safety." But it always based its philosophy upon the premise of original sin. Since the Fall, had men been left in a pure state of nature, all would have been Ishmaels; no man's life, family, or property would be secure. So, government was primarily a check on evil impulses; its function was negative rather than positive; it was to restrain violence, not to advance arts, sciences, technology. Yet, as Governor John Winthrop agreed during the first years of Massachusetts Bay, because *"salus populi suprema lex,"* there was a corollary (lurking out of sight) that government ought, once it restrained the lusts of these people, to do something more creative about making them comfortable.

In the negativistic emphasis of Protestant teachings, the reason for King George's violence and the consequent righteousness of resisting him were easy to make out. He and his ministers were violating the compact, so that he had become Ishmael. Law-abiding subjects were defending social barriers which, if once broken through, would cease to confine all social passions. By defying Britain they were preserving mankind from a descent into chaos. Resistance to a madman is not revolution; it is, in obedience to God, an exercise of the police power.

Yet what happens to particles of this logic when to it is joined the contention that by such resistance the righteous not only obey God but acquire wealth for themselves and their children? How can the soldier venture everything in the holy cause, after having confessed his depravity, if all the time he has a secret suspicion that by going through this performance he in fact is not so much repenting as gaining affluence for his society?

In most of the patriotic jeremiads the material inducement is entered—sometimes, we may say, smuggled in. It could not be left out. Yet once the machinery of national humiliation proved effective in producing the providential victory of the Americans, were they not bound to the prophecy that by their utilization of the form, they, and they alone, would bring about a reign of national bliss? But in that case how could a confession of unworthiness be sincere?

An uneasy awareness of the dilemma was present even in the early stages of agitation. Listen, for instance, to Samuel Williams, pastor of the Church in Bradford, delivering *A Discourse on the Love of Country*, December 15, 1774:

"As what should further confirm our attachment to our native country, it bids the fairest of any to promote *the perfection and happiness of mankind*. We have but few principles from which we can argue with certainty, what will be the state of mankind in future ages. But if we may judge the designs of providence, by the number and power of the causes that are already at work, we shall be led to think that the perfection and happiness of mankind is to be carried further in America, than it has ever yet been in any place." [32]

This passage is only one of hundreds in the same vein, and all wrestle with the same dubious contention: we have sinned, therefore we are afflicted by the tyranny of a corrupt Britain; we must repent and reform, in order to win the irresistible aid of Providence; once we have wholeheartedly performed this act, we shall be able to exert our freedom by expelling the violators of the compact; when we succeed we shall enter upon a prosperity and temporal happiness beyond anything the world has hitherto seen. But always implicit in this chain of reasoning was a vague suggestion that the people were being bribed into patriotism. And by universal admission, the occasion for a nation's deserting its Maker and surrendering to sensuality was always an excess of material comforts. So, was not the whole machinery an ironic device for bringing upon the children of the victors judgments still more awful than any that had previously been imposed?

The clergy had, in short, simplified the once massive complexity of the process of social regeneration by concentrating its terrorizing appeal upon a single hardship, the British government. Seventeenth-century theologians would have been more wary. They took pains to keep the list so long —draught, fires, earthquakes, insects, small-pox, shipwrecks— that while the people by their holy exertions might be let off this or that misery, they were sure to be tormented by some other. The Revolutionary divines, in their zeal for liberty, committed themselves unwittingly to the proposition that in this case expulsion of the British would automatically leave America a pure society. In their righteous anger, they painted gorier and gorier pictures of the depravity of England. Said President Langdon, "The general prevalence of vice has changed the whole face of things in the British govern-

[32] Samuel Williams, *A Discourse on the Love of Country*, Salem, 1775, p. 22.

ment"; [33] wherefore it had to follow that the sins of the colonial peoples, which brought down the Intolerable Acts, were in great part "infections" received from "the corruption of European courts." But then, once we innoculated ourselves against these contagions, would we not become a people washed white in the Blood of the Lamb?

The progress of events which led the patriots from their initial defense of "British liberties" to the radical plunge into independence also led them to this doctrinaire identification of religious exertion with the political aim. By 1776 Samuel West made it crystal clear:

"Our cause is so just and good that nothing can prevent our success but only our sins. Could I see a spirit of repentance and reformation prevail through the land, I should not have the least apprehension or fear of being brought under the iron rod of slavery, even though all the powers of the globe were combined against us. And though I confess that the irreligion and profaneness which are so common among us gives something of a damp to my spirits, yet I cannot help hoping, and even believing, that Providence has designed this continent for to be the asylum of liberty and true religion; for can we suppose that the God who created us free agents, and designed that we should glorify and serve him in this world that we might enjoy him forever hereafter, will suffer liberty and true religion to be banished from off the face of the earth?" [34]

What else, then, could President Ezra Stiles of Yale College preach upon, before the General Assembly of Connecticut, on May 8, 1783, but *The United States Elevated to Glory and Honor?*

"This will be a great, a very great nation, nearly equal to half Europe. . . . Before the millennium the English settlements in America may become more numerous millions than

[33] Thornton, p. 243.
[34] *ibid.*, p. 311.

the greatest dominion on earth, the Chinese Empire. Should this prove a future fact, how applicable would be the text, when the Lord shall have made his American Israel high above all nations which he has made, in numbers, and in praise, and in name, and in honor!" [35]

Still, the more closely we study this literature of exultation, the more we suspect that the New Englanders were dismayed by the very magnitude of their success. The Middle States were less inhibited. Most revelatory is George Duffield's *A Sermon Preached in the Third Presbyterian Church* of Philadelphia on December 11, 1783—the day that Congress could at long last conscientiously appoint a "Thanksgiving." It was now abundantly clear, said Duffield, that from the beginning the Revolution had been under providential direction. We have created a nation which shall receive the poor and oppressed: "here shall the husbandman enjoy the fruits of his labor; the merchant trade, secure of his gain; the mechanic indulge his inventive genius; and the sons of science pursue their delightful employment, till the light of knowledge pervade yonder yet uncultivated western wilds, and form the savage inhabitants into men." In the exuberance of triumph, Duffield permitted himself to say, in effect, that the jeremiad had also triumphed, and that we, being a completely reformed nation, need no longer be summoned to humiliation!

"A *day* whose evening shall not terminate in night; but introduce that joyful period, when the outcasts of Israel, and the dispersed of Judah, shall be restored; and with them, the fulness of the Gentile world shall flow to the standard of redeeming love: And the nations of the earth, become the kingdom of our Lord and Saviour. Under whose auspicious reign holiness shall universally prevail; and the noise and alarm of war be heard no more." [36]

[35] *ibid.*, p. 440.
[36] George Duffield, *A Sermon Preached in the Third Presbyterian Church*, Philadelphia, 1784, pp. 16–17, 18.

In this situation—if all the nation participated, as most of it did, in the assurances of Duffield's *te Deum*—there would be, at least for the moment, no further use for the jeremiad. A few New Englanders, along with President Witherspoon of Princeton, cautioned the people that while indeed God had blessed them beyond all expectation, they now had the further responsibility of perpetuating the reformation, but theirs were but feeble admonitions compared with the compulsions of the dark days of 1775. Because the program of salvation had been combined with the struggle for nationhood, American Protestants were obliged to see in the Treaty of Paris the fulfillment of prophecies. Ezra Stiles took as his text Deuteronomy xxvi.19, a verse that long had done yeoman's service as a club for beating backsliders, and then explained that on this occasion he selected it "only as introductory to a discourse upon the political welfare of God's American Israel, and as allusively prophetic of the future prosperity and splendor of the United States." [37] This by implication does pretend that the reformation had been entirely successful. So, with some reluctance, Stiles suggests that with the finish of the colonial era we have come also to the close of the jeremiad:

"And while we have to lament our Laodiceanism, deficient morals, and incidental errors, yet the collective system of evangelical doctrines, the instituted ordinances, and the true ecclesiastical polity, may be found here in a great degree of purity." [38]

Whereupon a chill strikes the exulting heart. If this be so, are we not, under the Providence of God, on leaving the exciting scenes both of war and spiritual conflict, now headed for a monotonous, an uninteresting prosperity, the flatness of universal virtue?

These people, however, had for a long time been disciplined to the expectation of woe. The government of the Confed-

[37] Thornton, p. 403.
[38] *ibid.*, p. 473.

eracy became mired in confusion, thus clouding once more any reading of God's design. While the States were devising a Constitution to correct this affliction, the blow was struck; but not in America—in Paris. At first, of course, the fall of the Bastille seemed to strengthen the alliance of social doctrine and religious hope. Shortly the fallacy became evident. Not that there was any serious threat in America of a reversion to the depraved state of nature which engulfed France in 1793; yet in this glorious republic the French Revolution brought home to the devout an immediate realization of the need for dissociating the Christian conception of life from any blind commitment to the philosophy of that Revolution. Indeed, they had no choice ultimately but to abandon the whole political contention of either of the two revolutions, and to seek at once some other program for Christian solidarity. They did not need to renounce the Declaration, nor even to denounce the Constitution, but only henceforth to take those principles for granted, yield government to the secular concept of the social compact, accept the First Amendment, and so to concentrate, in order to resist Deism and to save their souls, upon that other mechanism of cohesion developed out of their colonial experience, the Revival.

It took them until about the year 1800 to recast—or, as they believed, to recover—their history. Amid the great revivals which swept over Connecticut, Kentucky, and Tennessee in that year, which expanded into Georgia, Illinois, and for decades burned over northern New York, the Revolution was again and again presented as having been itself a majestic Revival. The leadership of Jefferson, Paine, and the rationalists was either ignored or explained away. The "Second Great Awakening" engendered the denominational forms of American Protestantism which still endure, but perhaps equally important was its work in confirming the American belief that the Revolution had not been at all revolutionary, but simply a protest of native piety against foreign impiety.

IV

Denominational historians tell us what the churches had to contend with following the Treaty of Paris. One fact seems indisputable: while Presbyterians and Congregationalists hesitated, Methodist itinerants rushed in. During the 1790's the major churches undertook a radical realignment of thinking, which for a century or more would determine their character.

The factors in this cultural crisis—complex though they were—can be, for narrative purposes, succinctly enumerated.

Despite the warnings of Provost Smith, the Protestant clergy preached so extravagant a Christian utopianism that with the end of the War they could only term what confronted them a demoralization beyond anything they had ever imagined. In 1795, for instance, the Methodist Church was calling for the resumption of fast days because of "our manifold sins and iniquities—our growing idolatry, which is covetousness and the prevailing love of the world . . . the profanation of the Sabbath . . . disobedience to parents, various debaucheries, drunkenness, and such like." [39] Relative to, say, the 1920's, the America of the 1790's may appear a reign of idyllic simplicity, but to organized religion it seemed morally abominable.

Coincident with this internal confusion came the French Revolution, that "volcano," as Robert Baird retrospectively called it in 1844, which "threatened to sweep the United States into its fiery stream." [40] It would not have set off such hysteria had not its excitements coincided with the frightening division of American society into parties, portending in the eyes of many an internal conflict. It is important, if we would make sense out of later developments, to insist that by no means all the religious—call them Calvinist, Evangelical, or simply Orthodox—went with Hamilton against Jefferson.

[39] Nathan Bangs, *A History of the Methodist Episcopal Church*, New York, 1839, II, 146.
[40] Robert Baird, *Religion in America*, New York, 1844, p. 102.

On the contrary, multitudes were not alienated by Jefferson's Deism. The publicity given by Henry Adams to Timothy Dwight's insane fears over Jefferson's election—Dwight's certainty that all the virgins of Connecticut would be raped—has been so played up in our histories that we forget how the Evangelicals were worried not so much about the President as about the whole apocalyptical scene. The Presbyterian General Assembly in May, 1798, bewailed innovations in Europe, the parades of devastation and bloodshed, but saw these as ominous because along with them had come "a general dereliction of religious principle and practice among our fellow-citizens, . . . a visible and prevailing impiety and contempt for the laws and institutions of religion, and an abounding infidelity which in many instances tends to Atheism itself." [41] By this time the churches supposed themselves once more in the predicament Edwards had diagnosed in 1740: the nation, having prospered, had become slovenly. Each by itself, with connivance, concluded that it was high time for another outpouring of God's Spirit, and then to their surprise found themselves engaged in a common enterprise which owed nothing to political agitation or to governmental encouragement. "We rejoice," said the Stonington Baptist Association in 1798, "that many of our brethren of different denominations have united in concert of prayer, and meet at stated season, to offer up fervant [sic] supplications, that God would avert his judgments." [42]

There was a dimension to their anxiety, however, which had hardly been present in 1740—the terrifying West. Kentucky and Tennessee were opened up, the Ohio Valley was ready for the stampede. The churches—Congregational, Baptist, Presbyterian, Lutheran, even the insurgent Methodist—were European institutions. In their several ways they had given religious sanction to the political break with Europe.

[41] Quoted in Charles R. Keller, *The Second Great Awakening in Connecticut*, New Haven, 1942, pp. 1–2.
[42] *ibid.*, p. 191.

Then, by 1800 or thereabouts, they had also to realize that they could no longer operate in terms of a provincial society huddled along the Atlantic coast, facing toward Europe; they had to find means for combating what everybody feared would be a plunge into barbarism, on the other side of the Appalachians, in a vast area stretching away from Europe. In the next decades the cry for saving the West swelled to a chorus of incitation infinitely more impassioned than had been the call for resistance to England. A view of the valleys of the two great rivers, said William Cogswell in 1833, is enough to make heaven weep, "enough to break any heart unless harder than adamant, and to rouse it into holy action, unless colder than the grave." [43]

To uncover the main spring of the "Second Great Awakening" one has to look in these directions, rather than to rest content with the conventional explanation that it was reaction against Deism and the Enlightenment. Actually, European Deism was an exotic plant in America, which never struck roots into the soil. "Rationalism" was never so widespread as liberal historians, or those fascinated by Jefferson, have imagined. The basic fact is that the Revolution had been preached to the masses as a religious revival, and had the astounding fortune to succeed. In a little more than a decade the Protestant conscience recognized anew that in the spiritual economy victory, especially the most complete victory, is bound to turn into failure. So the struggle had to be commenced once more. James McGready, Barton Warren Stone, and the two McGees were picking up at the end of the 1790's where the patriotic orators had relaxed. They were sustained by a sense of continuity.

There were, nevertheless, a few differences in their comprehension of the task. For these revivalists, it was no longer necessary to find space in their sermons for social theory. They might honor John Locke as much as George Washington, but

[43] William Cogswell, *The Harbinger of the Millennium*, Boston, 1833, p. 102.

could at best salute both in passing. Furthermore, they really had no way of holding the entire nation responsible for the observance of a covenant with Heaven. Clergymen of 1776 could plausibly present the tight little cluster of colonies as having been somehow all caught up within a special and particular bond, but after 1800, and even more after 1815, the country was too big, too sprawling, too amorphous. No Baptist, Presbyterian, or Methodist could pretend on national holidays to speak for the conscience of all churchmen. These two considerations so altered the bases of their campaign from what had served the First Awakening that they had to devise entirely new ones. They were required to risk an adventure unprecedented in history. Calling upon all the people to submit to a uniform moral law, they at the same time had to concede that American Christianity must and should accept a diversity of churches. We once, said the *Biblical Repository* in 1832, entertained Utopian ideas about great national religious institutions, but neither the state of the country nor the temper of the age will admit them: "Theological peculiarities and sectional feelings call for separate institutions." [44] If this configuration posed a threat of centrifugal force, then that had to be countered by the centripetal power of the Revival. Therefore the technique of revivalism had to be remodeled to serve precisely this function. Thus accepting the liberal consequences of the Revolution in the form of republican governments, and so abandoning the dream of theocracy, and equally surrendering (except for rhetorical flourish) the idea of a people in a national covenant with their Maker, these insurgents proposed to salvage the Protestant solidarity by the main force of spiritual persuasion. They summoned sinners to the convulsions of conversion; what in fact they were doing, even though few quite understood, was asserting the unity of a culture in pressing danger of fragmentation.

[44] *Biblical Repository*, IV, Andover, 1832, 79.

V

Of one thing patriotic sermons of the Revolution were supremely confident, even from the first stirrings of violence: with a free United States dawns the era of religious liberty. Massachusetts and Connecticut might have to construct a curious logic to explain just how this assurance was to be reconciled with their retention of a "standing order," yet whatever the devices by which they apologized for it, they stoutly added that all other denominations could and would enjoy perfect freedom. Samuel Cooper in 1800 betrayed his embarrassment by carefully quoting all the libertarian passages in the new Constitution, and further acknowledging that there exists a diversity of sentiments respecting the extent of civil power in religious matters. He would not enter into disputation, but he could frankly recommend, "where conscience is pleaded on both sides, mutual candour and love, and an happy union of all denominations in support of a government, which though human, and therefore not absolutely perfect, is yet certainly founded on the broadest basis of liberty, and affords equal protection to all." [45] Ezra Stiles permitted himself in 1783 conveniently to ignore the Connecticut system in his enthusiasm for prophesying that with our liberation from the Church of England and our attaining of freedom, we would restore the churches to primitive purity: "Religious liberty is peculiarly friendly to fair and generous disquisition." He was so persuaded that in a free market truth would prevail that he was willing to go to any lengths: "Here Deism will have its full chance; nor need libertines more to complain of being overcome by any weapons but the gentle, the powerful ones of argument and truth. Revelation will be found to stand the test to the ten thousandth examination." [46]

The prospect of glory for America lay not in this or that

[45] Cooper, pp. 36–37.
[46] Thornton, p. 471.

church, Stiles announced, but in the national virtue of all of them together: "We must become a holy people in reality, in order to exhibit the experiment, never yet fully made in this unhallowed part of the universe, whether such a people would be the happiest on earth." [47] Outside New England, preachers spoke unequivocally, asserting that all sects stood on a common level and that never again should there be any connection between religious profession and the rights of citizenship. In Connecticut after 1818 and in Massachusetts after 1833, ministers could happily join the chorus of freedom. Those who had fought most stoutly against disestablishment soon professed, as did Lyman Beecher, that it was a blessing to their churches.

Thus it was evident that the salvation of the nation which the revivalists of 1800 and of the following decades burned to accomplish had to be won, if won it might be, by their own exertions, with no assistance from any civil authority. They undertook their task without trepidation. They were aware that they were attempting an "experiment" unprecedented in Christian history, against the success of which past experience testified. This consideration only encouraged them. In the colonies there had come about a multiplicity of churches, a knack of getting along together, and a formal separation of church and state, by a process so natural as to make them see nothing extraordinary in their situation. True, they did recollect that formerly there had been nasty struggles, but these they banished from mind and ceased to dream of an established or uniform orthodoxy. There was clearly no cause to fear that either the federal or state governments, though thoroughly secularized, would ever become enemies of Christianity. If the civil powers could not actively foment a revival, they could likewise not hinder it. So at first the spiritual leaders saw nothing incongruous in their continuing to speak as though the whole nation professed itself still in covenant, as a unit, with Providence. Indeed when President

[47] Thornton, p. 487.

Washington proclaimed a day of thanksgiving for the inauguration of the Constitution in 1789, and another in 1795 over the suppression of the whiskey rebellion, the formula of national federation seemed still to prevail, and the churches promptly acted as of old.

The first tremors of disillusionment came when President Adams called for fasts in 1798 and 1799, ostensibly because of such standard afflictions as cholera and yellow fever. In the heat of the political contention, the Jeffersonians saw these gestures not as pious intercessions of the whole people before the throne of grace, but as Federalist plots to ensnare Republicans into praying for John Adams. It is not surprising then that Thomas Jefferson exposed the hollowness of the federal conception in 1802 by taking advantage of an awkward address from the Danbury Baptist Association (this minority in Connecticut was then objecting to being compelled to observe fast days appointed by the standing order) to announce that he would not longer, "as my predecessors did," proclaim such days. As he explained in a much-quoted letter of 1808, he considered the federal government prohibited by the Constitution from intermeddling with religious institutions, and that even to "recommend" a ceremonial observance would be indirectly to assume an authority over religion. It is not for the interest of the churches themselves, he said, "that the General Government should be invested with the power of effecting any uniformity of time or matter among them." [48] Wherefore, if the churches were to save this society and keep it righteous, though they might for a time employ the familiar language (as the Presbyterian Assembly did in 1798: "eternal God has a controversy with this nation"),[49] they soon were forced to recognize that in fact they now dealt with the Deity only as particular individuals gathered for historical, capricious

---

[48] Anson Phelps Stokes, *Church and State in the United States*, New York, 1950, I, 489–491.

[49] W. W. Sweet, *Religion on the American Frontier*, Vol. II, *The Presbyterians*, New York, 1936, p. 55.

reasons into this or that communion. They had to realize, at first painfully, that as a united people they had no contractual relationship with the Creator, and that consequently a national controversy with Him could no longer exist.

President Madison, despite his scruples, reverted to custom, and actually in 1812 chanted the ancient litany: we must acknowledge "the transgressions which might justly provoke the manifestations of His divine displeasure," we must seek His assistance "in the great duties of repentance and amendment" in order to counter Britain's Acts in Council.[50] But the magic had gone out of the spell. In the first place, the idea of James Madison sincerely using these phrases made it a rigmarole. Second, many good Christians, especially in New England, were so passionately opposed to the policy which was bringing on the hated war that they could not attribute the manifestations of displeasure as due to any transgressions of their own, but solely to the stupidity of the administration. They would respond to such an invitation from the White House not by assembling in churches to renew their covenant with Jehovah, but rather by gathering in a convention at Hartford, in order, if necessary, to break their covenant with anti-Federalist states. How obsolete the pattern had become, how indeed it no longer made sense and had to break up of itself, finally became evident in 1832 when Henry Clay was so misguided as to attempt to convert it into a stick for beating Andrew Jackson.

At the end of June in that year (the election was coming in the autumn), Clay introduced in the Senate a resolution to request that the President recommend a day of humiliation and prayer because the country was threatened with a cholera invasion. Clay had so little knowledge of the proper incantation—in the course of the debate he admitted that he was not a church member, but that even so he had "a profound respect for Christianity, the religion of my fathers, and for its rites, usages and its observances"—that he entirely omitted a

[50] Morris, p. 549.

recital of the sins of the nation which had drawn this visitation upon it. The most liberal of clerical orators in the Revolution would have been horrified at this violation of protocol! Instead, Clay proved at length that the Presidential recommendation "would be obligatory upon none," that it should be gratefully received by "all pious and moral men, whether members of religious communities or not."

Significantly enough, the Whigs rushed to Clay's support, even though some of them, like Frelinghuysen of New York, had once been Federalists and had formerly sneered at little Jimmy Madison's effort to play the prophet. But the Democrats would have none of it. Tazewell of Virginia scored heavily as he reaffirmed Jefferson's contention that Congress has no more power to make such a resolution than to enact any law concerning religious matter or right, but he scored more heavily when he denied that there was any threat to the mass of the nation from cholera. Once an affliction becomes so much a matter of debate that there can be no universal and instantaneous agreement upon its severity, then the glorious era of the covenant is terminated. In the House, Davis of South Carolina buried the resolution by branding the custom as "derived from our English ancestors," and said that if it were observed, it would increase alarm and so augment calamity.[51]

Despite the fumbling theology of the Whigs, Clay's resolution got lost in committee (Jackson was prepared to veto it had it ever emerged). However, in August, 1861, Lincoln did recommend a day of humility, and some of his language evoked memories of the past. Yet here the "affliction" was manifestly recognizable, and besides, by 1861, a succession of revivals and the prosperity of the "voluntary principle" had so reoriented American Protestantism within an uncovenanted piety that it could respond to the President's proclamation without anybody's giving a thought to the heavenly contract —at least, shall we say, in terms which the Puritan federalists

[51] *Annals, 22 Congress,* First Series (1832), pp. 1130–1132, 3834.

would have recognized. The emphasis of this day of humiliation was not really humiliation but a unanimous prayer "that
our arms may be blessed and made effective for the re-
establishment of law, order and peace throughout the country." This, of course, makes the fast day frankly an implement
of municipal policy, just what the Revolutionary proclamations are accused of being, but which they were only sub-
ordinately to their religious directive. The irony is that in
1861 the ceremony could be so openly devoted to the national
"happiness," because the religious injunction had for several
decades previously issued not from the covenantal relation of
the nation to God's designs but from a fervor of individual
piety aroused by the revivals and harnessed to religious action,
not through an established church but within a bewildering
variety of voluntaristic churches.

What gives both meaning and poignance to the story is
that at the very moment Lincoln issued his proclamation,
churches to the south of the Mason-Dixon Line—which in
theology, polity, and general piety were indeed the brethren
of those to the north—equally anxious prayers were being
offered for a blessing upon Confederate arms, and likewise
in the name of law and order. Between the Revolution and
the Civil War an alteration was worked in the mind of American Protestantism which is in fact a more comprehensive
revolution than either of the military irruptions. With the
political order separated from the ecclesiastical, yet not set
against it, the problem had become not how to enlist the
community into a particular political crusade for any social
doctrine, but how to preserve a spiritual unity throughout a
multitude of sects amid the increasing violence of political
dissension. On the one hand, the revival movement and the
extension of the voluntary system could not prevent the Civil
War, as conceivably the theology of the covenant might
have; but what these forces could do was to formulate a
religious nationalism which even the war could not destroy.
Whatever blood was shed and scars remained, the battles

were fought upon the assumption of a cultural similarity of the contestants, one with another, which could surmount the particular issues in dispute and thus become, after 1865, a powerful instrument of reunification.

VI

I do not mean to assert, as I hope is obvious, that the "jeremiad" form of the sermon—that inheritance from the covenant theology of the Old Testament, of Calvinism, of Puritanism—automatically ceased upon the miscarriage of Clay's resolution in 1832. It continued to be a staple in evangelical preaching. But never again would it have the sting of the seventeenth-century exercises, or of those of the Revolution. Without having behind it any living sense of a specific bond between the nation and God, it could survive only as a species of utilitarian exhortation.

For instance, Joel Parker discoursed in 1837 to the Presbyterian Congregation in New Orleans upon the Panic of 1837, which he presented as a novel "yet severe infliction." But when he asked whence it arose, he dwelt not upon the sins of the people, but almost entirely upon the educative effects of the experience. He entitled his homily, "Moral Tendencies of Our Present Pecuniary Distress," and though his adumbration of the moral effects by inference noted those tendencies which hitherto had been immoral, what really bore him up was such a reflection as "Our present pecuniary embarrassments tend ultimately to produce great good, by raising the tone of commercial integrity." [52] In other words, Parker was saying that if the besetting sin had been speculation, now, out of affliction, good men will learn caution, and so quickly step into the places of wealth vacated by the gamblers. Since these by definition will be virtuous, they, even when they become rich, will observe the Sabbath.

[52] Joel Parker, *Moral Tendencies of Our Present Pecuniary Distress*, New Orleans, 1837, p. 5.

Parker's effort is, perhaps, too slight to be taken very seriously, but the logic—or rather the rhetoric—to which it is reduced illustrates the problem that confronted a preacher who in the Jacksonian age endeavored to fire again the once-shattering blunderbuss of the jeremiad, even when he was specially favored by an outburst of cholera or even more by a financial panic spread across the whole nation. These calamities were not calamitous enough, severe though they were, to overcome the stubbornly persisting premise in the popular mind, deposited there both by the Declaration of Independence and by the successful jeremiads of the Revolution, that this people lived not in fear and trembling before a covenanted Jehovah, but as a race who go through sorrow, distress, reverses, in an ecstatic assurance of "happiness."

Adequately to unravel this tangle would take much space. To some extent it has variously been unraveled, in that analysts have one way or another perceived that the revival, although luridly wallowing in sin and hysterics, was anything but an indulgence in "Christian pessimism." [53] Aside from the obvious fact that revivalists in general—not merely Methodists but those professing, as did Finney, some form of "Calvinism"—so emphasized the ability of the sinner to acquire conversion as in effect to transform Calvinism (everywhere outside Old School Presbyterianism) into an operational Arminianism, even more fundamentally they made religious exultation an adjunct to the national vigor. Not to pile up citations, let us take one single but highly revelatory example, an article in *The Spirit of the Pilgrims* of 1831, entitled "The Necessity of Revivals of Religion to the Perpetuity of Our Civil and Religious Institutions." If one can resist the temptation to marvel that here is a naïve merging of Christianity with the culture beyond anything even imagined by Albrecht Ritschl, he can then decipher that it speaks out of a moment in the religious transformation of the col-

[53] Most recently and entertainingly by Bernard A. Weisberger, *They Gathered at the River*, Boston, 1958.

onies into a nation which remains, to say the least, crucial for all subsequent history of American Protestantism.

What is fascinating about this disquisition—though only because it is more articulate than most in the literature—is its admission that the real issue for American Christianity is "the corrupting influence of a pre-eminent national prosperity." On that basis, the essay accepts the basic challenge: is it a work beyond the power of God "to effect such a change of human character as will reconcile universal liberty and boundless prosperity, with their permanence and purity"? We suppose in advance that the author concludes on a note of Christian triumph. That forensic peroration does not count. What speaks to us is the primary definition, and then the anxiety, impossible to conceal, which gives the argument its thrust.

This anxiety is no longer dismay or pain because of ordeals to which the people have been subjected, not because of plagues or hurricanes, but a dread about the future. Will we be able to endure this prosperity? How can we, in the face of the "appalling" dangers which threaten the United States? And what are these? How deeply altered have become the very circumstances which Ezra Stiles, a half century before, found to be guarantees of American glory: the dangers arise "from our vast extent of territory, our numerous and increasing population, from diversity of local interests, the power of selfishness, and the fury of sectional jealousy and hate." The student is perplexed when dealing with such revivalists as Beecher and Finney as to just how much they believed their harvests were wrought by supernatural grace or how much they knew that they themselves stirred them up, engineered them by force of personality and lung-power. This exhortation in Beecher's journal—if not actually written by him, then surely it had his approval—suggests a realm of emotion in which the question might be disposed of: the Revival could be conceived as neither a descent from on high nor an artificial stimulation because it could be seen as an effort of religion to keep pace with the rush of American progress. It would thus cease to be a means of placating a vengeful deity and become the way so to change the nature of the citizens as to enable them to cope with their colossal nationality. "Let me then call the attention of my readers to our only remaining source of hope—GOD—and the interposition of his Holy Spirit, in great and general Revivals of Religion, to reform the hearts of this people, and make the nation good and happy." [54]

It is hardly too much to say that as the concept of the national covenant dissolved, depriving the jeremiad of its reason for being, the new form of religious excitation, the revivalistic preaching, fed not on the terrors which the population had passed but on the gory prospect of those to come. Concealed within this curious device is a secret assurance that if religion can be identified with nationality, or vice versa, then we can insure both goodness and happiness. When Americans talked to each other, they made a great show of the fear; when they turned to Europe, in order to explain this peculiar and apparently insane American ecclesiastical order, they revealed the confidence which inwardly sustained them. Robert Baird, for instance, had spent years in France as an agent for the Presbyterian Church, before his 1844 publication of *Religion in America*. Since it was addressed to an English and European public, there was no need for him to shout imprecations upon the disastrous consequences of prosperity, but simply and proudly to explain the beauties of American revivals and the efficient workings of the voluntary principle. By the time he was finished, foreign readers might get at least a glimmer of how the miracle operated: in a free democracy, with church and state entirely separated, amid what seemed a chaos of sects and orgiastic convulsions, the society could be called a "Christian" community. In fact, it was more thoroughly imbued with a Christian spirit than any in Europe.[55]

Certainly this paradox required explaining. We may doubt that even the judicious Baird succeeded in making French-

---

[54] *The Spirit of the Pilgrims*, IV, Boston, 1831, 467–479.
[55] Baird, pp. 105–129.

men and Englishmen understand. Certainly Alexis de Tocqueville pondered and pondered about the mystery, and his
pages on religion in *De la Démocratie en Amérique* are probably the least perceptive he ever wrote. They show that he
never could escape the puzzlement which fell upon him and
his companion, Gustave de Beaumont, shortly after they arrived in 1831 (the year of the piece in *The Spirit of the Pilgrims*), which Beaumont expressed in a letter from New York
after learning that at Sing Sing prison there was on successive
Sundays a rotation of ministers among the various churches:

"Actually, this extreme tolerance on the one hand toward
religions in general—on the other this considerable zeal of
each individual for his own religion, is a phenomenon I can't
yet explain to myself. I would gladly know how a lively and
sincere faith can get on with such a perfect toleration; how
one can have equal respect for religions whose dogmas differ;
and finally what real influence on the moral conduct of the
Americans can be exercised by their religious spirit, whose outward manifestations, at least, are undeniable."

Faced with sociological absurdity, the rational Frenchman
could only decide that in American religion there is more
breadth than depth, and that the competition among churches
must be attributed "to conceit and emulation rather than to
conviction and consciousness of the truth." [56] This would not
be the last time that Gallic logic failed to encompass the
spectacle of American irrationality.

Philip Schaff was German instead of French, and deeply
religious instead of priding himself on his liberalism. Furthermore he lived in America, became an American, studied it
with affection. He never could approve of the revivals, and
since he believed passionately in the unity of Christendom, he
was distressed by sectarianism. Yet when, after ten years in
this country, he revisited Germany and lectured about Amer-

[56] George Wilson Pierson, *Tocqueville and Beaumont in America*, New
York, 1938, p. 106.

ican Protestantism in Berlin, the resulting book, translated under the title *America* and published at New York in 1855, lovingly proclaimed "the United States are by far the most religious and Christian country in the world; and that, just because religion is there most free." His Prussian auditors remained skeptical, but they were shaken when Schaff solemnly informed them that in Berlin, a city of four hundred and fifty thousand, there were only forty churches; in New York, "to a population of six hundred thousand, there are over two hundred and fifty well-attended churches, some of them quite costly and splendid, especially in Broadway and Fifth Avenue." Schaff's book, which has been neglected by historians, is in many respects a more profound, a more accurate work than Tocqueville's overrated one, and the extent to which it achieves profundity is a consequence of his firm conviction that not any one of the present confessions would ever become exclusively dominant in America, "but rather, that out of the mutual conflict of all something wholly new will gradually arise." [57]

But precisely Schaff's use of the future tense was the most difficult thing for the returned German Lutheran to explain to his former colleagues. Whatever may become of venerable Europe, he said, "America is, without question, emphatically a land of the future." He hastened to say that this is not because Americans are more meritorious than Europeans, but because Providence has so arranged matters. This should not make Americans vain, but rather humble, "that they may faithfully and conscientiously fulfill their mission." [58] But also, during these years this prospect was what made them anxious. As the tension between the sections mounted, the appeal to religion—to revivalism and to the power of will expressed in free churches—to preserve unity became more and more agonized. No influence but religion, *The Spirit of the Pilgrims* had said in 1831, "can unite the local, jarring

[57] Philip Schaff, *America*, New York, 1855, pp. xii, 94, 97.
[58] *ibid.*, p. xvii.

interests of this great nation, and constitute us benevolently one." By 1856 a writer in *Bibliotheca Sacra* was pleading:

"Whether we will or not, we have within us a feeling of unity with all associated with us under the same institutions or laws. All are part of one great whole. It is not mere fancy, a mere prejudice; it is ordered so by our Creator; and, when we urge to the cultivation of national feeling, we but carry out His designs." [59]

It is, of course, a matter of historical fact that the slavery question proved so disruptive that not even this fervent religious nationalism could keep the great evangelical bodies from separating into southern and northern opponents. And from those prophetic divisions flowed eventually secession and all its woes. In that sense, the instinct of the revivals had been correct from their beginnings in 1800: that which should terrify religious souls in America was not the past but the future. Men must seek the Lord not because of what they have done or have suffered but so that they may be prepared to endure what is approaching. But the federal theology, the doctrine of the covenant and the call to humiliation as a method of gaining relief from affliction, was a creation of what Schaff called venerable Europe, and was supposedly extracted from the still more venerable Old Testament. Its entire emphasis was retrospective: the covenant had been made with Abraham, John Winthrop had committed the Puritan migration to a covenant back in 1630, the patriots of the Revolution called upon themselves to repent so that God would restore them to a blessing from which their transgressions had led them. The struggle was always to return, to get back to what, theoretically, the people, the communities, had once been. Therefore, among the many transformations wrought in the mentality of America between the Revolution and the Civil War was precisely this turning of the gaze from what had been, and could therefore be defined, to the illimitable

[59] *Bibliotheca Sacra*, XIII, Andover, 1856, 201.

horizon of the inconceivable. No doubt, as Schaff remarked, this achievement was not a result of the Americans' being more energetic or cleverer than other people (though they liked to boast that they were), but of circumstances—their isolation, their natural resources, their economic opportunity. Everything thus conspired to work an intellectual and moral transformation. In this drama the religious revolution plays a vital part, because in the pre-War society religion was all-pervasive. The piety that arose out of the process could not stave off the bloodshed. Perhaps we may even accuse it of prolonging the strife, of intensifying the ferocity. But it imparted a special character to this War which remains a part of its enduring fascination. Above all, by giving to American Protestantism an absolute dedication to the future, by leading it out of the covenant and into the current of nationalism, the religious experience of this period indelibly stamped an immense area of the American mind.

RELIGION AND MODERNITY, 1865–1914

STOW PERSONS

THE LATER DECADES of the nineteenth century have
commonly been regarded by historians as one of the
darker periods of American history. These were the
years of the Robber Barons and the Great Barbecue when the
pursuit of wealth through industrial exploitation and financial
manipulation blighted the cultural landscape. The religious
life of the times, as historians have reconstructed it, did not
escape the general malaise. Professor Schlesinger found the
last quarter of the nineteenth century to have been a "critical
period" in which the churches were faced with the necessity of
making basic readjustments consequent upon social, economic,
and intellectual changes.[1] Professor May sketched a drab
picture of somnolent ecclesiastical complacency aroused only
by successive "earthquakes" of industrial violence and depression.[2] The Roman Catholics, relative newcomers to the American scene, were, according to Father McAvoy, involved in
a "great crisis" over questions of Americanization and the
preservation of their ethnic and religious traditions.[3] These
characterizations all depicted a religious community at bay
before a secular culture with which it was unwilling or unable
to come to grips.

At the same time, there were more positive forces at work
within American religious life. The measure of congregational
autonomy and lay control that had come to characterize Protestantism in this country was such that the religious and secular aspects of life were remarkably sensitive and responsive
to each other. Certain great moral and social ideals were com-

[1] Arthur M. Schlesinger, "A Critical Period in American Religion,
1875–1900," *Proceedings of the Massachusetts Historical Society*, 64, June,
1932, pp. 523–547.
[2] Henry F. May, *Protestant Churches and Industrial America*, N.Y.,
1949, pp. 91–111.
[3] Thomas T. McAvoy, *The Great Crisis in American Catholic History*,
1895–1900, Chicago, 1957. See also Robert D. Cross, *The Emergence of
Liberal Catholicism in America*, Cambridge, Mass., 1957.

mon to both spheres, so that the individual readily played his various roles as citizen, workman, and church member. Under such circumstances it was extremely difficult if not impossible to say which role was dominant and which subordinate. The historian can point to many instances where spokesmen for various denominations undertook to mediate between religion and culture. And if they generally assumed it to be the function of religion to adapt itself to the secular culture, this was because the culture had been humanized and refined by influences emanating from the deep religious traditions of the American people.

Three ideological currents merged at the end of the nineteenth century to form the intellectual matrix of the modern age. The oldest of these was the Christian tradition in its Calvinistic Protestant form modified by denominational influences. The second was the democratic social ideology that had become firmly fixed in the American ethos during the nineteenth century. Most recently, a strong current of naturalistic ideas, a kind of popularized scientific philosophy arising out of positivism and evolution theory, was flowing through the intellectual class. The fusion of these traditions produced modernity as a world view. To the extent that it committed itself to a modern point of view, organized religion in America furnished a convenient scale for measuring the degree to which Americans committed themselves to modernity.

The Denominational Pattern

Comprehensive generalizations about American religious life in modern times are difficult to frame because of the number and variety of religious organizations and attitudes. The denominational pattern that had matured by the middle of the nineteenth century conformed closely to the contours of American social life. Under no other ecclesiastical system could the expressions of the religious spirit have been expected to reflect so immediately the character and outlook of the parishioners. No American region, class, or ethnic group was without a richly varied pattern of religious alternatives from which the individual could choose. The study of American religion should therefore provide a distinctive perspective from which to view the total culture.

The central feature of the religious scene was the denominational complex which had developed within the American civil framework of religious freedom. The denominations were voluntary and private associations of parishes, each of which served its own clientele. The denominations accepted one another's existence and, by the middle of the nineteenth century, had learned how to get along together peaceably. Adherents of denominational bodies (as opposed to churchmen or sectarians) made a characteristic distinction between church and state, or at least they defined the relationship in a peculiar way. This was one of the most important contributions of denominationalism to American culture. In the mind of the denominationalist the institutional separation of church and state was analogous to the distinction between religious and secular life. The religious and the secular represented a kind of partnership in which each individual participated. He was a citizen of both the spiritual and political worlds, with a dual citizenship comparable to that in state and nation. Each of these jurisdictions he acknowledged to be supreme in its own sphere, each equally worthy of loyalty and devotion, each subject to the constitutional provisions that fixed its bounds. The denominational adjustment resulting from such attitudes was neither theocratic nor Erastian; it was a new and distinctive form of dualism, the implications of which were to govern the Protestant approach to the most important doctrinal and ecclesiastical questions of the late nineteenth century.

It would be hard to deny the stability of the denominational system in post-Appomattox America. Each denomination had to meet the spiritual needs of its communicants if it were to survive. In practice, the total burden was divided among the several competing denominations according to criteria both

371

religious and social. In the larger communities, wherever several denominational parishes were to be found, a rough correlation could be made between social class and denominational affiliation. The underprivileged social and economic strata, with low educational levels and unsophisticated outlook, found in revivalistic parishes congenial affiliations that catered to their emotional and convivial needs. Several of the larger denominations, notably the Methodists and the Presbyterians, suffered schismatic divisions over the issue of revivalism. The middle classes generally preferred a more sedate and formal worship in which traditional dogmas were wedded to the individualistic ethic of the Gospel of Wealth.[4] Urban professionals and intellectuals who were sensitive to currents of opinion in the secular world were frequently drawn into that new phenomenon, the big city parish, centered on the resonant personality of a pulpit orator who blended the elements of an innocuous theology with discussion of current interests to produce a romantic individualism. By virtue of its capacity to fill each of these roles, denominational Protestantism fixed itself firmly in the American scene.

In the course of time, religious spokesmen were to view with mixed feelings the intimate adaptation of religion to culture accomplished by denominationalism. As apologists they could cite with satisfaction a proportionate increase in church membership for the period 1860–1910, from 23% of the total population in 1860 to 43% in 1910.[5] This was but one phase of a world-wide expansion of Christianity which reached its culmination at the beginning of the twentieth century. By the middle of that century, however, many students had come to question whether the statistics of growth had furnished a valid index of spiritual vitality.[6] Denominational influences

---

[4] Ralph H. Gabriel, *The Course of American Democratic Thought*, rev. ed., N.Y., 1956, pp. 151–169.

[5] Winfred E. Garrison, *The March of Faith; the Story of Religion in America Since 1865*, N.Y. and London, 1933, p. 264.

[6] Winthrop S. Hudson, *The Great Tradition of the American Churches*, N.Y., 1953. James H. Nichols, *Democracy and the Churches*, Phila., 1951.

had participated all too effectively in transforming Christianity into what Charles Norris Cochrane called a religion of culture, at the expense of the transcendent detachment that might have been expected of a religion less intimately implicated in the concerns of its communicants.

It is the principal object of the present chapter to indicate how the leaders of a representative denomination, the Congregationalists, contributed to the crystallization of the bundle of ideas we call modernity. It cannot be said that the denominations committed themselves unreservedly to the modern outlook. Whatever the attitudes of laymen may have been, many clerical spokesmen revealed a profoundly ambiguous feeling toward the modern ethos. Even when they participated actively in the formulation of the modern point of view, they implicitly acknowledged themselves to be in a peripheral position with respect to it. They seemed to imply that the modern world was not of their own making, and that they were free to reconcile themselves to it in its various aspects or not, as they wished. Economic life occupied its own autonomous sphere. Science was an enterprise with which religion had all too frequently clashed. The principal educational institutions, from school to university, had largely emancipated themselves from religious influences and control. The press was very largely secularized. From all of these enterprises denominational spokesmen felt themselves in some degree alienated. Wherever the sense of alienation was sufficiently keen, the individual was ripe to transfer his allegiance from denomination to sect. Contrasting attitudes toward modernity became, in fact, one of the chief means of distinguishing denominational from sectarian religion.

It was another distinctive feature of denominationalism that to a notable degree its more reflective representatives were able to detach themselves so far as to be able to view externally the relationship between religion and society. They frequently remarked that the age presented a unique challenge to the religious thinker. This challenge derived from the best knowledge of the time, from the prevailing sense of values, and from the interests and activities that occupied men. They presumed it to be their duty as religious thinkers to reinterpret religious truth in terms of the characteristics of the age. Not to do so would be failure to serve modern men, failure to show the universal relevance of religion, the courting of futility.

The modern age was democratic and individualistic. Its ideal was universal self-realization. To this end it sought to draw the entire community into ideological union, and to minimize social class differentials. Because it promised to advance these objectives education was hailed with enthusiasm. Education was not expected, however, to produce an intellectual or social elite, but rather the reverse. Education would level the community and bind it together, rather than divide or accentuate its differences. The notion of an intellectual elite was as repulsive to the modern mind as the notion of a political or racial elite. In any of its forms the concept of an elite challenged the modern ideal of one big happy community.

Modern ideas presupposed a cultural organicism in which it was at least questionable whether religion played anything more than a peripheral role. It was as though religion existed by sufferance, and might expect to make its contribution only by keying its message to secular ideas and interests. It did not occur to denominationalists that a relevant religious judgment might take the form of a condemnation of the age. The modern mind was supremely poised and confident. A relevant religion would have to conform to the convictions and values of the age because they were the product of experience and confirmed by the judgment of history.

The Challenge of Naturalism

The current of naturalistic thought that flowed strongly through American society in the wake of the convulsive struggle over the Union represented the sharpest and most dramatic departure from established traditions in the history of American intellectual life. Theretofore the cultivated mind had worked within well-established conventions of thought in which fundamental religious affirmations had become axioms to be taken for granted. Commonly received notions of the nature of the universe and the meaning of life were in harmony with the ancient teachings of religious orthodoxy. The scientific revolution of the seventeenth and eighteenth centuries had done surprisingly little to detach intellectual life in America from its traditional religious affiliations. Now, however, the full force of that revolution, previously damned up behind the flashboards of a stubborn traditionalism, burst in upon the American mind and within the space of a few years accomplished a radical alteration of thought.[7]

The effect of the naturalistic movement upon religion was to liquidate the capital with which theologians had long worked, and to drive them back to a fresh view of the fundamental questions to which they had previously been accustomed to furnish merely conventional answers. Was it still possible to deal with creation in religious terms? What was the status of man, of human nature, and of freedom? In a universe undergoing a continuous process of development how was one to deal with the problem of the revelation of religious truth? How was the history of such a world to be reconciled with the Christian promise of trial, judgment, and redemption? These questions cut to the very foundations of belief, and their answers doubtless required a radical recasting of philosophic as well as religious assumptions. The answers offered must not be in conflict with the established principles and findings of natural science. And they must bear sufficient resemblance to traditional religious affirmations so that the laity might continue to enjoy the consolations and assurances it required of its faith. None of these questions

[7] Stow Persons, *American Minds: A History of Ideas*, N.Y., 1958, pp. 217–235.

were new, but they were now put with an urgency arising from the success with which naturalism had attached itself to the scientific point of view with its rapidly growing prestige.

Naturalistic thought as it affected religion appeared in either of two forms. The first was the ideal or extreme form that emphasized materialism, determinism, and atheism or anti-theistic humanism. Naturalism in this form had relatively little influence in America.[8] Marxist materialists remained an isolated sect whose materialism was rejected or ignored even where their economic interpretation of history and politics was accepted. When Christian apologists in America attacked this form of naturalism they cited as examples such English and Continental positivists and rationalists as Huxley, Tyndall, Comte, and Spencer. Materialism was an ideal pole standing for a tendency of the age rather than a doctrine widely espoused in this country.

As early as 1871, President James McCosh of Princeton, a prominent Presbyterian theologian, took up the challenge of naturalism in lectures delivered at Union Theological Seminary on "Christianity and Positivism." [9] His object was to disengage scientific method and accomplishments from the embrace of the naturalistic philosophy, and to demonstrate further that there was nothing incompatible between scientific knowledge properly understood and the truths of revelation. In so doing he staked out in general terms the position to be commonly taken by Christian apologists throughout the period.

McCosh rejected categorically the basic naturalistic hypothesis that living protoplasm had emerged from inorganic materials by the process of spontaneous generation. By distinguishing between the "major assumptions" of the Biblical account of the creation and its verbal form, McCosh was able to maintain that there was no inconsistency between creation as described in Genesis and a scientifically acceptable account

[8] Sidney Warren, *American Freethought, 1860–1914*, N.Y., 1943.
[9] James McCosh, *Christianity and Positivism*, N.Y., 1871.

of the formation and development of the terrestrial globe. His principal concession was to accept the fact of "development." He sought to show that a scientifically acceptable theory of development was consistent with a figurative interpretation of Genesis as descriptive of successive phases of creation. It should be observed in fairness to all of those who sought comfort in a teleological version of "development" that in the generation following Darwin the scientists themselves were all too prone to equate evolution with development.

Unlike many of his contemporaries, McCosh was also acute enough to be able to distinguish between the causal theories of evolution, including natural selection, and the fact of evolution itself. He was aware of the formidable scientific objections to natural selection in its Darwinan form raised by Agassiz, Mivart, and others. Although he declared himself willing to accept it as a participating factor, he was not convinced that natural selection alone could have accomplished the entire process. In fact, it was one of McCosh's principal purposes as a Christian apologist to accommodate evolution to the traditional doctrine of design in nature, and he saw that the theory of natural selection with its dependence upon pure chance was the major obstacle to such an accommodation. He was persuaded that there was ample evidence of design in the organic unity and growth of the world, in the "collocation of things," in the fitting of parts to each other, all pointing toward an end "in which order and benevolence are manifested."

The Princeton theologian was emboldened to cling to a religious doctrine of creationism in the face of an authoritative developmental biology because he was one of the few men of his generation to realize that the evolutionists, notwithstanding the title of Darwin's epochal book, were much less concerned with ultimate origins than with transformations in process. An intense preoccupation with human and animal origins had been characteristic of the students of natural history during the previous two generations, an interest which indeed shaped the intellectual and psychological context in which evolutionary doctrines were received. But the evolutionists themselves were now commencing upon the task of shifting the focus of thought from beginnings and endings to the mid-passage. In so doing they were shaping an essential feature of the modern mentality. Although the materials that Darwin used so convincingly to document his evolutionary thesis included geological and paleontological data, the heart of his case lay in the contemporary evidences of transformation known to every observant horticulturist and stock-raiser. McCosh was free to believe what he liked about creation in the original sense because the evolutionists had no means of dealing with the subject, and in fact were rapidly losing interest in it.

Paradoxical though it may seem at first glance, the most significant consequence of evolutionism for intellectual history was not the recasting of traditional and conventional conceptions of the ultimate origins of life or the universe. The theory of evolution shifted attention away from origins, and fastened the modern consciousness firmly in its own present, shaping a world view as seen from the perspective of that present. We may as well follow established usage and call this new point of view modernity. Our immediate purpose is to inquire how quickly and effectively the spokesmen for the religious community adapted traditional beliefs to the modern outlook. It was a major achievement for a man like McCosh to perceive that there was nothing in a strict formulation of the doctrine of evolution that required the theologian to abandon his creationism. The real question was whether he could salvage its pertinence for a generation interested in other matters.

In a second form, an essentially humanistic theism, naturalism was far more influential. As such, it received expression not only among a few avowed theists but also in a sizable and influential segment of Protestantism. In forms variously designated as liberal, modernist, or progressive, this influence set up powerful currents among Congregationalists, Methodists, Episcopalians, Baptists, and Disciples. Unitarianism became almost wholly committed to it. Those who were influenced by humanistic theism were impelled to adapt their heritage of beliefs to "the spirit of the age," to begin with modern man, and to reconstruct a religion suited to his needs and opportunities.

Perhaps the earliest succinct expression of this point of view appeared within a year of McCosh's caveat against positivism. It was contained in a little volume entitled *The Religion of Humanity*, written by an erstwhile Unitarian, Octavius Brooks Frothingham,[10] who had recently reorganized his New York Unitarian parish as an independent Liberal Church. Frothingham's approach to religion rested on the naturalistic assumption of the social evolutionary emergence of mankind from darkest savagery into the light of civilization. While the stages of this process could doubtless be marked by various criteria, most pertinent and notable was the emergence of reason. Ultimately, perhaps, the force of rationality would furnish a sufficient motive for human action, but in the meanwhile moral inspiration or a passion for virtue remained necessary to counteract the baser passions that all men still experienced. The passion for virtue must spring from relevant religious convictions. Faith in Christ had been its traditional source; indeed, a mysterious religion of the supernatural had been appropriate and necessary in the coarse and violent times when men were still "moral pachyderms." But Protestantism had introduced the principle of reason, with the inevitable consequence that men discovered the difference between the Jesus of history and the Christ of myth. Christianity was now dying because the image of Christ the God-man no longer ruled the heart or conscience of Christendom.

[10] O. B. Frothingham, *The Religion of Humanity. An Essay*, N.Y., 1872. 3rd ed., 1875. See also Stow Persons, *Free Religion: An American Faith*, New Haven, 1947.

Romantic idealism and naturalistic evolutionism were neatly blended in Frothingham's Religion of Humanity. Declaring that "the interior spirit of any age is the Spirit of God," he thus identified God with the life of the mind in history. He found the law of evolution to be of great moral significance because it revealed society to be a self-developing organism containing within itself the source of all moral power. In the equation of evolution with progress, the natural and the moral were conveniently blended. Faith in natural powers thus became the modern faith, and what he considered a wholesome attitude replaced a morbid preoccupation with sin and despair. "Now, if one has a sin, he does his best to forget it, to outgrow it, to cover it up with new and better life. . . . The tacit assumption is that men forgive themselves, and are by men and God forgiven, when they rally to do better."

Doubtless the naturalist's most striking affirmation of faith lay in his conviction that truth was discoverable in the external order of nature and experience. He was a liberal and a democrat because the only authority he acknowledged was the universal obligation to search for truth. Science revealed the truths of the physical universe and history properly understood provided the key to the understanding of human nature and experience. The fundamental importance to the modern mind of a distinctive interpretation of history was to become increasingly apparent during the later years of the nineteenth century.

Frothingham's universal religion was cast in the conciliatory and traditionalist terms appropriate to a professed faith in collective experience. All the great religions of the world had reaffirmed in varying language certain common ideas: God, Revelation, Incarnation, Atonement, Providence, Immortality. Because science and philosophy were incapable of dealing with these ideas, they must remain the permanent subject matter of religion. Restated in terms relevant to current needs, they were the substance of the Religion of Humanity. The choice of this term was unfortunate, for it obliged Frothingham to dissociate his views from Comte's positivism. The materialistic atheism of the Enlightenment had in fact disappeared as men had come to realize that they could not dissociate the materialistic notions of law and cause from intelligence, will, and goodness. And so, while God remained unsearchable and unknowable, the universe was His embodied thought.

The ambiguities of the modern attitude toward history were clearly marked in Frothingham's theology. The evolutionary theory of development taught that men were products of the past. To deny the past, if it were possible, would be to deny human nature. The function of the preacher, Frothingham insisted, was to reconcile men to their humanity, which included the surviving animal element. Thus the perennial human struggle, in which the prudent man would summon divine aid, was the struggle between history and possibilities. But at the same time, there was a profound sense of a deep gulf separating the modern age from the past. The historians of a later day were to attribute this to the industrial revolution. To contemporary thinkers like Frothingham, however, the most persuasive indications of the unique character of the modern age were not industrial or material but moral, spiritual, and intellectual. Christianity was dying because its message had been couched in terms appropriate to the mentality of a less cultivated age. A religion of humanity must be centered upon the noblest elements of humanity; not upon a God-man but upon human possibilities. Its orientation must be toward the future realization of the divine potentialities in humanity. These potentialities were prefigured in the moral ideals that even now bound society together, namely, justice, kindliness, truth, equity, and love. The hope of immortality that all men professed should be fully satisfied in the realization of the immortality of influence. Just as men were formed by the past, they themselves would shape the future by the force of heredity, the power of ideals, and the influence of example.

The Religious Response

The historian of Congregationalist theology, Frank Hugh Foster, later expressed the belief that Christianity had to meet the challenge of naturalism if it were to survive.[11] Naturalism asserted the universal reign of law. These natural laws represented the limits of the powers of the deity, who could act only within nature and history. How could such a conception of deity be reconciled with traditional Christian convictions? For the portion of the Christian community that was sensitive to currents of contemporary opinion, questions like this could not be ignored. It is with that portion only that we are for the moment concerned.

The character of the religious response to the naturalistic challenge was determined by four convictions to which religious thinkers tenaciously clung. The first was a staunchly reaffirmed loyalty to the Christian revelation contained in Scripture. Surprisingly few Protestants were willing to follow the lead of Frothingham into a non-Christian theism. The very forces that were working to transform the Bible into a document recording the historical experiences out of which Christianity had grown were also sharpening those experiences as the vivid personal record of suffering and spiritual triumph to which Christians could still repair for inspiration and consolation.

A second commitment was the acceptance of science and an insistence that science and faith were not irreconcilably opposed. Science must not be permitted to become the exclusive possession of an irreligious or anti-religious naturalism. From this conviction emerged a characteristic distinction between nature and history. The validity of divine revelation was no longer to rest upon the authority of miracles that contravened the natural order but upon an understanding of history. This point of view was set forth by the Congregationalist theo-

11 Frank H. Foster, *The Modern Movement in American Theology*, N.Y., 1939, pp. 93–94.

logian, Newman Smyth, as early as 1879.[12] Smyth believed that the religion of Israel that had given birth to Christianity could not be understood naturalistically as the product of the circumstances of Jewish life. On the contrary, not only did it cut against the grain of the people who nurtured it, but it also emerged in stark contrast to the competing religions of Israel's near neighbors who lived in similar circumstances. The emergence of Judaeo-Christian religion in defiance of the probabilities represented the controlling influence of the divine in history.

Smyth acknowledged the mediatorial role of evolution theory in shifting the proofs of revelation from unique events to unique sequences of events. Science was a method of understanding and dealing with nature, valid so far as it went. On its authority men no longer acknowledged miraculous events that contravened the order of nature. But the principle of evolutionary development furnished a clue to the discovery of the supernatural at work within natural processes. The evidences of revelation were to be found in the events of history as seen not in isolation but in a complex pattern with unique meaning. So long as men discovered unique qualities in human experience, science could never displace the hand of the divine in history. The record of revelation thus became the record of the milestones in the development of spiritual values. In transferring the source of religious authority from nature to history Smyth was giving voice to a distinctively modern point of view.

A third conviction of the religious community was its commitment to the democratic ideology with its humane and ethical assumptions. The intellectual prestige of naturalism in the decades after the Civil War was great enough to command the assent of many intellectuals, whose professional and personal activities ceased to have any religious connection or content. Naturalism frequently led also to an authoritarian and undemocratic social philosophy. Under these circum-

---

[12] Newman Smyth, *Old Faiths in New Light*, N.Y., 1879. Rev. ed. 1891.

stances, the role of religious thinkers in preserving traditional values and in attempting to adapt them to changing circumstances has not received the attention it merited. The reaffirmation of the validity and universality of the Christian revelation was accompanied by an accommodation of doctrine to the humane and moral values of democracy. It would be difficult to account otherwise for the widespread tendency to reinterpret theological dogmas in moral terms. By the end of the century, the wing of Protestantism that was moving toward modernism had fairly thoroughly moralized its theology.

Finally, the view of history as constituting a social evolutionary development was taken over from naturalism and recast in terms consistent with a moralized and humanized theology. Human history recorded the steady ascent of man from conditions of primitive simplicity and irrationality to modern civilization with its progressive organization of life activities in the service of free, equal, and intelligent individuals. The indices of civilized progress included longer life expectancy and hence an increase in the population; accumulated goods and services, and a rising standard of living for all; scientific and technological advance; expanding literacy and educational opportunities; moral and spiritual refinement; effective social control; and democratic, equalitarian, and humanitarian social organization and relationships.

The conflicting demands of individuality and social solidarity that lay close to the heart of modernity could remain unresolved so long as they were subsumed under a devotion to the scientific outlook. Science appeared to offer a platform of agreement on which all men of good will could freely gather. Stubborn resistance to participation in methods or conclusions scientifically sanctioned was to be written off as a surviving relic of habits of thinking prevalent in less enlightened times. Education thus became the prime panacea which would furnish the key to the unsolved problems of the modern world. Many modern educators as well as laymen came to regard education as virtually synonymous with thinking scientifically. John Dewey, whose early connections with the liberal Congregationalists were close, was the principal exponent of this point of view. Congregationalists in turn had been familiar with the theory of Christian nurture since the days of Bushnell, and were well prepared for the substitution of religious education for evangelism.

Revelation and Experience

The impression that religion had ceased to occupy a central place in late nineteenth-century American life was apparent whenever denominational spokesmen called for "reconstruction" in religion. Thus Newman Smyth, a proponent of the "new theology" in Congregationalism, called for a "real and vital" theology which would be in intimate contact with "real life." In locating its authority in the Biblical past religion had been in danger of losing contact with the living God in the contemporary world.[13]

The reconstruction of religion involved several characteristically modern emphases. One of these was a strong conviction of the sacredness of the individual person and of his ethical life.[14] Experience in various forms became the touchstone of religious truth, as distinct from the authority of church, creed, or Scripture. But experience must be of the verifiable, rational type, susceptible of demonstration and analysis. It was in this vein that Theodore Munger of New Haven insisted that revelation rested upon reason. Christians, he held in 1883, accepted the substance of revelation not because of some external authority attached to it, but because in itself it was reasonable.[15] This was essentially the position taken by Channing more than half a century earlier. When Munger proposed to test faith by its reasonableness he seems

[13] *ibid.*, pp. xxiv–xxv.
[14] Henry C. King, *Reconstruction in Theology*, N.Y., 1901, cited in Foster, p. 173.
[15] Foster, p. 63.

to have meant the relevance of faith to experience. George A. Gordon of Boston, a disciple of Munger, admitted candidly that the working of miracles was extraneous to the real purpose of Jesus' teaching, which was moral and spiritual and which carried its own authority.[16]

The scientific attitude toward nature, together with the critical analysis of Scripture and religious history, thus had the effect of undermining some of the traditional authorities and driving the believer back to his one remaining resource, personal experience. It was not surprising, therefore, that the late nineteenth century should witness a new emphasis on the subjective approach to religion. Schleiermacher and Ritschl furnished theological models, and William James a manual of practical piety in his popular *Varieties of Religious Experience* (1902). But the former were Europeans, and James drew most of his examples from the literature of European monasticism. Had he used local materials his book might have been less popular. The fact was that the memory of struggles over revivalism was still too fresh in the minds of Protestant denominationalists to permit them to welcome the subjective approach. For them, "experience" must be restricted to the commonly verifiable events as disciplined by commitment to the scientific method.

The first result of the evolutionary view of history was to reduce the possibilities of human existence to the commonly verified experiences. The extraordinary events and miraculous episodes of the Bible must be ascribed to the primitive mentality of those who recorded them. An ever-increasing emphasis on the ethical substance of religion was inevitable as miracle and plenary inspiration lost their traditional authority. In Christology, the divinity of Christ was now presented in terms of perfection of moral and spiritual character, qualities in which He differed from ordinary mortals only in degree.

Although one might grant that this point of view did jus-

[16] *ibid.*, pp. 131–132.

tice to the facts of religious history, there still remained the question whether it rested on a valid concept of evolution. If the evolutionary analogy meant anything for human history it must surely provide a place for the true novelty or variation upon which social selection could operate. If religious experience were to be compressed within the common or universally verified experiences, how could the Kingdom be expected to come? A more considered view of the relation between revelation and experience in evolutionary terms was taken by George A. Gordon in 1901.[17] Instead of showing the compatibility of the event with its environing social conditions, after the manner of the prevailing historical positivism, Gordon followed Smyth, and insisted upon the unique character of the decisive religious event. The religion of Israel had flown in the face of history, surviving and maturing into Christianity in spite of all the probabilities to the contrary. Revelation could now be understood not as an event transcending the established limits of experience but as casting experience in a new form. It was the novel variation that defied expectation and mocked the efforts of social scientists to reduce experience to the routine sequences of behavior that admitted of categorization. Nevertheless, democracy and science were conspiring together to confirm the authority of experience as the touchstone of religious truth.

Immanence and History

No remark was more frequently heard in recent times than that the modern era was an age of change. At first glance it seemed paradoxical that this was an age fully conscious of its distinctive characteristics as an epoch in history, and at the same time emphatic in its insistence that no other period had experienced such revolutionary changes. The application of a rationalized technology to industrial production worked con-

---

[17] George A. Gordon, *The New Epoch for Faith*, Boston and N.Y., 1902.

sequences readily apparent to every reflective observer. It should not have been surprising in such an age that religious spokesmen, concerned as they were with the things that abide, should have been cast in a conservative role.

Those who commented upon change, including the social scientists who studied it most closely, did not for the most part appear to be particularly disturbed by it. There were several factors that might have accounted for this complacence. The consciousness of changes directly observed emerged from a background of ideas in which a philosophy of historical development had a prominent place. Whether overt changes produced the philosophy or vice versa is beside the point. The pervasive nineteenth-century belief in progress equated change with improvement. Progress had at first been a social and moral idea. But its overtones were readily transferred to the natural world with the coming of evolution theory. Nature's method was now understood to be that of "development," a term with which evolution was commonly equated, and which implied progressive improvement. These various conceptions of change coincided with, if they did not produce, the idea of social control. A static society could hardly have conceived of the notion of control, nor have attributed to it any practical significance. In a dynamic society the theory of social control was congenial to all of those impatient with the untidy course of events.

A strong sense of the unity of history as a single developmental process also played an important part in assisting the modern mind to minimize the hazards of change. This sense of unity was expressed in the assumption that the entire course of human history displayed the gradual elaboration of civilized institutions and values as men became ever more cultivated and humane. The naturalistic anthropologists had plotted the sequential development of mankind from primitive savagery through barbarism to civilization. The evils from which men still suffered were survivals of the benighted past. Civilization was still only skin deep, as James Harvey Robinson reminded his contemporaries; it should not surprise anyone if men occasionally reverted to the savagery of their forebears. Progress, however, was the basic secular trend, and the sharp edge of change was dulled by the cry of "evolution, not revolution."

Currently fashionable theories of dynamic psychology also strengthened the sense of the unity of history as a social evolutionary process. Just as the psychic identity of the individual survived in the successive phases of personal development, so a unifying thread of identity ran through the historical process. The past was acknowledged to be immensely influential in shaping the character of the present, even as the child survived in the man. Nevertheless, the modern mind was condescending toward the past because it had been outgrown. While in one sense the relationship was that of descent —in Darwin's phrase, descent with modification—in another sense it was better expressed in the idea of transcendence. The modern age looked upon the past with the same complacence with which the mature adult recalled his own childhood.

The appropriate culmination of the social process occurred with the emergence of democracy in recent times. "Democracy is the only subject for history," confidently declared Henry Adams, in 1884. To secular naturalists like Adams the prospect of democracy was exciting because it held forth the promise both of a new social physics and of a scientific historiography appropriate to a type of society in which all classes had been galvanized into activity, radiating social energy. But to the religious liberals the coming of democracy had quite a different significance. This was the moral and spiritual challenge presented by a society of free and responsible individuals. Traditional Christianity had never confronted such a situation. The marriage of Christianity and democracy inevitably shifted the constellation of religious virtues from the passive to the active type. Protestant denominationalists for the most part made the transition easily and largely unconsciously. For Catholics, on the other hand, democracy posed a real challenge. Isaac Hecker on the theoretical side and John Ireland on the practical attempted vigorously to make an adjustment; but they were resisted by powerful elements in the hierarchy, both in the United States and at Rome.

The central role of democracy in reorienting the outlook of Protestant denominationalists was seen in the fact that they now took it for granted that the Christian revelation was located entirely within history, and that its implications were to be fully worked out in the ongoing historical process. Any other view, such as one in which Christianity was regarded as a transcendent judgment upon history, would fail to satisfy the expectation that man's potentialities could be fully realized in the social order. Dedication to the democratic ideal consequently thrust upon the liberals a major theological commitment. This was the doctrine of divine immanence, the belief that the Spirit of God was identical with the creation itself, working within the social process to achieve its purpose in history.

Belief in the immanent deity was the distinctive theological doctrine of the precursors of modernism. Humanistic theists like Frothingham professed their faith in an immanent deity acting through such natural agencies as selection. The emphasis here fell upon the random and impersonal character of divine agency; the wind blew where it listeth. However, if one pressed on beyond the generalized action of divine selection to the specific instance where the novel variation occurred and undertook to show how that variation was the source of subsequent spiritual development, then one had isolated the action of the divine in history, and this could properly be declared to be a miraculous event in a specifically Christian sense. The life and work of Jesus Christ was such a variation.[18] Radiating out from that source, the divine spirit would eventually become incarnate in the whole human race.

[18] Newman Smyth, *Old Faiths in New Light*, pp. 33–61.

As Lyman Abbott put it, "what Jesus was, humanity is becoming." [19]

The meanings attached to the notion of immanence also reflected the modern spirit. Newman Smyth defined it as a process of divine education, in which all men, living and dead, were being prepared for the final blessing. Such a view, he felt, was more appropriate to the character of the age than that of Edwards, who regarded history as a work of redemption. It was also more pertinent than the theory of the evangelicals, who thought of the world as a place of probation. While these were indubitably aspects of the work of the Spirit, to emphasize them at the expense of the educative influence seemed "inhumane."

The dependence of the modern outlook upon an interpretation of history was vividly illustrated in the thought of George A. Gordon.[20] The impact of naturalism upon religion had altered the traditional relationship between Scriptural authority and the substance of religious truth. Historical and textual criticism on scientific principles forced Gordon to distinguish between "letter" and "spirit," and to concede that the spirit of truth was only imperfectly embodied in the letter of Scripture. How then was one to disentangle the truth from its imperfect vehicle of conveyance? Gordon sought guidance in an interpretation of history. It was a special version of the idea of progress.

The central theme of history was the emergence in the nineteenth century of the idea of a unified humanity. This had been an original religious insight, subsequently inhibited by rational, moral, and social forces. But in recent times, the combined impulses of the French Revolution, socialism, science, missionary activity, and American democracy had inevitably thrust the idea of humanity into the forefront of men's consciences. In vain did naturalism and pessimism seek

[19] Lyman Abbott, *Theology of an Evolutionist*, Boston and N.Y., 1897, p. 73.
[20] Gordon, pp. 291–381.

to depict humanity as a purely social phenomenon. The idea that man was by nature a religious being was rapidly spreading.

History as Gordon understood it was the study of reality through its temporal development; it was the record of the process by which truth developed its full character. In its most important aspect history was thus the history of thought. The present represented the most advanced truth, which was to be best understood, used, or improved upon by discovering through historical study how it had come to be. The best minds were those like Aristotle's that assimilated the thought of the past in order to evaluate it critically and augment it with new knowledge. The apprehension of the real world by thought, its potential mastery through intelligence, was progress. Human creativity in all its forms was "an evolution in response to the power of reality over man." The revelation of this reality to man would be complete when history was complete. "Faith thus becomes the attitude of the individual mind toward this historic process. . . . It is of the nature of insight, prophecy, and adventure; it sees, it anticipates, it is ready to take risks. And the help which comes to faith is through the new conception of history as the form that reality has taken. . . . Faith comes to mean sympathy with the race at its best; and the polemic of faith is then but the struggle of the individual to keep the race true to its highest insight and its grand, historic vocation."

In the study of history Gordon found three types of evidence of the existence of a moral order. One of these was the data of feelings or "instincts." Man's principal attachments to reality were effected through feelings, and Gordon was persuaded that whenever a train of thought had eventuated in stultifying skepticism, a way out was always at hand in a return to the "emotive, instinctive sources of knowledge." Another proof of the moral order lay in the universal data of humor. The bases of humor in false pretense, incongruity, and irony all testified to the pervasive character of the moral sense. Finally, conscience itself could only be an evolution out of the moral order of the universe. Gordon believed the idea of a historical theodicy to be the great achievement of the modern mind. This was the conviction that divine purposes would be fulfilled in and through the historical process. In its various guises as progress, evolution, or development, theodicy was the pervasive modern idea.

Enough has been said to indicate how far Gordon went toward transforming Christianity into a philosophy of history. In this philosophy faith in progress was the central element, determining the point of view from which the liberals faced the problem of religious belief. They could no longer accept the orthodox assumption that the full truth had been revealed in the Biblical past. For them, the past must be assimilated into the present in order to be useful. Its perennial elements must be constantly reinterpreted in the light of present needs, interests, and knowledge. New information and insights were constantly recasting the past in new colors and perspectives. Liberals spoke of a "progressive revelation," the ever-deepening understanding of past events which in themselves possessed a perhaps inexhaustible spiritual potential.

Newman Smyth had earlier declared the historical process to be a "providential development" which would culminate in the coming of the Kingdom of God. Although he followed Lessing in regarding the process as a work of divine education, he emphasized its essentially moral nature. He could be the more certain that the growth of conscience and of moral sentiment were the work of God because of the unquestioned assumption that they had undergone a steady process of refinement. One can see in retrospect that the attempt to justify religion by the criteria of evolutionary transformation depended on the identification of evolution with moral and spiritual progress. Without it the whole structure would have collapsed; without it, indeed, the design would never have been projected.

Church Unity

The religious liberals who undertook to reorient religious life in modern terms represented but a small segment of the Christian community. The democratic ideology which was an integral part of the modern outlook committed them irrevocably to equalitarian and universal social ideals which bore only incidental resemblance to the individualistic ethos of the middle classes which in fact they almost exclusively represented. Modernity was assumed to define the outlook and purposes of all men. It was the wave of the present, promising freedom and self-realization for all in a richer and better future. The element that came closest to betraying the social affiliations of the modernists was their strong emphasis upon education, which had traditionally been the primary concern of the middle and professional classes. Now, however, the principal burden of dissolving social class distinctions, equalizing opportunities, and equipping men to realize their potentials was placed upon education. This was the decisive animus in the transformation of education from a liberal to a social agency.

The same ambiguities surrounding the social affiliations and outlook of the liberals were present in their ecclesiastical thinking. For the most part they were content with the denominational pattern that was so intimately involved in the development of their point of view. Even the denominations like Congregationalism that had once enjoyed a privileged status as established churches had long since reconciled themselves to the denominational situation. But something of the earlier sense of community responsibility may well have survived in many of the leaders of these denominations to make them dissatisfied with the shrunken outlook that was characteristic of denominationalism. The very multiplicity of religious organizations suggested to reflective participants a distinction between the partial and perhaps imperfect embodiment of the religious spirit in a particular denomination and the total body of Christ's followers who constituted "the Church." The modern ideal envisaged not only a classless society but also a unified church.

Newman Smyth addressed himself specifically to this issue in 1908.[21] The accomplishment of Christian unity certainly required a catholic spirit, and where could one better begin than with Catholicism? A liberal movement appropriately calling itself modernist had emerged among the Catholics of England, France, and Italy at the end of the nineteenth century. Although, by the time that Smyth wrote, the movement had been condemned by the Papacy, Catholic modernists continued to protest their loyalty and to insist that they were misunderstood by the Vatican. Smyth ventured to hope that modernism would yet establish itself permanently within the Catholic Church and become the foundation of a reunified Christianity.

The new Catholicism that Smyth envisaged had its sources in critical and historical studies and in the evolutionary style of thinking. Its central beliefs were the immanence of God in man and the permanent presence of Christ in the church. The problem of ecclesiastical authority was to be solved by the democratization of the church. In order to enter the new church universal each branch of Christianity must confess and renounce its peculiar sin. Protestants must renounce their absolute independence. Roman Catholics must acknowledge the absolute Papacy to be destructive of the original democracy of the church.

Smyth was prepared to abandon Protestantism with little regret. Its great work was accomplished, and it now appeared to be disintegrating rather than forming new denominations. It had successfully established the spiritual liberty of the individual, a human right that could never be destroyed. On the other hand, it had failed to control the forces of modern life. Religion was no longer the master passion of the Prot-

---

[21] Newman Smyth, *Passing Protestantism and Coming Catholicism*, N.Y., 1908, 1916.

estant community, large elements of which displayed a vague religiosity without sustaining the obligations of specific denominational affiliation. Religious education was rapidly disintegrating. The indifference of intellectuals with Protestant backgrounds was becoming notorious. The time had come for Protestants to abandon their exclusive sectarianisms and immerse themselves in a movement appropriate to the needs and spirit of the age.

Catholics must similarly confess the shocking failure of their church to come to terms with modern culture. To men like Smyth, dedicated to freedom, democracy, progress, and science, the stubborn refusal of the Catholic Church to share their complacent assessment of modernity defied all of their expectations. The militant anticlericalism of Western Europe was the inevitable consequence of such folly. Smyth believed that the principle of papal authoritarianism served as a cloak for the domination of the church by reactionary interests. The modernists within the Catholic Church had professed obedience to ecclesiastical authority so far as that authority was consistent with "the mind of Christ." All men must submit to the authority of the collective conscience of the Christian community. This was the platform upon which the coming Catholicism was to be organized.

Sectarianism

It became the fashion in the early years of the twentieth century to speak of modernity as an epoch in history, whether one dated it from 1776, 1789, 1865, or from some other conventional landmark. As with any other period of history, it was convenient to assume that the entire community had committed itself to the modern ethos and that each individual bore its distinctive stamp. Proponents of the modern point of view frequently made this assumption explicit. They asserted that the modern outlook had triumphed completely over earlier attitudes, and that it had established itself as the permanent foundation on which subsequent developments would be erected. History was interpreted in these terms and the future was faced confidently in the assurance that it would grow inevitably out of the values and practices currently sanctioned. This was the appropriate social evolutionary expectation.

In these assumptions the modernists were doubtless mistaken. Society had not wholly committed itself to modernity, nor was it likely to do so. There was a common tendency among liberals to confuse industrialization and its products with a new mentality. Because mechanization touched virtually all Americans in various ways, there was a strong temptation to suppose that men's outlook had been correspondingly "rationalized." An inspection of the full range and diversity of American religious life between the Civil War and the First World War affords a convenient method for checking these assumptions of the modernists.

The impact of modernity upon the American mind, although massive, was by no means overwhelming. Denominational leaders were probably more conscious of this fact than were secularists. In several of the largest denominations they were witnesses to the struggle that left a widening chasm between modernists and traditionalists. As early as 1879, Newman Smyth observed that many of his colleagues were only too well aware of the distance that critical studies had carried them from many devout laymen and clerical associates in their own communions. The gulf between "modern" and "literal" reading of the Scriptures must have been at least as deep as any that had ever opened between parties calling themselves Christian. This situation was the more ominous because of the liberal conviction that sweet reason must prevail. There could be no lasting discrepancy between the best thought of the time and traditionally received opinions without great hazard to the community. Here was the peculiar danger in the modern situation. Learning was no longer the exclusive possession of a cloistered caste; it walked freely in the market place—and was proceeding to demonstrate that a little learning is a dangerous thing. Out of the widespread suspicion that learning was undermining faith emerged the religious indifference that was so characteristic of the modern era.[22]

The liberals undoubtedly accentuated their concern over this matter by the gratuitous assumption that, when confronted by a discrepancy between faith and knowledge, men would resolve the conflict by discarding faith. They assumed, in other words, that men required a unified world view, and that if it were fragmented, the authority of reason would be sufficient to undermine religious faith. This was a thoroughly modern attitude. Religious modernists differed from secularists only in the conviction that the secular point of view was self-defeating.

But did the facts of religious history confirm the modernist assumptions? Was it true that with the spread of knowledge the only alternatives would be a modernized faith or a corroding skepticism? Smyth may have been correct in believing that the denominations had achieved a stable equilibrium, but he overlooked the rapid proliferation of sectarian religious movements. The denominations had replaced the churches of an earlier era as the spawning grounds of sectarian movements. The years between the Civil War and the First World War were not inferior to other ages in the extent and variety of sectarian activity that they displayed.

An examination of certain aspects of Adventism will serve as a means of measuring the adequacy of the modernists' appraisal of the situation. The millennialist expectation of the coming of the Kingdom of God had been one of the major strands of American Protestant thought.[23] It was by no means confined to the Millerite and Mormon movements of the early nineteenth century. Elmer T. Clark has shown that

[22] Newman Smyth, *Old Faiths in New Light*, pp. 13–15.
[23] H. Richard Niebuhr, *The Kingdom of God in America*, Chicago and N.Y., 1937.

there was a steady growth of premillenarian sects during the subsequent period. He estimates that by mid-twentieth century there were forty or more sects with a combined membership of over a million in which premillennialism was a central doctrine. In addition, there were perhaps three million more millenarians in other conservative sects and denominations.[24]

Throughout American history the prevailing tendency among sectarian movements had been toward reconciliation with the environing culture, resulting in the transformation of sect into denomination. In the case of Millerite Adventism the transition occurred within a generation of the origin of the movement. After the failure of the Second Coming to occur as predicted in 1844, formal ecclesiastical organization was undertaken. It then became the official view that the Parousia would occur as a consequence of the world-wide preaching of the advent message and the conversion of a sufficient number of the faithful. This was a denominational point of view. It transformed the Second Coming from a divine judgment upon the world into an event dependent on human agency, namely, effective recruitment. The movement now had a long-range organizational objective to be pursued with approved denominational methods. But while the followers of Miller settled into denominational stability, successive waves of premillenarian enthusiasm during the late nineteenth century testified to the continuing pertinence of this belief for a large number of Americans.

The traditional sociological analysis of sectarian motivation, following Troeltsch, stressed underprivileged social status, misery, and sense of alienation out of which sectarian activity customarily emerged. The facts of American sect life are not always illumined by this socio-economic approach. It is amusing to read in Clark's account of the Millerite movement that, as the anticipated day of the Second Coming approached (Oct. 22, 1844), "men planted no crops, gave away

[24] Elmer T. Clark, *The Small Sects in America*, N.Y. and Nashville. Rev. ed. 1949, p. 34.

their money, discharged their employees, settled their accounts," and distributed gratis the latest editions of Adventist papers and periodicals.[25] Obviously such zealous liquidation cannot be explained as a product of poverty or persecution. One searches in vain for evidences of misery or any deep sense of the tragedy of life in Adventist literature. What it does reveal is at most a diffuse anxiety.

Millennialism in all of its forms represented a stubborn refusal to accept a modernist version of the historical process in which divine immanence was reconciled with events naturalistically conceived. Adventist expectations of the Second Coming based on Gospel predictions amounted to an assertion that history was comprehended within a divine providence that was ultimately extra-historical. The Bible contained the inspired and authoritative if somewhat obscure outline of God's program for the world. Blackstone's widely read tract, *Jesus Is Coming* (1908),[26] was intended to establish the authority of the inspired Biblical writers as the arbiters of modern history. Among the signs of the times pointing to the speedy Second Coming, Blackstone specified the transportation revolution and the rapid increase in literacy ("many shall run to and fro and knowledge shall be increased"); pestilence, famine, socialism, accumulating armaments, industrial conflict ("in the last days perilous times shall come"); spiritualism and Christian Science ("seducing spirits and doctrines of devils"); widespread apostasy due to Higher Criticism; and finally, the rise of Zionism foretelling the prophesied restoration of Israel. Had he written a generation later, Blackstone could have greatly enriched his catalogue of "signs of the times."

A principal object of this type of Adventism was to restore the authority of Scripture not so much over moral and social life as over the interpretation of history. It reflected bewilderment in the face of all the specialized authorities of modern life, and a desire to restore the unified and manageable au-

[25] *ibid.*, p. 36.
[26] William E. Blackstone, *Jesus Is Coming*, Chicago, 1908.

thority that the tradition of Scriptural literalism declared the Bible to represent. Rejection of modernity lay at the heart of sectarian millenarianism not because the sectarian was poor in the world's goods, nor because he was losing caste, but because he did not share the convictions and assumptions in terms of which the modernist interpreted his world.

One further aspect of sectarianism requires attention. The foregoing analysis has sought to elucidate sectarianism in terms of the needs and outlook of its communicants. But in any broad survey of the origins of American sect movements, it is readily apparent that many sects emerged out of ecclesiastical conflicts and divisions precipitated by aggressive clerical leaders who led out a devoted following for personal or institutional reasons. In many of these instances it is difficult to detect any distinctive content in the doctrines of the schismatics that would justify analysis in terms of their peculiar religious needs. In such cases it seems necessary to recognize the distinctive role of leadership.

Not only did the private and voluntary character of American Protestantism sanction aggressive leadership, but the whole tenor of American life encouraged it. The dynamic sect leader was a close counterpart of the energetic entrepreneur. His compensation was not principally monetary, but consisted of the more enduring satisfactions that a voluntary society could offer: the veneration of associates, institutional power, and the happiness that stemmed from activities well suited to talents and temperament. In order that the leader might have followers it was indeed necessary that he satisfy their social and religious needs. But we may also suppose that without his initiative those needs would often have remained unarticulated and unsatisfied. In late nineteenth-century America, with its fluid class lines, its geographical and occupational mobility, and its immature community life, all of which tended to. isolate the individual, the sect leader performed an important function. He furnished inspiration and guidance as well as religious discipline for many people who were unable to find these necessities in the dominant ethos.

RELIGION AND SCIENCE
IN AMERICAN PHILOSOPHY

JAMES WARD SMITH

I

Religious Tone and the Cosmic Sense in
American Philosophy

ROM 1620 to 1914 American thought was marked by a persistent optimism that courses of action can be justified by sweeping cosmic theories. Even our "pessimists," who deplored the actual course of events, retained the optimistic conviction that they understood ultimate truths which enabled them to judge and to condemn. The late Puritan could deplore the fact that the world was on the brink of disaster only because he was confident of his capacity to justify in terms of his cosmic theories specific courses of action which were *not* being followed. In his philosophical optimism rather than in his practical pessimism, he is typical of the main stream of American thought prior to 1914. No single fact about American philosophical thought since 1914 is more important than the loss of the confidence embodied in this "cosmic sense." The distinguishing mark of the 1920's and 1930's is its absence. If, as I believe, the 1950's have witnessed an attempt to grope back to that lost confidence, it is surely important that we examine with all the care at our command the sources of its collapse and the possibility of its being intelligently revived. Just this is the purpose of the present essay.

The "economic interpretation of history" and the psychoanalytic concept of "rationalization" have made us so intent upon finding causes of men's actions behind (and generally contrary to) the reasons they consciously supply that we run the danger of forgetting that the "causes" of men's actions are very often precisely the theoretical beliefs they provide as "reasons." There is, in short, such a thing as genuine purposeful behavior, and America has been full of it. Cosmic theories have been very real determinants in the course of our national life. The Puritans fled from England intent upon founding on earth a "Holy Commonwealth" which would realize God's cosmic (and very Calvinistic) purposes.[1] A century and a half later the Declaration of Independence based the founding of a new nation upon certain "self-evident truths" which proclaimed that men and nations are governed by God's cosmic (Newtonian-Lockean) laws.[2] By 1840 both Calvinism and Newtonian mechanism were considered highly suspect, but Emerson had as much confidence as either John Cotton or Thomas Jefferson that the American way of life could be justified by cosmic theories. Our political tradition of individualism and self-reliance was now the perfect expression of a new conception of the divine—Germanic, Platonic, mystical.[3] The Civil War, the advent of a developed theory of evolution, and the industrializing of society soon threw all of that out of gear, but before the century was over the ways of America were being justified by new visions of cosmic history, heavily influenced by the large theories of Hegel and Darwin.[4] Always there was present the "cosmic sense"—the continuous confidence that we *can* justify what

[1] For the best treatment of the genuineness of the settlers' theoretical "reasons," see Perry Miller, *The New England Mind, The Seventeenth Century*, New York, 1939, passim, but especially Chapter III.

[2] See Carl Becker, *The Declaration of Independence*, New York, 1922, especially Chapter II. Becker traces the steps whereby Colonial thinkers found themselves forced to provide "reasons" of a general philosophical kind. He finds that it was not accident that the Declaration appeals, for example, not to the rights of British citizens but to the rights of men.

[3] There is a real need for more serious philosophical study of thinkers such as Emerson, taking full account of the technical subtleties of Immanuel Kant and the later German romantic idealists. I have discussed this problem briefly in *Theme for Reason*, Princeton, 1957, pp. 39–49.

[4] There is an enormous literature concerning the impact upon American thought of the cosmic implications of evolution. See, for example, Stow Persons, ed., *Evolutionary Thought in America*, New Haven, 1950. This earlier publication of the Special Program in American Civilization at Princeton University sought to provide a synoptic study of the extent of the impact of evolutionary ideas. A large body of bibliographical material is available.

we are doing and what we stand for by reference to large and ambitious theories concerning the nature and the structure of the universe.

Our general theme may be stated in a preliminary way as follows: The cosmic sense of American philosophy was, while it lasted, universally religious in tone. At the same time, the religious tone was constantly coupled with an attempt to adjust to the deliverances of natural science. We shall argue, first, that the adjustment of religious world view to science in the seventeenth, eighteenth, and nineteenth centuries was persistently superficial; second, that the philosophical revolution of the twentieth century is predicated upon taking science seriously, and upon refusal to countenance superficial accommodation. If these two points can be clearly established, we can support two further claims: first, that the loss of cosmic sense can be understood only to the extent that we understand the points at which the demands of science had never been squarely met by our traditionally religious view of the world; second, that only by rectifying the failure of the past can an intelligent revival of cosmic sense flourish.

I do not wish to suggest that America's cosmic sense can be revived only by reinstating on a broad scale and in renewed confident form our traditional religious faith. The possible sources of cosmic sense far outstretch the narrow band of our traditional Christian, and largely Protestant, heritage. There may be force in the claim that no world view can have sufficient breadth of appeal in this country unless it rests upon a broadly conceived Hebraic-Christian base. (We are no longer sufficiently Protestant to ignore either Catholic or Jew.) Predictions concerning breadth of appeal, however, will form no part of our argument. We shall be content to consider the effort of theology to revive, and its effort to face the challenge of science in a more than superficial sense, as phases of a larger philosophical problem of revival.

Our claim that the traditional cosmic sense of America has been religious in tone calls for some clarification. The claim seems reasonably safe only so long as we refrain from over-scrupulous attention to details. As is so often the case in intellectual history, our confidence in a generalization is high only so long as we are content with a relatively vague over-all impression. What, after all, could be more obvious than our general impression that the tenor of American thought has been traditionally one of Protestant Christianity? And yet, when we come down to concrete cases, puzzlement increases. Paine and Jefferson were perhaps the leading intellectual figures in the closing decades of the eighteenth century—and both were vilified as "atheists." Few men better expressed the American mind of the early nineteenth century than did Emerson—and it is commonly said that Emerson was *not* a Christian. Unitarianism itself has often been denied and has indeed disclaimed the right to the label "Christian." And what are we to say of those two unique products of American religious history: Mormonism and Christian Science?

It might help a great deal if the concrete cases were examined more, rather than less, closely. The label "atheist" as applied to Paine was simply irresponsible slander. He proclaimed his belief in one God in no uncertain terms, and deplored the atheistic tendencies of the French revolution.[5] The case of Jefferson is more difficult, but one thing is clear: wherever his reflections led, they were reflections which grew out of deep concern with the Protestant Christian tradition of the West.[6] As for Unitarianism and Transcendentalism, each was successively a Protestant revolt within a continuing tradition of speculation on the part of New England ministers. Everything depends, of course, upon the sense in which we understand the word "Christian." There is a very real sense, for example, in which the tradition of Christian orthodoxy is overwhelmingly theistic. If we wish to emphasize this, we will

[5] See Alburey Castell's introductory essay in Thomas Paine, *The Age of Reason*, New York, 1948, pp. vii–xi.

[6] See Adrienne Koch, *The Philosophy of Thomas Jefferson*, New York, 1943, especially pp. 23–39, for a helpful treatment, but there has been no definitive philosophical study of Jefferson's religious views.

be inclined to say that any tendency to flirt with deism (Paine and Jefferson) falls outside the Christian pale. Similarly, any flirting with pantheism (Emerson) will fall outside the pale. But can we use our terms as strictly as this? [7] Theism may be overwhelmingly orthodox, but time and again the language of Protestant pulpits (and even of Catholic) has been channeled into the unorthodoxies of deism or pantheism.

Philosophers tend toward unorthodoxy. Therefore, it seems desirable here to use the phrase "Protestant Christian" in a sense broad enough to embrace unorthodoxies. In defining a Christian, are we to require positive belief in the divinity of Christ? Are we to require the doctrine of the Trinity? Are we to require literal commitment to the entirety of the Nicene Creed? Then we may as well forget the philosophers! Yet it is surely important that many philosophers, especially American philosophers prior to 1914, are immersed in a Protestant Christian heritage. In this broader sense, the questions a man asks are more important than the answers he gives. Unorthodox conclusions may emerge from a focus of attention upon problems drawn entirely from the tradition. Unitarians were Calvinists in revolt, but this made them by the same token an offshoot of the Calvinist tradition. Emerson was a minister in revolt against the new orthodoxies of Unitarianism, but he remained a Protestant minister even in his naughtiest moments. Paine's proclamation of deism shocked the

---

[7] The three technical terms "deism," "pantheism," and "theism" should be used strictly. "Deism" is the label for the view that God and the world are wholly distinct, related only by the act of creation. "Pantheism" is the label for the view that God and the world are identical in some sense. Literal identity is seldom seriously meant even by such an extreme advocate of the view as Spinoza; ordinarily God is said to constitute the "real essence" of the world. "Theism" is a bridge position. Theism always requires at least two key terms: "immanence" and "transcendence." Insofar as the theist insists on God's immanence in the world, he aligns himself with pantheism; insofar as he insists on God's transcendence, he aligns himself with deism.

While technical terms such as these should be strictly used, a word like "Christian," unless one clearly states one's reasons for providing it with a rigid definition, had best be used in studies such as the present one with general and flexible meaning.

orthodox, but his motivating purpose was in fact to defend the core of the Christian heritage as he saw it. Even Mormonism, however empty philosophically, was a product of broader currents within the stream of nineteenth-century American Protestantism. Joseph Smith did not add a book to the Vedanta.

It comes then to this: that the intellectual historian has need of that "vague over-all impression" to which we earlier referred. The vague need not be confused or sloppy; the over-precise may direct our attention away from significant general features. American philosophy prior to 1914 was not only incurably cosmic; it was also persistently and doggedly Christian in emphasis. Unorthodoxies of one sort or another have been legion, but the general outlines of our cosmic sense have always clearly discernible sources in the Protestant Christian tradition. Before 1914 revolt was always against orthodoxy, never against the tradition as such. Only against this background can the truly revolutionary character of the twentieth century be understood, for after the First World War the object of revolt does for the first time become the tradition as such. To understand this more serious revolt, let us turn our attention to the problem of science.

II

Religion and Science: Preliminary Remarks [8]

Any philosophy at any period in history must do what justice it can to the deliverances of the best empirical science of its day. There always have been, and there doubtless will continue to be, periods in which philosophers either willfully reject or unwittingly ignore natural science. All too often the responsibility for such default can be traced to preoccupa-

[8] Philosophical distinctions are sometimes entirely ignored both by theologians and by cultural historians. Since my argument depends upon careful attention to the distinctions here drawn, I plead for patience with these few dry and analytical pages. With Section III the meat of my argument begins.

tion with religious or other highly metaphysical matters. Few lessons of intellectual history are more striking than this: a point of view which ignores or fails to keep abreast of science will not in the long run win out. In all continuing traditions, there follows after every rejection of science a move to accommodate. The religious tradition is no exception to this rule, and our concern in this paper is not with those religious philosophers who have unwisely ignored science. It is rather with those who, while persisting in the attempt to interpret America's destiny in cosmic and religious terms, have faced the need of accommodating the best that science had to offer them.

When we speak of "accommodating science" we must at once be alert to the ambiguities of the word "science." There are few matters in which systematic philosophers and intellectual historians could be of more assistance to each other than in this. Too frequently intellectual historians use the word "science" with insufficient care. We are repeatedly informed, for example, that the late eighteenth century is an "age of science." But this might be understood in very different senses, and while true enough in one sense it might be egregiously mistaken in another. If we are to avoid serious confusion, there are at least two fundamental distinctions to be kept in mind.

Philosophers are inclined to lay considerable stress upon the difference between pure science and applied science. The difference is by no means an easy one to make precise. In a rough and ready way we can see that the inventions of a plow, a telephone, and a hydrogen bomb are accomplishments of applied science. The concern of pure science is with the theories which pave the way for such inventions. The pure science of physics, for example, is concerned with the development of a theory which will describe the nature of matter; applied physics manipulates matter in accordance with the theory in vogue. Obviously there is a theoretical base presupposed in all applied science; just as obviously, the results of application will continuously stimulate both advance and change at the level of pure theory. At a minimum, however, there are two senses in which, viewed from this standpoint, an age may be "scientific" in spirit. It may be so in the sense that it is more than usually productive of conceptual insight at the theoretical level, or it may be so in the sense that it is prolific in the invention of gadgetry and appliances. As we shall see, late eighteenth-century America produced little in the first sense, though it seethed with activity in the second sense.

There is, however, a second, and equally important, distinction which cuts across the distinction between pure science and applied science. One may, when using the word "science," wish to refer to a given body of data, laws, and interpretations. Let us speak in this sense of the *corpus* of science, and note that the attitude of an individual or of an age toward science may be conceived simply as an attitude toward this corpus. One uses the word "science" quite differently when referring not to any given body of facts or laws or interpretations, but rather to a unique methodological spirit of inquiry. One may accommodate the corpus of science and remain impervious to its method, and this is true whether the corpus in question is that of pure or of applied science. The housewife may accept and accommodate her dishwasher and her television set without the slightest understanding of the spirit of invention which produced them. Just so, a theologian may accept and accommodate the theory of evolution or the principles of quantum mechanics without in the least being affected by the spirit of inquiry which produced them. These distinctions will be essential to the following reading of American intellectual history.

We have earlier referred to the "cosmic sense" in philosophy, and in so doing we have doubtless put the reader on his guard that metaphysical matters are in the wind. It is impossible to record the numerous and weighty reasons why so many recent philosophers, especially in the English-speaking world, have tried to place metaphysics in disrepute. Some of us believe that the enterprise need not be as disreputable as it is often made out to be, but out of the debate has emerged one important insight which we must take note of. If by "metaphysics" we mean the attempt to formulate a set of highly general concepts in terms of which we contend that the "ultimate" or "real" nature of the world can be "explained," or "described," or at a very minimum "discussed," we must face an obvious consequence. One mark of a successful metaphysical system so conceived will be the impossibility of confronting it with a fact which cannot be explained or described or discussed in terms of the system. This is both a logical and a historical matter. As a matter of history, the mark of a strong and continuing metaphysical tradition is always its capacity to adjust to new and unanticipated facts; as a matter of logic, it is evident that a system designed to discuss everything without exception must never find itself at a loss in the attempt to discuss anything in particular. If it finds itself at a loss, it has failed.

We may readily concede that some weapons in the arsenal of past metaphysics are of dubious value. One of the weapons recently subjected to most violent attack is the weapon of that notorious pair of concepts: "appearance" and "reality." It has been remarked that with these weapons at one's disposal, vast advantages may be reaped at the expense of very little intellectual effort. These terms provide a ready-made device for labeling any recalcitrant fact "mere appearance." Other devices may be equally suspect, but it still has not been shown that all of metaphysics is a bag of conjurer's tricks. The important facts are these: that the human mind has shown a remarkable tendency to grope for over-all perspective on the nature of things, and this tendency cannot be eradicated overnight; that *several* continuing metaphysical traditions have shown remarkable vitality, and have adjusted themselves with undeniable agility to new facts and new discoveries; and that *one* of these continuing traditions has been that which broadly characterizes the Judaeo-Christian heritage of the West.

It is of the utmost importance that this last fact be stressed. The core of the religious heritage of the West is patently metaphysical. Not all metaphysics need be religious, and a difficult job it is to state with clarity the conditions under which a metaphysic is properly called "religious." Conversely, however, all religion is in essence metaphysical. We speak, of course, of religious institutions and of religious experiences. We sometimes so preoccupy ourselves with the description of institutions and of experiences that we fail to see that the "religious" quality of both derives from a more basic sense in which they either perpetrate or express a distinctive way of viewing the world as a whole. A sociologist may be struck by institutional similarities between the Vatican and the Kremlin; a psychologist may note striking parallels between the experiences of devout Catholic communicants and dedicated party cell workers. One obscures at one's peril, however, the fact that the world view of Communism is the antithesis (and avowedly so) of what we traditionally classify as a religious world view. Dialectical materialism is a metaphysical system of concepts which is self-consciously anti-religious. The often used phrase "religion of Communism" obscures this, and is therefore perilous.

It is fortunately not my task to identify those features which are common to the several world views of the major religious traditions such as Buddhism, Hinduism, Christianity, and the rest. Suffice it to say that the Christian tradition, as one member of the set, has managed to keep its "shape"—its identifiable pattern—amidst a most amazing variation in detail. The variety of detail is in its way a measure of the conceptual strength of its own common core. The Christian tradition has adjusted again and again to new facts and new theories. Its protagonists have used every known weapon in the metaphysical arsenal. In particular, they have continuously attempted to adjust to the changing scene of science. This essay will examine some of the ways in which American philosophers have made this adjustment.

Consider, now, the following two conditions: first, that a religiously minded philosopher's primary concern may well be with a set of metaphysical concepts explicitly designed to enable him to discuss anything whatsoever; second, that his interest in science may be in its *corpus*—i.e., with a given body of facts and formulas. Surely assimilation of the latter to the former is not likely to present any insuperable difficulties. Our hypothetical philosopher's capacity to translate the corpus of science into the terminology of his general conceptual scheme is no more nor less than a sign that his scheme is doing what it is designed to do. There is, moreover, no obvious reason why other conceptual schemes might not equally well accomplish the same feat. I stress that the corpus of theoretical science is as easily assimilated in this sense as is the corpus of applied science. There is nothing in the corpus of contemporary science—whether the science of quantum mechanics or the science of rocket missiles—which will stump an acute neo-Thomist who is agile in the manipulation of a conceptual system devised in the thirteenth century. By the same token, in America's past, the Puritan metaphysician had little difficulty in discussing Newtonian science in his own terms; and at a later date, although some Christian ministers were horrified by the facts and theories of evolution, it did not take men like James McCosh very long to discover that the traditional concepts of Christian metaphysics were strong enough to adjust and to adapt to the new facts.

Nevertheless, the demand that a metaphysical system of concepts "do justice to" the best science of its time may have a different and a much more difficult sense. In this stronger sense, science is not assimilated until the spirit of its method is understood. In this regard it cannot seriously be claimed that either the Puritan metaphysician or James McCosh succeeded. From this distinction between a weak and a strong way of meeting the intellectual demands of science I derive a definition of the phrase "superficial accommodation." Accommodation is "superficial" if it is accomplished merely by showing that the corpus of science can be discussed without fiasco in a specialized terminology. Accommodation is "real" only to the extent that it rests upon a painstaking understanding of the method of science and upon taking seriously the success of that method as a way of understanding the nature of things.

With these preliminary matters out of the way, we can now turn to our main themes. In the following section I argue that the accommodation of religion to science in America was persistently superficial from the seventeenth century through the latter nineteenth century. We shall then be prepared to discuss the impact on American religion of an attitude toward science which was not superficial.

III

Religion and Science: Superficial Accommodations

Little need be said concerning the Puritan adjustment to Newtonian science. By 1700 Puritan Harvard was teaching the new science and on the whole teaching it well.[9] But it has long been recognized that the open-armed reception of Newtonian science by the Puritan was an acceptance of the corpus only, and in no way involved serious concession to the methodological spirit of science. The Puritan acceptance of the Newtonian corpus was based upon assurance that nothing in it would detract from God's omnipotence and majesty, and this assurance was bolstered by the tone in which the Newtonian scientists and Newton himself spoke. The Puritan theologians never themselves seriously adopted the method of science, and never ceased to approach the problems of physics

---

[9] See Samuel Eliot Morison, *Harvard College in the Seventeenth Century*, Cambridge, Mass., 1936, Chapters X and XI.

with a moralizing rather than an objective and inquiring spirit. In short, they "took little part either in advancing new theories or in retarding their development . . . the whole matter was regarded as indifferent or secondary." [10] Thus at the very outset of our history a religious philosophy in vogue made the mistake of adjusting to science only in the superficial sense. Commendable though it was that religious thinkers kept abreast of and accepted a major revolution of science, they nonetheless did so in such a way as to miss the deeper implications. Perhaps for this very reason the science they accepted ate away at the inside of their system and eventually caused trouble. It may well be that one cannot merely accept the corpus of science, discussing it in one's own terms, and remain for long uninfluenced by the deeper spirit.

It would be absurd to say, as a matter of logic, that Puritanism *could not* adjust to science in any but a superficial sense. An accident of history must not be misread as a necessary theoretical entailment. That Puritan doctrine might have adjusted to science in a deeper sense is one of the principal lessons to be learned from careful study of the works of Jonathan Edwards. This remarkable New England theologian manifests as much capacity as either Berkeley or Hume to understand the deeper implications of the scientific spirit.[11] Parrington's remark that Edwards is an "anachronism," the claim that in his mature theological writings he abandoned the early promise of a scientifically oriented philosophical spirit, has been thoroughly discredited.[12] Every one of Edwards' mature theological works is a monumental attempt

[10] Perry Miller, *The New England Mind; The Seventeenth Century*, p. 219. I am especially indebted to Miller's section, pp. 213–222.

[11] On this point we owe much to Perry Miller's study *Jonathan Edwards*, William Sloane Associates, 1949, although a definitive study has yet to be written. An excellent brief study is contained in the introduction to Faust and Johnson, eds., *Jonathan Edwards, Representative Selections*, New York, 1935, pp. xi–xcviii. See also, for brief comment, Herbert W. Schneider, *A History of American Philosophy*, New York, 1946, p. 20.

[12] Vernon Louis Parrington, *Main Currents in American Thought*, New York, 1927, Vol. I, Book II, Part I, Chapter II. Note chapter title and see especially p. 162.

to reinterpret basic Calvinist axioms in the light of precisely that scientifically oriented philosophical spirit which he never lost. Careful study of these works will reveal that what gradually changes in the process is not Edwards' philosophical spirit but the whole tone and tenor of the Calvinist axioms under discussion. The conception of depravity which emerges in the subtle argument of *The Nature of True Virtue;* the conception of determinism so brilliantly defended in *Freedom of the Will;* and the account of man's access to knowledge of God in *The Treatise on the Religious Affections*—each of these is a striking example of what new meaning can be injected into an old concept when genuine effort to attend to the implications of the scientific spirit is present.[13]

The failure of Edwards—not merely the failure of being rejected, but more importantly the failure of being universally misunderstood—is in itself a sign of the superficiality of the common adaptation of the Puritan mentality to the new science. It was all very well to accept the facts and laws of Newtonian science; but when devotion to the underlying spirit produced obvious changes in the purport of basic church axioms, the time had come *not* to understand.

Edwards, of course, was rejected on two sides. Looking backward, he was rejected by Calvinists unwilling to re-examine basic axioms. Looking forward, he was rejected by all those "enlightened" eighteenth-century souls who trumpeted the new scientific spirit and failed to see that this spirit

---

[13] The point concerning *The Treatise on the Religious Affections* is covered by Perry Miller in his *Jonathan Edwards,* already cited. Miller goes perhaps too far in attributing to Edwards views later expressed by William James. The conception of depravity in *The Nature of True Virtue* is well explained in the introduction to Faust and Johnson, but much more needs to be written about it. Edwards' idea that depravity consists in the "interestedness" of all choice is really a far cry from the usual theological conceptions of the Fall. It is in fact a corollary of the Lockean psychology of *Freedom of the Will* when combined with a subtle pantheist conception of true virtue as identification of oneself with Being. That the determinism of *Freedom of the Will* is influenced by Newtonianism has long been recognized, but that Edwards came close to foreseeing Kant's view of causality has not been recognized.

could imply anything in religion other than the superficialities of "deism." Intellectual historians of the period too seldom recognize that Edwards, in defense of the "wormy and moth-eaten" doctrines of Calvin, revealed a far deeper understanding of the spirit of science than did the trumpeters of a "scientific" or "rational" religion. Edwards stands between two quite different ways of superficially accommodating science and religion.

The *intention* of the Enlightenment was not superficial. The late eighteenth century was motivated by a genuine desire to apply a method which had achieved such success in physics and astronomy to the perennially recalcitrant areas of ethics, political philosophy, and theology. Unhappily, their understanding of the scientific method, especially in America, was itself demonstrably superficial. And at no point was it quite so superficial as at the point where they proclaimed its capacity to settle the religious issue.

The works of John Locke were the fountainhead, throughout the English-speaking world, of the eighteenth-century empiricist movement. At heart this movement was an attempt to bring philosophy to terms with what was then understood to be the major implications of taking the method of science seriously. But the careful student will take pains to distinguish two currents of thought which flowed from Locke. On the one hand there was the widespread and popular current of optimism, practicalism, and secularism. On the other hand there was a subtle and esoteric development of skeptical and far from practical philosophical speculation best represented by Berkeley and Hume. The popular current made, as is usual, the more noise; and cultural historians of the period often make generalizations remarkably inapplicable to Berkeley and to Hume. Meanwhile the esoteric current, seldom attended to and more seldom understood, had to await, as is usual, a more favorable time to be recognized at its true value.

Nowhere more than in America were the popular and short-lived products of the thought of Locke more dominant,

and the permanent and esoteric products less understood.[14]
True, the works of Edwards and the American Samuel Johnson parallel those of Berkeley, but neither had any significant
effect on the American mind of the later eighteenth century.
In each case the reason was primarily religious. Edwards'
thought was enmeshed in the defense of a dying Calvinist
past, and Johnson's held tainted by his conversion to Anglicanism. Not by accident do the cultural historians so often
commit the mistake of relegating Edwards and Johnson to
earlier chapters, divorcing them from the intellectual revolution of the eighteenth century.[15] A historian immersed in
literature more typical of late eighteenth-century America
is apt to miss the fact that Edwards and Johnson were the
most advanced thinkers produced in the country during the
century; by the same token he is likely to fail in providing
any adequate account of the most significant philosophical
tendencies in the Western world at large during the period.
The late eighteenth century in America means "Enlightenment" in the narrow, and in the last analysis superficial,
sense.[16] It is this temper that we must understand if we are

[14] I shall have more to say about Hume at a later stage of this essay;
see also footnote 36. No American philosopher of the eighteenth or early
nineteenth century understood Hume's central doctrines. Hume is, in
spite of his deceptively clear style of writing, an extraordinarily difficult
philosopher to comprehend, and few of his readers anywhere properly
understood him. Certainly historians of American thought, who have read
perhaps mainly the comments by eighteenth- and nineteenth-century Americans on him, repeatedly reveal serious ignorance of Hume's position. See,
for example, the references to Hume as a "materialist" by Merle Curti,
The Growth of American Thought, New York, 1943, pp. 163–164.

[15] See, for example: Parrington; Curti; Schneider; Joseph L. Blau,
Men and Movements in American Philosophy, New York, 1952; W. H.
Werkmeister, *A History of Philosophical Ideas in America*, New York,
1949; P. R. Anderson and M. H. Fisch, *Philosophy in America*, New
York, 1939; W. G. Muelder and L. Sears, *The Development of American
Philosophy*, New York, 1940.

[16] The word "Enlightenment" is a troublesome one. It is occasionally
used in very broad senses which would make inappropriate any claim
that late eighteenth-century America was an especially outstanding expression of it. (See, e.g., Hayes's use of the term as a label for the tendency,
starting with the Reformation and continuing into the present, to disseminate learning among the masses: Carlton J. Hayes, *The Political and*

to understand the second major attempt in this country to weld science and religion together in a thoroughly superficial way.

Much has been written about the spirit of science in late eighteenth-century America. The Age of Reason, unlike the Puritan age, was deeply affected by the methodological *spirit* of science. There was unquestionably an increase in the conviction that open-minded observation and controlled experiment are the keys to unlocking the secrets of the natural world.[17] In one sense, the adulation of Newton and Locke was not superficial. There may have been dogmatic certainty that the world is neater, simpler, and more mechanistic than the science of later centuries has borne out, but every period in human history has unfortunately its dogma, and behind this one was at least the salutary sense that controlled observation must take precedence over tradition if we are to come to grips with the truth about things. In another sense, however, superficiality was rampant. Most historians have rightly seen that the American emphasis was upon the utilitarian and practical applications of science rather than upon its speculative base.[18] The practical emphasis was largely upon experiments which

Cultural History of Modern Europe, New York, 1933. Or see Ernst Cassirer's article on "Enlightenment" in *The Encyclopaedia of the Social Sciences*, in which the sense of the word is associated with the modern tendency, starting with Bacon and Descartes, to shift the basis of Western thought from theology to science.) The narrower sense of the term, as a label for a movement in late eighteenth-century thought which was particularly strong in France and America, will be found clearly stated both in the Oxford English Dictionary and in Webster's Unabridged. There is, however, a marked difference. The OED uses the expression "a shallow and pretentious" movement, whereas Webster used such adjectives as "lively," "keen," and "vigorous." Even the writers of dictionaries occasionally find objectivity difficult. I am inclined to agree with the OED.

[17] See Clinton Rossiter, *The First American Revolution*, New York, 1953, p. 210.

[18] Notice the emphasis in the following passage from Max Savelle, *Seeds of Liberty*, New York, 1948, pp. 145–146: "The sweep of science in America was part and parcel of the so-called Enlightenment of Europe; at the same time, in its wide popularization, in the emphasis upon utility, and in its application to the practical, daily affairs of life by the ingenuity of the Americans, it was peculiarly American." See also Savelle, p. 102, and Curti, p. 95.

amplified European theories already widely prevailing; some was upon mere gadgetry. The main thing upon which philosophical depth depends was almost wholly absent, for there was little or no critical examination of the speculative basis of Newtonian science. At bottom the period was one of dogmatic certainty and hence of theoretical superficiality.

Benjamin Franklin is rightly viewed as a symbol of the period, as Thomas Edison may be viewed as a symbol of a much later period during which America worshiped the corpus of science while paying little or no attention to its speculative base. The fame of Franklin's kite is symbolic of the emphasis on gadgetry. Franklin's work in electricity was not without its theoretical importance, but his kite was a dramatic device for demonstrating a theory already widely recognized. It never occurred to Franklin, as it did to Cadwallader Colden, to criticize and challenge Newton's *theory*. Indeed, as far as I can discover, Colden seems to stand alone among colonial Americans as a theoretical innovator. And no one understood David Hume.

The prevalence of dogmatic assurance concerning the theoretical basis of science produced an over-hasty confidence that mechanistic explanation is possible in morals and religion. Not always hasty. Benjamin Rush's experiments in the Philadelphia jail were remarkably careful preliminaries to what would many years later become scientific studies in the psychology of crime. Interestingly enough, Rush had to be secretive about his work. He, like Colden, was not typical of the times. It was more typical to proclaim that rigorous law governs the behavior of men—without too much detail.

Our main concern is with the impact of all this science-worship upon religion, and nowhere did the spokesmen of the new spirit more obviously founder. On the one hand, they most assuredly did not establish what they claimed, and, on the other hand, the subsequent history of science entirely failed to bear them out.

To perceive that they did not establish what they claimed,

we need only look briefly at the argument from design. The claim was that the religious question could be settled by empirical demonstration. Few groups have more loudly claimed that the virtue of what they said lay in its empirical demonstrability, yet so seldom offered any demonstrations. The argument from design, purporting to prove that God exists, is one of the few cases in which the proclaimed demonstration is in fact offered. The unfortunate truth is that it has no empirical force whatever. Is there anything empirical about the claim that from the observed order and design of the world one can justly conclude that there must be a divine designer? Clearly not; the inference from the existence of order to the necessary existence of a cause for that order rests upon an assumed premise for which at the very least it would be difficult to say what would count as empirical support. The premise is that the existence of order is antecedently improbable. Only if the chance existence of order (of *any* kind) is less probable than the chance existence of disorder is there any force to the demand that we must posit a cause of the existence of order. And this premise, whether it be justifiable or not, is by no stretch of anyone's imagination a premise of an empirical kind. A moment's reflection will reveal that no evidence could possibly bear on the issue one way or another. It follows that the argument from design, whatever else it may be, is certainly not an empirical argument. It is therefore not the type of argument which can have any of the virtue the Enlightenment claimed for it.[19]

Perhaps a more convincing way to show the superficiality of the claim is to show how badly it failed to weather the test of time. True science was supposed to convert us all to deism, but as science continued to progress and to flourish in the nineteenth and twentieth centuries, deism is of all the theological alternatives the one least often encountered. Particu-

[19] An empirical argument may, of course, contain non-empirical premises, provided they are clearly established truths of logic. In the present case, however, the non-empirical premise has no logical force whatever.

larly with the advent of evolution, the tendency of those who took science seriously was to conceive of God increasingly as immanent in the world process.[20] Extreme pantheism was as rare as deism, but versions of theism which laid special stress on the concept of immanence were to set the style for later versions of scientific theology. Viewed simply as a prediction, the Enlightenment's claim that science would support the cause of deism was plainly a mistake.

All of this means that the Enlightenment, like Puritanism, integrated religion and science only in a superficial sense. In the last analysis Thomas Paine fares no better than the Calvinist clergy. He, too, accepted Newtonian science primarily as a "corpus." He dogmatically accepted the facts and laws with little appreciation of the complex spirit of the method.[21] His proclamation of deism was as uncritical as the Calvinist's proclamation of divine inscrutability. He too mouthed religious concepts which did not genuinely grow out of the method he proclaimed.

During the first half of the nineteenth century science played a comparatively minor role in shaping the American mind. The age of romanticism did not take science seriously. Emerson, the most perceptive intellect of the period, preached wisely on the matter, but there is very little evidence that he practiced what he preached. He insisted (to use the terminology of his 1836 essay on *Nature*) that man must discipline his "Understanding" before his "Reason" can be allowed to sally forth into the realm of transcendent truth. This meant, of course, that a thorough training in empirical science [22] is a necessary prerequisite to sober rational vision. But

[20] See Stow Persons, "Evolution and Theology in America," the final essay in Stow Persons, ed., *Evolutionary Thought in America*, pp. 427–428.

[21] See Thomas Paine, *The Age of Reason*, pp. 45–47.

[22] Here, as elsewhere, it is necessary to be conversant with German Philosophy if one is to grasp the import of Emerson. Kant had differentiated the two "faculties": Understanding and Reason. Understanding is the faculty which imposes "categories" upon the phenomena of experience and thus makes inductive science possible. Reason is the faculty which asks categorial questions about things as they are, independent of experi-

there is little evidence that Emerson subjected himself to any such thorough training. Scholars have claimed that he was ahead of his time in grasping the essence of later evolutionary philosophy, and so indeed he was. But there was little science in his soul, and less genuine empiricism. His warped conception of Locke and of Hume is symptomatic of this fact. The nineteenth century did not take science seriously until the full impact of Darwin and of Spencer was felt. And nowhere more than in America did this impact reverberate with religious overtones.

This was the second major scientific revolution to be faced by American theologians, and it is interesting to contrast the two. The Newtonian revolution was met by the Puritan clergy with remarkable calm. The Darwinian revolution was met by the nineteenth-century clergy with hostility and polemic. To be sure, the fact that Puritanism accepted Newtonian science did not prevent its ultimate destructive effect. Was the late nineteenth-century clergy dimly aware of this fact? No matter; the battle they themselves fought was a losing battle, and it was not long before the intelligent Christian apologists moved to recoup their losses. Our concern in this essay is not with the open resistance of such men as Charles Hodge; our concern is with the overtures of peace and rapprochement of such men as James McCosh. The attempt of the peacemakers to establish a common ground between Christian theology and evolutionary science is our third and final example of "superficial accommodation."

The thesis requires little defense. What, after all, was accomplished by the peacemakers? So long as one was not too

---

ence; and according to Kant Reason does not yield knowledge. Post-Kantian philosophers (including Emerson) differ with him as to the capacities of Reason. They all conceive of Reason as in one way or another a source of a superior kind of knowledge. But they inherit from Kant the use of the word "Understanding" as a label for the faculty whereby man achieves scientific or inductive knowledge of experienced objects (as distinct from "things-in-themselves"). Thus, when Emerson speaks of disciplining the Understanding he is to be understood as referring to all training in inductive or empirical science.

literalistic in his reading of the Bible, so long as one concentrated on the general metaphysical concepts of the Christian tradition, he was bound sooner or later to discover that these are general enough to adjust to anything contained in evolutionary science. Sporadic variation could be discussed in the terminology of Divine intervention and miracle; the origin of species could be discussed in the terminology of God's purposes; the concept of creation could itself be adjusted to the facts of continuous development through time. As Asa Gray clearly saw, species are logically as distinct as they ever were, however compelling the evidence that in fact they emerge but slowly in time. The logic of God's mind, the logic of the creative act, the logic of divine intervention, and the logic of continuous divine government are in no way altered by a mere temporal complication of the facts. Literalism might be embarrassed by the new discoveries, but the subtle metaphysical temperament need have no fear.[23]

The only thing to be feared was that somebody would wake up to the fact that this kind of metaphysical or purely terminological accommodation *was* superficial. Perhaps a goodly number of alternative metaphysical schemes could adjust to the facts of evolution with equal ease. Precisely this kind of awakening, precisely this kind of complete disillusion with metaphysics, is one of the most important products of religious speculation in late nineteenth-century America. And the surprising thing—too often ignored by studies of this period—is that this awakening first occurred among liberal Protestant theologians. It did not originate in academic schools; it originated in the Protestant pulpit.

While McCosh, Gray, LeComte, Savage, and Johnson labored to translate the facts of evolution into the terminology of Christian metaphysics, a second group of men labored to expunge metaphysics from the Christian church. This did not

---

[23] One of the best summary treatments of this period is the article by Stow Persons cited in footnote 20. A fuller grasp of the point made here can be obtained by reading the authors he discusses.

happen overnight; two important factors led up to it. There is first the long history of the gradually increasing humanization of Christian concepts in American Protestantism. Puritanism itself had, prior to its demise, gradually humanized its concepts. As deism was transformed into Unitarianism, and as Unitarianism gave way to Transcendentalism, the humanizing of basic religious concepts was again at work. The proliferation of Protestant sects in the nineteenth century abetted this tendency, for it became increasingly difficult to find among Protestant groups any clear-cut doctrinal common ground. Increasingly, what was common among Protestants was a human attitude rather than a metaphysical point of view.[24] This was one of the factors at work. The other was that fundamental Protestantism *had* resisted evolution on doctrinal and metaphysical grounds. That their battle was soon lost led to embarrassment among the Protestant clergy. In moving to recoup their losses, they fastened on the claim that metaphysics was not their bailiwick anyway. They took refuge in the claim that the essence of Christianity lies in its ethical and social teachings. Protestantism disowned metaphysics and proclaimed a "Religion of Humanity" and a "Social Gospel."

With these movements our subject shifts. We pass from superficial attempts on the part of theological metaphysics to accommodate science, to a period of disillusion with theological metaphysics. Movements within the Protestant churches are a prelude to climactic developments in professional philosophy. Eventually the evolution controversy forced philosophers to take science seriously. There emerged two schools

---

[24] I am here trying to impress upon the reader the extent to which religion was losing its metaphysical nerve during this period. Needless to say, there was still a great deal of metaphysical presupposition on the part of the most metaphysically timid. Nobody has ever succeeded in rooting all metaphysical assumptions out of his talk, least of all the Christian ministers. Here I focus attention on a tendency very prevalent in my own youth—a tendency, of course, not conveying the entire picture. For other aspects see the articles in the present volume by Sydney Ahlstrom and Daniel Williams.

of thought which were to dominate the twentieth-century American mind, each school deriving in its own way from its emphasis on science a disillusion with traditional metaphysics. These were the schools of pragmatism and positivism. The influence of pragmatism on American Protestantism cannot be understood unless one sees that the disillusion of the latter was already being produced by the very forces that were setting the former in motion. America was on a grand scale losing its "cosmic sense," and the churches themselves were affected by that very temper which was to pave the way for two major movements in technical philosophy.

IV

The Challenge of Science Understood: Disillusion

At the outset, pragmatism was well intentioned enough. It began with Charles Sanders Peirce's claim that any difference in meaning, however fine, must make some sensible difference in the course of experience.[25] No man understood science better than Peirce, and he saw that the essence of the scientific spirit lies in the demand that the meaning of any hypothesis be spelled out by detailed specification of the *differences* that would be entailed if that hypothesis, rather than an alternative, were true. This principle is the logical basis of all experiment. It is also the leverage for rooting out all merely verbal thought and argument. But Peirce used his principle for other than destructive purposes. The theological hypothesis made, according to him, an enormous difference, and he expended a good deal of energy in working out an evolutionary theology. Some commentators have argued that there is no bridge between Peirce's methodologi-

---

[25] In this connection see C. S. Peirce's classic essay "How to Make Our Ideas Clear," available in numerous collections of his writings. For the differences between the pragmatisms of Peirce, James, and Dewey, see James Ward Smith, "Pragmatism, Realism and Positivism in the United States," *Mind*, LXI, N.S. no. 242, April 1952, pp. 190–208.

cal demand for "laboratory philosophy" and his constant flights of metaphysical imagination. In Peirce's own mind there was a very solid bridge, for he repeatedly argued that his theistic metaphysic made a considerable difference in experience. It is to that extent a testable hypothesis.

Peirce's writings, however, were virtually unknown, and his pragmatic rule became an important influence upon American thought only through the midwifery of William James. James expanded the rule into a philosophical theory which went much further than Peirce intended. For James, the claim that the meaning of a hypothesis consists in the sensible difference it would make is transformed into the claim that any concept means no more nor less than what is done with it. And this claim led him in turn to the conclusion that truth is nothing but a successful doing. Most of this far transcends, and in certain respects contradicts, Peirce's intentions, but when he came to religious questions James adopted a line which had marked affinities to Peirce.

There are two closely related aspects of James's approach to religion. On the one hand, he insisted that there are certain questions concerning which a man must make up his mind one way or the other—that there is no genuine compromise between believing or disbelieving. Some of these questions, and the existence of God is one of them, cannot be answered by appeal to direct evidence. With respect to such questions, therefore, James argues that pragmatic empiricism will recognize the necessity of transcending the limits of direct evidence. This first aspect of James's approach is contained in the doctrine of "the will to believe." [26] On the other hand, and this is unquestionably James's major contribution to the history of religious thought, he argued that indirect testing of the religious hypothesis could be secured by careful and detailed psychological studies. His monumental work, *The Varieties of Religious Experience*, is a comprehensive attempt to show that, although we cannot

[26] William James, *The Will to Believe*, London, 1897.

directly test the religious hypothesis, we can carefully document the difference it makes in the life history of the believer.[27] And James's claim is, of course, that it makes a difference for the better, a difference toward fuller and more integrated life. Pragmatism is still on the side of the angels.

What never occurred to James was that his way of justifying religious "over-beliefs" might be used by someone else as a basis of condemning them. The climax of pragmatism is reached in the writings of John Dewey. Approaching religion in the manner initiated by James, Dewey moves inexorably to the conclusion that there are basic commitments, alternative to those of theological metaphysics, which are more successful as integrative factors in human life. The object of Dewey's attack is metaphysics at large, but religious metaphysics in particular suffers heavy punishment in the process. One finds in Dewey's writings two different lines of attack which are not perhaps as incompatible as may on first sight appear. One line of attack is that metaphysical thinking *does* make a difference in human life—for the worse. It is said to block inquiry, to make our thinking dogmatic and stagnant, to close our minds to the exciting possibilities of increased application of the scientific method. The other line is that metaphysical thinking really makes no difference at all. It is froth which obscures the real forces making for difference. These real forces are always concrete events and purposes in time, and the method for understanding them is the experimental method of science. Dewey clearly wishes to make both of these attacks upon religious metaphysics. The former stresses the contingent fact that men who accept theories of a certain type are adversely affected in their intellectual life; the latter stresses the logical fact that those same theories may be entirely barren of predictive consequences.

Dewey's positive thesis is that effective and ennobling action must be divorced from the pretense of metaphysical

[27] William James, *The Varieties of Religious Experience*, London, 1902.

foundations. His professed goal is to divorce the meaning of the adjective "religious" from the traditional sense of the noun "religion." The intent of this divorce will be seen at once in the following quotations. First, the definition of "religious":

"Any activity pursued in behalf of an ideal end against obstacles and in spite of threats of personal loss because of conviction of its general and enduring value is religious in quality." [28]

What, then, of "religion"?

"If I have said anything about religions and religion that seems harsh, I have said those things because of a firm belief that the claim on the part of religions to possess a monopoly of ideals and of the supernatural means by which alone, it is alleged, they can be furthered, stands in the way of the realization of distinctively religious values inherent in natural experience. For that reason, if for no other, I should be sorry if any were misled by the frequency with which I have employed the adjective 'religious' to conceive of what I have said as a disguised apology for what have passed as religions. The opposition between religious values as I conceive them and religions is not to be bridged. Just because the release of these values is so important, their identification with the creeds and cults of religions must be dissolved." [29]

Of course, one cannot forever keep a noun and an adjective in a state of divorce. A new sense of the noun "religion" began to be coupled with Dewey's adjective. We began to speak of the religion of science and of the religion of communism.

Dewey's explicit warning that his words not be read as disguised apology for "what have passed as religions" has caused some wonderment that what he said was so cordially received by liberal Protestantism. For this reason it is im-

[28] John Dewey, *A Common Faith*, New Haven, 1934, p. 27.
[29] *ibid.*, pp. 27–28.

portant to notice how well the Religion of Humanity and the Social Gospel had prepared the way for him. Dewey's *A Common Faith,* published in 1934, did not say anything likely to shock a clergy already favorably disposed to the writings of Shailer Mathews and Walter Rauschenbusch. Long before pragmatism reached its destructive phase, Protestant theologians had themselves lost confidence in their capacity to support a special type of metaphysics or world view. Listen to Walter Rauschenbusch in *Christianity and the Social Crisis,* published in 1907:

"Since the second century, and especially since the great doctrinal controversies of the fourth century, dogma came to be regarded as the essence of Christianity. A man must assent to the true doctrine, and if he held that, the fundamental requirement of religion was fulfilled. But when dogmatic and speculative questions absorbed the religious interest, less of it was left for moral and social questions. . . .

"The mass of men are not able to comprehend speculation; but if they see their intellectual leaders vociferating about the incomprehensible, they will echo the catchwords with an ardor equal to their ignorance. In them the constant insistence on dogma induced an unthinking submission of intellect which dried up those powerful springs of free faith and will that had made primitive Christianity so productive. . . .

"A type of Christianity in which pagan superstition and Greek intellectualism had paralyzed the original social and ethical impetus, was in no condition to undertake the immense task of reorganizing social relations on a Christian basis. Even the personality of Jesus, which is the unceasing source of revolutionary moral power in Christianity, was almost completely obscured by the dogmatic Christ of the Church." [30]

There you have it—the metaphysical heritage of the Chris-

[30] Walter Rauschenbusch, *Christianity and the Social Crisis,* New York, 1919, pp. 178–179.

tian West shrugged off as "pagan superstition and Greek intellectualism"! What could Dewey say that would shock a clergy accustomed to this?

The Social Gospel, like the Religion of Humanity, played down the role of world view in Christianity and played up the role of moral and social teaching. Christ, it was said in effect, was no metaphysician. He was a social and moral reformer. The speculative systems of Christianity were the products of Platonism and of petty medieval pedants. Protestantism had always taught that the Catholic doctrine of intercession was contrary to the fundamental Christian spirit. The extremity of Protestantism now emerged; it could really go no further, for it was claimed that nothing so interceded between Christ and mankind as did the whole history of theologizing metaphysics. Liberal Protestantism sought boldly to de-theologize itself. The present writer, reared in devout Protestant surroundings, well remembers the most frequent precept of his early religious training in the 1920's and 1930's: "Religion consists in a life well led." Here is Shailer Mathews in 1933:

"It became increasingly clear that theology was a phase of a religious movement and that as such it could not be understood as if detached from the operations of social groups. A theology which serves as a basis and test for the integrity of a group life is very different from truths abstractly considered. It must be approached from the social and historical fact rather than from metaphysics." [31]

And as late as 1946 Willard L. Sperry, Dean of the Harvard Divinity School, commends the view that "Christianity is a quality of life rather than a fixed system of doctrine." [32]

Religion's retreat from metaphysics was evident not only in the Social Gospel, not only in the tendency to measure

[31] Shailer Mathews, "Theology as a Group Belief," quoted by Herbert W. Schneider, *Religion in 20th Century America*, Cambridge, Mass., 1952, p. 129.
[32] Willard L. Sperry, *Religion in America*, New York, 1946, p. 138. His reference is to Father Tyrrell.

one's degree of religious conviction by the amount of one's contributions to Community Chest and Foreign Missions, but also in the spreading tendency to psychologize one's approach to religion. William James's stirring of the waters produced a gushing stream of influence in twentieth-century America; the tidal wave of Freudian psychology did the rest. The clergy, still unconsciously smarting under its apparent metaphysical defeat at the hands of evolutionary science, sought refuge in the science of individual as well as of social psychology. James provided them with the battle cry that religious beliefs integrated personality; their reading of psychoanalysis now convinced them that for centuries religious practice had been based upon sound psychological principles. "Peace of Mind" became the rage. Protestant, Catholic, and Jew could join forces in the claim that, quite apart from wrangles over esoteric doctrinal differences, the psychological habits of religious conviction are healthy.

In these ways and in many others, the defenders of religion shifted their grounds of argument from those of traditional metaphysics to new grounds that were de-theologizing religion itself. Even the ecumenical movement among Protestant groups has often, though by no means always,[33] been achieved at the expense of loss in metaphysical tone. Differences in the content of belief, differences in the details of metaphysical doctrine, are minimized, while similarities in moral and ethical commitment and in therapeutic psychology are stressed. Where Presbyterians and Baptists unite, the metaphysical wrangle over determinism is not likely to be seriously discussed. Thus, the destructive tone of pragmatism and positivism was not new. And yet, if not new, the matter was put in such a way as to evoke at last a reaction. By the

---

[33] My impression is that during recent years there has been a marked increase in the metaphysical emphasis among proponents of the ecumenical movement. This would be difficult to document, as would also be, for example, the impression that such organizations as the YMCA have recently sensed the dangers inherent in thinking of Christianity as a wholly social or ethical movement.

mid-thirties one can trace the rise of counter currents. An increasing number of theologians, not only in America but abroad, began to sense that the core of the Christian religion is after all metaphysical, and that to abandon the metaphysics is to abandon the essence of Christianity. The philosophical movements made the danger clear. The new tendency in theology, variously [34] represented by Reinhold Niebuhr, Paul Tillich, Karl Barth, and Emil Brunner, is rooted in attack upon the claims of pragmatism and positivism; and, conversely, it is rooted in a reawakening of the metaphysical and theological tone of religion.

Thus far we have said nothing of the grounds of the positivist attack on religion. Once again the object of attack is metaphysics as such, but before we consider the attack in detail we must, in order to avoid a misunderstanding which is all too prevalent, note certain trends in the development of the positivist movement. It began with a destructive blast against all, or almost all, previous philosophy. The foundation of the movement was the work of a small group of men, the "Vienna Circle," all of whom were deeply influenced by revolutionary developments in the sciences of mathematics and physics. The basis of their argument was the claim that if one properly understands the method of science he will see that there are two and only two sets of precise conditions, one or the other of which must be met by any proposition which purports to mean anything at all. This argument, used as a formidable bludgeon, sets the tone of the first or *enfant terrible* stage of positivism. But the members of the Vienna Circle themselves changed their minds with remarkable rapidity as time went on, and before long the single-mindedness which marked the opening or destructive phase of the move-

[34] I stress the word "variously." The theologians here listed represent very different approaches, and in some cases wage violent intellectual warfare with each other. But all represent the trend I am discussing. Perhaps the clearest example is Tillich, and I have heard those who still disapprove of too much metaphysics in Protestantism proclaim that Tillich is not "really" a Christian!

ment was largely lost. At the present time there are so many different schools of thought which have stemmed from this origin that the usefulness of the word "positivism" has almost reached the zero point. One sometimes feels that the word is now used only as a term of opprobrium by those who dislike, without fully understanding, the philosophical tendencies by which they are surrounded. In any event, the following account of the "positivist" attack upon metaphysics is intended as a summary of the argument of the *enfant terrible* stage.[35] It was very wicked indeed; and most so-called "positivists" have since retreated from it in one way or another. While wicked, however, it was a healthy shock, and it probably produced more genuine cogitation on the part of twentieth-century philosophers than any other single argument.

It will be noticed that pragmatism became anti-metaphysical at a late stage in its development, while positivism began with an attack on metaphysics. In its attitude toward religion, pragmatism during its early stages was motivated by friendly intentions; only gradually did its capacity to destroy become evident. Positivism, on the other hand, while opening with a destructive bellow, has shown an increasing tendency to make peace. In its more recent stages of development it has waved the olive branch not only at metaphysics in general but at religious mysticism in particular. Philosophical movements often develop in unanticipated directions. In the present instance, however, the interesting historical accident is that the late destructive phase of pragmatism and the early destructive phase of positivism came at roughly the same time. The time was the period of the 1920's and 1930's.

So much by way of historical comment. What, then, was the ground of the early positivist attack? In essence, the argument hinged on a logically revamped version of prin-

---

[35] The most readable statement of the *enfant terrible* line of argument is A. J. Ayer, *Language, Truth and Logic*, London, 1936, especially Chapter VI.

ciples enunciated by David Hume in the eighteenth century. The positivists, like Hume, were trying to take the method of science seriously, and, like him, they concluded that there are two and only two ways in which we can seriously claim that what we say has clear cognitive meaning. On the one hand, we may appeal to the logical criteria of consistency (ultimately to the principle of non-contradiction); on the other hand, we may appeal to evidence as a basis for justifying our predictions as to matters of fact. Hume had suggested that there is a strict "either-or" here: that, on the one hand, no matter of fact can be established by appeal to logical principles alone; that, on the other hand, the appeal to logical principle is entirely independent of what matters of fact may be. Hume also insisted that theoretical certainty is always merely a matter of logical inevitability, and that matters of fact are never certain. No prediction, no description, nothing which passes as "knowledge of matters of fact" is more than a guess based upon whatever degree of probability our acquaintance with available evidence warrants.[36]

The early positivists simply tightened up Hume's thesis. Perhaps the strongest weapon at their disposal was the widely heralded demonstration early in the century that all mathematics is strictly deducible from a small set of primitive logical axioms—that, therefore, mathematics (pure mathematics as distinct from applied mathematics) is true no matter what the facts may be.[37] A rigid line (first suggested by

[36] This paragraph states succinctly the central thesis in Hume, the force of which was missed by most of his contemporaries, and certainly by all the Americans who saw fit to refer to him. Kant, of course, saw the point, and his entire philosophy rests upon his attempt to answer Hume. Kant insisted that Hume's two pigeonholes were not enough—even for science.

[37] It would be difficult to overestimate the influence on philosophy in the twentieth century of A. N. Whitehead and Bertrand Russell, *Principia Mathematica*, 3 vols., Cambridge, Eng., 1910–1913. The successful deduction of mathematics from a small set of primitive logical axioms was the most important single factor in the widespread revolt from the concept of the "synthetic a priori" on which so much previous philosophy had depended. Starting with Kant, mathematical propositions had been taken as the model of the synthetic a priori. The view that all of mathematics is analytic destroyed this model at one blow.

Leibniz in the seventeenth century) between logical truth and empirical truth was the foundation of the positivist argument. Consider any statement. If it is true by logical principles alone, it will be true no matter what the facts are. The alternative is that its truth (or falsity) will depend upon what the facts are found to be. In the latter case the statement is no more nor less than a hypothesis, the truth of which will depend upon contingent happenings in the course of events. In the former case its truth is a matter of logic—that is to say, highly rigorous but purely formal.

The bludgeon of this argument was formidable. It was comparatively easy to show that a great deal of what we say does not conform to either of the models set up. Consider one of the favorite examples of this: Shelley's line, "Life like a dome of many colored glass stains the white radiance of eternity." Now, clearly, no amount of careful logic will demonstrate that such a sentence is true, no matter what the facts may be. It is not a theorem in an axiomatic system containing only logical premises. Is it, then, a hypothesis for which one can set up crucial experiments? Clearly, we are told, it is not; surely nothing could *happen* that would establish that what is here said is false. Therefore, the argument continues, what is here said is in no strict sense *either* true *or* false. And that means that, whatever emotional response it may evoke, it does not in the strict sense say anything at all. This too simple example may stand as a model of the treatment accorded virtually all of traditional metaphysics by the early destructive phase of positivism. The inferences for religious metaphysics are clear.

Thus positivists, like pragmatists, were saying during the thirties that the propositions of religious metaphysics are, from a cognitive standpoint, nonsense. Both groups, in their own way, based this conclusion upon inferences drawn from careful study of the methodology of science. The agreement goes further than this, for both groups were led to classify religious talk under the heading of the emotive and the irrational. The positivists tended to classify it as poetry, the pragmatists as a biological organism's striving for integration. There was one very important difference. The positivists, in their precise way insisting that science is itself the essence of rationality and of cognitive objectivity, drew a sharp line between science on the one hand and the poetic vagaries of religion on the other. The pragmatists, however, tended to regard science itself as mere behavior on the part of biological organisms. Thus in pragmatism the line between science and religion is drawn at another point, and less precisely. Science is striving that works, while religion in the traditional sense is striving that thwarts and obstructs.

Were we to stop here, with the period between the two world wars, we would have to say that the American mind had gone the full distance. It seemed finally and irrevocably to have discarded its "cosmic sense." One side of the coin was a naïve faith in the capacity of science and of practical ingenuity to solve all of our problems and to sell our way of life to the rest of the world. The other side of the coin was an almost total loss of faith in cosmic ideas. We not only refused to follow in the footsteps of our predecessors in offering cosmic and Christian justification of our way of life; we even prided ourselves on our refusal. It was a conscious and almost defiant mood manifestly evident in, of all places, the Protestant pulpits themselves. Then came the depression and a second world war.

V

Recovery from Disillusion

The disillusion of the 1920's is often attributed to World War I and to Prohibition. I cannot but feel that this is a superficial reading of the period. It seems to me little short of nonsense to attribute the lawlessness of the country to Prohibition. Prohibition merely provided an area in which the lawless spirit could express itself; it was a superficial rather than a fundamental cause of the disease of the times. As for the First World War, it is true that we went into it fired with the enthusiasm and the idealism of Woodrow Wilson's ringing speech of April 2, 1917; and it is true that by the war's end little or none of that enthusiasm and idealism remained. On the other hand, we entered the Second World War fired with the idealism of Franklin Roosevelt's four freedoms, and we have since lived to face a deterioration of America's position throughout the world; but we are *not* now disillusioned in the same sense as were the 1920's. Our cosmic concern is on the increase rather than on the wane. Our religion and our art are flourishing; the contrast with the twenties could hardly be more extreme. Why is this?

No account of the contrast between the two postwar periods, the 1920's and the 1950's, will be complete which fails to emphasize the importance of our different attitudes toward science. War stimulates advance in both theoretical and applied science, and World War I produced just enough awareness of the possibilities of scientific advance to generate unprecedented optimism. The economic optimism of the Coolidge era was a by-product of this temper. The nation's idols were Thomas Edison, Henry Ford, and Charles Lindbergh. One of the most marked features of the era was the disillusionment of the artist; this went hand in hand with our religious and metaphysical nonchalance. Where there courses abroad a spirit that practical science can solve all problems, neither the artist nor the preacher will sense that he has an important role to fulfill. The nation was on a rampage of this-worldly self-confidence. The first sobering blow was the great depression and the collapse of the Coolidge state of mind. Then came World War II, which caused once more a tremendous advance in science. Only, this time the advance was literally *too* much. Hiroshima instilled not confidence in science but the first national shudder of terror. Science became overnight a source not of national self-confidence but of sober stocktaking and dread. The real source of our disillusionment with art and religion after World War I was our optimism that science could solve all human problems. The real source of the revival of art and religion after World War II has been a disillusionment with science which began with the depression and culminated at Hiroshima. We most assuredly do not respect science less, but we are far less naïve about its relation to human values.

To the extent that philosophy reflects this general temper, both pragmatism and positivism have given way. Dewey's writings no longer reflect the national temper.[38] The "pragmatic" appeal, the present version of the claim that we must look to what works in the practical context, is increasingly associated with the *limits* of science rather than with science-*worship*.[39] And positivism, as I have suggested, has variously matured into far less destructive forms. Virtually no one now seriously maintains that science alone is going to solve all our problems.

One may be tempted to conclude without further ado that a thorough and perceptive grasp of the method of science and its limitations will no longer produce disillusionment with religion, but may indeed lend support to it. Such a conclusion has already been advocated by several best-sellers. Unfortunately, many proponents of religion who argue in this fashion paint with brush strokes far too sweeping on a canvas far too broad. To put the matter bluntly, they are plunging headlong back into the same old superficial mode of adaptation of which

[38] One of the most noticeable signs of Dewey's loss of influence upon the popular American mind is the ill favor in which "progressive education" is increasingly being held.

[39] See, for example, Willard van Orman Quine's constant appeal in his more recent writings to the "pragmatic" as the only escape from certain extremely puzzling logical and theoretical difficulties. But Quine always contrasts the pragmatic escape and the scientific solution, as is perhaps sufficiently evident in the following typical passage: "Each man is given a scientific heritage plus a continuing barrage of sensory stimulation; and the considerations which guide him in warping his scientific heritage to fit his continuing sensory promptings are, where rational, pragmatic." This is the concluding sentence of "Two Dogmas of Empiricism" in *From a Logical Point of View*, Cambridge, Mass., 1953, p. 46.

we have found previous centuries so full. But what must be achieved is detailed understanding of precisely those points at which destructive pragmatism and positivism went wrong. To a large extent the foundations of both of those movements were sound, and their demand that the method of science be respected is not to be shrugged away. The defender of religion cannot proceed as though nothing has been learned since 1900. The burden is on him to show that he has kept abreast of these movements and can say in detail what went wrong. This is the present guise of the demand that real rather than superficial justice be done to the method of science.

Let us consider first the demands of positivism. It is now generally conceded that it is a mistake to hold that there are two, and only two, ways of talking sense. Most of the important things we need to say fail, like Shelley's line, to satisfy the rigorous criteria either of logically demonstrable theorems or of strictly empirical hypotheses. And if this is so, it follows that a great deal more work needs to be done by way of examining our decision procedures where these rigorous criteria are inapplicable. It is a mistake of the most serious kind to suppose that the failure of early positivism provides a carte blanche for the babblers of nonsense. The positivist work of that period has in no sense been undermined; the careful description of the difference between logical and empirical truth, and the rigorous demands made upon those who claim they are enunciating either, still stand. It does not follow from the fact that we must also talk in other ways, that any and all irresponsible talk becomes, by the waving of some magic wand, respectable. In theology, as elsewhere, the burden inherited from our bout with positivism is this: we must state with the utmost care the rules governing our decision procedures, and this is most urgently true at just those points where we disclaim the two sets of rules which early positivism set up as the two exclusive models.

We hear much at the present time of "Christian Existentialism." The label is not easy to pin down, and it is always difficult to pass judgment upon new and current trends. But the so-called "Christian Existentialists" seem to me, at times, to be playing with fire. They rightly see that the models of early positivism will not do. They rightly see that we must constantly *decide* in the absence of proof either deductive or inductive. But they make the mistake of interpreting this as a carte blanche for irrationality. Notice that we concede the game to the early positivists if we concede that we are being "rational" only to the extent that we function either as mathematical logicans or as inductive engineers. It is all very well to insist on decision in the absence of proof; but this makes it only the more important to formulate alternative rules governing rational or reasonable decision. The philosophical defense of religion cannot be simply negative. It is not enough to say what sort of thing religious talk is not. It is not enough to say that it is like poetry, or that it is a form of committing oneself, where what is meant is that poetry and committing oneself do *not* satisfy the rigorous demands entailed in the two standard ways of "proving." We need also to provide a detailed positive account of the standards to which a reasonable man will appeal in such cases. If religion is like poetry, the question to be asked is: what are to be our standards of judgment when dealing with poetry? And, of course, religion is not all poetry. The theologian cannot therefore simply take refuge behind the poet's apron. He has a large and difficult task to perform if he is to earn our respect.

A closely related danger in recent theology lies in the marked increase of the appeal to paradox. This is a return to Hegelianism which cannot be countenanced by the philosopher. The appeal to paradox solves nothing.[40] A genuine

[40] After reading Daniel Williams' article in the present volume, I contemplated altering this remark. Williams, on pp. 471 and 494, treats in a more favorable tone the theological appeal to the concept of paradox. I feel, however, that I must stick by my philosophical guns. We philosophers may very well be wrong, but nothing short of frank and open debate is going to convince us.

paradox involves flat contradiction, and, as Kant (who was a far more sensible philosopher than Hegel) rightly saw, if we find ourselves saying both of two genuinely contradictory propositions, something is wrong. Whatever mistakes the early positivists may have made about the limitations of their models, they were certainly sound in their logic. They were right in showing that where an axiomatic system implies a contradiction, it is logically unsound. It is high time the theologians faced this fact. It may well be that much of their appeal to paradox is rooted in a vague and imprecise use of the word "paradox"; but let them not claim this is a virtue. Here as elsewhere the crying need is for methodological precision. We are increasingly aware that science itself cannot proceed without basic commitments, basic axioms, and basic procedural principles; and the same is true of theology. In theology, as in science, the key to rational self-respect is clarity and precision in stating the rules which govern debate and decision procedure.

If these are the problems inherited from positivism, a closely related problem is inherited from pragmatism. It arises from a question which is embedded in the shift from James to Dewey. James argued that Christian cosmic beliefs work; Dewey argued that down-to-earth unmetaphysical naturalistic beliefs work better. In one sense the present American temper constitutes an endorsement of James, for we hear on all sides the plea for a return to cosmic sense. There is surely an increase of awareness that Dewey's ultra-naturalistic practicalism has in fact not worked very well. More and more, the clear heads in the nation are proclaiming the need for recommitment on ultimate issues. We are facing in Russia, in the Near East, and in the Far East, cultures which are extraordinarily vocal in their expression of cosmic perspective. We know that we disagree, that our traditions are rooted in a different way of viewing things; but we find that in our preoccupation with the practical we have lost our capacity to defend cosmic principle. Hence James's claim that cosmic commitments "work" best is winning out. Unfortunately, that is only the beginning of the matter. The question now is, what *do* we stand for? Do we still know; and when we are pushed to the wall, do we have any rigorous standards of judgment to which we can appeal in the attempt to convince others that we are right?

It need hardly be said that these are difficult questions, and when we tackle them we must not be glib or superficial. The troublesome thing about many current defenses of the religious perspective is that, like James's, they are so formulated that Dewey's inferences could still be drawn from them. Our defense of a cosmic stand must be frankly cosmic. Exclusive concern, for example, with the support of empirical psychology is not enough. The usual form in which one encounters the "peace of mind" argument or the "guide to positive living" argument leads one to ask: why does one need anything more than good sound untheological psychology? The theologians sometimes manifest delight in their ability to assimilate certain fundamental teachings of psychoanalysis. But they go at times so far that one loses the cosmic religious sense. Their enthusiastic talk would at times imply that a savage suddenly but thoroughly trained in the techniques of psychoanalysis would, without ever having heard of the Bible or of Jesus Christ, be well on the road to being a Christian. This simply will not do. The defense of religious belief must be direct, not peripheral. Psychology is not a substitute for theology. If James's line is to be guarded against Dewey's inference, the cosmic content of religious belief must be soberly and clearly defined, and the procedures used in the decisions governing our argument must be brought out into the open. If there is to be an end to the hostility which has recently characterized the relations between theology and philosophy, there must be a beginning of agreement as to matters of careful methodology. The key to avoiding superficiality is precision and care concerning method. Fortunately, if only we are bold enough to try, the time is ripe for this.

TRADITION AND EXPERIENCE
IN AMERICAN THEOLOGY

DANIEL D. WILLIAMS

T HEOLOGY is responsible for the interpretation of the
faith of a religious community. It will hardly be
disputed that there is an interaction between the national history and culture and the ferment of theological
ideas. The nature of this relationship, however, is complex.
The Christian community transcends national boundaries.
Theology has its roots in the Scripture and tradition of this
supranational community. The work of Biblical criticism, of
church history, of systematic theology goes on in the wider
context of the experience of the church. The problems and
the contributions of theological work may have no special
relationship to national peculiarities.

At the same time it is clear that the history of Christian
thought shows a continual encounter between the Christian
faith and the thought and life of the cultures in which the
church exists. The rise of empires and nations has formed
not only the political but also much of the spiritual context
in which the Christian faith has been stated. While there is,
therefore, no American theology, there is a theological development peculiar to the American experience. The situation
of the church in the United States has been different from
every other in Christian history. Here all the Christian
communions, and every other religious faith and group, have
existed side by side, and none has been either favored or
encumbered by religious establishment except for the New
England experiment with theocracy and the few Southern
Anglican establishments which survived into the early national period. This status of the church in the new nation,
and the growth of the American consciousness with its
democratic faith, have provided a new set of problems for
theology. Many aspects of this new experience of the church

443

have left distinctive marks on much American theology, and for that matter upon all American religious thought.

Sydney Ahlstrom's survey of the theological history, with its variety of trends and schools, should put us on guard concerning the danger of generalizations on our theme. There is further warning in the fact that interpreters of American Christianity have taken sharply different points of view concerning its spirit and direction. European critics have looked for what they regard as distinctively American themes in American theology. The familiar characteristics of optimism, activism, and democratic individualism are held to be determinative for much American theology, especially that of liberal Protestantism and its social gospel. Often this leads to a theological critique which holds that these liberal tendencies, derived from the Enlightenment and reinforced by the American type of democracy, have dissipated the foundations of Christian faith.[1]

In contrast to this criticism one could adopt a quite different perspective and stress the tenacity of all the confessional traditions in the American scene. Many Lutheran groups, Baptists, Episcopalians, and, of course, the Roman Catholic Church have maintained traditional doctrinal positions in the face of all the threats and enticements of modern culture.

Clearly theologians have reacted in a variety of ways to the American experience. The theological spectrum runs from the Calvinism of Jonathan Edwards at one end to the transcendentalism of Ralph Waldo Emerson at the other, with many mediators such as William Ellery Channing, Theodore Parker, Horace Bushnell, and contemporary neo-evangelicals in between. The spectrum includes the broad strain of Biblical evangelical piety which underlies popular fundamentalism and the intellectualistic Biblicism of J. Gresham Machen. It includes the ethical modernism of Harry Emerson

[1] See George Hammar, *Christian Realism in Contemporary American Theology*, Uppsala, Sweden, 1940.

Fosdick, which reflects also this Protestant piety. If we explain the social gospel and its classic interpreter, Walter Rauschenbusch, by reference to American problems, we must also seek what is distinctively American in the work of Reinhold Niebuhr, who began his work within liberal Protestant theology but is the outstanding critic of some of its positions.

Taking the risk of generalization, I shall assert that there has been a distinguishing characteristic of American theology, but it is not found in the traits usually assigned to it. This common element does not consist in agreement upon particular doctrines, but in a way of thinking about the relation of doctrine to the religious life and to the life of the church. American theologians who take part in ecumenical discussions not infrequently will be heard to express a sense of common understanding in the face of the theological styles characteristic of churches in other nations. The reason is that the Americans are likely to have a distinctive sense of theological method. When we say this, we use the term "method" in a broad sense. It includes the theologian's view of his materials and the criteria of theological judgment. It includes his way of understanding how experience enters into the development and criticism of theological categories. Theological method is significantly determined by the kind of freedom the theologian believes he has in dealing with the tradition and with new experience. The American theologian has tended to be oriented not so much to a confessional position as to a variety of positions, and to a search for an experiential unity beneath formal differences.

Three aspects of this distinctive orientation can be designated with the terms "empiricism," "pluralism," and "catholicity." In the American situation there is generally an expectancy of theological revision. There is an emphasis upon perceiving the relation between dogma and concrete experience, and a concern to exhibit the connection between Christian faith and an intelligible world view, often by philosophical means. There has been a capacity to respond to new impulses from movements in European theology and to give them usually a distinctive American stamp.

We may agree that there is a certain tendency to extremism in American theology. When confessional rigidity is found, it is likely to be very rigid, perhaps in part in defense against the fluidity in the open stream of religious ideas. When radical modernizing tendencies appear, they often move toward a total theological reconstruction in the light of a new insight. While these extremes are significant for recognizing certain underlying characteristics because they exaggerate them, we ought not to give too much attention to the extreme positions because this would be to miss the more important structural characteristics of American religious thought.

This analysis derives primarily from an examination of the Protestant theologies in the American scene. An adequate interpretation of Roman Catholic and Jewish theology in this context would require interpreters who stand within those viewpoints. No doubt important qualifications of positions here taken would appear, but all American religious groups have had to come to terms with the vitalities and structures of American society, and there are definite parallels in the Roman Catholic and Jewish theologies for the trends here described in the Protestant tradition. There are increasing prospects in mid-twentieth century for a more vigorous theological conversation between the major faiths.

We do not forget that American Christianity is largely the result of the deposit of European traditions in this country. American theologians have studied in the theological and philosophical schools all over the world. Winds of doctrine arising on the European continent and in Britain, and now in Asia, blow across the American intellectual frontiers. Eastern Orthodox theologies are beginning to be communicated in the American scene. Many of the distinguished leaders of American theological thought have come from other countries and have made their major contributions in America. In some sense what is peculiarly "American" is just this experience of being in the situation where every tradition has its open hearing. This has had its effect on the interpretation of the Christian faith which stands above all national and parochial forms and yet is involved in them.

It remains by way of introduction to say only that this characterization of American theology is an essay in understanding, not a defense of any position. That would be another task entirely.

I. Empiricism in American Theology

"Experience" is a protean word. All theology has roots in experience which gives material for reflection, a source of insight, and an object of ultimate reference for religious dogma, since the faith must be shown to be relevant to what men in a given culture think and feel.

In using the term "empiricism" to point to this important strand in American theology, we use the word as referring to a broad attitude toward experience, rather than as confined to the philosophical doctrine of knowledge, though we must not ignore the influence of the philosophical empiricisms on American theological thought. The significance of "empiricism" here lies both in its reference to a certain attitude toward the place of experience in attaining theological truth, and also to the distinctive elements in what Americans take to be the content of experience. Even in technical American philosophy and theology the term "experience" has a broad connotation. It is not restricted to sense data. It embraces the concreteness of human deeds and feelings. George Santayana's comment on this element in the American consciousness is pertinent:

"The American is wonderfully alive, and his vitality not having found a suitable outlet, makes him appear agitated on the surface; he is always letting off an unnecessarily loud blast of incidental steam. Yet his vitality is not superficial; it is inwardly prompted, and as sensitive and quick as a magnetic needle. He is inquisitive, and ready with an answer to any question that he may put to himself of his own accord; but if you try to pour instruction into him on matters that do not touch his own spontaneous life, he shows the most extraordinary powers of resistance and oblivescence; so that he is often remarkably expert in some directions and surprisingly obtuse in others. He seems to bear lightly the sorrowful burden of human knowledge. In a word, he is young."[2]

Santayana's phrase "his own spontaneous life" gives the clue to the common thread which runs through the diverse theologies of Edwards and Emerson, through the pietists for whom "experience" means the event of regeneration, and through the liberals for whom it may mean the process of moral decision and action. Santayana does stress "optimism," but while this is related to many aspects of the content of the American experience, it is not as decisive as many interpreters have held. Experience can have many contents.

We can distinguish five principal aspects of the incorporation of experience into the method and content of Christian theology as developed by American theologians. These are, first, the treatment of religious experience as a source of knowledge of God; second, the use of religious experience as the sign of vitality in religious faith; third, the emphasis on experience as the testing ground for moral character and for the achievement of moral goals; fourth, the viewing of experience as the field for cooperation among people of differing doctrinal persuasions; and, finally, the modernist use of present experience for criticism and interpretation of traditional doctrines and practices. After discussing the appearance of these themes in American theology we shall

[2] George Santayana, *Character and Opinion in the United States*, New York, 1956, pp. 110–111.

describe the empirical theology in which the interpretation of experience has been made the foundation of theological method.

A. Experience and Knowledge of God. Most of these aspects of the appeal to experience can be documented in the commanding figure of Jonathan Edwards. His lifelong search to bring Scripture, nature, and rational intelligibility into one structure can be traced through his journal. The underlying principle is well summarized by Perry Miller as "finding in things an intelligibility not transcending them but immanent in them." [3] When Edwards searched in nature for typological examples of divine truths he felt no danger of abandoning his Biblical faith to a humanistic reflection on the divine purpose. The disclosure of that purpose in Scripture has its analogues and confirmation in those traces of the divine will and plan which the mind, illumined by faith and grace, can discern in the order of nature and in the human heart. This is how all the Puritans could justify their turning to philosophy, not as a rival to faith, but as its exemplification. Thus Edwards' treatise on the freedom of the will was a theological defense of Calvinist doctrine couched largely in philosophical terms.[4] Of course there is nothing peculiarly American in this assertion of the capacity of reason to express the structures of religious faith. Such a synthesis of mysticism and rationalism is characteristic of Christian Platonism and Augustinianism which have affirmed the fusing of faith and reason in the white heat of divine illumination. But this tradition has found distinctive materials and emphases in the American scene.

First, there is the feeling for nature itself as an earnest of the divine faithfulness and an expression of the divine beauty. Edwards' love for the intricacy and order of nature is unflagging:

[3] Jonathan Edwards, *Images or Shadows of Divine Things*, ed. Perry Miller, New Haven, 1948, p. 29.
[4] Jonathan Edwards, *Freedom of the Will*, ed. Paul Ramsey, New Haven, 1957, especially Part IV, section 13.

"We can conceive of nothing more beautiful of an external kind than the beauties of nature here, especially the beauty of the more animated parts of this world. We never could have conceived of these if we had not seen them; and now we can think of nothing beyond them; and therefore the highest beauties of art consist in imitation of them." [5]

Alongside this we may put the statement of Horace Bushnell, who stands in between Edwards and the later liberal theology:

"It is not even supposable that organic natures, injured and disordered, as we have seen that human bodies are by sin, should propagate their life in a progeny unmarred and perfect. If we speak of sin as action, their children may be innocent, and so far may reveal the loveliness of innocence; still the crystalline order is broken; the passions, tempers, appetites are not in the proportion of harmony and reason, the balance of original health is gone by anticipation, and a distempered action is begun, whose affinities are with evil rather than with good." [6]

In what Bushnell says of "the crystalline order" and the "balance of original health" one sees his faith in an essentially good human nature, always capable of being realized, yet obstructed by sin.

Clearly "nature" includes "human nature" in typical American usage. It certainly is not to be opposed to the distinctively human, though one cannot say that the characteristic American feeling for nature stresses only the continuity of man with his physical environment. Emerson and the Transcendentalists, for example, are too good idealists to affirm any simple reconciliation between man and the order of physical causes and laws. The American experience includes far too much of the battle with an intractable wilderness and the stubborn effort to extract from nature her wealth to picture

[5] Quoted from Edwards, "Miscellanies" in Miller, ed., p. 35.
[6] Horace Bushnell, *Nature and the Supernatural*, New York, 1858, pp. 177–178.

nature as the simple and yielding companion of man. It has been rather the experience of man set in a larger environment which poses him problems while offering resources for their solution. Nature does yield in part to man's cooperation, and human nature is plastic to the forces which have produced man. Thus, to see human nature and physical nature in a constant interplay of challenge and adjustment, of accommodation and response, is congenial to the kind of experience Americans have had, and it has helped to shape the theological vision of the relation of nature and its Creator. As Edwards again comments:

"Man is made with his feet on the earth and with his posture erect and countenance toward heaven, signifying that he was made to have heaven in his eyes, and the earth under his foot." [7]

Interest in the varieties of religious experience, so important to later empirical theology, appears also in Edwards. For him, of course, there are no degrees of status under the judgment of God. All share in the Fall and live in bondage until the gracious act of God renews the heart and will. Yet Edwards experienced the variety of responses to his own preaching. He saw the passion, unpredictability, and eccentricity of religious emotion. In his *Treatise Concerning Religious Affections* he never surrenders the conviction that the work of grace is always and essentially the same; but he recognizes the multiplicity of possible human responses to the divine prompting, and the extraordinary manifestations of feelings which may attend the movement of the Holy Spirit. From Edwards' *Treatise* to William James's Gifford Lectures on *The Varieties of Religious Experience* is not a very long step. James, too, respects the empirical diversity of religious emotions, and is unwilling to insist on one type of spiritual experience as normative. This conviction that genuine religion may be variously expressed has come to the aid of the

[7] Edwards, *Images or Shadows of Divine Things,* p. 88.

American attempt to conceive of a community bound together by the religious spirit in spite of doctrinal divisions.

It is Edwards, also, who makes clear that a positive attitude toward the revelation of the divine in nature need not involve a sentimental obscuring of the dark side of the creation:

"This world is all over dirty. Everywhere it is covered with that which tends to defile the feet of the traveller. Our streets are dirty and muddy, intimating that the world is full of that which tends to defy the soul, that worldly objects and worldly concerns and worldly company tend to pollute us." [8]

There are romantic overtones in Horace Bushnell's musing on the grand story of evolution; yet he shows the triumph of the evangelical spirit over a simple deism:

"This whole tossing, rending, recomposing process, that we call geology, symbolizes evidently, as in the highest reason it should, the grand spiritual catastrophe, and Christian new-creation of man . . . What we see is the beginning conversing with the end, and Eternal Forethought reaching across the tottering mountains and boiling seas. . . . and all the long eras of desolation, and refitted bloom and beauty, represented in the registers of the world, are but the epic in stone, of man's great history before the time." [9]

This attempt to read the outlines of the drama of salvation in the face of nature by no means entails for Bushnell the view that experience offers an ultimate criterion of judgment over the special revelation of Scripture. Some theologians, Americans among them, have taken that position, but others have not. What Puritans and the nineteenth-century evangelicals did share with later immanentists and liberals was the conviction that the face of nature carefully surveyed

[8] *ibid.*, p. 94.
[9] Bushnell, p. 206.

would yield outlines of the divine purpose and a knowledge of the divine presence.

The story of how the categories of Edwardsean Calvinism hardened into stereotypes imposed with pathological rigidity upon the surging vitalities of American culture has often been told.[10] Edwards himself is not exempt from responsibility for a distortion of the relation of the divine anger to the divine mercy. The categories of original sin, election, and regeneration which had been used to interpret the convictions of the Protestant Reformation came to be formulated without a sense of their flexibility in application to life. They became an abstract set of symbols about which violent intellectual battles were fought, but which really needed to be reinterpreted in order that their relevance to the experience of a new civilization could be shown. Their truth became obscured in the measure that their conformation to experience was lost from sight.

B. Experience as the Principle of Vital Religion. A second aspect of the significance of "experience" in American theology stems from the pietistic strand in American Christianity, which overlaps with the Puritan tradition while it has its distinctive sources in European pietism and the revivalism of the frontier. When the term "religious experience" is used in American theology, it generally connotes, implicitly if not explicitly, the kind of experience through which men believe they are made new through the grace of God. Conversion and regeneration were the heart of vital religion for both Puritan and sectarian pietists. Therefore, "religious experience" does not suggest that which is purely subjective, incommunicable, and peculiar to the individual as in a later individualistic era it has sometimes done. In the religion of

[10] Frank H. Foster, *A Genetic History of the New England Theology*, Chicago, 1907; Joseph Haroutunian, *Piety versus Moralism*, New York, 1932; Shelton Smith, *Changing Conceptions of Original Sin*, New York, 1955.

pietism "experience" means that wrestling with God which all men must go through on their way to salvation. It is, therefore, communicable through faithful witness. It is shared in the communities of personal faith and common worship which the Holy Spirit creates.

It was inevitable that pietists would discover in the camp meetings, and amid the clash of rival sectarian doctrines, that the emotional patterns of the conversion experience could become the liturgy and sacrament of the religious fellowship. The revival, the hymns, the preaching for decision, and the excitement of the converting work of the Spirit, were the very enactment of the drama of salvation. When theologians of the later nineteenth century began to work out a theological method in which Christian experience was taken as the ultimate criterion of truth they could draw upon the materials provided by the pietistic faith.

As a major stimulus and resource for a theology of experience in the nineteenth century there came from Germany the influence of F. D. E. Schleiermacher. Schleiermacher combined his Moravian piety with the intellectual and emotional sophistication of German romanticism. His influence in America, partly mediated through the influence of Samuel Taylor Coleridge, is of especial importance in the development of the systematic appeal to experience. The Congregationalist Lewis French Stearns' lectures in 1890, *The Evidence of Christian Experience*, and the Baptist theologian William Newton Clarke's *An Outline of Christian Theology* in 1894 are prime examples of theological construction rooted in pietistic experience and seeking a Christian apologetic for the new intellectual situation.[11]

What must be kept in mind in understanding American theology is that when the religious empiricists of the late nineteenth and early twentieth centuries tried to relate the

[11] Lewis French Stearns, *The Evidence of Christian Experience*, New York, 1890. William Newton Clarke, *An Outline of Christian Theology*, Cambridge, Mass., 1894.

knowledge of God to scientific ways of knowing by giving a broader philosophical interpretation of the role of experience in knowledge, most of them had the overtones of the evangelical spirit in their religious consciousness. Men find in their experience, in part at least, what history and tradition have sensitized them to expect therein.

C. EXPERIENCE AS MORAL TESTING GROUND FOR FAITH. It is true that the oft-remarked optimism of American culture has shaped and reinforced the content of the appeal to experience. There has always been a task at hand in the construction of the future. Hence personal morality and social action are a proving ground for religious and ethical convictions. Even Puritans like Jonathan Edwards and Samuel Hopkins, who insisted that the work of grace in the human heart was a miracle beyond any direct observation, were concerned to assert that faith would prove itself by its fruits. As the "New Light" Calvinists became more and more involved in the revivalism of the nineteenth century, this moralistic emphasis increased. The Christian was admonished to display the accepted pattern of moral behavior in order to "prove" his membership in the elect.[12] One factor which undoubtedly encouraged orthodox Christians to make more of this stress was the freedom with which deists and free thinkers reduced the core of religion to a few basic beliefs and the practical exhibition of moral qualities. Is not practical, decent, humane behavior enough? Meeting this challenge, apologists for Christianity could not afford to leave out the demand for moral fruits of faith and to try to show that evangelical piety was the source of lasting moral loyalty.

An instance of this need is found in the social gospel movement which represented a prophetic witness against a piety grown formal and protected behind the social and economic *status quo*. But the social gospel had to make its appeal effective by interpreting the areas of social injustice and

[12] E. Porter, *Letters on the Religious Revivals Which Prevailed about the Beginning of the Present Century*, Boston, 1858.

conflict in terms which made positive contact with evangelical piety. Such terms as "social sin" and the "redemption of society" connected the efforts of social reform with the categories of Christian experience. The social gospel can be understood as seeking to correct an irrelevant piety by upholding the necessity of proving the validity of Christian conviction through the search for social justice. It is clear that much of the power of Walter Rauschenbusch's writing lay in his ability to interpret the categories of sin and grace in relation to social issues.[13]

D. EXPERIENCE AS AN AID TO UNITY AMID RELIGIOUS DIVERSITY. The diversity of the Christian communions and of religious faiths in the American scene has been extremely important in reinforcing the appeal to experience both as a sign of religious community and as a systematic theological principle. Where men must enter into some kind of cooperation and understanding amid doctrinal diversity, an appeal to a common experience underlying differing symbols may be the only possible means for securing a basis for understanding. It also leads to the creation of new symbols which are endowed with the power of supporting social unity. "Brotherhood," "our Father's God, author of liberty," "democracy," became symbolic concepts, invested with religious and moral feeling, which transcend the differences between traditional faiths. We can see how American evangelicalism has been torn between the need to proclaim a positive core of doctrine, and the need to make the appeal for religious commitment broad enough to embrace a variety of doctrines. One circumstance underlining this latter need has been the growth of the voluntary religious societies. Major issues of public policy for the churches and for the community can only be dealt with if the voluntary societies which seek to influence the nation are open to men on some basis which lies deeper than special sectarian beliefs. When, for example, the American Missionary Association was founded in 1846, "any

[13] Walter Rauschenbusch, *A Theology for the Social Gospel*, New York, 1918.

person of evangelical sentiments . . . who is not a slave-holder, or in the practice of other immoralities," was invited to join.[14] The Lutheran Samuel S. Schmucker, whose passion for Christian unity and cooperation outran considerably his interest in Lutheran confessional tradition, was enthusiastic in 1839 about the Sunday School system as he looked forward to the day of millennial triumph when "the minor peculiarities of sect will be thrown into the background, and Christians meet on the broad platform of the Bible." [15]

Such impatience with theological formulas which set men against one another is an authentic element in most religious feeling. The desire to discover unity amidst doctrinal diversity in the instances just noted undoubtedly is motivated also by the need for national unity. Further, there is often an element of anti-intellectualism in this eagerness to overcome dogmatic strife.

Whatever the ingredients, the attitude is there, and it has been significant in the religious situation out of which American theology has come and to which it must address itself. A pluralism of religious sects and doctrines has required any theology not content with a pure confessionalism to search for the thread of common experience which runs through a variety of doctrinal expressions. When new scientific knowledge, the concept of evolution, and the results of Biblical criticism posed increasingly sharper problems for Christian faith as the nineteenth century drew to its close, the appeal to religious experience loomed up as a viable method of apologetics. Thus theological empiricism in America has been strengthened not only by its intellectual ability to cope with science, but also by a spirit of social and ecclesiastical cooperation, and the search for experiential unity among diverse symbols.

[14] *A Brief History of the Origin and Growth of the American Missionary Society*, New York, 1876. Quoted in John Bodo, *The Protestant Clergy and Public Issues, 1812–1848*, Princeton, 1954, p. 110. I am indebted to Dr. Bodo's valuable study for this and the following quotation and for many insights into the impact of the national experience on theology.

[15] Samuel S. Schmucker, "The happy adaptation of the Sabbath-school system to the peculiar wants of our age and country," Philadelphia, 1839, p. 17.

E. EXPERIENCE AND TRADITION. If the conclusion here arrived at seems to give too much weight to modernizing tendencies in a theological complex which has certainly exhibited every kind of traditionalism, it must be remembered that we are pointing to the way in which experience enters into the interpretation of the faith, not to any one view of the content of that experience. It is further clear that the appeal to experience in the modernist movement itself functioned in part as a conservative principle. It preserved the relevance of traditional doctrines to changing situations. Theological empiricism is not always to be associated with revolutionary attacks on tradition. As in Western history generally, empiricism has often been used to defend conservative positions or to support gradualistic theories of development and reform.

Yet it must be recognized that "experience" as a methodological category can be used as a fulcrum for leverage against traditional ideas which are disliked or rejected. The modernists' appeal to experience was certainly used to support liberal humanistic values against doctrines of total depravity. Channing's attack on Calvinism, for example, is premodernist in method, but the argument from experience is clearly present in his critique of the orthodox religious system:

"By shocking, as it does, the fundamental principles of morality, and by exhibiting a severe and partial Deity, it tends strongly to pervert the moral faculty, to form a gloomy, forbidding, and servile religion, and to lead men to substitute censoriousness, bitterness, and persecution for a tender and impartial charity. We think, too, that this system, which begins with degrading human nature, may be expected to end in pride; for pride grows out of a consciousness of high distinctions, however obtained, and no distinction is so great as that which is made between the elected and abandoned of God." [16]

[16] William Ellery Channing, *Unitarian Christianity*, first published 1819, New York, 1957, p. 25.

Every Christian theology includes the criteria of scriptural authority, of church tradition, and of human experience. The interrelations of these factors may be variously conceived, and we can understand some of the underlying forces in the American theological development only by seeing that there has been an assertion of the dynamic interrelations of all three.

II. The Rise of Theological Empiricism

We turn to one group of American theologians who sought to reconstruct Christian doctrine by making the appeal to experience the foundation of theological method. In singling out the empirical modernism of the Chicago school, which developed its major contribution beginning about 1890 and had its highest point of influence near 1930, we are not holding that this school is typical and representative of American theology as a whole. It is not. It belongs to the modernist movement which made a self-conscious identification with scientific and historical methods, whereas much of American theology, Catholic and Protestant, has preserved the traditional forms of authority and ecclesiastical dogma. The position of the empiricists has always drawn sharp criticism both from theological conservatives and from philosophical theologians who have sought idealistic or Kantian methods for the adjustment of religious belief to science. Humanists and rationalists have generally remained unconvinced by attempts to defend the evangelical doctrines through reinterpretation by scientific method. If, however, we see the development of empirical theology in relation to the considerations we have been urging with respect to the meaning of "experience" in the American scene, it is possible to understand how this radical modernism could arise within the evangelical tradition of American Christianity. We may regard this school as an outcropping of a vein of religious thought and attitude which runs underneath the surface of much of American Christianity, and which has been an ingredient in many types of

459

theology, even those which differ in many ways from the characteristic positions of the empiricists.

While the position we are examining was especially prominent at the University of Chicago, its development and influence were not confined to that university. There is in the background William James's radical empiricism and pragmatism with its important relations to the philosophies of John Dewey, George Herbert Mead, and Charles Peirce. The sociologist Albion W. Small was a teacher of the Baptist Shailer Mathews who came to Chicago in 1894 to teach New Testament history. Mathews, later Dean of the Chicago Divinity School, became a leader in the application of social historical analysis to Christian doctrine, and went on to develop a systematic theological method on the basis of his theory of the relation of doctrine to social behavior.[17] Other theologians in the original group were George Burman Foster, whose theology moved steadily toward a functional analysis of the meaning of religious doctrines in their fulfillment of human needs; Gerald Birney Smith, interpreter of modernism; and the Congregationalist theologian, Clarence A. Beckwith, in the Chicago Theological Seminary. The application of empirical historical method to New Testament criticism was developed by Shirley Jackson Case. Henry Nelson Wieman, Presbyterian minister and theologian who studied philosophy at Harvard University, came to the Divinity School of the University of Chicago in 1927, and there developed his philosophy of religion and reinterpretation of the Christian faith through a new conception of the range and competence of empirical method in religious thought.

There is no full study of the development of the Chicago school, but there are excellent general accounts in Herbert W. Schneider's *History of American Philosophy*, and in Douglas Clyde Macintosh's *The Problem of Religious Knowl-*

---

[17] Shailer Mathews, *New Faith for Old, an Autobiography*, New York, 1936.

edge.[18] Macintosh was G. B. Foster's student. He later developed his own empirical theological method at the Yale Divinity School. His *Theology as an Empirical Science*, written in 1919, stands as a classic expression of the whole movement, though Macintosh was always more inclined to provide for a realm of "overbeliefs" above those empirically testable than were the more radical of the Chicago modernists.[19] The Chicago development was not an isolated affair of university intellectualism. Through The American Institute for Sacred Literature, pamphlets and books stating the new point of view on the Scriptures and the faith were made accessible and were widely read throughout Protestant churches in the Middle West.

A. THE PHILOSOPHICAL BACKGROUND OF AMERICAN EMPIRICISM. An analysis of the development of the epistemological strands in American theology involves a look at the general problem of the relation of philosophical thought to theology. All the philosophical traditions have been represented in America, and many of them have influenced theology. German and French idealism, Lockean empiricism, Scottish common sense, Kantian critical philosophy, and, more lately, British philosophical analysis and continental existentialism have all been present. American pragmatism drew upon both empirical and idealistic traditions, and in turn influenced American theologians. There is, for example, the direct influence of John Dewey's philosophy on Henry Nelson Wieman. Through George A. Coe, among others, pragmatism influenced the religious education movement, which developed a theological perspective combining Christian faith, democratic rationalism, and progressive educational theory.[20]

[18] Herbert W. Schneider, *A History of American Philosophy*, New York, 1946, ch. 33. Douglas Clyde Macintosh, *The Problem of Religious Knowledge*, New York, 1940.
[19] Douglas Clyde Macintosh, *Theology as an Empirical Science*, New York, 1919. Cf. his debate with Henry N. Wieman in *Is There a God?*, Chicago, 1932.
[20] George A. Coe, *What Is Christian Education?*, New York, 1929.

Without denying the complexity of the philosophical influences in American theology, one may say that, whereas modern European theology since the decline of idealism has been dominated by the Kantian adjustment of religious faith to science by means of the restriction of metaphysical reason, American theology has found Platonism and other realistic types of philosophic thought more congenial. It has been less shy of metaphysical speculation in theology. The empirical strand in theology built upon this confidence in metaphysics. It asserted a continuity between divine action and human response. It found immanentism in metaphysics congenial even when traditional doctrines of transcendence were also preserved.[21] This remark must be made with caution since the Kantian restriction on knowledge of the noumenal realm, especially as developed theologically in the Ritschlian movement, has also had strong representation in American theology. Even in the empirical positions of Shailer Mathews and D. C. Macintosh there is an acceptance of an ultimate barrier between human experience and direct knowledge of the divine. Yet in both these theologians there is confidence in the capacity of experience to reveal, indirectly at least, man's relationship to "the personality producing forces" (Mathews) and the response of the divine reality to man's "religious adjustment" (Macintosh). The Methodist personalist, Borden Parker Bowne, came by way of Hegel and Lotze's idealism to a position beyond the Kantian critical philosophy. Josiah Royce's idealism, developed by William Ernest Hocking, influenced many theologians, especially through Royce's interpretation of community in *The Problem of Christianity*, and through Hocking's view of religious experience in *The Meaning of God in Human Experience*. American pragmatism moved from the historical and dialectical rationalism of

---

Harrison S. Elliott, *Can Religious Education Be Christian?*, New York, 1940.

[21] See H. W. Schneider, *A History of American Philosophy*, Part VI, and passim for the critique of Kantian epistemology in nineteenth-century American thought.

Hegel to the empiricism of James and Peirce. Evolutionary science and metaphysics led the pragmatists to seek the meaning of ideas in their functional significance for the biological and social processes.

While these new philosophical concepts seemed to provide theologians with resources for adjusting faith to the new world-view, they led others to a deeper skepticism about traditional theology and toward positivism and humanism. Comtean positivism in the last half of the nineteenth century proposed a humanistic philosophy as an alternative to Christianity following the shock which Darwinism gave to orthodoxy. The Free Religious Association promoted the humanistic gospel. Robert G. Ingersoll, gifted orator and rationalistic critic, proclaimed the Holy Trinity of Science: reason, observation, and experience.[22] Andrew D. White had a much more positive attitude toward the values of religious experience than many rationalists, but his *History of the Warfare of Science with Theology in Christendom,* published in 1896, stood as a classic affirmation of the necessity for reconstruction of theological tradition. Theologians who sought to remain within the Christian community and to preserve faith in the divine grace which judges and renews the human spirit, found themselves in a situation where a convincing defense of Christianity required acknowledgment of the claims of scientific method. Could the new empiricism be used to defend the faith?

The work of the empirical theologians, it is clear, must be understood as an apologetic movement. It was an attempt to answer atheism and humanism on the common ground of human experience and scientific knowledge. The task was conceived on a broad scale which included the development of both historical-critical and systematic-constructive methods. It included a concern for the ethical expression of the gospel

---

[22] Robert G. Ingersoll, *Works,* Dresden ed., 1900, I, 86. Quoted in R. H. Gabriel, *The Course of American Democratic Thought,* New York, 1940, p. 181, 2nd ed., p. 192. Chapter 15 of this book gives an excellent survey of the new positivism and humanism.

in the search for social justice. It tried to preserve and communicate the Christian tradition by reinterpreting theological symbols in a new intellectual situation.

B. EMPIRICAL THEOLOGY IN THE CHICAGO SCHOOL. Two of the Chicago theologians already named, Shailer Mathews and Henry Nelson Wieman, were central figures in this theological development. Mathews' work was always explicitly theological as he sought to interpret the Christian tradition in the light of a theory of the social process and its ideological products. In *The Faith of Modernism* he proposed as the key to the new standpoint the doctrine of Christianity's concern with personal values, their decisive exemplification in the spirit of Jesus, and their expression in various cultural and religious forms throughout the history of the church. Human life was analyzed in categories appropriate to the search for fulfillment of psycho-physical organisms, who need to discover, share, and criticize emerging values through the process of social adjustment.[23] Jesus Christ expresses and unifies the personal values of human existence. The Christian community is the social expression of man's response to the attitude and values expressed in Jesus' life.

So far this was familiar modernist doctrine, but Mathews had a special thesis about the language and symbols in which the faith is expressed. His "pattern theory" of theology was a generalization of the view that dogmatic symbols can be understood through discovery of their origin and function in social experience. The church has drawn the categories and symbols for the expression of its faith from the structures of group behavior. "King," "Lord," "Judge," "dying and rising," are cultural patterns and symbols which have been used by the community of faith for the expression of its spiritual experience. Many of these basic symbols are political in origin.

Mathews applied this analysis to the idea of God, which he always regarded as a symbol functioning in human experience to help man adjust to the cosmic source and goal of his life.

[23] Shailer Mathews, *The Faith of Modernism*, New York, 1924.

"God is our idea of the personality producing forces," Mathews asserted.[24] *What* the God-idea symbolizes is objective and ontological. It is the reality of the divine power on which we depend. But the way in which men understand God, including all the personal attributes suggested by the traditional doctrine, is through symbols drawn from human experience. In his books *The Growth of the Idea of God* and *The Atonement and the Social Process,* Mathews carried through with this method.[25] He supported his analysis by a critical review of the history of Christian doctrine in which the major theological symbols were interpreted as attempts to find adequately functioning concepts for the guidance of religious adjustment to the demands and crises of social life. What is distinctive here was not simply the view that religious symbols have social origins. That is a common presupposition of modern historical criticism. But the point important for systematic theology was that this empirical understanding of the social function of theological dogmas was to be brought into organic relationship to the religious meaning of those dogmas. Religion is social and cosmic adjustment. Orthodox theology is "transcendentalized politics." [26]

Mathews rejected the humanist position that God is a projection of human ideals. The symbols have an outward and ontological reference. Yet the willingness to regard all symbols for the divine as rooted in the relativities of human experience may threaten the objectivity of faith. George Burman Foster and Edward Scribner Ames at Chicago seemed to go further than Mathews in loosening the emphasis on the objective content of faith.[27] It was this problem of the objective criterion for human appropriation of divine truth which

[24] Shailer Mathews, *The Growth of the Idea of God,* New York, 1931.
[25] Shailer Mathews, *The Atonement and the Social Process,* New York, 1930.
[26] *ibid.,* p. 33.
[27] See D. C. Macintosh's account of Foster in *The Problem of Religious Knowledge,* pp. 97–119. Cf. Edward Scribner Ames, *Religion,* New York, 1929.

Henry N. Wieman set out to solve by one of the most radical generalizations of the claims of empirical method in theology yet to appear in American thought.

Under the stimulus of the metaphysics of Alfred North Whitehead and the empiricism of John Dewey, Wieman sought a doctrine of God which would express the immediate relationship of God and man in the process of existence, and yet would provide for a rational and experiential check upon all human conceptions of God. The clue he developed consisted in defining God as the source of the values disclosed in experience. The structure of increasing value is not created by man, but is an order against which human errors and false valuations find themselves measured and tested. Thus for exploratory purposes in theology, God is defined as "that behavior of the universe . . . which preserves and increases to the maximum the total good of all human living where right adjustment is made." [28]

Wieman's first book, *Religious Experience and Scientific Method*, sought to put religion in its right relationship to scientific knowledge by demonstrating that rigorous intellectual inquiry can guide religious devotion only so long as precise concepts are recognized to be abstractions from the concreteness of man's experience of the divine reality. Openness to the depth and mystery of God is the meaning of mysticism. [29] In subsequent books Wieman developed the definition of God in such terms as "the process of progressive integration," "the creative event," and the "growth of qualitative meaning." He asserted more explicitly that the method of religious inquiry can be scientific since it seeks rigorous definition of the realities discoverable in experience, and requires the testing of all concepts through observation of the processes of human living. Thus God "is more than we can think." What we can know of God is that he is that activity in exist-

[28] Henry Nelson Wieman, *The Wrestle of Religion with Truth*, New York, 1927, p. 62.
[29] *ibid.*, ch. XII.

ence which creates value and is accessible to observation, as is every other existential process.

While Wieman's thought led him toward a philosophy of religion expressed in terms quite different from those of the theological tradition, his work was carried on within the context of Christian faith. He has continued to interpret the major Christian concepts in the light of his metaphysical position. His major work, *The Source of Human Good*, contains Christological and eschatological doctrines, an interpretation of the church, and an explicit assertion that his religious thought stands within the Judaeo-Christian tradition.[30]

It might be said that this radical extension of the use of empirical method in theology differs so widely from traditional theological methods that it cannot be considered relevant to the analysis of Christian thought in America. We have acknowledged that this development is not typical of the broad stream of confessional theologies in America; but it is an expression in radical form of the faith that experience yields knowledge of God, which has characterized much American religious thought. The empirical movement, it should be said, influenced many theologians who never completely accepted all its theses. Walter Marshall Horton, John C. Bennett, and Robert Lowry Calhoun are among the theologians who incorporated elements of empirical method and yet did not accept its restrictions on the transcendent dimension in the divine revelation.[31] Anglican modernism, represented at the turn of the century in America by William Porcher DuBose, kept a balance between adjustment to mod-

[30] Cf. the present writer's essay "Henry Nelson Wieman as Christian Theologian" in a forthcoming volume on Wieman's theology in *The Library of Living Theology*, ed. Robert Brettall and Charles Kegley. Cf. also Henry N. Wieman, *The Source of Human Good*, Chicago, 1946; H. N. Wieman, *Man's Ultimate Commitment*, Carbondale, Ill., 1958.

[31] Walter Marshall Horton and H. N. Wieman, *The Growth of Religion*, Chicago, 1938. Cf. W. M. Horton, *Theology in Transition*, New York, 1943, pp. xv–xviii. John C. Bennett, *Social Salvation*, New York, 1935, and *Christian Realism*, New York, 1941; Robert L. Calhoun, *God and the Common Life*, New York, 1935.

ern categories and maintenance of the traditional forms.[32]

The modernist method as we have been describing it has not been confined to discussion among academics. Empirical theology, to take one instance, has been for a quarter of a century the theological foundation of the training of ministers in the Iliff Theological Seminary, Denver, Colorado, a seminary of the Methodist church. Its proponent in this school is William H. Bernhardt, who studied at the Chicago Divinity School, and who has developed a systematic empirical approach to Christian doctrine.[33] Strong influences from the empirical theologies are found in many American theological schools and in the preaching and teaching of many churches. While such a development, certainly remarkable within Christendom, is not a majority voice in the American situation, those who stand within the movement do not regard it as a deviation from the Christian tradition, but as a necessary phase of the task of relating the faith of the Christian church to the life and thought of the modern world.

C. The Reaction against Empirical Theology. The story of the reaction against liberalism and modernism in the twentieth century is a familiar aspect of the theological development not only in America but in Protestant thought everywhere. We can ask whether this criticism, which is directed against many of the positions taken by the empirical theologians, displays any special characteristics in the American scene. If so, the thesis that American theology does show distinguishing features which run through diverse standpoints would be supported. To some extent this is the case. The critique of liberalism in theology and of empirical method has been supported by American theologians, not only as a reassertion of a more traditional doctrine of revelation, but also on the ground that *experience itself* requires a reappraisal of

[32] William Porcher Dubose, *Unity in the Faith,* ed. W. Norman Pittenger, Greenwich, 1957. Cf. W. P. Dubose, *The Reason of Life,* New York, 1911.

[33] William Henry Bernhardt's writings are mainly found in *The Iliff Review,* Denver. A bibliography and survey of his thought by several writers are in *The Iliff Review,* Winter, 1954.

the liberal view of man and the nature of his knowledge of God. The experiences of a tragic history are now in the 1940's and 50's asserted against the confidence in "scientific empiricism" as a sufficient method in theology. Put in another way, the characteristic American polemic against the empirical theology seeks to show how the Biblical conception of revelation and the main themes of evangelical faith are more relevant to human experience than are the categories of growth, experiment, and social adjustment which played so large a role in the empirical viewpoint. It is typical of the "neo-evangelical" movement in American theology that it continues to relate Christian doctrine to general categories of value, ethical responsibility, and religious experience, even though these categories are brought under the judgment of the Biblical revelation. Experience is transcended in the knowledge of God, but it is not eliminated from that knowledge.

Two volumes written in the transition from the liberal period to the mid-century reaction exemplify the way in which the theological movement kept the appeal to experience while shifting from one theological standpoint to another. Both volumes are associated with the career of Douglas Clyde Macintosh. In 1931 he edited a volume of essays entitled *Religious Realism*. The writers shared a common restlessness with the subjective tendencies in liberalism and were seeking a reorientation of theology based upon a clear affirmation of the objectivity of the divine ground of faith.[34] Henry N. Wieman, H. Richard Niebuhr, and Macintosh, the editor, were among the contributors. Many of the writers had participated in the empirical movement, but the volume expressed a concern to recover emphasis upon divine judgment on human ideals and a recognition of the limits of human effort in history. H. Richard Niebuhr's essay is of especial interest partly because of his reference to the appearance on the continental horizon of Paul Tillich's religious socialism with its theme of "belief-ful realism" as the corrective to liberal idealism. A year later

[34] *Religious Realism*, ed. Douglas Clyde Macintosh, New York, 1931.

Niebuhr translated Tillich's *The Religious Situation,* with an introduction for American readers.[35] Tillich's theology represented, as in subsequent development it has continued to do, a synthesis of the doctrine of revelation with philosophical reason and other cultural forms of response to revelation. *Religious Realism* marked a stage in the reconsideration of the nature of religious experience and of the adequacy of the liberal and modernist phase of theological reconstruction.

In a later volume of essays written in honor of Douglas Clyde Macintosh in 1937, eleven of his former students presented him with a series of reflections entitled *The Nature of Religious Experience.* Nearly all the writers expressed dissatisfaction with empirical theology. J. Seelye Bixler, for example, declared that "the resort to empiricism in religion has raised at least as many problems as it has solved"; but the solution did not lie for him in a separation of faith from reason. He argued for "spiritual idealism in which objects are no longer existences in time and space, but bearers of an essence, a quality which illumines them with a light that never was on sea or land." [36] In the same volume H. Richard Niebuhr developed the relations of value theory and theology. He raised objections to the way in which modern theology has tried to assert the "value which God has for faith," thus making of value an ideal abstracted from the givenness of religious experience. He says, however, that "a more adequate value theory would be able to overcome these difficulties." [37] In his theological construction, which has widely influenced American thought, H. Richard Niebuhr has reinterpreted the concept of revelation so as to hold that the human search for value is corrected and transformed by the Christian revelation, but the relevance of man's experience of goodness and justice to the understanding of revelation is main-

[35] Paul Tillich, *The Religious Situation,* tr. with a preface by H. Richard Niebuhr, New York, 1932.
[36] *The Nature of Religious Experience, Essays in Honor of Douglas Clyde Macintosh,* New York, 1937, pp. 91–92.
[37] *ibid.,* p. 113.

tained.[38] He seeks to combine the objectivism of Karl Barth's doctrine of revelation with an acknowledgment of the relativity of human experience in appropriating that revelation. This relativistic emphasis is influenced by Ernst Troeltsch, and also has affinities with the empirical theology.

There is no more instructive example of the way in which the issues between the liberal and post-liberal schools can be formulated in experiential terms than the critique of liberalism in Reinhold Niebuhr's theology. As a student of Macintosh at the Yale Divinity School he found the narrow concentration on epistemological problems uncongenial. As his essay in *The Nature of Religious Experience* shows, he saw in myth and other symbolic expressions of religion a depth and adequacy which he missed in the "scientific" definitions of the objects of religious concern.[39] An important source of his critical reflections on liberal theology came through firsthand observation of the working of the modern industrial system as it bore upon the fate of workers in automobile factories in Detroit, Michigan. His book *Moral Man and Immoral Society* in 1932 represented his break with the liberal theology. It is a critical analysis of the conflict between moral ideals and political realities.[40] It confronted liberal religion with historical realities. As he developed his theology in *The Nature and Destiny of Man*, Niebuhr made explicit use of Søren Kierkegaard's doctrine of the paradoxes which faith presents to reason.[41] In these Gifford Lectures he developed the thesis that the experience of modern culture displays the inadequacy of man's effort to complete the meaning of his life through historical progress. Human experience points toward the necessity of a transcendent perspective within which the limits

[38] H. Richard Niebuhr, *The Meaning of Revelation*, New York, 1941. Cf. *Faith and Ethics; the Theology of H. Richard Niebuhr*, ed. Paul Ramsey, New York, 1957.
[39] Reinhold Niebuhr, "The Truth in Myths" in *The Nature of Religious Experience*.
[40] Reinhold Niebuhr, *Moral Man and Immoral Society*, New York, 1932.
[41] Reinhold Niebuhr, "Coherence, Incoherence, and the Christian Faith" in *Christian Realism and Political Problems*, New York, 1953, pp. 175ff.

of human life are exposed and the truth of the divine mercy is known, even though experience itself cannot furnish that perspective. It rests ultimately on faith. Niebuhr thus asserts a theological judgment based on Biblical faith as more relevant to the cultural problem than any alternative. But the interpretation of the Biblical faith and the demonstration of its relevance depends upon a continual dialectic with the data of historical experience.[42] In a later book, *The Self and the Dramas of History,* Niebuhr continues his critique of scientific empiricism as incapable of grasping the freedom and responsibility of the self. These strictures against empiricism are balanced by an appreciation of the "wisdom of common sense" through which, Niebuhr holds, the Western democratic nations have come close to the insight of the Christian faith that human community depends upon the humility which can acknowledge human sin and the need for divine mercy. He here expresses precisely the position which sees "experience" as leading toward the insights provided by Christian faith, yet of itself unable to produce the ultimate truth of revelation which is above all empirical demonstration:

"But ideally we have merely approached a situation in Western political history in which we have discovered by tortuous experience, that liberty and equality are strictly compatible only in the heart of perfect love." [43]

Niebuhr has argued against Karl Barth that a reliance on scriptural authority without the experiential dimension in the appropriation of the scriptural truth distorts the real situation of man before God and tends to obscure the relevance of the gospel to human life.[44]

This "experiential" component of American theology is in

---

[42] Reinhold Niebuhr, *The Nature and Destiny of Man,* 2 vols., New York, 1941–43. Also, Reinhold Niebuhr, *Faith and History,* New York, 1949.

[43] Reinhold Niebuhr, *The Self and the Dramas of History,* New York, 1955, p. 200.

[44] See the exchange of views between Reinhold Niebuhr and Karl Barth in *The Christian Century,* vols. 65:2 and 66:1, 1948–1949.

part the consequence of a certain impatience with confessionalism and traditionalism as insufficient in themselves to provide
theological norms and existential relevance. The emphasis
on experience expressed the conviction that developments
in modern science and history are pertinent to the understanding of the meaning of the gospel. It required the relating of
theological thought to specific areas of Christian concern such
as social justice, religious education, and psychological therapy.
Perhaps the most important root of theological empiricism
was the belief, derived from the Christian faith and present in
the American consciousness from the Puritans and Edwards
to the present, that a sufficiently faithful and realistic attention
to the direction of historical events will disclose the hand
and judgment of God. American theological empiricism in
all its forms has an inward relation to the doctrine of Providence, whether this be expressed in Calvinist determinism, in
ideas of progress, or in the criticism of progressive optimism.

III. The Theology of Church and Community

In searching for distinctive contributions of American theology, we may adopt the hypothesis that some aspects of what
is characteristically American will be found where the life of
the American people in their churches and communities has
been examined from a theological standpoint and where the
interpretation of this American experience has become a
problem for theologians.

Four major areas for theological reflection are suggested
by this general topic. First, there is the doctrine of the church
and the general question of the nature of the religious community in the light of the experience of the American churches.
Second, there is the relation of church and state. Third, there
is the broader question of the foundations of the political
community in the light of the American experience. Here a
nation has sought to weld together the ethical and religious
resources of many religious traditions, and to find the terms

473

upon which a common national loyalty can be related to this diversity of faiths. Finally, there is the theology of history and the place of the nation in the economy of redemption. How has theology in America come to terms with ideas of the national mission and destiny, and how far has there appeared a distinctively theological critique both of the values and the temptations to *hybris* in the American democratic faith?

All these questions are interrelated. The national ideals and the sense of the vocation of American democracy have been bound up with the hope for the success of a pluralistic national community with its non-established churches and its cooperative ethical ventures transcending doctrinal differences. This is not to say that either the theologies which have asserted the mission of democracy or those which have criticized this ideology have held identical views of the church and the state and their proper relationships. Theologies have differed on these issues, not only across the lines of Roman Catholic, Protestant, and Jewish faiths, but within them. Whatever its position, every theology in America has sooner or later had to analyze the life of the American community, the place of religious groups within it, the foundations of its ethical order, and the course and crises of its historical development.

A. How Democracy Became a Theological Problem. To risk generalization again, it can be said that while theology in America has always developed theories of the significance of the democratic way of life and its bearing on the vocation of the nation, it is not until the twentieth century with its two world wars that the issues involved in American democratic life have been exposed in their full complexity. New England theocrats and democratic rationalists had their opposing views of the ethical and religious foundations of democracy, but aside from the lingering defense of the New England establishment there was a general acceptance of the principle of separation of church and state, and a common acceptance of the distinctive mission of America to realize a new form of political community in which the dignity of the individual and his freedom were upheld. Doctrines which well served in the first century and a half of the republic's life have in the middle of the twentieth century demanded a new analysis.

There are at least four reasons why theology, since the two world wars, has had to reexamine some well-worn formulas in the interpretation of the national life and destiny.

The first reason is that the earliest formative theory of the place of the church in the new nation—that developed by the Puritan theocratic idealists—proved itself incapable of maintaining its power to shape the American political faith. We need not repeat here the story of the contribution of the Puritan and Separatist church theories to the shaping of constitutional democracy through the doctrine of human rights, the growth of the town meeting, and the practice of congregational democracy. Nor need we discount the importance of that contribution. But the fact is that the rejection of religious establishment in the American Constitution was derived partly from the need for freedom of sectarian religious groups, such as those for whom Roger Williams spoke, and partly from the insights of rationalists, deists, and free thinkers who saw that no establishment was possible without creating hopeless divisions in the body politic. Hence the *theological* ground for disestablishment was a compound of sectarian theology and rational political foresight. There was no compelling theological rationale to which Christian churches could point as the adequate interpretation of the new situation. The thought of Roger Williams is an important exception because of his probing reflection on which powers are appropriate for the secular government and which powers must be restricted if the spiritual life is to be free. Williams' analysis, however, was not subjected to systematic and critical review as time went on, either by his own followers or by others.

A second factor which affected the way in which theologians regarded the theological significance of the new nation was the general confidence that the new order, which would show the way to humanity's better life, was being realized. Confidence in democratic institutions was linked with belief in the national destiny. Jonathan Edwards had spoken positively, though with a proper restraint, in his history of the work of redemption about the opportunities for the church that were being opened up on the American continent.[45] The Puritan conception of the nation as the New Israel consolidated and reinforced this hopeful spirit. We shall examine more closely this view of the national destiny and the sober reflections about it which arose over the issues of slavery and the Civil War. But even here the assurance that the basic values of American life were a light to guide the world was not really shaken. Theodore Parker, the transcendentalist preacher and theologian, first spoke of "The American Idea," though Horace Bushnell had clearly anticipated the phrase.[46] In the later nineteenth century liberal theologians, caught up in the progressive enthusiasms of evolutionary philosophies and national growth, anticipated the triumph of democracy as the fulfillment of the divine purpose in history.

A third factor lying behind the comparative quiet on such issues as the relation of church and state has been that the general constitutional arrangements were so overwhelmingly supported, or at least accepted, that no serious issue such as the relation of the state to public and parochial schools, for example, could reach the stage of widespread theological discussion. Certainly there have been conflicts, even violent ones, throughout American history between religious groups; but these have been for the most part sporadic, unreflective, indecisive, and certainly not productive of illuminating theological debate until very recent times.[47] It was not until the Amer-

---

[45] Jonathan Edwards, *A History of the Work of Redemption, Works,* New York, 1843, Vol. I, pp. 468–469.

[46] Horace M. Kallen, *Cultural Pluralism and the American Idea,* Philadelphia, 1956, p. 196. Theodore Parker, *The Aspect of Freedom in America,* (1852) in *Works,* London, 1863, Vol. iv, 77ff.

[47] Anson Phelps Stokes, *Church and State in the United States,* 3 vols., New York, 1950, is the major review of the history.

ican churches found themselves living so closely together in society and undergoing the sharp impact of the vast changes in patterns of life in the twentieth century that the nature of a community in which all religious groups participate freely has been recognized as a challenge to theological analysis.

It should also be remembered that the sheer pace of expansion of the churches' life has tended to outrun theological reflection on the relationships they sustain to the larger community and to one another. For many of the confessional groups, the history of their American experience until well into the twentieth century is filled with the task of consolidating the polities and doctrinal positions inherited from many immigrant groups, the establishment of new churches in new communities, the development of voluntary religious societies to deal with the multitude of practical problems, and provisions for general education and religious education in schools and colleges.[48]

A fourth factor somewhat inhibiting theological analysis has been the deep strain of moralism in the approach of the American churches to the problem of community. This familiar theme, traced by many historians, must be given its due weight. American religious thinkers of nearly every shade of opinion have tended to formulate the issues of democratic life in terms of the right and wrong of empire, slavery, freedom, economic systems, and political ideals. Certainly the theological relevance of these moral judgments is not to be set aside. But it has become clear in our later national history that not until the ethical issues are exposed in their complex relations to the forms of social power can the ultimate problems of moral judgment in history be fully seen. The social gospel movement with all its passion for social justice contributed very little to sociological theory or the theology of society. By and large in American thought until very late it

[48] Conrad Bergendoff, *The Doctrine of the Church in American Lutheranism*, Philadelphia, 1956, gives a clear description of the problems of the Lutheran groups in their moves to consolidate their church order and doctrinal position.

was the secular philosophers, the jurists and politicians such as Abraham Lincoln, the critical historians such as Brooks and Henry Adams, and literary critics such as Nathaniel Hawthorne and Walt Whitman, who were the more realistic analysts of democratic problems.

The emergence after World War II of a theological critique of democracy itself and of the "American experiment" is one of the distinguishing features of the recent theological situation. It is difficult to give a neat outline of the emerging positions. In general, the conflict between a basically liberal-rationalist view of democracy and one which holds that the doctrines of the Fall and human sin are pertinent to the understanding of the nature and needs of democracy has come to the fore. Thus the perennial issues between Augustinian and Pelagian views of man and salvation reappear in the theological view of the democratic state.

B. The Doctrine of the Church. In spite of the varied sociological conditions under which the churches live in America and the development of new forms of church life, American theologians have not given major attention to ecclesiology. When statements about the nature of the church are made in ecumenical discussions among American groups, they tend to reflect the traditional positions, often showing clearly their European origins or reflecting the special circumstances which brought forth a new American denomination. This in part stems from the fact that, as the churches come into a face-to-face relationship, each tends to make sure first of its own identity.

There have been tendencies in American church life toward the modification of many practices in church government. These include some emphasis on "democracy" in such matters as the election of bishops, ministers, and other officers, and in the establishment of the equality of women in ecclesiastical offices.[49] Some community churches, people's churches, and

[49] *ibid.*, for a study of democratizing tendencies in American churches with continental backgrounds.

ethical culture societies have conceived the religious community as a company of spiritual seekers not bound by any of the traditional faiths, though not necessarily disavowing them. This view of the religious community or church sometimes is put forward as an advance toward the more inclusive religious society, which can overcome the fragmentation created by the inherited differences of tradition. Other liberal doctrines of the church are founded upon religious philosophies which seek to elicit the spiritual impulses latent within secular culture and the truth inherent in the wide variety of man's religious experience. Thus religious pluralism tends to develop a special type of "catholicity" of its own in which religious divisiveness is to be overcome through the creation of a more inclusive social body for the nurture of the religious spirit.[50]

For the sources of new ecclesiological conceptions within the American churches, one may look more specifically at the kinds of internal and external adjustments which the churches have made in order to survive on a basis of voluntary membership and support in the complex American community. Specifically, there is the development of the councils of churches in cities, states, and the nation, which have become important instruments for the furtherance of cooperative church projects, and which try to bring the consolidated force of church judgment to bear on contemporary issues. It is significant that a thoughtful interpreter of this development of interchurch councils has recently urged a more adequate theological analysis of these new structures.[51] Upon what basis do the denominational bodies cooperate in the growing number of activities which require something more than individual denominational support? Also, the question arises of the broader basis of cooperation between Protestants, Roman Catholics, Ortho-

[50] Will Herberg, *Protestant, Catholic, and Jew*, New York, 1956; cf. John Herman Randall, Jr., "The Churches and the Liberal Tradition," in *Annals American Academy of Political Science*, March 1948, p. 150.
[51] Truman Douglass, "Our Cooperative Witness to Our Oneness in Christ," *The Christian Century*, Vol. lxxv, no. 2, Jan. 8, 1958, pp. 41–44.

dox, and Jews in chaplaincies, in community programs of religious instruction in the schools and colleges, and numerous other projects which require examination of the spiritual and ethical bases of the American community. Here again a pluralistic community has developed forms of "catholicity" appropriate to the requirements of such cooperation, yet without violating the authority which each group accepts in its faith and practice. The increasing concern about theological criteria for interpreting and judging activities of churches which bring them into close relationship to one another is a sign that the basic problems of religious community are becoming more sharply identified.

The internal life of the American churches also raises some new problems for theological interpretation. It may be that the most important insight into the nature of the church derived from the American experience will come through a discovery of the vitality and the problems of the "voluntary" religious community. Here the offices and functions of ministry, teaching, and worship are intimately related to the common life. The office of ministry, whatever the traditional interpretation of its authority, takes on characteristics of group leadership and responsibility. It requires the capacity of the minister to elicit from the company of Christians the disciplines and action appropriate to a Christian congregation. The lay church member may participate responsibly in a community of faith and life.[52]

C. CHURCH AND STATE. There are signs that a searching discussion of the traditional American conceptions of the relation of church and state is on the horizon. This is not only because of increasing concern over such issues as public education, which divide Catholics and Protestants, but also because there are emerging viewpoints within both Catholic and

[52] H. Richard Niebuhr, *The Purpose of the Church and Its Ministry*, New York, 1956. Cf. report of the Oberlin Conference on Faith and Order, *The Nature of the Unity We Seek*, ed. Paul S. Minear, St. Louis, 1958. I am indebted to Dr. James Luther Adams for his insight into the significance of the principle of voluntary association in American life.

Protestant thought which suggest a fresh attack on the whole problem. One may point to the development of a Catholic interpretation of the democratic state in the work of the Jesuit John Courtney Murray and others. A thesis is being stated concerning the separation between the spiritual sphere in which conscience has its obligations to the authority of the church, and the sphere of the citizen with obligations to the political community.[53] On the Protestant side there are increasing signs of restlessness with the negativism of a doctrine which asserts separation without clarifying positive modes of common action by which the church may make its witness effective in the state. In Anson Phelps Stokes's *Church and State in the United States* and William Adams Brown's *Church and State in Contemporary America,* Christian thinkers have produced two important reviews of the history of the problem.[54] It remains to be seen whether out of the present ferment some fundamental theological doctrine of the state satisfactory to Protestant or Catholic, or both, can come. Nothing less than the fundamental problem of the basis of human social existence is involved in the question of how men of different faiths can live and work together.

D. Toward a Theology of the Human Community. In 1887 an American Catholic leader, Isaac Hecker, argued against the adequacy of Protestant Christianity for American life on the ground that the Calvinist tradition of total depravity and the determinism which is linked with it could not support the freedom and the human effort necessary to make democracy work.[55] Had Hecker's thesis been considered seriously by Protestant theologians, a significant discussion of

[53] John Courtney Murray, "Contemporary Orientations of Catholic Thought on Church and State in the Light of History," *Cross-Currents,* Autumn, 1951. Cf. R. J. Henle, S.J., "Dr. Kallen's Idea of Americanism and Cultural Relativism" in H. M. Kallen, *Cultural Pluralism and the American Idea,* pp. 145ff.

[54] For Stokes see n. 44. William Adams Brown, *Church and State in Contemporary America,* New York, 1936.

[55] Isaac Thomas Hecker, *The Church and the Age,* New York, 1896, pp. 64–99.

fundamental problems in the theology of democratic life might have been forthcoming. Nearly forty years of history were necessary in order to bring to the fore the issue Hecker raised. His own program, with its concern to assert American values in the life of American Catholicism, was soon to run into difficulties, and the force of his thrust toward a Catholic theory of democracy was spent.[56] On the Protestant side, such Calvinists as were willing in the late nineteenth century to support the traditional doctrines of depravity and the bondage of the will were so entrenched in a dogmatic conservatism that they were not much concerned with a reappraisal of the Christian doctrine of man. The liberal Protestants had already got rid of Calvinist determinism in the name of the same human freedom and ethical responsibility for which Hecker was arguing, and they believed they had a doctrine of man consonant with the democratic ideal and adequate to its defense.

The decisive turn in the theological-ethical analysis of the democratic faith in the twentieth century has been the criticism of this liberal synthesis. There has been a reassertion of the relevance of the Reformation doctrines of sin and of justification by faith alone, and a recognition of the tragic character of all history as relevant to the defense of democratic theory. The central figure in this discussion is Reinhold Niebuhr, whose theological ethic has been concerned throughout with the reexamination of the foundations of democracy. While he criticizes liberal optimism about man, he holds that neither traditional Lutheranism nor Calvinism adequately recognized the balance between human capabilities and limitations which is necessary to a true estimate of the problems of the democratic community. He has found values in the positions of the "left wing sects" of the Reformation, even though their assertion of radical freedom was made within a rather simple and utopian expectation of the new age in history. Reinhold

---

[56] A full account is in Thomas T. McAvoy, *The Great Crisis in American Catholic History, 1895–1900,* Chicago, 1957.

Niebuhr's writings, along with those of H. Richard Niebuhr, represent a new turn in the search for a Protestant theology of community. One cannot say that all the implications of the new doctrine are clear. The inconceivably rapid developments of a technological society make the effort at formulation of a contemporary Christian politics and ethics difficult in the extreme, but some of its main lines can be stated.

There is first a more explicit theological defense of the principle of disestablishment, not only on the ground of the general values of religious freedom, but also on the ground that this is the most healthy and desirable situation for religion and for the church. The position now being taken, both by Catholic and by Protestant theologians, that there is a sphere of the common life in which no special advantages ought to be provided for any religious group, is defended as necessary for the spiritual health of the churches, so that they will rely upon persuasion rather than coercion and thus be relatively free of the corruptions which attend a monopoly of spiritual symbols and control.[57] The freedom of the community for the hearing of all religious claims in a free market of ideas is defended on Christian grounds. This position has significance for the growing problem of the relationship of religious groups in the world community. It is the maturing of a doctrine of the pluralistic society in which the diversity of faiths is held together in an "orchestration." It rests upon the conviction that in the realm of the spirit only a free commitment can be a genuinely religious response.

A second thesis looks toward some reconciliation of the extreme emphasis on man as sinner with belief in his capacity for that response to ethical claims which a free society must expect. In one sentence Reinhold Niebuhr has stated the decisive point: "Man's capacity for justice makes democracy possible; but man's inclination to injustice makes democracy

[57] Jacques Maritain, *The Rights of Man and Natural Law*, New York, 1943, pp. 81–83. William Ernest Hocking, *Man and the State*, New Haven, 1927, especially pp. 437ff. Cf. James Hastings Nichols, *Democracy and the Churches*, Philadelphia, 1951.

necessary." [58] Democracy must use every possible strategy for putting restrictions upon the overbearing use of power, and for requiring the claims and pretensions of every group, no matter how high the ideals they profess, to be submitted to public criticism. At the same time a view of man and of divine grace which denies any real capacity for effective human decision and action in history will undercut the democratic process. Thus the task of a Christian anthropology is to achieve a sufficiently clear estimate of the relation between man's pursuit of cultural values and the ultimate dimension of man's life before God. The following statement by Merrimon Cuninggim, of the Perkins School of Theology, leans somewhat toward the more liberal type of theological appraisal of the ethical needs of democracy, yet it is fairly representative of the more recent attempts to hold democratic values and the Christian faith together:

"These, then, are among the positive virtues of freedom that the man of religious faith will expound and seek to emulate: sense of community, brotherhood, respect for truth, and fair play. Taken together they come close to being what the Christian means by love in human relationships. Freedom is not full-fledged Christian love, but it is at the gateway to love." [59]

The tone here is characteristically American, and the qualification in the last sentence keeps an acknowledgment of the transcendent reference of faith.

It is characteristic also of American theology to insist that empirical description of the behavior of the church gives essential data for a theological doctrine of the church. H. Richard Niebuhr's study, *The Social Sources of Denominationalism*, and Liston Pope's *Millhands and Preachers*, a sociological analysis of the behavior of churches in the conflicts

---

[58] Reinhold Niebuhr, *The Children of Light and the Children of Darkness*, New York, 1945, p. xi.

[59] Merrimon Cuninggim, *Freedom's Holy Light*, New York, 1955, p. 163.

of an industrial community, are representative essays which seek to hold together theological and empirical dimensions of the church's life. The present interest of the ecumenical movement in the so-called "non-theological" factors in the relations of Christian communions is a confirmation of the validity of this aspect of the American approach to ecclesiology.[60]

IV. American Destiny and the Theology of History

National self-consciousness has been one of the formative elements in American theology from the earliest days of the venture on the new continent. The problems posed by the creation of the new nation gave rise to a series of theological interpretations of American nationhood. These have been characterized by an interweaving of a sense of the peculiar significance of America's place in world history with the Christian faith in the Providence of God. Reinhold Niebuhr says:

"From the earliest days of its history to the present moment, there is a deep layer of Messianic consciousness in the mind of America." [61]

And there is insight in Max Lerner's comment on one ingredient in American religious feeling:

"It might be truer to say, however, that instead of finding their democratic faith in supernatural religion, Americans have tended to find their religious faith in various forms of belief about their own existence." [62]

As we examine the way in which the special vocation of America has become a theological concept, we may pause to

[60] H. Richard Niebuhr, *The Social Sources of Denominationalism*, New York, 1929. Liston Pope, *Millhands and Preachers*, New Haven, 1942. Cf. H. Dodd, G. R. Cragg, and Jacque Ellul, "Social and Cultural Factors in Church Divisions," Faith and Order Commission Papers, no. 10, London, 1952.

[61] Reinhold Niebuhr, *The Irony of American History*, New York, 1952, p. 69.

[62] Max Lerner, *America as a Civilization*, New York, 1957, p. 715.

ask what ought to be expected from Christian theology as it reflects upon any national experience and the patriotic loyalties of men. What kind of contribution should theology make to the understanding of national pride and hope?

When we look back on three hundred years of American theology, we are apt to feel, with some justification, that what has been lacking has been a certain balance, a critical restraint derived from an independent Christian perspective in the midst of national emotions, a capacity for self-criticism born of the knowledge of the judgment of God upon all nations. Christian thought in America seems to bear out the view that the tendency to identify the special genius and power of one's own nation as of peculiar worth in the Kingdom of God is a universal human trait. Theologians do not escape it. In America the tendency has persistently taken the form of a struggle with the ideals, actualities, and disillusionments of the democratic hope.

It is not necessary to review here the entire history of the doctrine of America as the New Israel, with its extreme expressions in early Puritanism and its subsequent versions in liberal theology. H. Richard Niebuhr has shown how the doctrine of the sovereignty of God in history became the ground theme of American theology, and how it can be found in theologies of many varieties.[63]

In the first half of the nineteenth century it is possible to recognize two distinct developments in the interpretation of the national existence. The heirs of the Puritan tradition, most of them New England Calvinists, took the problem of the religious foundation of the state extremely seriously. There were still some remnants of the establishment to defend. As even these were given up, the question of how people were to be reached with the Christian gospel and brought to a regenerate life became for these Puritans the critical problem.

To these upholders of the theocratic tradition the virtue

[63] H. Richard Niebuhr, *The Kingdom of God in America*, Chicago, 1937. Arthur E. Holt, *This Nation Under God*, Chicago, 1939.

must be granted of having perceived the issue of how the religious foundations of the national life could be preserved. Their schemes for carrying out their vision, however, left much to be desired. The interpretations they gave of American nationhood and of the problems of preserving its moral strength make rather painful reading today. They are filled with self-congratulatory remarks upon the mission of America to lead the world to democracy without very much self-searching concerning the ultimate problems of either church or community. The matters singled out for criticism in the national life are generally represented by those things which opposed the inherited values and virtues of Protestant New England. There are moral criticisms of Mormonism, intemperance, the manners of the frontier, and there are pleas for sabbath observance. The more serious disputes over the War of 1812 and the Mexican War seem to be motivated from the New England side by a fear lest the larger nation "get out of hand," that is, get beyond the reach of New England influence. Western pietists were more ready for national expansion, justifying it partly on the ground of increased opportunity for missionary work. In fairness, some heroic efforts at securing humane and statesmanlike treatment of the Indians should be mentioned.

John Bodo has provided an illuminating survey of theological and sermonic essays during this period from 1812 to 1848.[64] Something of the flavor of the early nineteenth-century spirit is present in Bodo's quotation from Richard B. Storrs' challenge to the Sunday School Union to double its efforts against "Sectarianism," "Romanism," "Infidelity," and "Atheism," because "the prospective influences going forth from us to affect the destinies of the world" demanded as much.[65]

This appeal to the providential mission of the nation is sometimes coupled with warnings of divine judgment should

[64] Bodo, *The Protestant Clergy and Public Issues, 1812–1848*.
[65] Richard S. Storrs, *The Importance of Religiously Instructing the Young*, Philadelphia, 1845, p. 33. Quoted in Bodo, p. 242.

the nation fail in its duties. These, however, appear to have mainly a rhetorical function, since they rarely lead to any searching self-criticism. They are used to bolster the case against the sins of groups other than one's own. It was a period in which the young nation was beginning to feel its expansive power, and there was a strong tendency to say that the fulfillment of the national hopes depended upon consistency of adherence to the inherited moral and religious values.

The real crisis for the theological interpretation of the national existence came with the slavery issue and the Civil War. We are concerned here only with the way in which this crisis modified the theological understanding of history. Of course, much of the religious interpretation followed the lines of sectional perspective on the issues. Christians were divided over whether slavery was an absolute wrong which should be abolished immediately at whatever consequence for the Union, or whether it was a natural and valuable arrangement in harmony with the will of God, or whether, admitting its evil, some way should be found to let the institution die gradually. Many in North and South supported the African colonization plan to "solve" the problem by eliminating the Negroes from the national life. In the earlier part of the nineteenth century, colonization was favored by many New England theologians and preachers who rejected the radical position of the abolitionists, and who were not at all sanguine about the prospects for national peace and unity if the two races tried to live together.[66]

Threatening, as it did, the existence of the union of the states, the Civil War posed for theologians on both sides the question of the significance of American nationhood in the perspective of the faith that there is a divine will being worked out in history. It is clearer to us now than it could be to anyone at that time that the Civil War was the turning point in the emergence of the new nation. It meant the establishment for the foreseeable future of a unified national life, and was the

[66] Bodo, ch. v.

beginning of the American emergence with growing power in the community of the nations. And it brought the end of slavery.

It is true that much of what theologians of the time said about the war expressed a rather simple view of the alliance of Providence either with the North or with the South. Even Horace Bushnell can be quoted, as he is by Ralph Henry Gabriel, in a paean of righteous affirmation of the North's cause.[67] The confederacy and the system of slavery had their Biblical defenders also.

There were, however, a few men on both sides who sensed a deeper significance in the struggle. A study by William Clebsch singles out three theologians who tried to understand the meaning of the conflict by relating their faith in Providence to the sense of a divine judgment upon the guilt of the whole nation, and to the suffering of the war as leading to a new life for the nation. The three are Horace Bushnell; Philip Schaff, the theologian of the Reformed Church; and a Southern Episcopal Bishop, Stephen Elliott.[68]

Elliott, the Southerner, at first conceived of the Confederacy as the continuation of the real American nation, with a regard for the rights of states and communities. For Bushnell and Schaff the war with its suffering was the way to the rebirth of true national unity. All three theologians refused to identify one side as blameless and the other as completely guilty. All shared a contrition about slavery, at least about its manifest evils, and saw it as a burden of guilt upon the whole people. All acknowledged that the agony of the war could be understood as manifesting the divine judgment and retribution.

Bushnell and Schaff held the special view that the suffering

[67] Ralph H. Gabriel, *The Course of American Democratic Thought*, 2d ed., New York, 1956, p. 115.

[68] William Clebsch, *Baptism of Blood: A Study of Christian Contributions to the Interpretation of the Civil War in American History*. Unpublished dissertation in the Union Theological Seminary, New York, Library, 1957. I am much indebted to this study and to Dr. Wilhelm Pauck for calling it to my attention.

was the instrument by which the nation would be purged of the sins which had brought about the conflict, and would experience a new birth. Both used the symbol "baptism by blood." Said Schaff, "this very baptism of blood entitles us also to hope for a glorious regeneration." [69] We have to try to realize the extent to which even these comparatively liberal Calvinists were working with a conception of Providence which allowed them to search for explicit traces of the divine design in contingent historical circumstances. Neither of these went so far as the later liberal theologian, Theodore T. Munger, who tried to specify the way in which every aspect of the war, even its length and the geographical location of the battlefields, formed parts of the divine plan.[70]

Another note was sounded by Bushnell. He said that the great sin which was being paid for was the failure in the founding of the nation to recognize that God must be the author of a true and lasting community. He attacked the deistic and rationalistic theory of the creation of the democracy by voluntary contract. The Declaration of Independence was "a fusion of Puritan church order and the doctrine of the French Encyclopedia." [71] Bushnell believed that the war would result in a new national consciousness which would rest on a deeper foundation than the illusion of a man-made compact. There would be a new conviction of the indissoluble unity of a people called by God for a special witness. As Bushnell penetrated deeply into the issue of what must go into the formation of a national consciousness, he produced an apologetic for the Puritan answer to this question. Insofar as it was an oversimplified answer it was another instance of the failure of the heirs of the Puritan tradition to see the

[69] Philip Schaff in *The Christian Intelligencer*, New York, 1866, Vols. 9:2, 10:1. Quoted in Clebsch, p. 135.

[70] Theodore T. Munger, "Providence and the War," *Hoosac Valley News*, May 30, 1885. Quoted in Clebsch, p. 230.

[71] Horace Bushnell, "Popular Government by Divine Right" in *Building Eras in Religion*, New York, 1881. Cf. "The Doctrine of Loyalty" in *Work and Play*, New York, 1881, and *Reverses Needed*, Hartford, 1861.

difficulty of identifying particular historical events with the divine will, and their failure to estimate correctly the creative elements in rationalistic and secular theories of democracy. Certainly the Civil War did not eliminate the secular interpretation of democracy or destroy the faith which it expressed.

The interpreters of the social gospel in the last quarter of the nineteenth century and the first quarter of the twentieth were more careful about identifying particular events with the will of God. This was partly because their progressive scheme of history had taken on some new dimensions. The elimination of war and the establishment of economic justice were now viewed as the goals of the divine work in history, and there was some new realism about the involvement of all nations in social evils. There is, for example, Walter Rauschenbusch's chapter entitled "The Kingdom of Evil" in his *Theology for the Social Gospel*, with its indictment of collective systems of exploitation. The hope for a just society was combined with a universalistic optimism. The First World War was interpreted as a prelude to universal peace. Not many insights into the tragic depths of history are to be found in that period. It was out of the disillusioned decades after World War I that a sober rethinking of the meaning of history began to come.

If theological interpretations of the vocation of the nation in history have often been uncritical, they have still posed a fundamental problem for all Christian theology. History is made by nations and empires. Postwar realistic theology has reasserted the relevance of theological categories to the interpretation of history, while it has criticized the formulas of earlier pietism. The struggles of the past to understand the distinctive significance of the American nation may have provided experiences, memories, and that trial and error through which a more mature theology of history can come into being.

V. The Vision of God

Theology properly begins and ends with the doctrine of God. If all human experience affects man's appropriation of God's self-revelation, we are entitled to ask what there may be in any national experience which has shaped and modified the doctrine of God. Surely the experience of the Hebrews is fundamental for the revelation to which the Bible gives witness, a point the American Puritans were quite conscious of when they thought of their own national destiny. In 1831 Edgar Quinet in the *Revue des Deux Mondes* prophesied:

"A new idea of God will surge from the lakes of Florida and the peaks of the Andes; in America will begin a new religious era, and will be born a new idea of God." [72]

This may be dubious prophecy from a Christian point of view which holds that God, the Logos of all things, has already decisively disclosed Himself. Further, if we consider the themes which are most consistently present in American theology—the sovereignty of God, the presence of the divine spirit in nature, the sense of an unfinished world, and the evolutionary concept of the divine working through time and history, we see that none of these is the exclusive possession of American theology.

Still it is true that some aspects of the American consciousness have tended to make certain ideas about God congenial. There is the theme of God's working in time which has received special attention from theologians such as Theodore Parker, Edgar S. Brightman, and Henry N. Wieman.[73] The metaphysics of Bergson and Whitehead and of others influenced by evolutionary conceptions have been attractive to

[72] Edgar Quinet in *Revue des Deux Mondes*, quoted in Robert Spiller et al., *Literary History of the United States*, New York, 1953, p. 214.

[73] E. S. Brightman was a philosopher of religion, but his thought is intimately related to the personalistic school of theology developed at the Boston University School of Theology. Cf. his *The Problem of God*, New York, 1930.

some American theologians as providing a certain openness and unfinishedness in the creation. The theme of God as cosmic worker appears, for example, in the carefully balanced theology of Robert Lowry Calhoun in his *God and the Common Life*.[74] This is not to say that any one metaphysical outlook is necessary to the doctrines of God developed in America. Rather, a plurality of metaphysical outlooks has been present. Nor has the relation of man and God been overly "democratized" by theologians who have kept a clear perception of the categories of sin and grace. There is at the same time characteristic acceptance of the idea that God is to be understood as creative spirit, and that man in some sense shares in the creative task.

If we keep in mind the combination of empiricism and pluralism in the American approach to religious thought, we see that one source of insight into the doctrine of God has been the belief in the variety of forms through which God can be known. Even when American theologians stress the confessional standpoint in religious faith and acknowledge the impossibility of standing outside one's own faith, they are likely to hold a pluralistic confessionalism which asserts that God may be known in a variety of theologies. The sectarian traditions in American life have here, as elsewhere, often encouraged the view that the work of the Holy Spirit transcends historical forms, and that knowledge of God is to be sought in personal experience, without too great reliance on traditional structures of piety or liturgy. The liberal theologies explicitly affirm the value of a plurality of symbols as yielding richness and depth to knowledge of God.[75] One American theologian remarked in a discussion, "I believe in the necessity

[74] Robert L. Calhoun, *God and the Common Life*, New York, 1935, chs. 4–5.
[75] For a philosophical defense of a pluralism of religious symbols see John Herman Randall, Jr., "Naturalistic Humanism" in F. E. Johnson, ed., *Patterns of Faith in America Today*, New York, 1957. E. E. Aubrey's *Living the Christian Faith*, New York, 1939, ch. IV, is one of the important theological analyses of the pluralistic elements in American culture and their influence on theology.

of different theological parties just as I believe in the necessity of different political parties." A type of Hegelian synthesis in which the divine is known as the reconciliation of polarities, an idea which the Catholic Isaac Hecker found congenial and to which Christian idealists like Josiah Royce and William Ernest Hocking have given philosophical expression, offers possibilities for a theology of religious language and symbolism freed of the restrictiveness of traditional confessionalism. Those who have learned to value highly a richness of diversity held together in a community of life may be expected to be interested in the idea of a useful diversity in man's language about the One God.

The contribution of theology in a national culture can be understood in various ways. Some would hold that theology serves man best by divesting itself as completely as possible of all cultural involvements and by witnessing to the absolute judgment of God upon all human life. But if theology must do its work by taking the risk of participation in the clash of human values, since faith is relevant to the common life, then it will make its contribution by moving from problem to problem, from witness to self-criticism, as it regards all life in the light of faith in the Creator and Redeemer.

Christian theology in America has been engaged in the shaping of the American tradition, and has had special problems in relation to that tradition and experience. Where it has not remained aloof from secular ideals and values, it has run the risk of reflecting those values without sufficient criticism of them. Yet it has struggled to bring to birth some new insights into the way in which the gospel and the church can exist in a national life where many religious ideas and commitments are held together in the one community. It is a problem comparable to that which the human family faces on a world scale for a long time to come. If theologians have had to say quite bluntly, "the fact remains that there can be no faith in God so long as he is regarded as a sort of confirmatory appendage to the American way of life," [76] at the same time they have sought for an understanding of the relation between the Christian faith and the human quest for liberty and community which, with all its distortions, has been an authentic element in the American experience.

[76] David E. Roberts, "The Christian Gospel and the American Way of Life," in *What the Christian Hopes for in Society*, New York, 1957, p. 73.

INDEX

146, 148, 150-153, 154-155, 156-
157, 160; Orthodox, 129-131,
132, 136, 138, 139, 142, 144-146,
147, 149, 153, 154-155, 212;
American Reform Movement,
131-144, 145, 146-147, 153-154,
155, 156, 158; Conservative
Movement, 147-151, 153, 154,
155-156; Reconstructionist Movement, 156, 160; Black Jews, 227.
See also anti-Semitism; Zionism
justice, social, *see* reform, social

kabbalah, 123
Kallen, Horace, 150
Kant, Immanuel, 263, 267, 289,
403n, 415n, 421n-422n, 434n,
441, 459, 461, 462
Kaplan, Mordecai M., 149, 156
Karo, Joseph, 124-125, 126
Karson, Marc, 100n
Keane, John J., 97
Keely, Patrick C., 113
Keil, William, 192
Kelpius, Johannes, 191, 192, 209,
218
Kierkegaard, Søren, 311, 312, 315-
316, 471
Kingdom of God, 8, 40, 56, 209,
210, 211, 213, 216, 242, 296, 297,
387, 393, 398, 403, 486
Kingsley, Charles, 321n
Knights of Labor, 97-98
Know-Nothing Party, 166, 279
Knudsen, A. C., 289
Kohler, Kaufmann, 135-137, 138
Kohlmann, Anthony, 83
Kohut, Alexander, 145, 146
Krauth, Charles P., 272, 276-279
Krotana, 218
Ku Klux Klan, 118, 139, 166
Kurtz, Benjamin, 272, 276

Labadists, 208-209
labor movement, 140, 143, 146.
See also unions, trade
LaFarge, John, 107
Landmark controversy, 303, 304n
Lane Theological Seminary, 259
Langdon, Samuel, 328, 330, 337-
339, 340, 346

language: Bushnell's theory of, 281-
282; Mathews' theory of, 464-
465; and theology, 494
Laud, Archbishop, 27, 238
law, natural: contrasted with divine
law, 21, 46-47, 48-49, 382; as ex-
pression of divine law, 69-70, 114,
245, 317
leader, as core of religious move-
ment, 26, 169, 181, 200-202, 217,
219, 401
LeConte, Joseph, 423
Lee, Ann, 181, 201, 202, 209, 212
Leeser, Isaac, 131, 132
Lehmann, Peter, 192
Leibniz, G. W., 435
Leipzig, University of, 273
Lemurian Fellowship, 218
Lenhart, John M., 78n
Leo XIII, 99, 100, 116
Lerner, Max, 221, 485
Leuba, James, 220
Levellers, 39
Lewis, Edwin, 313
Liberal Catholic Church, 218
liberalism, theological, 182, 185,
232, 251, 271, 275, 279-285, 286-
298, 303, 304, 307, 308, 309, 310-
311, 312, 315, 316, 317, 379, 428,
430, 444, 445, 448, 452, 468, 469,
470, 471-472, 479, 486, 493
liberty, 31, 332, 341, 346, 347, 355,
395, 472. *See also* freedom
Liebman, Joshua L., 11, 156
Lincoln, Abraham, 232, 359, 360,
478
Lindbergh, Charles, 437
literature and Protestantism, 24
Locke, John, 50, 244, 245, 248, 249,
258, 263, 328, 334, 338, 342, 353,
403, 415n, 416, 418, 422, 461
Loehe, William, 274n
logic, 423, 434, 435, 439, 441
Lollards, 170
Lord's Supper, *see* Eucharist
Lotze, Rudolph Hermann, 288, 306,
462
Louis XVI, 333
Lowrie, Walter, 312
Luther, Martin, 18, 27, 29, 34, 35,
38, 39, 44, 186, 188, 230, 240,
249, 270, 275, 312

333, 336, 341, 350, 359, 360, 368, 386, 444, 445, 454, 455, 456, 487, 493

Pillar of Fire, 26

Pittsburgh declaration of 1885, 137, 138, 144, 154

Pius XI, 99

Pius XII, 120

Plan of Union, Presbyterian-Congregationalist, 61, 260, 265

Plato, 208

Platonism, 403, 430, 462; Christian, 249, 449. *See also* neo-Platonism

Plotinus, 259

pluralism: religious, 6, 17, 25-26, 51, 142, 162-165, 173n, 219, 232, 272, 354, 394, 445, 456-457, 479, 483, 493; cultural, 103, 118, 150, 194, 474, 480, 483. *See also* denominationalism

Plymouth Brethren, 53

poetry, 436, 440

politics (political life), 21, 63, 170, 194, 314, 471, 473, 483; and covenant theology, 328, 333, 334-343, 344, 347, 356, 360; and scientific spirit, 416

polygamy, 215, 216

Pontius Pilate, 317

Pope, Liston, 484

Populism, 101

positivism, 370, 376, 379, 381, 387, 425, 431, 432-436, 438-441, 463

Powderly, Terence V., 97, 98

Power, John, 81

pragmatism, 47, 150, 159, 161, 324, 425-432, 433, 435, 436, 438-439, 441-442, 460, 461, 462-463

preaching, 45, 56, 240, 248, 253, 273, 293, 333, 364, 381, 399, 454. *See also* jeremiad

predestination, 7, 34, 180, 278, 306

Presbyterianism, 19, 25, 26, 27, 61-62, 77, 165, 184n, 195, 196, 197, 234, 236, 239, 243, 246, 259, 260, 261-266, 267, 280, 306, 325, 326, 331, 340, 348, 351, 352, 354, 357, 361, 362, 364, 372, 376, 431, 460; Cumberland, 26, 54, 195; Associate, 53; United, 61; Orthodox Presbyterian Church, 184n

press, 79-80, 82, 108, 112, 130-131, 133, 373

Preston, John, 237, 239, 241

Princeton Theological Seminary, 261-264, 266, 267

Princeton University, 12-13, 247, 260, 261, 331, 349, 376, 403n

progress, 21, 56, 127, 134, 139, 141, 151, 161, 216, 253, 286, 287, 298, 315, 363, 380, 384, 388, 389, 391, 392, 393, 396, 471, 473

progressivism, 101, 140, 141, 143, 379

Prohibition, 436

Protestant Episcopal Church, *see* Episcopalianism

Protestantism, 4-5, 14-15, 20-71, 74, 76, 82, 83, 84, 85, 86, 88, 93, 95, 107, 116, 118, 119, 120, 132, 133, 140, 162-231; as movement, 22-36, 41, 42, 71; order in, 22, 24, 30, 31, 36-47, 62, 63, 71; history of, 25-28, 29, 32-36, 322-368; reformation in, 23, 24, 32-36, 37, 38, 39, 40; and protest, 26-32, 35, 37, 38, 39, 40, 45, 48, 66; unity in, 36, 59-65, 165-166, 185, 366, 456-457; and culture, 51, 57-59, 65-71; and modernism, 369-401 *passim*. *See also* science; theology

Protestants and Other Americans United for Separation of Church and State, 118

Psychiana, 218

psychoanalysis, 157, 402, 431, 442

psychology, 10, 11, 24, 220, 222, 244, 248, 306, 311, 415n, 426, 431, 442, 473; dynamic, 389

Purcell, John B., 96n

Puritanism, 7, 19, 25, 27, 38, 39, 41, 74, 84, 171, 185, 193, 204, 213, 222, 223, 233, 234, 236-243, 246, 247, 248, 253, 261, 269, 270, 276, 307, 313, 317, 325, 330, 332, 334, 340, 359, 361, 367, 402, 403, 412, 413-415, 421, 422, 424, 449, 452, 453, 455, 473, 475, 476, 486, 490, 492

Purnell, Benjamin, 26

Purple Mother, 218